THE

NIGHT-SIDE OF NATURE;

OR,

Ghosts and Ghost-Seers.

BY

CATHERINE CROWE,

AUTHORESS OF "SUSAN HOPLEY," "LILLY DAWSON," "ARISTODEMUS," ETC.

"Thou com'st in such a questionable shape,
That I will speak to thee."

NEW YORK:
J. S. REDFIELD, CLINTON HALL.
BOSTON:—B. B. MUSSEY & CO.

1850.

PREFACE.

In my late novel of "Lilly Dawson," I announced my intention of publishing a work to be called "The Night-Side of Nature;" this is it.

The term "Night-Side of Nature" I borrow from the Germans, who derive it from the astronomers, the latter denominating that side of a planet which is turned from the sun, its *night-side*. We are in this condition for a certain number of hours out of every twenty-four; and as, during this interval, external objects loom upon us but strangely and imperfectly, the Germans draw a parallel between these vague and misty perceptions, and the similar obscure and uncertain glimpses we get of that veiled department of nature, of which, while comprising as it does, the solution of questions concerning us more nearly than any other, we are yet in a state of entire and wilful ignorance. For science, at least science in this country, has put it aside as beneath her notice, because new facts that do not fit into old theories are troublesome, and not to be countenanced.

We are encompassed on all sides by wonders, and we can scarcely set our foot upon the ground, without trampling upon some marvellous production that our whole life and all our faculties would not suffice to comprehend. Familiarity, however, renders us insensible to the ordinary works of nature; we are apt to forget the miracles they comprise, and even, sometimes, mistaking words for conceptions, commit the error of thinking we understand their mystery. But there is one class of these wonders with which, from their comparatively rare occurrence, we do not become familiar; and these, according to the character of the mind to which they are presented, are frequently either denied as ridiculous and impossible, or received as evidences of supernatural interference—interrnptions of those general laws by which God governs the universe; which latter mistake arises from our only seeing these facts without the links that connect them with the rest of nature, just as in the faint light of a starlit night we might distinguish the tall mountains that lift their crests high into the sky, though we could not discern the low chain of hills that united them with each other.

There are two or three books by German authors, entitled 'The Night-Side," or "The Night-Dominion of Nature," which are on subjects, more or less analogous to mine. Heinrick Schubert's is the most celebrated among them; it is a sort of cosmogony of the world, written in a spirit of philosophical mysticism—too much so for English readers in general.

In undertaking to write a book on these subjects myself, I wholly disclaim the pretension of *teaching* or of enforcing opinions. My object is to suggest inquiry and stimulate observation, in order that we may endeavor, if possible, to discover something regarding our psychical nature, as it exists here in the flesh; and as it is to exist hereafter, out of it.

If I could only induce a few capable persons, instead of laughing at these things, to look at them, my object would be attained, and I should consider my time well spent.

CONTENTS.

THE

NIGHT-SIDE OF NATURE.

CHAPTER I.

INTRODUCTION.

"Know ye not that ye are the Temple of God, and that the Spirit of God dwelleth in you?"—1 CORINTHIANS, iii. 16.

MOST persons are aware that the Greeks and Romans entertained certain notions regarding the state of the soul, or the immortal part of man, after the death of the body, which have been generally held to be purely mythological. Many of them doubtless are so, and of these I am not about to treat; but among their conceptions, there are some which, as they coincide with the opinions of many of the most enlightened persons of the present age, it may be desirable to consider more closely. I allude here particularly to their belief in the tripartite kingdom of the dead. According to this system, there were the Elysian fields, a region in which a certain sort of happiness was enjoyed; and Tartarus, the place of punishment for the wicked; each of which was, comparatively, but thinly inhabited. But there was also a mid-region, peopled with innumerable hosts of wandering and mournful spirits, who, although undergoing no torments, are represented as incessantly bewailing their condition, pining for the life they once enjoyed in the body, longing after the things of the earth, and occupying themselves with the same pursuits and objects as had formerly constituted their business or their pleasure. Old habits are still dear to them, and they can not snap the link that binds them to the earth.

Now, although we can not believe in the existence of Charon, the three-headed dog, or Alecto, the serpent-haired fury, it may be worth while to consider whether the persuasion of the ancients with regard to that which concerns us all so nearly—namely, the destiny that awaits us when we have shaken off this mortal coil—may not have some foundation in truth: whether it might not be a remnant of a tradition transmitted from the earliest inhabitants of the earth, wrested by observation from nature, if not communicated from a higher source: and also whether circumstances of constant recurrence in all ages and in all nations, frequently observed and recorded by persons utterly ignorant of classical lore, and unacquainted, indeed, with the dogmas of any creed but their own, do not, as well as various passages in the Scriptures, afford a striking confirmation of this theory of a future life; while it, on the other hand, offers a natural and convenient explanation of their mystery.

To minds which can admit nothing but what can be explained and demonstrated, an investigation of this sort must appear perfectly idle: for while, on the one hand, the most acute intellect or the most powerful logic can throw little light on the subject, it is, at the same time—though I have a confident hope that this will not always be the case—equally irreducible within the present bounds of science; meanwhile, experience, observation, and intuition, must be our principal if not our only guides. Because, in the seventeenth century, credulity outran reason and discretion; the eighteenth century, by a natural reaction, threw itself into an opposite extreme. Whoever closely observes the signs of the times, will be aware that another change is approaching. The contemptuous skepticism of the last age is yielding to a more humble spirit of inquiry; and there is a large class of persons among the most enlightened of the present, who are beginning to believe that much which they had been taught to reject as fable, has been, in reality, ill-understood truth. Somewhat of the mystery of our own being, and of the mysteries that compass us about, are beginning to loom upon us—as yet, it is true, but obscurely; and, in the endeavor to follow out the clew they offer, we have but a feeble light to guide us. We must grope our way through the dim path before us, ever in danger of being led into error, while we may confidently reckon on being pursued by the shafts of ridicule—that weapon so easy to wield, so potent to the weak, so weak to the wise—which has delayed the births of so many truths, but never stifled one. The pharisaical skepticism which denies without investigation, is quite as perilous, and much more contemptible, than the blind credulity which accepts all that it is taught without inquiry; it is, indeed, but another form of ignorance assuming to be knowledge. And by *investigation*, I do not mean the hasty, captious, angry notice of an unwelcome fact, that too frequently claims the right of pronouncing on a question; but the slow, modest, pains-taking examination, that is content to wait upon Nature, and humbly follow out her disclosures, however opposed to preconceived theories or mortifying to human pride. If scientific men could but comprehend how they discredit the science they really profess, by their despotic arrogance and exclusive skepticism, they would surely, for the sake of that very science they love, affect more liberality and candor. This reflection, however, naturally suggests another, namely, do they really love science, or is it not too frequently with them but the means to an end? Were the love of science genuine, I suspect it would produce very different fruits to that which we see borne by the tree of knowledge, as it flourishes at present; and this suspicion is exceedingly strengthened by the recollection that, among the numerous students and professors of science I have at different times encountered, the real worshippers and genuine lovers of it, for its own sake, have all been men of the most single, candid, unprejudiced, and inquiring minds, willing to listen to all new suggestions, and investigate all new facts; not bold and self-sufficient, but humble and reverent suitors, aware of their own ignorance and unworthiness, and that they are yet but in the primer of

Nature's works, they do not permit themselves to pronounce upon her disclosures, or set limits to her decrees. They are content to admit that things new and unsuspected may yet be true; that their own knowledge of facts being extremely circumscribed, the systems attempted to be established on such uncertain data, must needs be very imperfect, and frequently altogether erroneous; and that it is therefore their duty, as it ought to be their pleasure, to welcome as a stranger every gleam of light that appears in the horizon, let it loom from whatever quarter it may.

But, alas! poor Science has few such lovers! *Les beaux y eux de sa cassette,* I fear, are much more frequently the objects of attraction than her own fair face.

The belief in a God, and in the immortality of what we call the soul, is common to all nations; but our own intellect does not enable us to form any conception of either one or the other. All the information we have on these subjects is comprised in such hints as the Scripture here and there give us: whatever other conclusions we draw, must be the result of observation and experience. Unless founded upon these, the opinion of the most learned theologian or the most profound student of science that ever lived, is worth no more than that of any other person. They know nothing whatever about these mysteries; and all *à priori* reasoning on them is utterly valueless. The only way, therefore, of attaining any glimpses of the truth in an inquiry of this nature, where our intellect can serve us so little, is to enter on it with the conviction that, knowing nothing, we are not entitled to reject any evidence that may be offered to us, till it has been thoroughly sifted, and proved to be fallacious. That the facts presented to our notice appear to us absurd, and altogether inconsistent with the notions our intellects would have enabled us to form, should have no weight whatever in the investigation. Our intellects are no measure of God Almighty's designs; and, I must say, that I do think one of the most irreverent, dangerous, and sinful things man or woman can be guilty of, is to reject with scorn and laughter any intimation which, however strangely it may strike upon our minds, and however adverse it may be to our opinions, may possibly be showing us the way to one of God's truths. Not knowing all the conditions, and wanting so many links of the chain, it is impossible for us to pronounce on what is probable and consistent, and what is not; and, this being the case, I think the time is ripe for drawing attention to certain phenomena, which, under whatever aspect we may consider them, are, beyond doubt, exceedingly interesting and curious; while, if the view many persons are disposed to take of them be the correct one, they are much more than this. I wish, also, to make the English public acquainted with the ideas entertained on these subjects by a large proportion of German minds of the highest order. It is a distinctive characteristic of the thinkers of that country, that, in the first place, they do think independently and courageously; and, in the second, that they never shrink from promulgating the opinions they have been led to form, however new, strange, heterodox, or even absurd, they may appear to others. They do not succumb, as people do in this country, to the fear of ridicule; nor are they in danger of the odium that here pursues those who deviate from established notions; and the consequence is, that, though many fallacious theories and untenable propositions may be advanced, a great deal of new truth is struck out from the collision; and in the result, as must always be the case, what is true lives and is established, and what is false dies and is forgotten. But here, in Britain, our critics and colleges are in such haste to strangle and put down every new discovery that does not emanate from themselves, or which is not a fulfilling of the ideas of the day, but which, being somewhat opposed to them, promises to be troublesome from requiring new thought to render it intelligible, that one might be induced to suppose them divested of all confidence in this inviolable law; while the more important and the higher the results involved may be, the more angry they are with those who advocate them. They do not quarrel with a new metal or a new plant, and even a new comet or a new island stands a fair chance of being well received; the introduction of a planet appears, from late events, to be more difficult; while phrenology and mesmerism testify that any discovery tending to throw light on what most deeply concerns us, namely, our own being, must be prepared to encounter a storm of angry persecution. And one of the evils of this hasty and precipitate opposition is, that the passions and interests of the opposers become involved in the dispute: instead of investigators, they become partisans; having declared against it in the outset, it is important to their petty interests that the thing shall not be true; and they determine that it *shall* not, if they can help it. Hence, these hasty, angry investigations of new facts, and the triumph with which failures are recorded; and hence the wilful overlooking of the axiom that a thousand negatives can not overthrow the evidence of one affirmative experiment. I always distrust those who have declared themselves strongly in the beginning of a controversy. Opinions which, however rashly avowed, may have been honest at first, may have been changed for many a long day before they are retracted. In the meantime, the march of truth is obstructed, and its triumph is delayed; timid minds are alarmed; those who dare not or can not think for themselves, are subdued; there is much needless suffering incurred, and much good lost; but the truth goes quietly on its way, and reaches the goal at last.

With respect to the subjects I am here going to treat of, it is not simply the result of my own reflections and convictions that I am about to offer. On the contrary, I intend to fortify my position by the opinions of many other writers; the chief of whom will, for the reasons above given, namely, that it is they who have principally attended to the question, be Germans. I am fully aware that in this country a very considerable number of persons lean to some of these opinions, and I think I might venture to assert that I have the majority on my side, as far as regards ghosts—for it is beyond a doubt that many more are disposed to believe than to confess—and those who do confess, are not few. The deep interest with which any narration of spiritual appearances bearing the stamp, or apparent stamp, of authenticity is listened to in every society, is one proof that, though the fear of ridicule may suppress, it can not extinguish that intuitive persuasion, of which almost every one is more or less conscious.

I avow, that in writing this book, I have a higher aim than merely to afford amusement. I wish to engage the earnest attention of my readers; because I am satisfied that the opinions I am about to advocate, seriously entertained, would produce very beneficial results. We are all educated in the belief of a future state, but how vague and ineffective this belief is with the majority of persons, we too well know; for although, as I have said above, the number of those who are what is called believers in ghosts and similar phenomena is very large, it is a belief that they allow to sit extremely lightly on their minds. Although they feel that the evidence from within and from without is too strong to be altogether set aside, they have never permitted themselves to weigh the significance of the facts. They are afraid of that bugbear, Superstition—a title of opprobrium which it is very convenient to attach to whatever we do not believe ourselves. They forget that nobody has a right to call any belief superstitious, till he can prove that it is unfounded. Now, no one that lives can assert that the reappearance of the dead is impossible; all he has a right to say is, that he does not believe it; and the interrogation that should immediately follow this declaration is, "Have you devoted your life to sifting all the evidence that has been adduced on the other side, from the earliest periods of history and tradition?" and even though the answer were in the affirmative, and that the investigation had been conscientiously pursued, it would be still a bold inquirer that would think himself entitled to say, the question was no longer open. But the rashness and levity with which mankind make professions of believing and disbelieving, are, all things considered, phenomena much more extraordinary than the most extraordinary ghost-story that ever was related. The truth is, that not one person in a thousand, in the proper sense of the word, believes anything; they only fancy they believe, because they have never seriously considered the meaning of the word and all that it involves. That which the human mind can not conceive of, is apt to slip from its grasp like water from the hand; and life out of the flesh falls under this category. The observation of any phenomena, therefore, which enabled us to master the idea, must necessarily be extremely beneficial; and it must be remembered, that one single thoroughly well-established instance of the reappearance of a deceased person, would not only have this effect, but that it would afford a demonstrative proof of the deepest of all our intuitions, namely, that a future life awaits us.

Not to mention the modern Germans of eminence, who have devoted themselves to this investigation, there have been men remarkable for intellect in all countries, who have considered the subject worthy of inquiry. Among the rest, Plato, Pliny, and Lucien; and in our own country, that good old divine, Dr. Henry Moore, Dr. Johnson, Addison, Isaac Taylor, and many others. It may be objected that the eternally-quoted case of Nicolai, the bookseller at Berlin, and Dr. Ferriar's "Theory of Apparitions," had not then settled the question; but nobody doubts that Nicolai's was a case of disease; and he was well aware of it himself, as it appears to me, everybody so afflicted, is. I was acquainted with a poor woman, in Edinburgh, who suffered from this malady, brought on, I believe, by drinking; but she was perfectly conscious of the nature of the illusions; and that temperance and a doctor were the proper exorcists to lay the spirits. With respect to Dr. Ferriar's book, a more shallow one was assuredly never allowed to settle any question; and his own theory can not, without the most violent straining, and the assistance of what he calls *coincidences*, meet even half the cases he himself adduces. That such a disease, as he describes, exists, nobody doubts; but I maintain that there are hundreds of cases on record, for which the explanation does not suffice; and if they have been instances of spectral illusion, all that remains to be said, is, that a fundamental reconstruction of the theory on that subject is demanded.

La Place says, in his "Essay on Probabilities," that "any case, however apparently incredible, if it be a recurrent case, is as much entitled, under the laws of induction, to a fair valuation, as if it had been more probable beforehand." Now, no one will deny that the case in question possesses this claim to investigation. Determined skeptics may, indeed, deny that there exists any well-authenticated instance of an apparition; but that, at present, can only be a mere matter of opinion; since many persons, as competent to judge as themselves, maintain the contrary; and in the meantime, I arraign their right to make this objection till they have qualified themselves to do so, by a long course of patient and honest inquiry; always remembering that every instance of error or imposition discovered and adduced, has no positive value whatever in the argument, but as regards that single instance; though it may enforce upon us the necessity of strong evidence and careful investigation. With respect to the evidence, past and present, I must be allowed here to remark on the extreme difficulty of producing it. Not to mention the acknowledged carelessness of observers and the alleged incapacity of persons to distinguish between reality and illusion, there is an exceeding shyness in most people, who, either have seen, or fancied they have seen, an apparition, to speak of it at all, except to some intimate friend; so that one gets most of the stories second-hand; while even those who are less chary of their communications, are imperative against their name and authority being given to the public. Besides this, there is a great tendency in most people, after the impression is over, to think they may have been deceived; and where there is no communication or other circumstance rendering this conviction impossible, it is not difficult to acquire it, or at least so much of it as leaves the case valueless. The seer is glad to find this refuge from the unpleasant feelings engendered; while surrounding friends, sometimes from genuine skepticism, and sometimes from good-nature, almost invariably lean to this explanation of the mystery. In consequence of these difficulties and those attending the very nature of the phenomena, I freely admit that the facts I shall adduce, as they now stand, can have no scientific value; they can not in short, enter into the region of science at all, still less into that of philosophy. Whatever conclusions we may be led to form, can not be founded on pure induction. We must confine ourselves wholly within the region of opinion; if we venture beyond which, we shall assuredly founder. In the beginning, all sciences have been but a collection of facts, afterward to be examined, compared, and weighed, by intelligent minds. To the vulgar, who do not see the universal law which governs the universe, everything out of the ordinary course of events, is a prodigy; but to the enlightened mind there are no prodigies; for it perceives that in both the moral and the physical world, there is a chain of uninterrupted connection; and that the most strange and even apparently contradictory or supernatural fact or event will be found, on due investigation, to be strictly dependent on its antecedents. It is possible, that there may be a link wanting, and that our investigations may, consequently, be fruitless; but the link is assuredly there, although our imperfect knowledge and limited vision can not find it.

And it is here the proper place to observe, that, in undertaking to treat of the phenomena in question, I do not propose to consider them as supernatural; on the contrary, I am persuaded that the time will come, when they will be reduced strictly within the bounds of science. It was the tendency of the last age to reject and *deny* everything they did not understand; I hope it is the growing tendency of the present one to *examine* what we do not understand. Equally disposed with our predecessors of the eighteenth century to reject the supernatural, and to believe the order of nature inviolable, we are disposed to extend the bounds of nature and science, till they comprise within their limits all the phenomena, ordinary and extraordinary, by which we are surrounded. Scarcely a month passes that we do not hear of some new and important discovery in science. It is a domain in which nothing is stable, and every year overthrows some of the hasty and premature theories of the preceding ones; and this will continue to be the case as long as scientific men occupy themselves each with his own subject, without studying the great and primal truths — what the French call *les verités mères* — which link the whole together. Meantime, there is a continual unsettling. Truth, if it do not emanate from an acknowledged authority, is generally rejected; and error, if it do, is as often accepted; while, whoever disputes the received theory, whatever it be—we mean especially that adopted by the professors of colleges—does it at his peril. But there is a day yet brooding in the bosom of time, when the sciences will be no longer isolated; when we shall no longer deny, but be able to account for, phenomena apparently prodigious, or have the modesty, if we can not explain them, to admit that the difficulty arises solely from our own incapacity. The system of centralization in statistics seems to be of doubtful advantage; but a greater degree of centralization appears to be very much needed in the domain of science. Some improvement in this respect might do wonders, particularly if reinforced with a slight infusion of patience and humility into the minds of scientific men; together with the recollection that facts and phenomena, which do not depend on our will, must be waited for—that we must be at their command, for they will not be at ours.

But to return once more to our own subject. If we do believe that a future life awaits us, there can be nothing more natural than the desire to obtain some information as to what manner of life that is to be for which any one of us may, before this time to-morrow, have exchanged his present mode of being. That there does not exist a greater interest with regard to this question in the mind of man, arises partly from the vague, intangible kind of belief he entertains of the fact; partly from his absorption in worldly affairs, and the hard and indigestible food upon which his clerical shepherds pasture him—for, under dogmatic theology, religion seems to have withered away to the mere husk of spiritualism; and partly, also, from the apparent impossibility of pursuing the inquiry to any purpose. As I said before, observation and experience can alone guide us in such an inquiry; for, though most people have a more or less intuitive sense of their own immortality, intuition is silent as to the mode of it; and the question I am anxious here to discuss with my readers is, whether we have any facts to observe, or any experience from which, on this most interesting of all subjects, a conclusion may be drawn. Great as the difficulty is of producing evidence, it will, I think, be pretty generally admitted that, although each individual case, as it stands alone, may be comparatively valueless, the amount of recurrent cases forms a body of evidence that, on any other subject, would scarcely be rejected; and since, if the facts are accepted, they imperatively demand an explanation — for, assuredly, the present theory of spectral illusions can not comprise them — our inquiry, let it terminate in whatever conclusion it may, can not be useless or uninteresting. Various views of the phenomena in question may be taken; and although I shall offer my own opinions and the theories and opinions of others, I insist upon none. I do not write to dogmatise, but to suggest reflection and inquiry. The books of Dr. Ferriar, Dr. Hibbert, and Dr. Thatcher, the American, are all written to support one exclusive theory; and they only give such cases as serve to sustain it. They maintain that the whole phenomena are referrible to nervous or sanguineous derangement, and are mere subjective illusions; and whatever instance can not be covered by this theory, they reject as false, or treat as a case of extraordinary coincidence. In short, they arrange the facts to their theory, not their theory to the facts. Their books can not, therefore, claim to be considered as anything more than essays on a special disease; they have no pretence whatever to the character of investigations. The question, consequently, remains as much an open one as before they treated it; while we have the advantage of their experience and information, with regard to the peculiar malady that forms the subject of their works. On that subject it is not my intention to enter; it is a strictly medical one, and every information may be obtained respecting it in the above-named treatises, and others emanating from the faculty.

The subjects I do intend to treat of are the various kinds of prophetic dreams, presentiments, second-sight, and apparitions; and, in short, all that class of phenomena which appears to throw some light on our physical nature, and on the probable state of the soul after death. In this discussion, I shall make free use of my German authorities, Doctors Kerner, Stilling, Werner, Eschenmayer, Ennemoser, Passavent, Schubert, Von Meyer, &c., &c.; and I here make a general acknowledgment to that effect, because it would embarrass my book too much to be constantly giving names and references, although, when I quote their words literally, I shall make a point of doing so; and because, also, that, as I have been both thinking and reading much on these subjects for a considerable time past, I am, in fact, no longer in a condition to appropriate, either to them or to myself, each his own. This, however, is a matter of very little consequence, as I am not desirous of claiming any idea as mine that can be found elsewhere. It is enough for me, if I succeed in making a tolerably clear exposition of the subject, and can induce other people to reflect upon it.

CHAPTER II.

THE DWELLER IN THE TEMPLE.

It is almost needless to observe, that the Scriptures repeatedly speak of man as a tripartite being, consisting of spirit, soul, and body: and that, according to St. Paul, we have two bodies—a natural body and a spiritual body; the former being designed as our means of communication with the external world—an instrument to be used and controlled by our nobler parts. It is this view of it, carried to a fanaticism, which has led to the various and extraordinary mortifications recorded of ascetics. As is remarked by the Rev. Hare Townshend, in a late edition of his book on mesmerism, in this fleshly body consists our organic life; in the body which we are to retain through eternity, consists our fundamental life. May not the first, he says, "be a temporary development of the last, just as leaves, flowers, and fruits, are the temporary developments of a tree? And in the same manner that these pass and drop away, yet leave the principle of reproduction behind, so may our present organs be detached from us by death, and yet the ground of our existence be spared to us continuously."

Without entering into the subtle disputes of philosophers, with regard to the spirit, a subject on which there is a standing controversy between the disciples of Hegel and those of other teachers, I need only observe that the Scriptures seem to indicate what some of the heathen sages taught, that the spirit that dwells within us is the spirit of God, incorporated in us for a period, for certain ends of his own, to be thereby wrought out. What those ends are, it does not belong to my present subject to consider. In this spirit so imparted to us, dwells, says Eschenmayer, the conscience, which keeps watch over the body and the soul, saying, "Thus shalt thou do!" And it is to this Christ addresses himself when he bids his disciples become perfect, like their Father in heaven. The soul is subject to the spirit; and its functions are, *to will*, or *choose*, *to think*, and *to feel*, and to become thereby cognizant of the true, the beautiful, and the good; comprehending the highest principle, the highest ideal, and the most perfect happiness. The *Ego*, or *I*, is the resultant of the three forces, Pneuma, Psyche, Soma—spirit, soul, and body.

In the spirit or soul, or rather in both conjoined, dwells, also, the power of *spiritual seeing*, or *intuitive knowing;* for, as there is a spiritual body, there is a spiritual eye, and a spiritual ear, and so forth; or, to speak more correctly, all these sensuous functions are comprised in one universal sense, which does not need the aid of the bodily organs; but, on the contrary, is most efficient when most freed from them. It remains to be seen whether, or in what degree, such separation can take place during life; complete it can not be till death; but whoever believes sincerely that the divine spirit dwells within him, can, I should think, find no difficulty in conceiving that, although from the temporary conditions to which that spirit is subjected, this universal faculty is limited and obscured, it must still retain its indefeasible attribute.

We may naturally conclude that the most perfect state of man on earth consists in the most perfect unity of the spirit and the soul; and to those who in this life have attained the nearest to that unity will the entire assimilation of the two, after they are separated from the body, be the easiest; while to those who have lived only their intellectual and external life, this union must be extremely difficult, the soul having chosen its part with the body, and divorced itself, as much as in it lay, from the spirit. The voice of conscience is then scarcely heard; and the soul, degraded and debased, can no longer perform its functions of discerning the true, the beautiful, and the good.

On these distinct functions of the soul and spirit, however, it is not my intention to insist, since it appears to me a subject on which we are not yet in a condition to dogmatize. We know rather more about our bodies, by means of which the soul and spirit are united and brought into contact with the material world, and which are constructed wholly with a view to the conditions of that world; such as time, space, solidity, extension, &c., &c. But we must conceive of God as necessarily independent of these conditions. To Him, all times and all places must be for ever present; and it is *thus* that he is omniscient and omnipresent; and since we are placed by the spirit in immediate relation with God and the spiritual world, just as we are placed by the body in immediate relation with the material world, we may, in the first place, form a notion of the possibility that some faint gleams of these inherent attributes may, at times, shoot up through the clay in which the spirit has taken up its temporary abode; and we may also admit, that through the connection which exists between us and the spiritual world, it is not impossible but that we may, at times, and under certain conditions, become cognizant of, and enter into more immediate relation with it. This is the only postulate I ask; for, as I said before, I do not wish to enforce opinions, but to suggest probabilities, or at least possibilities, and thus arouse reflection and inquiry.

With respect to the term *invisible world*, I beg to remind my readers, that what we call *seeing* is merely the function of an organ constructed for that purpose in relation to the external world; and so limited are its powers, that we are surrounded by many things in that world which we can not see without the aid of artificial appliances and many other things which we can not see even with them; the atmosphere in which we live, for example, although its weight and mechanical forces are the subjects of accurate calculation, is entirely imperceptible to our visual organs. Thus, the fact that we do not commonly see them, forms no legitimate objection to the hypothesis of our being surrounded by a world of spirits, or of that world being inter-diffused among us. Supposing the question to be decided that we do sometimes become cognizant of them, which, however, I admit it is not, since, whether the apparitions are subjective, or objective, that is, whether they are the mere phenomena of disease, or real out-standing appearances, is the inquiry I desire to promote—but, I say, supposing that question were decided in the affirmative, the next that arises is, how, or by what means do we see them; or, if they address us, hear them? If that universal sense which appears to me to be inseparable from the idea of spirit, be once admitted, I think there can be no difficulty in answering this question; and if it be objected that we are conscious of no such sense, I answer, that both in dreams and in certain abnormal states of the body, it is frequently manifested. In order to render this more clear, and, at the same time, to give an interesting instance of this sort of phenomenon, I will transcribe a passage from a letter of St. Augustine to his friend Evadius (Epistola 159. Antwerp edition).

"I will relate to you a circumstance," he writes, "which will furnish you matter for reflection. Our brother Sennadius, well known to us all as an eminent physician, and whom we especially love, who is now at Carthage, after having distinguished himself at Rome, and with whose piety and active benevolence you are well acquainted, could yet, nevertheless, as he has lately narrated to us, by no means bring himself to believe in a life after death. Now, God, doubtless, not willing that his soul should perish, there appeared to him one night, in a dream, a radiant youth of noble aspect, who bade him follow him; and as Sennadius obeyed, they came to a city where, on the right side, he heard a chorus of the most heavenly voices. As he desired to know whence this divine harmony proceeded, the youth told him that what he heard were the songs of the blessed; whereupon he awoke, and thought no more of his dream than people usually do. On another night, however, behold! the youth appears to him again, and asks him if he knows him; and Sennadius related to him all the particulars of his former dream, which he well remembered. 'Then,' said the youth, 'was it while sleeping or waking that you saw these things?'—'I was sleeping,' answered Sennadius. 'You are right,' returned the youth, 'it was in your sleep that you saw these things; and know, O Sennadius, that what you see now is also in your sleep. But if this be so, tell me where then is your body?'—'In my bedchamber,' answered Sennadius. 'But know you not,' continued the stranger, 'that your eyes, which form a part of your body, are closed and inactive?'—'I know it,' answered he. 'Then,' said the youth, 'with what eyes see you these things?' And Sennadius could not answer him; and as he hesitated, the youth spoke again, and explained to him the motive of his questions. 'As the eyes of your body,' said he, 'which lies now on your bed and sleeps, are inactive and useless, and yet you have eyes wherewith you see me and these things I have shown unto you; so after death, when these bodily organs fail you, you will have a vital power, whereby you will live, and a sensitive faculty, whereby you will perceive. Doubt, therefore, no longer that there is a life after death.' And thus," said this excellent man, "was I convinced, and all doubts removed."

I confess there appears to me a beauty and a logical truth in this dream that I think might convince more than the dreamer.

It is by the hypothesis of this universal sense, latent within us—an hypothesis which, whoever believes that we are immortal spirits, incorporated for a season in a material body, can scarcely reject—that I seek to explain those perceptions which are not comprised within the functions of our bodily organs. It seems to me to be the key to all or nearly all of them, as far as our own part in the phenomena extends. But, supposing this admitted, there would then remain the difficulty of accounting for the partial and capricious glimpses we get of it; while in that department of the mystery which regards apparitions, except such as are the pure result of disease, we must grope our way, with very little light to guide us, as to the conditions and motives which might possibly bring them into any immediate relation with us.

To any one who has been fortunate enough to witness one genuine case of clairvoyance, I think the conception of this universal sense will not be difficult, however the mode of its exercise may remain utterly incomprehensible. As I have said above—to the great Spirit and Fountain of life, all things, in both space and time, must be present. However impossible it is to our finite minds to conceive this, we must believe it. It may, in some slight degree, facilitate the conception to remember that action, once begun, never ceases—an impulse given is transmitted on for ever; a sound breathed reverberates in eternity; and thus the past *is* always present, although, for the purpose of fitting us for this mortal life, our ordinary senses are so constituted as to be unperceptive of these phenomena. With respect to what we call *the future*, it is more difficult still for us to conceive it as present; nor, as far as I know, can we borrow from the sciences the same assistance as mechanical discoveries have just furnished me with in regard to the past. How a spirit sees that which has not yet, to our senses, taken place, seems certainly inexplicable. *Foreseeing* it is not inexplicable: we foresee many things by arguing on given premises, although, from our own finite views, we are always liable to be mistaken. Louis Lambert says: "Such events as are the product of humanity, and the result of its intelligence, have their own causes, in which they lie latent, just as our actions are accomplished in our thoughts previous to any outward demonstration of them; presentiments and prophecies consist in the intuitive perception of these causes." This explanation, which is quite conformable with that of Cicero, may aid us in some degree as regards a certain small class of phenomena; but there is something involved in the question much more subtle than this. Our dreams can give us the only idea of it; for there we do actually see and hear, not only that which never was, but that which never will be. Actions and events, words and sounds, persons and places, are as clearly and vividly present to us as if they were actually what they seem; and I should think that most people must be somewhat puzzled to decide in regard to certain scenes and circumstances that live in their memory, whether the images are the result of their waking or sleeping experience. Although by no means a dreamer, and without the most remote approximation to any faculty of presentiment, I know this is the case with myself. I remember also a very curious effect being produced upon me, when I was abroad, some years ago, from eating the unwholesome bread to which we were reduced, in consequence of a scarcity. Some five or six times a day I was seized with a sort of vertigo, during which I seemed to pass through certain scenes, and was conscious of certain words, which appeared to me to have a strange connection, with either some former period of my life, or else some previous state of existence. The words and the scenes were on each occasion precisely the same: I was always aware of that, and I always made the strongest efforts to grasp and retain them in my memory, but I could not. I only knew that the thing *had been*; the words and the scenes were gone. I seemed to pass momentarily into another sphere and back again. This was purely the result of disorder; but, like a dream, it shows how we may be perceptive of that which is not, and which never may be; rendering it, therefore, possible to conceive that a spirit may be equally perceptive of that which shall be. I am very far from meaning to imply that these examples remove the difficulty: they do not explain the thing; they only show somewhat the mode of it. But it must be remembered that when physiologists pretend to settle the whole question of apparitions by the theory of spectral illusions, they are exactly in the same predicament. They can supply examples of similar phenomena; but how a person, perfectly in his senses, should receive the spectral visits of, not only friends, but strangers, when he is thinking of no such matter—or by what process, mental or optical, the figures are conjured up—remains as much a mystery as before a line was written on the subject.

All people and all ages have believed, more or less, in prophetic dreams, presentiments, and apparitions; and all historians have furnished examples of them. That the truths may be frequently distorted and mingled with fable, is no argument against those traditions; if it were, all history must be rejected on the same plea. Both the Old and New Testaments furnish numerous examples of these phenomena; and although Christ and the apostles reproved all the superstitions of the age, these persuasions are not included in their reprehensions.

Neither is the comparative rarity of these phenomena any argument against their possibility. There are many strange things which occur still more rarely, but which we do not look upon as supernatural or miraculous. Of nature's ordinary laws, we yet know but little; of their aberrations and perturbations, still less. How should we, when the world is a miracle and life a dream, of which we know neither the beginning nor the end! We do not even know that we see anything as it is, or rather, we know that we do not. We see things but as our visual organs represent them to us; and were those organs differently constructed, the aspect of the world would to us be changed. How, then, can we pretend to decide upon what is and what is not?

Nothing could be more perplexing to any one who read them with attention, than the trials for witchcraft of the seventeenth century. Many of the feats of the ancient thaumaturgists and wonder-workers of the temples might have been nearly as much so, but these were got rid of by the easy expedient of pronouncing them fables and impostures: but, during the witch-mania, so many persons proved their faith in their own miraculous powers by the sacrifice of their lives, that it was scarcely possible to doubt their having some foundation for their own persuasion, though what that foundation could be, till the late discoveries in animal magnetism, it was difficult to conceive; but here we have a new page opened to us which concerns both the history of the world and the history of man, as an individual; and we begin to see that that which the ignorant thought supernatural, and the wise impossible, has been both natural and true. While the scientific men of Great Britain, and several of our journalists, have been denying and ridiculing the reports of these phenomena, the most eminent physicians of Germany have been quietly studying and investigating them, and giving to the world, in their works, the results of their experience. Among the rest, Dr. Joseph Ennemoser, of Berlin, has presented to us in his two books on "Magic," and on "The Connection of Magnetism with Nature and Religion," the fruits of his thirty years' study of this subject—during the course of which he has had repeated opportunities of investigating all the phenomena, and of making himself perfectly familiar with even the most rare and perplexing. To any one who has studied these works, the mysteries of the temples and of the witch-trials are mysteries no longer; and he writes with the professed design, not to make science mystical, but to bring the mysterious within the bounds of science. The phenomena, as he justly says, are as old as the human race. Animal magnetism is no new development, no new discovery. Inseparable from life, although, like many other vital phenomena, so subtle in its influences, that only in abnormal cases it attracts attention, it has exhibited itself more or less in all ages and in all countries. But its value as a medical agent is only now beginning to dawn on the civilized world, while its importance in a higher point of view is yet perceived by but few. Every human being who has ever withdrawn himself from the strife, and the turmoil, and the distraction, of the world without, in order to look within, must have found himself perplexed by a thousand questions with regard to his own being, which he would find no one able to solve. In the study of animal magnetism, he will first obtain some gleams of a light which will show him that he is indeed the child of God! and that, though a dweller on the earth, and fallen, some traces of his divine descent, and of his unbroken connection with a higher order of being, still remain to comfort and encourage him. He will find that there exists in his species the germs of faculties that are never fully unfolded here on earth, and which have no reference to this state of being. They exist in all men, but in most cases are so faintly elicited as not to be observable; and when they do shoot up here and there, they are denied, disowned, misinterpreted, and maligned. It is true that their development is often the symptom and effect of disease, which seems to change the relations of our material and immaterial parts; it is true that some of the phenomena resulting from these faculties are stimulated by disease, as in the case of spectral illusions; and it is true that imposture and folly intrude their unhallowed footsteps into this domain of science, as into that of all others: but there is a deep and holy well of truth to be discovered in this neglected by-path of nature, by those who seek it, from which they may draw the purest consolations for the present, the most ennobling hopes for the future, and the most valuable aid in penetrating through the letter into the spirit of the Scriptures.

I confess it makes me sorrowful when I hear men laughing, scorning, and denying this their birthright; and I can not but grieve to think how closely and heavily their clay must be wrapped about them, and how the external and sensuous life must have prevailed over the internal, when no gleam from within breaks through to show them that these things are true.

CHAPTER III.

WAKING AND SLEEPING; AND HOW THE DWELLER IN THE TEMPLE SOMETIMES LOOKS ABROAD.

To begin with the most simple — or rather, I should say, the most ordinary — class of phenomena, for we can scarcely call that simple, the mystery of which we have never been able to penetrate — I mean dreaming — everybody's experience will suffice to satisfy them that their ordinary dreams take place in a state of imperfect sleep, and that this imperfect sleep may be caused by any bodily or mental derangement whatever, or even from an ill-made bed, or too much or too little covering; and it is not difficult to conceive that the strange, confused, and disjointed visions we are subject to on these occasions, may proceed from some parts of the brain being less at rest than the others; so that, assuming phrenology to be fact, one organ is not in a state to correct the impressions of another. Of such vain and insignificant visions, I need scarcely say it is not my intention to treat; but, at the same time, I must observe, that when we have admitted the above explanation, as far as it goes, we have not, even in regard to *them*, made much progress toward removing the difficulty. If dreaming resembled thinking, the explanations might be quite satisfactory; but the truth is, that dreaming is not thinking, as we think in our waking state, but is more analogous to thinking in delirium or acute mania, or in that chronic condition which gives rise to sensuous illusions. In our ordinary normal state, conceiving of places or persons does not enable us to see them or hold communion with them, nor do we fancy that we do either. It is true, that I have heard some painters say that, by closing their eyes and concentrating their thoughts on an object, they can bring it more or less vividly before them, and Blake professed actually to see his sitters when they were not present; but whatever interpretations we may put upon this curious faculty, his case was clearly abnormal, and connected with some personal peculiarity, either physical or psychical; and, after making the most of it, it must be admitted that it can enter into no sort of comparison with that we possess in sleep, when, in our most ordinary dreams, untrammelled by time or space, we visit the uttermost ends of the earth, fly in the air, swim in the sea, listen to beautiful music and eloquent orations, behold the most charming as well as the most loathsome objects; and not only see, but converse with our friends, absent or present, dead or alive. Every one, I think, will grant that there is the widest possible difference between conceiving of these things when awake, and dreaming them. When we dream, we do, we see, we say, we hear, &c., &c., that is, we believe at the time we do so; and what more can be said of us when we are awake, than that we *believe* we are doing, seeing, saying, hearing, &c. It is by external circumstances, and the results of our actions, that we are able to decide whether we have actually done a thing or seen a place, or only dreamt that we have done so; and as I have said above, after some lapse of time we are not always able to distinguish between the two. While dreaming, we frequently ask ourselves whether we are awake or asleep; and nothing is more common than to hear people say, "Well, I think I did, or heard, so and so; but I am not sure whether it was so, or whether I dreamt it." Thus, therefore, the very lowest order of dreaming, the most disjointed and perplexed, is far removed from the most vivid presentations of our waking thoughts; and it is in this respect, I think, that the explanations of the phenomena hitherto offered by phrenologists, and the metaphysicians of this country, are inadequate and unsatisfactory; while, as regards the analogy between the visions of sleep and delirium, whatever similarity there may be in the effects, we can not suppose the cause to be identical: since, in delirium the images and delusions are the result of excessive action of the brain, which we must conclude to be the very reverse of its condition in sleep. Pinel certainly has hazarded an opinion that sleep is occasioned by an efflux of blood to the head, and consequent compression of the brain—a theory which would have greater weight were sleep more strictly periodical than it is; but which, at present, it seems impossible to reconcile with many established facts.

Some of the German physiologists and psychologists have taken a deeper view of this question of dreaming, from considering it in connection with the phenomena of animal magnetism; and although their theories differ in some respects, they all unite in looking toward that department of nature for instruction. While one section of these inquirers, the Exegetical Society of Stockholm included, calls in the aid of supernatural agency, another, among whom Dr. Joseph Ennemoser, of Berlin, appears to be one of the most eminent, maintains that the explanation of the mystery is to be chiefly sought in the great and universal law of polarity, which extends not only beyond the limits of this earth, but beyond the limits of this system, which must necessarily be in connection with all others; so that there is thus an eternal and never-ceasing inter-action, of which, from the multiplicity and contrariety of the influences, we are insensible, just as we are insensible to the pressure of the atmosphere, from its impinging on us equally on all sides.

Waking and sleeping are the day and night sides of organic life, during which alternations an animal is placed in different relations to the external world, and to these alternations all organisms are subject. The completeness and independence of each individual organism, are in exact ratio to the number and completeness of the organs it develops; and thus the locomotive animal has the advantage of the plant or the zoophyte, while, of the animal kingdom, man is the most complete and independent; and, although still a member of the universal whole, and therefore incapable of isolating himself, yet better able than any other organism to ward off external influences, and comprise his world within himself. But, according to Dr. Ennemoser, one of the consequences of this very completeness is a weak and insignificant development of instinct; and thus the healthy, waking, conscious man, is, of all organisms, the least sensible to the impressions of this universal inter-communication and polarity; although, at the same time, partaking of the nature of the plant and the animal, he is subject, like the first, to all manner of atmospheric, telluric, and periodic influences; and frequently exhibits, like the second, peculiar instinctive appetites and desires, and, in some individual organizations, very marked antipathies and susceptibilities with regard to certain objects and influences, even when not placed in any evident relation with them.

According to this theory, sleep is a retrograde step—a retreating into a lower sphere; in which condition, the sensuous functions being in abeyance, the instincts somewhat resume their sway. "In sleep and in sickness," he says, "the higher animals and man fall in a physico-organical point of view, from their individual independence, or power of self-sustainment; and their polar relation, that is, their relation to the healthy and waking man, becomes changed from a positive to a negative one; all men, in regard to each other, as well as all nature, being the subjects of this polarity. It is to be remembered, that this theory of Dr. Ennemoser's was promulgated before the discoveries of Baron von Reichenback in magnetism were made public, and the susceptibility to magnetic influences in the animal organism, which the experiments of the latter go to establish, is certainly in its favor; but while it pretends to explain the condition of the sleepers, and may possibly be of some service in our investigations into the mystery of dreaming, it leaves us as much in the dark as ever, with respect to the cause of our falling into this negative state; an inquiry in which little progress seems to have been hitherto made.

With respect to dreaming, Dr. Ennemoser rejects the physiological theory, which maintains, that in sleep, magnetic or otherwise, the activity of the brain is transferred to the ganglionic system, and that the former falls into a subordinate relation. "Dreaming," he says, "is the gradual awakening of activity in the organs of imagination, whereby the presentation of sensuous objects to the spirit, which had been discontinued in profound sleep, is resumed. Dreaming," he adds, "also arises from the secret activity of the spirit in the innermost sensuous organs of the brain, busying the fancy with subjective sensuous images, the objective conscious day-life giving place to the creative dominion of the poetical genius, to which night becomes day, and universal nature its theatre of action; and thus the supersensuous or transcendent nature of the spirit becomes more manifest in dreaming than in the waking state. But, in considering these phenomena, man must be viewed in both his psychical and physical relations, and as equally subject to spiritual as to natural operations and influences; since, during the continuance of life, neither soul nor body can act quite independently of the other; for, although it be the immortal spirit which perceives, it is through the instrumentality of the sensuous organs that it does so; for of absolute spirit without body, we can form no conception."

What is here meant seems to be, that the brain becomes the world to the spirit, before the impressions from the external world do actually come streaming through by means of the external sensuous organs. The inner spiritual light illumines, till the outward physical light overpowers and extinguishes it. But in this state the brain, which is the storehouse of acquired knowledge, is not in a condition to apply its acquisitions effectively; while the intuitive knowledge of the spirit, if the sleep be imperfect, is clouded by its interference.

Other physiologists, however, believe, from the numerous and well-attested cases of the transference of the senses, in disease, to the pit of the stomach, that the activity of the brain in sleep *is* transferred to the epigastric region. The instances of this phenomenon, as related by Dr. Petetin and others, having been frequently published, I need not here quote. But, as Dr. Passavant observes, it is well known that the functions of the nerves differ in some animals; and that one set can supply the place of another; as in those cases where there is a great susceptibility to light, though no eyes can be discovered.

These physiologists believe, that, even during the most profound sleep, the spirit retains its activity, a proposition which, indeed, we can not doubt; "it wakes, though the senses sleep, retreating into its infinite depths, like the sun at night; living on its spiritual life undisturbed, while the body sinks into a state of vegetative tranquillity. Nor does it follow that the soul is unconscious in sleep because in waking we have frequently lost all memory of its consciousness; since, by the repose of the sensuous organs, the bridge between waking and sleeping is removed, and the recollections of one state are not carried into the other."

It will occur here to every one, how often in the instant of waking we are not only conscious that we have been dreaming, but are also conscious of the subject of the dream, which we try in vain to grasp, but which eludes us, and is gone for ever the moment we have passed into a state of complete wakefulness.

Now, with respect to this so-called dreaming in profound sleep, it is a thing no one can well doubt who thoroughly believes that his body is a temple built for the dwelling of an immortal spirit; for we can not conceive of spirit sleeping, or needing that restoration which we know to be the condition of earthly organisms. If, therefore, the spirit wakes, may we not suppose that the more it is disentangled from the obstructions of the body the more clear will be its perceptions; and that, therefore, in the profound natural sleep of the sensuous organs we may be in a state of clear-seeing. All who have attended to the subject are aware that the clear seeing of magnetic patients depends on the depth of their sleep; whatever circumstance, internal or external, tends to interrupt this profound repose of the sensuous organs, inevitably obscures their perceptions.

Again, with respect to the not carrying with us the recollections of one state into the other, should not this lead us to suspect that sleeping and waking are two different spheres of existence; partaking of the nature of that *double life*, of which the records of human physiology have presented us with various instances wherein a patient finds himself utterly divested of all recollection of past events and acquired knowledge, and has to begin life and education anew, till another transition takes place, wherein he recovers what he had lost, while he at the same time loses all he had lately gained, which he only recovers, once more, by another transition, restoring to him his lately-acquired knowledge, but again obliterating his original stock, thus alternately passing from one state to the other, and disclosing a double life—an educated man in one condition, a child learning his alphabet in the next!

Where the transition from one state to another is complete, memory is entirely lost; but there are cases in which the change, being either gradual or modified, the recollections of one life are carried more or less into the other. We know this to be the case with magnetic sleepers, as it is with ordinary dreamers; and most persons have met with instances of the dream of one night being continued in the next. Treviranus mentions the case of a student who regularly began to talk the moment he fell asleep, the subject of his discourse being a dream, which he always took up at the exact point at which he had left it the previous morning. Of this dream he had never the slightest recollection in his waking state. A daughter of Sir George Mackenzie, who died at an early age, was endowed with a remarkable genius for music, and was an accomplished organist. This young lady dreamed, during an illness, that she was at a party, where she had heard a new piece of music, which made so great an impression on her by its novelty and beauty, that, on awaking, she besought her attendants to bring her some paper, that she might write it down before she had forgotten it—an indulgence which, apprehensive of excitement, her medical attendant unfortunately forbade; for, apart from the additional psychological interest that would have been attached to the fact, the effects of compliance, judging from what ensued, would probably have been soothing rather than otherwise. About ten days afterward, she had a second dream, wherein she again found herself at a party, where she descried on the desk of a pianoforte, in a corner of the room, an open book, in which, with astonished delight, she recognised the same piece of music, which she immediately proceeded to play, and then awoke. The piece was not of a short or fugitive character, but in the style of an overture. The question, of course, remains, as to whether she was composing the music in her sleep, or, by an act of clairvoyance, was perceiving some that actually existed. Either is possible, for, although she might have been incapable of composing so elaborate a piece in her waking state, there are many instances on record of persons performing intellectual feats in dreams, to which they were unequal when awake. A very eminent person assured me that he had once composed some lines in his sleep (I think it was a sonnet) which far exceeded any of his waking performances of that description.

Somewhat analogous to this sort of double life is the case of the young girl mentioned by Dr. Abercrombie and others, whose employment was keeping cattle, and who slept for some time, much to her own annoyance, in the room adjoining one occupied by an itinerant musician. The man, who played exceedingly well, being an enthusiast in his art, frequently practised the greater part of the night, performing on his violin very complicated and difficult compositions; while the girl, so far from discovering any pleasure in his performances, complained bitterly of being kept awake by the noise. Some time after this, she fell ill, and was removed to the house of a charitable lady, who undertook the charge of her; and here, by-and-by, the family were amazed by frequently hearing the most exquisite music in the night, which they at length discovered to proceed from the girl. The sounds were those of a violin, and the tuning and other preliminary processes were accurately imitated. She went through long and elaborate pieces, and afterward was heard imitating, in the same way, the sounds of a pianoforte that was in the house. She also talked very cleverly on the subjects of religion and politics, and discussed with great judgment the characters and conduct of persons, public and private. Awake, she knew nothing of these things; but was, on the contrary, stupid, heavy, and had no taste whatever for music. Phrenology would probably interpret this phenomenon by saying that the lower elements of the cerebral spinal axis, as organs of sensation, &c., &c., being asleep, the cluster of the higher organs requisite for the above combinations were not only awake, but rendered more active from the repose of the others: but to me it appears that we here see the inherent faculties of the spirit manifesting themselves, while the body slept. The same faculties must have existed when it was in a waking state, but the impressions and manifestations were then dependent on the activity and perfection of the sensuous organs, which seem to have been of an inferior order; and consequently, no rays of this in-dwelling genius could pierce the coarse integument in which it was lodged.

Similar unexpected faculties have been not unfrequently manifested by the dying, and we may conclude to a certain degree from the same cause, namely, that the incipient death of the body is leaving the spirit more unobstructed. Dr. Steinbech mentions the case of a clergyman, who, being summoned to administer the last sacraments to a dying peasant, found him, to his surprise, praying aloud in Greek and Hebrew, a mystery which could be no otherwise explained than by the circumstance of his having, when a child, frequently heard the then minister of the parish praying in those languages. He had, however, never understood the prayers, nor indeed paid any attention to them; still less had he been aware that they lived in his memory. It would give much additional interest to this story had Dr. Steinbech mentioned how far the man now, while uttering the words, understood their meaning; whether he was aware of what he was saying, or was only repeating the words by rote.

With regard to the extraordinary faculty of memory manifested in these and similar cases, I shall have some observations to make in a subsequent part of this book.

Parallel instances are those of idiots, who, either in a somnambulic state, or immediately previous to death, have spoken as if inspired. At St. Jean de Maurinne, in Savoy, there was a dumb *cretin*, who, having fallen into a natural state of somnambulism, not only was found to speak with ease, but also to the purpose; a faculty which disappeared, however, whenever he awoke. Dumb persons have likewise been known to speak when at the point of death.

The possibility of suggesting dreams to some sleepers by whispering in the ear, is a well-known fact; but this can doubtless only be practicable where the sensuous organs are partly awake. Then, as with magnetic patients in a state of incomplete sleep, we have only revery and imagination in place of clear-seeing.

The next class of dreams are those which partake of the nature of second sight, or prophecy, and of these there are various kinds; some being plain and literal in their premonitions, others allegorical and obscure; while some also regard the most unimportant, and others the most grave events of our lives. A gentleman engaged in business in the south of Scotland, for example, dreams that on entering his office in the morning, he sees seated on a certain stool a person formerly in his service as clerk, of whom he had neither heard nor thought for some time. He inquires the motive of the visit, and is told that such and such circumstances having brought the stranger to that part of the country, he could not forbear visiting his old quarters, expressing at the same time a wish to spend a few days in his former occupation, &c., &c. The gentleman, being struck with the vividness of the illusion, relates his dream at breakfast, and, to his surprise, on going to his office, there sits the man, and the dialogue that ensues is precisely that of the dream! I have heard of numerous instances of this kind of dream, where no previous expectation nor excitement of mind could be found to account for them, and where the fulfilment was too exact and literal, in all particulars, to admit of their being explained away by the ready resource of "an extraordinary coincidence." There are also on record, in both this country and others, many perfectly well-authenticated cases of people obtaining prizes in the lottery, through having dreamed of the fortunate numbers. As many numbers, however, may have been dreamed of that were not drawn prizes, we can derive no conclusion from this circumstance.

A very remarkable instance of this kind of dreaming occurred a few years since to Mr. A—— F——, an eminent Scotch advocate, while staying in the neighborhood of Loch Fyne, who dreamed one night that he saw a number of people in the street following a man to the scaffold. He discovered the features of the criminal in the cart distinctly; and, for some reason or other, which he could not account for, felt an extraordinary interest in his fate—insomuch that he joined the throng, and accompanied him to the place that was to terminate his earthly career. This interest was the more unaccountable, that the man had an exceedingly unprepossessing countenance, but it was nevertheless so vivid as to induce the dreamer to ascend the scaffold, and address him, with a view to enable him to escape the impending catastrophe. Suddenly, however, while he was talking to him, the whole scene dissolved away, and the sleeper awoke. Being a good deal struck with the lifelike reality of the vision, and the impression made on his mind by the features of this man, he related the circumstance to his friends at breakfast, adding that he should know him anywhere, if he saw him. A few jests being made on the subject, the thing was forgotten.

On the afternoon of the same day, the advocate was informed that two men wanted to speak to him, and, on going into the hall, he was struck with amazement at perceiving that one of them was the hero of his dream!

"We are accused of a murder," said they, "and we wish to consult you. Three of us went out, last night, in a boat; an accident has happened; our comrade is drowned, and they want to make us accountable for him." The advocate then put some interrogations to them, and the result produced in his mind by their answers was a conviction of their guilt. Probably the recollection of his dream rendered the effects of this conviction more palpable; for one addressing the other, said in Gaelic, "We have come to the wrong man; he is against us."

"There is a higher power than I against you," returned the gentleman; "and the only advice I can give you is, if you are guilty, fly immediately." Upon this, they went away; and the next thing he heard was, that they were taken into custody on suspicion of the murder.

The account of the affair was, that, as they said, the three had gone out together on the preceding evening, and that in the morning the body of one of them had been found on the shore, with a cut across his forehead. The father and friend of the victim had waited on the banks of the lake till the boat came in, and then demanded their companion; of whom, however, they professed themselves unable to give any account. Upon this, the old man led them to his cottage for the purpose of showing them the body of his son. One entered, and, at the sight of it, burst into a passion of tears; the other refused to do so, saying his business called him immediately home, and went sulkily away. This last was the man seen in the dream.

After a fortnight's incarceration, the former of these was liberated; and he then declared to the advocate his intention of bringing an action of damages for false imprisonment. He was advised not to do it. "Leave well alone," said the lawyer; "and if you'll take my advice, make off while you can." The man, however, refused to fly: he declared that he really did not know what had occasioned the death of his comrade. The latter had been at one end of the boat, and he at the other; when he looked round, he was gone; but whether he had fallen overboard, and cut his head as he fell, or whether he had been struck and pushed into the water, he did not know. The advocate became finally satisfied of this man's innocence; but the authorities, thinking it absurd to try one and not the other, again laid hands on him: and it fell to Mr. A—— F—— to be the defender of both. The difficulty was, not to separate their cases in his pleading; for, however morally convinced of the different ground on which they stood, his duty, professionally, was to obtain the acquittal of both, in which he finally succeeded, as regarded the charge of murder. They were, therefore, sentenced to two years' imprisonment; and, so far as the dream is concerned, here ends the story. There remains, however, a curious sequel to it.

A few years afterward, the same gentleman being in a boat on Loch Fyne, in company with Sir T—— D—— L——, happened to be mentioning these curious circumstances, when one of the boatmen said that he "knew well about those two men; and that a very strange thing had occurred in regard to one of them." This one, on inquiry, proved to be the subject of the dream; and the strange thing was this: On being liberated, he had quitted that part of the country, and in process of time had gone to Greenock, and thence embarked in a vessel for Cork. But the vessel seemed fated never to reach its destination; one misfortune happened after another, till at length the sailors said: "This won't do; there must be a murderer on board with us!" As is usual, when such a persuasion exists, they drew lots three times, and each time it fell on that man! He was consequently put on shore, and the vessel went on its way without him. What had become of him afterward was not known.

A friend of mine, being in London, dreamed that she saw her little boy playing on the terrace of her house in Northumberland; that he fell and hurt his arm, and she saw him lying apparently dead. The dream recurred two or three times on the same night, and she awoke her husband, saying she "feared something must have happened to Henry." In due course of post, a letter arrived from the governess, saying that she was sorry to have to communicate that, while playing on the terrace that morning, Master Henry had fallen over a heap of stones, and broken his arm; adding that he had fainted after the accident, and had lain for some time insensible. The lady to whom this dream occurred is not aware having ever manifested this faculty before or since.

Mrs. W—— dreamed that she saw people ascending by a ladder to the chamber of her step-son John; wakes, and says she is afraid he is dead, and that there was something odd in her dream about a watch and a candle. In the morning a messenger is sent to inquire for the gentleman, and they find people ascending to his chamber-window by a ladder, the door of the room being locked. They discover him dead on the floor, with his watch in his hand, and the candle between his feet. The same lady dreamed that she saw a friend in great agony, and that she heard him say they were tearing his flesh from his bones. He was some time afterward seized with inflammation, lay as she had seen him, and made use of those exact words.

A friend of mine dreamed lately that somebody said her nephew must not be bled, as it would be dangerous. The young man was quite well, and there had been no design of bleeding him; but on the following morning he had a tooth drawn, and an effusion of blood ensued, which lasted some days, and caused a good deal of uneasiness.

A farmer, in Worcestershire, dreamed that his little boy, of twelve years old, had fallen from the wagon and was killed. The dream recurred three times in one night; but, unwilling to yield to superstitious fears, he allowed the child to accompany the wagoner to Kidderminster fair. The driver was very fond of the boy, and he felt assured would take care of him; but, having occasion to go a little out of the road to leave a parcel, the man bade the child walk on with the wagon, and he would meet him at a certain spot. On arriving there, the horses were coming quietly forward, but the boy was not with them; and on retracing the road, he was found dead, having apparently fallen from the shafts, and been crushed by the wheels.

A gentleman, who resided near one of the Scottish lakes, dreamed that he saw a number of persons surrounding a body, which had just been drawn out of the water. On approaching the spot, he perceives that it is himself, and the assistants are his own friends and retainers. Alarmed at the lifelike reality of the vision, he resolved to elude the threatened destiny by never venturing on the lake again. On one occasion, however, it became quite indispensable that he should do so; and, as the day was quite calm, he yielded to the necessity, on condition that he should be put ashore at once on the opposite side, while the rest of the party proceeded to their destinations, where he would meet them. This was accordingly done: the boat skimmed gayly over the smooth waters, and arrived safely at the rendezvous, the gentlemen laughing at the superstition of their companion, while he stood smiling on the bank to receive them But, alas! the fates were inexorable: the little promontory that supported him had been undermined by the water; it gave way beneath his feet, and life was extinct before he could be rescued. This circumstance was related to me by a friend of the family.

Mr. S—— was the son of an Irish bishop, who set somewhat more value on the things of this world than became his function. He had always told his son that there was but one thing he could not forgive, and that was, a bad marriage—meaning, by a bad marriage, a poor one. As cautions of this sort do not, by any means, prevent young people falling in love, Mr. S—— fixed his affections on Lady O——, a fair young widow, without any fortune; and, aware that it would be useless to apply for his father's consent, he married her without asking it. They were consequently exceedingly poor; and, indeed, nearly all they had to live on was a small sinecure of forty pounds per annum, which Dean Swift procured for him. While in this situation, Mr. S—— dreamed one night that he was in the cathedral in which he had formerly been accustomed to attend service; that he saw a stranger, habited as a bishop, occupying his father's throne; and that, on applying to the verger for an explanation, the man said that the bishop was dead, and that he had expired just as he was adding a codicil to his will in his son's favor. The impression made by the dream was so strong, that Mr. S—— felt that he should have no repose till he had obtained news from home; and as the most speedy way of doing so was to go thero himself, he started on horseback, much against the advice of his wife, who attached no importance whatever to the circumstance. He had scarcely accomplished half his journey, when he met a courier, bearing the intelligence of his father's death; and when he reached home, he found that there was a codicil attached to the will, of the greatest importance to his own future prospects; but the old gentleman had expired, with the pen in his hand, just as he was about to sign it!

In this unhappy position, reduced to hopeless indigence, the friends of the young man proposed that he should present himself at the vice-regal palace, on the next levee day, in hopes that some interest might be excited in his favor; to which, with reluctance, he consented. As he was ascending the stairs, he was met by a gentleman whose dress indicated that he belonged to the church.

"Good Heavens!" said he, to the friend who accompanied him, "who is that?"

"That is Mr. ——, of so and so."

"Then he will be bishop of L——!" returned Mr. S——; "for that is the man I saw occupying my father's throne."

"Impossible!" replied the other; "he has no interest whatever, and has no more chance of being a bishop than I have."

"You will see," replied Mr. S——; "I am certain he will."

They had made their obeisance above, and were returning, when there was a great cry without, and everybody rushed to the doors and windows to inquire what had happened. The horses attached to the carriage of a young nobleman had become restiff, and were endangering the life of their master, when Mr. —— rushed forward, and, at the peril of his own, seized their heads, and afforded Lord C—— time to descend, before they broke through all restraint, and dashed away. Through the interest of this nobleman and his friends, to whom Mr. —— had been previously quite unknown, he obtained the see of L——. These circumstances were related to me by a member of the family.

It would be tedious to relate all the instances of this sort of dreaming which have come to my knowledge, but were they even much more rare than they are, and were there none of a graver and more mysterious kind, it might certainly occasion some surprise that they should have excited so little attention. When stories of this sort are narrated, they are listened to with wonder for the moment, and then forgotten, and few people reflect on the deep significance of the facts, or the important consequences to us involved in the question, of how, with our limited faculties, which can not foretell the events of the next moment, we should suddenly become prophets and seers.

The following dream, as it regards the fate of a very interesting person, and is, I believe, very little known, I will relate, though the story is of somewhat an old date :—Major André, the circumstances of whose lamented death are too well known to make it necessary for me to detail them here, was a friend of Miss Seward's, and, previously to his embarkation for America, he made a journey into Derbyshire, to pay her a visit, and it was arranged that they should ride over to see the wonders of the Peak, and introduce André to Newton, her minstrel, as she called him, and to Mr. Cunningham, the curate, who was also a poet.

While these two gentlemen were awaiting the arrival of their guests, of whose intentions they had been apprised, Mr. Cunningham mentioned to Newton, that on the preceding night, he had had a very extraordinary dream, which he could not get out of his head. He had fancied himself in a forest; the place was strange to him; and, while looking about, he perceived a horseman approaching at great speed, who had scarcely reached the spot where the dreamer stood, when three men rushed out of the thicket, and, seizing his bridle, hurried him away, after closely searching his person. The countenance of the stranger being very interesting, the sympathy felt by the sleeper for his apparent misfortune awoke him; but he presently fell asleep again, and dreamed that he was standing near a great city, among thousands of people, and that he saw the same person he had seen seized in the wood brought out and suspended to a gallows. When André and Miss Seward arrived, he was horror-struck to perceive that his new acquaintance was the antitype of the man in the dream.

Mr. C——, a friend of mine, told me the other day, that he had dreamed he had gone to see a lady of his acquaintance, and that she had presented him with a purse. In the morning he mentioned the circumstance to his wife, adding that he wondered what should have made him dream of a person he had not been in any way led to think of; and, above all, that she should give him a purse. On that same day, a letter arrived from that lady to Mrs. C——, containing a purse, of which she begged her acceptance. Here was the imperfect foreshadowing of the fact, probably from unsound sleep.

Another friend lately dreamed, one Thursday night, that he saw an acquaintance of his thrown from his horse; and that he was lying on the ground with the blood streaming from his face, which was much cut. He mentioned his dream in the morning, and being an entire disbeliever in such phenomena, he could not account for the impression made on his mind. This was so strong, that on Saturday, he could not forbear calling at his friend's house; who, he was told, was in bed, having been thrown from his horse on the previous day, and much injured about the face.

Relations of this description having been more or less familiar to the world in all times and places, and the recurrence of the phenomena too frequent to admit of their reality being disputed, various theories were promulgated to account for them; and indeed, there scarcely seems to be a philosopher or historian among the Greeks and Romans who does not make some allusion to this ill-understood department of nature; while, among the eastern nations, the faith in such mysterious revelations remains even yet undiminished. Spirits, good and evil, or the divinities of the heathen mythology, were generally called in to remove the difficulty; though some philosophers, rejecting this supernatural interference, sought the explanation in merely physical causes.

In the druidical rites of the northern nations, women bore a considerable part: there were priestesses, who gave forth oracles and prophecies, much after the manner of the Pythonesses of the Grecian temples, and no doubt drawing their inspiration from the same sources; namely, from the influences of magnetism, and from narcotics. When the pure rites of Christianity seperseded the heathen forms of worship, tradition kept alive the memory of these vaticinations, together with some of the arcana of the druidical groves; and hence, in the middle ages, arose the race of so-called witches and sorcerers, who were partly impostors, and partly self-deluded. Nobody thought of seeking the explanation of the facts they witnessed in natural causes; what had formerly been attributed to the influence of the gods, was now attributed to the influence of the devil;

and a league with Satan was the universal solvent of all difficulties.

Persecution followed, of course; and men, women, and children, were offered up to the demon of superstition, till the candid and rational part of mankind, taking fright at the holocaust, began to put in their protest, and lead out a reaction, which, like all reactions, ran right into the opposite extreme. From believing everything, they ceased to believe anything; and, after swallowing unhesitatingly the most monstrous absurdities, they relieved themselves of the whole difficulty, by denying the plainest facts; while what it was found impossible to deny, was referred to *imagination*—that most abused word, which explained nothing, but left the matter as obscure as it was before. Man's spiritual nature was forgotten; and what the senses could not apprehend, nor the understanding account for, was pronounced to be impossible. Thank God! we have lived through that age, and in spite of the struggles of the materialistic school, we are fast advancing to a better. The traditions of the saints who suffered the most appalling tortures, and slept or smiled the while, can scarcely be rejected now, when we are daily hearing of people undergoing frightful operations, either in a state of insensibility, or while they believe themselves revelling in delight; nor can the psychological intimations which these facts offer, be much longer overlooked. One revelation must lead to another; and the wise men of the world will, ere long, be obliged to give in their adherence to Shakspere's much quoted axiom, and confess that "there *are* more things in heaven and earth than are dreamt of in their philosophy."

CHAPTER IV.

ALLEGORICAL DREAMS, PRESENTIMENT, ETC.

It has been the opinion of many philosophers, both ancient and modern, that in the original state of man, as he came forth from the hands of his Creator, that knowledge which is now acquired by pains and labor was intuitive. His material body was given him for the purpose of placing him in relation with the material world, and his sensuous organs for the perception of material objects, but his soul was a mirror of the universe, in which everything was reflected, and, probably, is so still, but that the spirit is no longer in a condition to perceive it. Degraded in his nature, and distracted by the multiplicity of the objects and interests that surround him, man has lost his faculty of spiritual seeing; but in sleep, when the body is in a state of passivity, and external objects are excluded from us by the shutting up of the senses through which we perceive them, the spirit, to a certain degree freed from its impediments, may enjoy somewhat of its original privilege. "The soul, which is designed as the mirror of a superior spiritual order" (to which it belongs), still receives in dreams, some rays from above, and enjoys a foretaste of its future condition; and, whatever interpretation may be put upon the history of the Fall, few will doubt that, before it, man must have stood in a much more intimate relation to his Creator than he has done since. If we admit this, and that, for the above-hinted reasons, the soul in sleep may be able to exercise somewhat of its original endowment, the possibility of what is called prophetic dreaming may be better understood.

"Seeing in dreams," says Ennemoser, "is a self-illumining of things, places, and times;" for relations of time and space form no obstruction to the dreamer: things, near and far, are alike seen in the mirror of the soul, according to the connection in which they stand to each other; and, as the future is but an unfolding of the present, as the present is of the past, one being necessarily involved in the other, it is not more difficult to the untrammelled spirit to see what *is* to happen, than what has *already* happened. Under what peculiar circumstances it is that the body and soul fall into this particular relative condition, we do not know, but that certain families and constitutions are more prone to these conditions than others, all experience goes to establish. According to the theory of Dr. Ennemoser, we should conclude that they are more susceptible to magnetic influences, and that the body falls into a more complete state of negative polarity.

In the histories of the Old Testament we constantly find instances of prophetic dreaming, and the voice of God was chiefly heard by the prophets in sleep; seeming to establish that man is in that state more susceptible of spiritual communion, although the being thus made the special organ of the Divine will, is altogether a different thing from the mere disfranchisement of the embodied spirit in ordinary cases of clear seeing in sleep. Profane history, also, furnishes us with various instances of prophetic dreaming, which it is unnecessary for me to refer to here. But there is one thing very worthy of remark, namely, that the allegorical character of many of the dreams recorded in the Old Testament, occasionally pervades those of the present day. I have heard of several of this nature, and Oberlin, the good pastor of Ban de la Roche, was so subject to them, that he fancied he had acquired the art of interpreting the symbols. This characteristic of dreaming is in strict conformity with the language of the Old Testament, and of the most ancient nations. Poets and prophets, heathen and Christian, alike express themselves symbolically, and, if we believe that this language prevailed in the early ages of the world, before the external and intellectual life had predominated over the instinctive and emotional, we must conclude it to be the natural language of man, who must, therefore, have been gifted with a conformable faculty of comprehending these hieroglyphics; and hence it arose that the interpreting of dreams became a legitimate art. Long after these instinctive faculties were lost, or rather obscured, by the turmoil and distractions of sensuous life, the memories and traditions of them remained, and hence the superstructure of jugglery and imposture that ensued, of which the gipsies form a signal example, in whom, however, there can be no doubt that some occasional gleams of this original endowment may still be found, as is the case, though more rarely, in individuals of all races and conditions. The whole of nature is one large book of symbols, which, because we have lost the key to it, we can not decipher. "To the first man," says Hamann, "whatever his ear heard, his eye saw, or his hand touched, was a living word; with this word in his heart and in his mouth, the formation of language was easy. Man saw things in their essence and properties, and named them accordingly.

There can be no doubt that the heathen forms of worship and systems of religion were but the external symbols of some deep meanings, and not the idle fables that they have been too frequently considered; and it is absurd to suppose that the theology which satisfied so many great minds had no better foundation than a child's fairy tale.

A maid-servant, who resided many years in a distinguished family in Edinburgh, was repeatedly warned of the approaching death of certain members of that family, by dreaming that one of the walls of the house had fallen. Shortly before the head of the family sickened and died, she said she had dreamed that the main wall had fallen.

A singular circumstance which occurred in this same family, from a member of which I heard it, is mentioned by Dr. Abercrombie. On this occasion the dream was not only prophetic, but the symbol was actually translated into fact.

One of the sons being indisposed with a sore throat, a sister dreamed that a watch, of considerable value, which she had borrowed from a friend, had stopped; that she had awakened another sister and mentioned the circumstance, who answered that "something much worse had happened, for Charles's breath had stopped." She then awoke, in extreme alarm, and mentioned the dream to her sister, who, to tranquillize her mind, arose and went to the brother's room, where she found him asleep and the watch going. The next night the same dream recurred, and the brother was again found asleep and the watch going. On the following morning, however, this lady was writing a note in the drawing-room, with the watch beside her, when, on taking it up, she perceived it had stopped; and she was just on the point of calling her sister to mention the circumstance, when she heard a scream from her brother's room, and the sister rushed in with the tidings that he had just expired. The malady had not been thought serious; but a sudden fit of suffocation had unexpectedly proved fatal.

This case, which is established beyond all controversy, is extremely curious in many points of view; the acting out of the symbol, especially. Symbolical events of this description have been often related, and as often laughed at. It is easy to laugh at what we do not understand; and it gives us the advantage of making the timid narrator ashamed of his fact, so that if he do not wholly suppress it, he at least insures himself by laughing, too, the next time he relates it. It is said that Goethe's clock stopped the moment he died; and I have heard repeated instances of this strange kind of synchronism, or magnetism, if it be by magnetism that we are to account for the mystery. One was told me very lately by a gentleman to whom the circumstances occurred.

On the 16th of August, 1769, Frederick II., of Prussia, is said to have dreamed that a star fell from heaven and occasioned such an extraordinary glare that he could with great difficulty find his way through it. He mentioned the dream to his attendants, and it was afterward observed that it was on that day Napoleon was born.

A lady, not long since, related to me the following circumstance: Her mother, who was at the time residing in Edinburgh, in a house one side of which looked into a wynd, while the door was in the High street, dreamed that, it being Sunday morning, she had heard a sound which attracted her to the window; and, while looking out, had dropped a ring from her finger into the wynd below; that she had, thereupon, gone down in her night-clothes to seek it, but when she reached the spot it was not to be found. Returning, extremely vexed at her loss, as she re-entered her own door she met a respectable looking young man, carrying some loaves of bread. On expressing her astonishment at finding a stranger there at so unseasonable an hour, he answered by expressing his at seeing her in such a situation. She said she had dropped her ring, and had been round the corner to seek it; whereupon, to her delighted surprise, he presented her with her lost treasure. Some months afterward, being at a party, she recognized the young man seen in her dream, and learned that he was a baker. He took no particular notice of her on that occasion; and, I think, two years elapsed before she met him again. This second meeting, however, led to an acquaintance, which terminated in marriage..

Here the ring and the bread are curiously emblematic of the marriage, and the occupation of the future husband.

Miss L——, residing at Dalkeith, dreamed that her brother, who was ill, call her to his bedside and gave her a letter, which he desired her to carry to their aunt, Mrs. H——, with the request that she would "deliver it to John." (John was another brother, who had died previously, and Mrs. H—— was at the time ill.) He added that "he himself was going *there* also, but that Mrs. H—— would be *there* before him." Accordingly, Miss L—— went, in her dream, with the letter to Mrs. H——, whom she found dressed in white, and looking quite radiant and happy. She took the letter, saying she was going *there* directly, and would deliver it.

On the following morning Miss L—— learned that her aunt had died in the night. The brother died some little time afterward.

A gentleman who had been a short time visiting Edinburgh, was troubled with a cough, which, though it occasioned him no alarm, he resolved to go home to nurse. On the first night of his arrival he dreamed that one half of the house was blown away. His bailiff, who resided at a distance, dreamed the same dream on the same night. The gentleman died within a few weeks.

" This symbolical language, which the Deity appears to have used" (witness Peter's dream, Acts ii., and others) "in all his revelations to man, is in the highest degree, what poetry is in a lower, and the language of dreams, in the lowest, namely, the original natural language of man; and we may fairly ask whether this language, which here plays an inferior part, be not, possibly, the proper language of a higher sphere, while we, who vainly think ourselves awake, are, in reality, buried in a deep, deep sleep, in which, like dreamers who imperfectly hear the voices of those around them, we occasionally apprehend, though obscurely, a few words of this divine tongue." (*Vide Schubert.*)

This subject of sleeping and waking is a very curious one, and might give rise to strange questionings. In the case of those patients above mentioned, who seem to have two different spheres of existence, who shall say which is the waking one, or whether either of them be so? The speculations of Mr. Dove on this subject merited more attention, I think, than they met with when he lectured in Edinburgh. He maintained that, long before he had paid any attention to magnetism, he had arrived at the conclusion that there are as many states or conditions of mind beyond sleep as there are on this side of it; passing through the different stages of dreaming, revery, contemplation, &c., up to perfect vigilance. However this be, in this world of appearance, where we see nothing as it is, and where, both as regards our moral and physical relations, we live in a state of continual delusion, it is impossible for us to pronounce on this question. It is a common remark, that some people seem to live in a dream, and never to be quite awake; and the most cursory observer can not fail to have been struck with examples of persons in this condition, especially in the aged.

With respect to this allegorical language, Ennemoser observes, that, "since no dreamer learns it of another, and still less from those who are awake, it must be natural to all men."

How different too, is its comprehensiveness and rapidity, to our ordinary language! We are accustomed, and with justice, to wonder at the admirable mechanism by which, without fatigue or exertion, we communicate with our fellow-beings; but how slow and ineffectual is human speech compared to this spiritual picture-language, where a whole history is understood at a glance! and scenes that seem to occupy days and weeks, are acted out in ten minutes. It is remarkable that this hieroglyphic language appears to be the same among all people; and that the dream-interpreters of all countries construe the signs alike. Thus, the dreaming of deep water denotes trouble, and pearls are a sign of tears.

I have heard of a lady who, whenever a misfortune was impending, dreamed that she saw a large fish. One night she dreamed that this fish had bitten two of her little boy's fingers. Immediately afterward a schoolfellow of the child's injured those two very fingers by striking him with a hatchet; and I have met with several persons who have learned, by experience, to consider one particular dream as the certain prognostic of misfortune.

A lady who had left the West Indies when six years old, came one night, fourteen years afterward, to her sister's bedside, and said, "I know uncle is dead. I have dreamed that I saw a number of slaves in the large store-room at Barbadoes, with long brooms, sweeping down immense cobwebs. I complained to my aunt, and she covered her face and said, 'Yes, he is no sooner gone than they disobey him.'" It was afterward ascertained that Mr. P—— had died on that night, and that he had never permitted the cobwebs in this room to be swept away, of which, however, the lady assures me she knew nothing; nor could she or her friends conceive what was meant by the symbol of the cobwebs, till they received the explanation subsequently from a member of the family.

The following very curious allegorical dream I give, not in the words of the dreamer, but in those of her son, who bears a name destined, I trust, to a long immortality:—

"WOOER'S ABBEY-COTTAGE, DUNFERMILIINE-IN-THE-WOODS,
"*Monday morning*, 31*st May*, 1847.

"DEAR MRS. CROWE: *That* dream of my mother's was as follows: She stood in a long, dark, empty gallery: on her one side was my father, and on the other my eldest sister Amelia; then myself, and the rest of the family, according to their ages. At the foot of the hall stood my youngest sister Alexes, and above her my sister Catherine—a creature, by-the-way, in person and mind, more like an angel of heaven than an inhabitant of earth. We all stood silent and motionless. At last IT entered—the unimagined *something*, that, casting its grim shadow before, had enveloped all the trivialities of the preceding dream in the stifling atmosphere of terror. It entered, stealthily descending the three steps that led from the entrance down into the chamber of horror: and my mother *felt* IT *was Death!* He was dwarfish, bent, and shrivelled. He carried on his shoulder a heavy axe; and had come, she thought, to destroy 'all her little ones at one fell swoop.' On the entrance of the shape, my sister Alexes leaped out of the rank, interposing herself between him and my mother. He raised his axe and aimed a blow at Catherine—a blow which, to her horror, my mother could not intercept, though she had snatched up a three-legged stool, the sole furniture of the apartment, for that purpose. She could not, she felt, fling the stool at the figure without destroying Alexes, who kept shooting out and in between her and the ghastly thing. She tried in vain to scream; she besought my father, in agony, to avert the impending stroke; but he did not hear, or did not heed her, and stood motionless, as in a trance. Down came the axe, and poor Catherine fell in her blood, cloven to 'the white halse bane.' Again the axe was lifted, by the inexorable shadow, over the head of my brother, who stood next in the line. Alexes had somewhere disappeared behind the ghastly visitant; and, with a scream, my mother flung the footstool at his head. He vanished, and she awoke.

"This dream left on my mother's mind a fearful apprehension of impending misfortune, 'which would not pass away.' It was *murder* she feared; and her suspicions were not allayed by the discovery that a man (some time before discarded by my father for bad conduct, and with whom she had, somehow, associated the *Death* of her dream) had been lurking about the place, and sleeping in an adjoining outhouse on the night it occurred, and for some nights previous and subsequent to it. Her terror increased. Sleep forsook her; and every night, when the house was still, she arose and stole, sometimes with a candle, sometimes in the dark, from room to room, listening, in a sort of waking nightmare, for the breathing of the assassin, who, she imagined, was lurking in some one of them. This could not last. She reasoned with herself; but her terror became intolerable, and she related her dream to my father, who, of course, called her a fool for her pains, whatever might be his real opinion of the matter.

"Three months had elapsed, when we children were all of us seized with scarlet fever. My sister Catherine died almost immediately—sacrificed, as my mother in her misery thought, to her (my mother's) over-anxiety for Alexes, whose danger seemed more imminent. The dream-prophecy was in part fulfilled. I also was at death's door—given up by the doctors, but not by my mother: she was confident of my recovery; but for my brother, who was scarcely considered in danger at all, but on whose head *she had seen* the visionary axe impending, her fears were great; for she could not recollect whether the blow had or had not descended when the spectre vanished. My brother recovered, but relapsed, and barely escaped with life; but Alexes did not. For a year and ten months the poor child lingered, and almost every night I had to sing her asleep—often, I remember, through bitter tears, for I knew she was dying, and I loved her the more as she wasted away. I held her little hand as she died; I followed her to the grave—the last thing that I have *loved* on earth. And *the dream was fulfilled.*

"Truly and sincerely yours, J. NOEL PATON."

The dreaming of coffins and funerals, when a death is impending, must be considered as examples of this allegorical language. Instances of this kind are extremely numerous. Not unfrequently the dreamer, as in cases of second-sight, sees either the body in the coffin, so as to be conscious of who is to die, or else is made aware of it from seeing the funeral-procession at a certain house, or from some other significant circumstance. This faculty, which has been supposed to belong peculiarly to the highlanders of Scotland, appears to be fully as well known in Wales and on the continent, especially in Germany.

The language of dreams, however, is not always symbolical. Occasionally, the scene, that is transacting at a distance, or that is to be transacted at some future period, is literally presented to the sleeper, as things appear to be presented in many cases of second-sight, and also in clairvoyance; and, since we suppose him (that is, the sleeper) to be in a temporarily magnetic state, we must conclude that the degree of perspicuity, or translucency of the vision, depends on the degree of that state. Nevertheless, there are considerable difficulties attending this theory. A great proportion of the prophetic dreams we hear of are connected with the death of some friend or relative. Some, it is true, regard unimportant matters, as visits, and so forth; but this is generally, though not exclusively, the case only with persons who have a constitutional tendency to this kind of dreaming, and with whom it is frequent; but it is not uncommon for those who have not discovered any such tendency, to be made aware of a death: and the number of dreams of this description I meet with is very considerable. Now, it is difficult to conceive what the condition is that causes this perception of an approaching death; or why, supposing, as we have suggested above, that, when the senses sleep, the untrammelled spirit *sees*, the memory of this revelation, if I may so call it, so much more frequently survives than any other, unless, indeed, it be the force of the shock sustained—which shock, it is to be remarked, always wakes the sleeper; and this may be the reason that, if he fall asleep again, the dream is almost invariably repeated.

I could fill pages with dreams of this description which have come to my knowledge, or been recorded by others.

Mr. H——, a gentleman with whom I am acquainted—a man

engaged in active business, and apparently as little likely as any one I ever knew to be troubled with a faculty of this sort—dreamed that he saw a certain friend of his dead. The dream was so like reality, that, although he had no reason whatever to suppose his friend ill, he could not forbear sending in the morning to inquire for him. The answer returned was, that Mr. A—— was out, and was quite well. The impression, however, was so vivid, that, although he had nearly three miles to send, Mr. H—— felt that he could not start for Glasgow, whither business called him, without making another inquiry. This time his friend was at home, and answered for himself, that he was very well, and that somebody must have been hoaxing H——, and making him believe otherwise. Mr. H—— set out on his journey, wondering at his own anxiety, but unable to conquer it. He was absent but a few days (I think three); and the first news he heard on his return was, that his friend had been seized with an attack of inflammation, and was dead.

A German professor lately related to a friend of mine, that, being some distance from home, he dreamed that his father was dying, and was calling for him. The dream being repeated, he was so far impressed as to alter his plans, and return home, where he arrived in time to receive his parent's last breath. He was informed that the dying man had been calling upon his name repeatedly, in deep anguish at his absence.

A parallel case to this is that of Mr. R—— E—— S——, an accountant in Edinburgh, and a shrewd man of business, who relates the following circumstance as occurring to himself. He is a native of Dalkeith, and was residing there, when, being about fifteen years of age, he left home on a Saturday, to spend a few days with a friend at Prestonpans. On the Sunday night he dreamed that his mother was extremely ill, and started out of his sleep with an impression that he must go to her immediately. He even got out of bed with the intention of doing so, but, reflecting that he had left her quite well, and that it was only a dream, he returned to bed, and again fell asleep. But the dream returned, and, unable longer to control his anxiety, he arose, dressed himself in the dark, quitted the house, leaping the railings that surrounded it, and made the best of his way to Dalkeith. On reaching home, which he did before daylight, he tapped at the kitchen-window, and, on gaining admittance, was informed that on the Saturday evening, after he had departed, his mother had been seized with an attack of British cholera, and was lying above, extremely ill. She had been lamenting his absence extremely, and had scarcely ceased crying, "Oh, Ralph, Ralph! what a grief that you are away!" At nine o'clock he was admitted to her room; but she was no longer in a condition to recognise him, and she died within a day or two.

Instances of this sort are numerous, but it would be tedious to narrate them, especially as there is little room for variety in the details. I shall therefore content myself with giving one or two specimens of each class, confining my examples to such as have been communicated to myself, except where any case of particular interest leads me to deviate from this plan. The frequency of such phenomena may be imagined, when I mention that the instances I shall give, with few exceptions, have been collected with little trouble, and without seeking beyond my own small circle of acquaintance.

In the family of the above-named gentleman (Mr. R—— E—— S——), there probably existed a faculty of presentiment; for, in the year 1810, his elder brother being assistant-surgeon on board the "Gorgon," war-brig, his father dreamed that he was promoted to the "Sparrowhawk," a ship he had then never heard of—neither had the family received any intelligence of the young man for several months. He told his dream, and was well laughed at for his pains; but in a few weeks a letter arrived announcing the promotion.

When Lord Burghersh was giving theatrical parties at Florence, a lady (Mrs. M——, whose presence was very important) excused herself one evening, being in great alarm from having dreamed in the night that her sister, in England, was dead, which proved to be the fact.

Mr. W——, a young man at Glasgow college, not long since dreamed that his aunt in Russia was dead. He noted the date of his dream on the window-shutter of his chamber. In a short time the news of the lady's death arrived. The dates, however, did not accord; but, on mentioning the circumstance to a friend, he was reminded that the adherence of the Russians to the old style reconciled the difference.

A man of business, in Glasgow, lately dreamed that he saw a coffin, on which was inscribed the name of a friend, with the date of his death. Some time afterward he was summoned to attend the funeral of that person, who, at the time of the dream, was in good health, and he was struck with surprise on seeing the plate of the coffin bearing the very date he had seen in his dream.

A French gentleman, Monsieur de V——, dreamed, some years since, that he saw a tomb, on which he read very distinctly, the following date—23d June, 184—; there were, also, some initials, but so much effaced that he could not make them out. He mentioned the circumstance to his wife; and for some time, they could not help dreading the recurrence of the ominous month; but, as year after year passed, and nothing happened, they had ceased to think of it, when at last the symbol was explained. On the 23d of June, 1846, their only daughter died at the age of seventeen.

Thus far the instances I have related seem to resolve themselves into cases of simple clairvoyance, or second sight in sleep, although, in using these words, I am very far from meaning to imply that I explain the thing, or unveil its mystery. The theory above alluded to, seems as yet, the only one applicable to the facts, namely, that the senses, being placed in a negative and passive state, the universal sense of the immortal spirit within, which sees, and hears, and knows, or rather, in one word, *perceives*, without organs, becomes more or less free to work unclogged. That the soul is a mirror in which the spirit sees all things reflected, is a modification of this theory; but I confess I find myself unable to attach any idea to this latter form of expression. Another view, which I have heard suggested by an eminent person, is, that if it be true, as maintained by Dr. Wigan, and some other physiologists, that our brains are double, it is possible that a polarity may exist between the two sides, by means of which the negative side may, under certain circumstances, become a mirror to the positive. It seems difficult to reconcile this notion with the fact, that these perceptions occur most frequently when the brain is asleep. How far the sleep is perfect and general, however, we can never know; and of course, when the powers of speech and locomotion continue to be exercised, we are aware that it is only partial, in a more or less degree. In the case of magnetic sleepers, observation shows us, that the auditory nerves are aroused by being addressed, and fall asleep again as soon as they are left undisturbed. In most cases of natural sleep, the same process, if the voice were heard at all, would disperse sleep altogether; and it must be remembered that, as Dr. Holland says, sleep is a fluctuating condition, varying from one moment to another, and this allowance must be made when considering magnetic sleep also.

It is by this theory of the duality of the brain, which seems to have many arguments in its favor, and the alternate sleeping and waking of the two sides, that Dr. Wigan seeks to account for the state of double or alternate consciousness above alluded to; and also, for that strange sensation which most people have experienced, of having witnessed a scene, or heard a conversation, at some indefinite period before, or even in some earlier state of existence. He thinks that one half of the brain being in a more active condition than the other, it takes cognizance of the scene first; and that thus the perceptions of the second, when they take place, appear to be a repetition of some former experiences. I confess this theory, as regards this latter phenomenon, is to me eminently unsatisfactory, and it is especially defective in not accounting for one of the most curious particulars connected with it, namely, that on these occasions people not only seem to recognise the circumstances as having been experienced before; but they have, very frequently, an actual foreknowledge of what will be next said or done.

Now, the explanation of this mystery, I incline to think, may possibly lie in the hypothesis I have suggested; namely, that in profound, and what appears to us generally to have been dreamless sleep, we are clear-seers. The map of coming events lies open before us, the spirit surveys it; but with the awaking of the sensuous organs, this dream-life, with its aerial excursions, passes away, and we are translated into our other sphere of existence. But, occasionally, some flash of recollection, some ray of light from this visionary world, in which we have been living, breaks in upon our external objective existence, and we recognise the locality, the voice, the very words, as being but a reacting of some foregone scenes of a drama.

The faculty of presentiment, of which everybody must have heard instances, seems to have some affinity to the phenomenon last referred to. I am acquainted with a lady, in whom this faculty is in some degree developed, who has evinced it by a consciousness of the moment when a death was taking place in her family, or among her connections, although she does not know who it is that has departed. I have heard of several cases of people hurrying home from a presentiment of fire; and Mr. M—— of Calderwood was once, when absent from home, seized with such an anxiety about his family, that without being able in any way to account for it, he felt himself impelled to fly to them and remove them from the house they were inhabiting; one wing of which fell down immediately afterward. No notion of such a misfortune had ever before occurred to him, nor was there any reason whatever to expect it; the accident originating from some defect in the foundations.

A circumstance, exactly similar to this, is related by Stilling, of Professor Böhm, teacher of mathematics at Marburg; who being one evening in company, was suddenly seized with a conviction that he ought to go home. As however, he was very comfortably taking his tea, and had nothing to do at home, he resisted the admonition; but it returned with such force that at length he was obliged to yield. On reaching his house, he found everything as he had left it; but he now felt himself urged to remove his bed from the corner in which it stood to another; but as it had always stood there, he resisted this impulsion also. However, the resistance was vain, absurd as it seemed, he felt he must do it; so he summoned the maid, and with her aid, drew the bed to the other side of the room; after which he felt quite at ease and returned to spend the rest of the evening with his friends. At ten o'clock the party broke up, and he retired home and went to bed and to sleep. In the middle of the night, he was awakened by a loud crash, and on looking out, he saw that a large beam had fallen, bringing part of the ceiling with it, and was lying exactly on the spot his bed had occupied.

A young servant girl in this neighborhood, who had been several years in an excellent situation, where she was much esteemed, was suddenly seized with a presentiment that she was wanted at home; and, in spite of all representations, she resigned her place, and set out on her journey thither; where, when she arrived, she found her parents extremely ill, one of them mortally, and in the greatest need of her services. No intelligence of their illness had reached her, nor could she herself in any way account for the impulse. I have heard of numerous well-authenticated cases of people escaping drowning from being seized with an unaccountable presentiment of evil when there were no external signs whatever to justify the apprehension. The story of Cazotte, as related by La Harpe, is a very remarkable instance of this sort of faculty; and seems to indicate a power like that possessed by Zschokke, who relates, in his autobiography, that frequently while conversing with a stranger, the whole circumstances of that person's previous life were revealed to him, even comprising details of places and persons. In the case of Cazotte, it was the future that was laid open to him, and he foretold, to a company of eminent persons, in the year 1788, the fate which awaited each individual, himself included, in consequence of the revolution then commencing. As this story is already in print, I forbear to relate it.

One of the most remarkable cases of presentiment I know, is, that which occurred, not very long since, on board one of her majesty's ships, when lying off Portsmouth. The officers being one day at the mess-table, young Lieutenant P—— suddenly laid down his knife and fork, pushed away his plate, and turned extremely pale. He then rose from the table, covering his face with his hands, and retired from the room. The president of the mess, supposing him to be ill, sent one of the young men to inquire what was the matter. At first Mr. P—— was unwilling to speak, but on being pressed, he confessed that he had been seized by a sudden and irresistible impression that a brother he had then in India was dead. "He died," said he, "on the 12th of August, at six o'clock; I am perfectly certain of it!" No arguments could overthrow this conviction, which, in due course of post, was verified to the letter. The young man had died at Cawnpore, at the precise period mentioned.

When any exhibition of this sort of faculty occurs in animals, which is by no means unfrequent, it is termed *instinct;* and we look upon it, as what it probably is, only another and more rare development of that intuitive knowledge which enables them to seek their food, and perform the other functions necessary for the maintenance of their existence and the continuance of their race. Now, it is remarkable, that the life of an animal is a sort of dream-life; their ganglionic system is more developed than that of man, and the cerebral less; and since it is, doubtless, from the greater development of the ganglionic system in women that they exhibit more frequent instances of such abnormal phenomena as I am treating of, than men, we may be, perhaps, justified in considering the faculty of presentiment in a human being as a suddenly-awakened instinct; just as in an animal it is an intensified instinct.

Everybody has either witnessed or heard of instances of this sort of presentiment, in dogs especially. For the authenticity of the following anecdote I can vouch, the traditions being very carefully preserved in the family concerned, from whom I have it. In the last century, Mr. P——, a member of this family, who had involved himself in some of the stormy affairs of this northern part of the island, was one day surprised by seeing a favorite dog, that was lying at his feet, start suddenly up and seize him by the knee, which he pulled—not with violence, but in a manner that indicated a wish that his master should follow him to the door. The gentleman resisted the invitation for some time, till at length, the perseverance of the animal rousing his curiosity, he yielded, and was thus conducted by the dog into the most sequestered part of a neighboring thicket, where, however, he could see nothing to account for his dumb friend's proceeding, who now lay himself down, quite satisfied, and seemed to wish his master to follow his example, which, determined to pursue the adventure and find out, if possible, what was meant, he did. A considerable time now elapsed before the dog would consent to his master's going home; but at length he arose and led the way thither, when the first news Mr. P—— heard was, that a party of soldiers had been there in quest of him; and he was shown the marks of their spikes, which had been thrust through the bed-clothes in their search. He fled, and ultimately escaped, his life being thus preserved by his dog

Some years ago, at Plymouth, I had a brown spaniel that regularly, with great delight, accompanied my son and his nurse in their morning's walk. One day she came to complain to me that Tiger would not go out with them. Nobody could conceive the reason of so unusual a caprice; and, unfortunately, we did not yield to it, but forced him to go. In less than a quarter of an hour he was brought back, so torn to pieces, by a savage dog that had just come ashore from a foreign vessel, that it was found necessary to shoot him immediately.

CHAPTER V.

WARNINGS.

This comparison between the power of presentiment in a human being and the instincts of an animal, may be offensive to some people; but it must be admitted, that, as far as we can see, the manifestation is the same, whatever be the cause. Now, the body of an animal must be informed by an immaterial principle—let us call it soul or spirit, or anything else; for it is evident that their actions are not the mere result of organization; and all I mean to imply is, that this faculty of foreseeing must be inherent in intelligent spirit, let it be lodged in what form of flesh it may; while, with regard to what instinct is, we are, in the meanwhile, in extreme ignorance, *Instinct* being a word which, like *Imagination*, everybody uses, and nobody understands.

Ennemoser and Schubert believe, that the instinct by which animals seek their food, consists in polarity, but I have met with only two modern theories which pretend to explain the phenomena of presentiment; the one is, that the person is in a temporarily-magnetic state, and that the presentiment is a kind of clairvoyance. That the faculty, like that of prophetic dreaming, is constitutional, and chiefly manifested in certain families, is well established; and the very unimportant events, such as visits, and so forth, on which it frequently exercises itself, forbid us to seek an explanation in a higher source. It seems, also, to be quite independent of the will of the subject, as it was in the case of Zschokke, who found himself thus let into the secrets of persons in whom he felt no manner of interest, while, where the knowledge might have been of use to him, he could not command it. The theory of one half of the brain in a negative state, serving as a mirror to the other half, if admitted at all, may answer as well, or better, for these waking presentiments, than for clear-seeing in dreams. But, for my own part, I incline very much to the views of that school of philosophers who adopt the first and more spiritual theory, which seems to me to offer fewer difficulties, while, as regards our present nature, and future hopes, it is certainly more satisfactory. Once admitted that the body is but the temporary dwelling of an immaterial spirit, the machine through which, and by which, in its normal states, the spirit alone can manifest itself, I can not see any great difficulty in conceiving that, in certain conditions of that body, their relations may be modified, and that the spirit may perceive, by its own inherent quality, without the aid of its material vehicle; and, as this condition of the body may arise from causes purely physical, we see at once why the revelations frequently regard such unimportant events.

Plutarch, in his dialogue between Lamprius and Ammonius, observes, that if the demons, or protecting spirits, that watch over mankind, are disembodied souls, we ought not to doubt that those spirits, even when in the flesh, possessed the faculties they now enjoy, since we have no reason to suppose that any new ones are conferred at the period of dissolution; for these faculties must be inherent, although temporarily obscured, and weak and ineffective in their manifestations. As it is not when the sun breaks from behind the clouds that he first begins to shine, so it is not when the soul issues from the body, as from a cloud that envelops it, that it first attains the power of looking into the future.

But the events foreseen are not always unimportant, nor is the mode of the communication always of the same nature. I have mentioned above some instances wherein danger was avoided, and there are many of the same kind recorded in various works; and it is the number of instances of this description, corroborated by the universal agreement of all somnambulists of a higher order, which has induced a considerable section of the German psychologists to adopt the doctrine of guardian spirits—a doctrine which has prevailed, more or less, in all ages, and has been considered by many theologians to be supported by the Bible. There is in this country, and I believe in France, also, though with more exceptions, such an extreme aversion to admit the possibility of anything like what is called supernatural agency, that the mere avowal of such a persuasion is enough to discredit one's understanding with a considerable part of the world, not excepting those who profess to believe in the Scriptures. Yet, even apart from this latter authority, I can not see anything repugnant to reason in such a belief. As far as we see of nature, there is a continued series from the lowest to the highest; and what right have we to conclude that we are the last link of the chain? Why may there not be a gamut of beings? That such should be the case, is certainly in accordance with all that we see; and that we do not see them, affords, as I have said above, not a shadow of argument against their existence; man, immersed in business and pleasure, living only his sensuous life, is too apt to forget how limited those senses are, how merely designed for a temporary purpose, and how much may exist of which they can take no cognizance.

The *possibility* admitted, the chief arguments against the *probability* of such a guardianship, are the interference it implies with the free-will of man, on the one hand, and the rarity of this interference, on the other. With respect to the first matter of free-will, it is a subject of acknowledged difficulty, and beyond the scope of my work. Nobody can honestly look back upon his past life without feeling perplexed by the question, of how far he was, or was not, able at the moment to resist certain impulsions, which caused him to commit wrong or imprudent actions; and it must, I fear, ever remain a *quæstio vexata*, how far our virtues and vices depend upon our organization—an organization whose constitution is beyond our own power, in the first instance, although we may certainly improve or deteriorate it; but which we must admit, at the same time, to be, in its present deteriorated form, the ill result of the world's corruption, and the inherited penalty of the vices of our predecessors, whereby the sins of the fathers are visited upon the children unto the third and fourth generation.

There is, as the Scriptures say, but one way to salvation, though there are many to perdition—that is, though there are many wrongs, there is only one right; for truth is one, and our true liberty consists in being free to follow it; for we can not imagine that anybody seeks his own perdition, and nobody, I conceive, loves vice for its own sake, as others love virtue, that is, because it *is* vice: so that, when they follow its dictates, we must conclude that they are not free, but in bondage, whose ever bond-slave they be, whether of an evil spirit, or of their own organization; and I think every human being, who looks into himself, will feel that he is in effect then only *free* when he is obeying the dictates of virtue; and that the language of Scripture, which speaks of sin as a bondage, is not only metaphorically but literally true.

The warning a person of an impending danger or error implies no constraint; the subject of the warning is free to take the hint or not, as he pleases; we receive many cautions, both from other people and from our own consciences, which we refuse to benefit by.

With regard to the second objection, it seems to have greater weight; for although the instances of presentiment are very numerous, taken apart, they are certainly, as far as we know, still but exceptional cases. But here we must remember that an influence of this sort might be very continuously, though somewhat remotely, exercised in favor of an individual, without the occurrence of any instance of so striking a nature as to render the interference manifest; and certain it is that some people—I have met with several, and very sensible persons too—have all their lives an intuitive persuasion of such a guardianship existing in relation to themselves. That in our normal states it was not intended we should hold sensible communion with the invisible world, seems evident; but nature abounds in exceptions; and there may be conditions regarding both parties, the incorporated and the unincorporated spirit, which may at times bring them into a more intimate relation. No one who believes that consciousness is to survive the death of the body, can doubt that the released spirit will then hold communion with its congeners; it being the fleshly tabernacles we inhabit which alone disables us from doing so at present. But since the constitutions of bodies vary exceedingly, not only in different individuals, but in the same individuals at different times, may we not conceive the possibility of there existing conditions which, by diminishing the obstructions, render this communion practicable within certain limits? For there certainly are recorded and authentic instances of presentiments and warnings, that with difficulty admit of any other explanation; and that these admonitions are more frequently received in the state of sleep than of vigilance, rather furnishes an additional argument in favor of the last hypothesis; for if there be any foundation for the theories above suggested, it is then that, the sensuous functions being in abeyance and the external life thereby shut out from us, the spirit would be most susceptible to the operations of spirit, whether of our deceased friends or of appointed ministers, if such there be. Jung Stelling is of opinion that we must decide from the aim and object of the revelation, whether it be a mere development of the faculty of presentiment, or a case of spiritual intervention; but this would surely be a very erroneous mode of judging, since the presentiment that foresees a visit may foresee a danger, and show us how to avoid it, as in the following instance:—

A few years ago, Dr. W——, now residing at Glasgow, dreamed that he received a summons to attend a patient at a place some miles from where he was living; that he started on horseback; and that, as he was crossing a moor, he saw a bull making furiously at him, whose horns he only escaped by taking refuge on a spot inaccessible to the animal, where he waited a long time, till some people, observing his situation, came to his assistance and released him. While at breakfast on the following morning, the summons came; and, smiling at the odd *coincidence*, he started on horseback. He was quite ignorant of the road he had to go; but by-and-by he arrived at the moor, which he recognised, and presently the bull appeared, coming full tilt toward him. But his dream had shown him the place of refuge, for which he instantly made; and there he spent three or four hours, besieged by the animal, till the country people set him free. Dr. W—— declares that, but for the dream, he should not have known in what direction to run for safety.

A butcher named Bone, residing at Holytown, dreamed a few years since that he was stopped at a particular spot on his way to market, whither he was going on the following day to purchase cattle, by two men in blue clothes, who cut his throat. He told the dream to his wife, who laughed at him; but, as it was repeated two or three times and she saw he was really alarmed, she advised him to join somebody who was going the same road. He accordingly listened till he heard a cart passing his door, and then went out and joined the man, telling him the reason for so doing. When they came to the spot, there actually stood the two men in blue clothes, who, seeing he was not alone, took to their heels and ran.

Now, although the dream was here probably the means of saving Bone's life, there is no reason to suppose that this is a case of what is called *supernatural intervention*. The phenomenon would be sufficiently accounted for by the admission of the hypothesis I have suggested, namely, that he was aware of the impending danger in his sleep, and had been able, from some cause unknown to us, to convey the recollection into his waking state.

I know instances in which, for several mornings previous to the occurrence of a calamity, persons have awakened with a painful sense of misfortune, for which they could not account, and which was dispersed as soon as they had time to reflect that they had no cause for uneasiness. This is the only kind of presentiment I ever experienced myself; but it has occurred to me twice, in a very marked and unmistakable manner. As soon as the intellectual life, the life of the brain, and the external world, broke in, the instinctive life receded, and the intuitive knowledge was obscured. Or, according to Dr. Ennemoser's theory, the polar relations changed, and the nerves were busied with conveying sensuous impressions to the brain, their sensibility or positive state now being transferred from the internal to the external periphery. It is by the contrary change that Dr. Ennemoser seeks to explain the insensibility to pain of mesmerized patients.

A circumstance of a similar kind to the above occurred in a well-known family in Scotland, the Rutherfords of E——. A lady dreamed that her aunt, who resided at some distance, was murdered by a black servant. Impressed with the liveliness of the vision, she could not resist going to the house of her relation, where the man she had dreamed of (whom I think she had never before seen) opened the door to her. Upon this, she induced a gentleman to watch in the adjoining room during the night; and toward morning, hearing a foot upon the stairs, he opened the door and discovered the black servant carrying up a coal-scuttle full of coals, for the purpose, as he said, of lighting his mistress's fire. As this motive did not seem very probable, the coals were examined, and a knife found hidden among them, with which, he afterward confessed, he intended to have murdered his mistress, provided she made any resistance to a design he had formed of robbing her of a large sum of money which he was aware she had that day received.

The following case has been quoted in several medical works, at least in works written by learned doctors, and on that account I should not mention it here, but for the purpose of remarking on the extraordinary facility with which, while they do not question the fact, they dispose of the mystery :—

Mr. D——, of Cumberland, when a youth, came to Edinburgh, for the purpose of attending college, and was placed under the care of his uncle and aunt, Major and Mrs. Griffiths, who then resided in the castle. When the fine weather came, the young man was in the habit of making frequent excursions with others of his own age and pursuits; and one afternoon he mentioned that they had formed a fishing-party, and had bespoken a boat for the ensuing day. No objections were made to this plan; but in the middle of the night, Mrs. Griffiths screamed out, "The boat is sinking!—oh, save them!" Her husband said he supposed she had been thinking of the fishing-party, but she declared she had never thought about it at all, and soon fell asleep again. But, ere long, she awoke a second time, crying out that she "saw the boat sinking!"—"It must have been the remains of the impression made by the other dream," she suggested to her husband, "for I have no uneasiness whatever about the fishing-party." But on going to sleep once more, her husband was again disturbed by her cries: "They are gone!" she said, "the boat has sunk!" She now really became alarmed, and, without waiting for morning, she threw on her dressing-gown, and went to Mr. D——, who was still in bed, and whom with much difficulty she persuaded to relinquish his proposed excursion. He consequently sent his servant to Leith with an excuse, and the party embarked without him. The day was extremely fine when they put to sea, but some hours afterward a storm arose, in which the boat foundered—nor did any one of the number survive to tell the tale!

"This dream is easily accounted for," say the learned gentlemen above alluded to, "from the dread all women have of the water, and the danger that attends boating on the frith of Forth!" Now, I deny that all women have a dread of the water, and there is not the slightest reason for concluding that Mrs. Griffiths had. At all events, she affirms that she felt no uneasiness at all about the party, and one might take leave to think that her testimony upon that subject is of more value than that of persons who never had any acquaintance with her, and who were not so much as born at the time the circumstance occurred, which was in the year 1731. Besides, if Mrs. Griffiths's dread arose simply from "the dread all women have of the water," and that its subsequent verification was a mere coincidence, since women constantly risk their persons for voyages and boating excursions, such dreams should be extremely frequent—the fact of there being any accident impending or not, having, according to this theory, no relation whatever to the phenomenon. And as for the danger that attends boating on the frith of Forth, we must naturally suppose that, had it been considered so imminent, Major Griffiths would have at least endeavored to dissuade a youth that was placed under his protection from risking his life so imprudently. It would be equally reasonable to explain away Dr. W——'s dream, by saying that all gentlemen who have to ride across commons are in great dread of encountering a bull—commons in general being infested by that animal!

Miss D——, a friend of mine, was some time since invited to join a pic-nic excursion into the country. Two nights before the day fixed for the expedition, she dreamed that the carriage she was to go in was overturned down a precipice. Impressed with her dream, she declined the excursion, confessing her reason, and advising the rest of the party to relinquish their project. They laughed at her, and persisted in their scheme. When, subsequently, she went to inquire how they had spent the day, she found the ladies confined to their beds from injuries received, the carriage having been overturned down a precipice. Still, this was only a coincidence!

Another specimen of the haste with which people are willing to dispose of what they do not understand, is afforded by a case that occurred not many years since in the north of Scotland, where a murder having been committed, a man came forward, saying that he had dreamed that the pack of the murdered pedlar was hidden in a certain spot; where, on a search being made, it was actually found. They at first concluded he was himself the assassin, but the real criminal was afterward discovered; and it being asserted (though I have been told erroneously) that the two men had passed some time together, since the murder, in a state of intoxication, it was decided that the crime and the place of concealment had been communicated to the pretended dreamer—and all who thought otherwise were laughed at; "for why," say the rationalists, "should not Providence have so ordered the dream as to have prevented the murder altogether?"

Who can answer that question, and whither would such a discussion lead us? Moreover, if this faculty of presentiment be a natural one, though only imperfectly and capriciously developed, there may have been no design in the matter: it is an accident, just in the same sense as an illness is an accident; that is, not without cause, but without a cause that we can penetrate. If, on the other hand, we have recourse to the intervention of spiritual beings, it may be answered that we are entirely ignorant of the conditions under which any such communication is possible; and that we can not therefore come to any conclusions as to why so much is done, and no more.

But there is another circumstance to be observed in considering the case, which is, that the dreamer is said to have passed some days in a state of intoxication. Now, even supposing this had been true, it is well known that the excitement of the brain caused by intoxication has occasionally produced a very remarkable exaltation of certain faculties. It is by means of either intoxicating draughts or vapors that the soothsayers of Lapland and Siberia place themselves in a condition to vaticinate; and we have every reason to believe that drugs, producing similar effects, were resorted to by the thaumaturgists of old, and by the witches of later days, of which I shall have more to say hereafter. But, as a case in point, I may here allude to the phenomena exhibited in a late instance of the application of ether, by Professor Simpson, of Edinburgh, to a lady who was at the moment under circumstances not usually found very agreeable. She said that she was amusing herself delightfully by playing over a set of quadrilles which she had known in her youth, but had long forgotten them; but she now perfectly remembered them, and had played them over several times. Here was an instance of the exaltation of a faculty from intoxication, similar to that of the woman who, in her delirium, spoke a language which she had only heard in her childhood, and of which, in her normal state, she had no recollection.

That the inefficiency of the communication, or presentiment, or whatever it may be, is no argument against the fact of such dreams occurring, I can safely assert, from cases which have come under my own knowledge. A professional gentleman, whose name would be a warrant for the truth of whatever he relates, told me the following circumstance regarding himself.

He was, not very long since, at the seaside with his family, and, among the rest, he had with him one of his sons, a boy about twelve years of age, who was in the habit of bathing daily, his father accompanying him to the water-side. This had continued during the whole of their visit, and no idea of danger or accident had ever occurred to anybody. On the day preceding the one appointed for their departure, Mr. H——, the gentleman in question, felt himself after breakfast surprised by an unusual drowsiness, which, having vainly struggled to overcome, he at length fell asleep in his chair, and dreamed that he was attending his son to the bath as usual, when he suddenly saw the boy drowning, and that he himself had rushed into the water, dressed as he was, and brought him ashore. Though he was quite conscious of the dream when he awoke, he attached no importance to it; he considered it merely a dream — no more; and when, some hours afterward, the boy came into the room, and said, "Now, papa, it's time to go — this will be my last bath" — his morning's vision did not even recur to him. They walked down to the sea, as usual, and the boy went into the water, while the father stood composedly watching him from the beach, when suddenly the child lost his footing, a wave had caught him, and the danger of his being carried away was so imminent, that, without even waiting to take off his great-coat, boots, or hat, Mr. H—— rushed into the water, and was only just in time to save him.

Here is a case of undoubted authenticity, which I take to be an instance of clear-seeing, or second-sight, in sleep. The spirit, with its intuitive faculty, saw what was impending; the sleeper remembered his dream, but the intellect did not accept the warning; and, whether that warning was merely a subjective process — the clear-seeing of the spirit — or whether it was effected by any external agency, the free-will of the person concerned was not interfered with.

I quote the ensuing similar case from the "Frankfort Journal," June 25, 1837: "A singular circumstance is said to be connected with the late attempt on the life of the archbishop of Autun. The two nights preceding the attack, the prelate dreamed that he saw a man who was making repeated efforts to take away his life, and he awoke in extreme terror and agitation from the exertions he had made to escape the danger. The features and appearance of the man were so clearly imprinted on his memory, that he recognised him the moment his eye fell upon him, which happened as he was coming out of church. The bishop hid his face, and called his attendants, but the man had fired before he could make known his apprehensions. Facts of this description are far from uncommon. It appears that the assassin had entertained designs against the lives of the bishops of Dijon, Burgos, and Nevers."

The following case, which occurred a few years since in the north of England, and which I have from the best authority, is remarkable from the inexorable fatality which brought about the fulfilment of the dream: Mrs. K——, a lady of family and fortune in Yorkshire, said to her son, one morning on descending to breakfast: "Henry, what are you going to do to-day?"

"I am going to hunt," replied the young man."

"I am very glad of it," she answered. "I should not like you to go shooting, for I dreamed last night that you did so, and were shot. The son answered, gayly, that he would take care not to be shot, and the hunting party rode away; but, in the middle of the day, they returned, not having found any sport. Mr. B——, a visiter in the house, then proposed that they should go out with their guns and try to find some woodcocks. "I will go with you," returned the young man, "but I must not shoot, to-day, myself; for my mother dreamed last night I was shot; and, although it is but a dream, she would be uneasy."

They went, Mr. B—— with his gun, and Mr. K—— without. But shortly afterward the beloved son was brought home dead: a charge from the gun of his companion had struck him in the eye, entered his brain, and killed him on the spot. Mr. B——, the unfortunate cause of this accident and also the narrater of it, died but a few weeks since.

It is well known that the murder of Mr. Percival, by Bellingham, was seen in sleep by a gentleman at York, who actually went to London in consequence of his dream, which was several times repeated. He arrived too late to prevent the calamity; neither would he have been believed, had he arrived earlier.

In the year 1461, a merchant was travelling toward Rome by Sienna, when he dreamed that his throat was cut. He communicated his dream to the innkeeper, who did not like it, and advised him to pray and confess. He did so, and then rode forth, and was presently attacked by the priest he had confessed to, who had thus learned his apprehensions. He killed the merchant, but was betrayed, and disappointed of his gains, by the horse taking fright and running back to the inn with the money-bags.

I have related this story, though not a new one, on account of its singular resemblance to the following, which I take from a newspaper paragraph, but which I find mentioned as a fact in a continental publication:—

"SINGULAR VERIFICATION OF A DREAM.—A letter from Hamburgh contains the following curious story relative to the verification of a dream. It appears that a locksmith's apprentice, one morning lately, informed his master (Claude Soller) that on the previous night he dreamed that he had been assassinated on the road to Bergsdorff, a little town at about two hours' distance from Hamburgh. The master laughed at the young man's credulity, and, to prove that he himself had little faith in dreams, insisted upon sending him to Bergsdorff with one hundred and forty rix dollars, which he owed to his brother-in-law, who resided in the town. The apprentice, after in vain imploring his master to change his intention, was compelled to set out at about 11 o'clock. On arriving at the village of Billwaerder, about half-way between Hamburgh and Bergsdorff, he recollected his dream with terror; but perceiving the baillie of the village at a little distance, talking to some of his workmen, he accosted him, and acquainted him with his singular dream, at the same time requesting that, as he had money about his person, one of his workmen might be allowed to accompany him for protection across a small wood which lay in his way. The baillie smiled, and, in obedience to his orders, one of his men set out with the young apprentice. The next day, the corpse of the latter was conveyed by some peasants to the baillie, along with a reaping-hook which had been found by his side, and with which the throat of the murdered youth had been cut. The baillie immediately recognised the instrument as one which he had on the previous day given to the workman who had served as the apprentice's guide, for the purpose of pruning some willows. The workman was apprehended, and, on being confronted with the body of his victim, made a full confession of his crime, adding that the recital of the dream had alone prompted him to commit the horrible act. The assassin, who is thirty-five years of age, is a native of Billwaerder, and, previously to the perpetration of the murder, had always borne an irreproachable character."

The life of the great Harvey was saved by the governor of Dover refusing to allow him to embark for the continent with his friends. The vessel was lost, with all on board; and the governor confessed to him, that he had detained him in consequence of an injunction he had received in a dream to do so.

There is a very curious circumstance related by Mr. Ward, in his "Illustrations of Human Life," regarding the late Sir Evan Nepean, which I believe is perfectly authentic. I have at least been assured, by persons well acquainted with him, that he himself testified to its truth.

Being, at the time, secretary to the admiralty, he found himself one night unable to sleep, and urged by an undefinable feeling that he must rise, though it was then only two o'clock. He accordingly did so, and went into the park, and from that to the home office, which he entered by a private door, of which he had the key. He had no object in doing this; and, to pass the time, he took up a newspaper that was lying on the table, and there read a paragraph to the effect that a reprieve had been despatched to York, for the men condemned for coining.

The question occurred to him, Was it indeed despatched? He examined the books and found it was not; and it was only by the most energetic proceedings that the thing was carried through, and reached York in time to save the men.

Is not this like the agency of a protecting spirit, urging Sir Evan to this discovery, in order that these men might be spared, or that those concerned might escape the remorse they would have suffered for their criminal neglect?

It is a remarkable fact, that somnambules of the highest order believe themselves attended by a protecting spirit. To those who do not believe, because they have never witnessed, the phenomena of somnambulism, or who look upon the disclosures of persons in that state as the mere raving of hallucination, this authority will necessarily have no weight; but even to such persons the universal coincidence must be considered worthy of observation, though it be regarded only as a symptom of disease. I believe I have remarked elsewhere, that many persons, who have not the least tendency to somnambulism or any proximate malady, have all their lives an intuitive feeling of such a guardianship; and, not to mention Socrates and the ancients, there are, besides, numerous recorded cases in modern times, in which persons, not somnambulic, have declared themselves to have seen and held communication with their spiritual protector.

The case of the girl called Ludwiger, who, in her infancy, had lost her speech and the use of her limbs, and who was earnestly committed by her mother, when dying, to the care of her elder sisters, is known to many. These young women piously fulfilled their engagement till the wedding-day of one of them caused them to forget their charge. On recollecting it, at length, they hastened home, and found the girl, to their amazement, sitting up in her bed, and she told them that her mother had been there and given her food. She never spoke again, and soon after died. This circumstance occurred at Dessau, not many years since, and is, according to Schubert, a perfectly-established fact in that neighborhood. The girl at no other period of her life exhibited any similar phenomena, nor had she ever displayed any tendency to spectral illusions.

The wife of a respectable citizen, named Arnold, at Heilbronn, held constant communications with her protecting spirit, who warned her of impending dangers, approaching visiters, and so forth. He was only once visible to her, and it was in the form of an old man; but his presence was felt by others as well as herself, and they were sensible that the air was stirred, as by a breath.

Jung Stilling publishes a similar account, which was bequeathed to him by a very worthy and pious minister of the church. The subject of the guardianship was his own wife, and the spirit first appeard to her after her marriage, in the year 1799, as a child, attired in a white robe, while she was busy in her bed-chamber. She stretched out her hand to take hold of the figure, but it disappeared. It frequently visited her afterward, and in answer to her inquiries it said, "I died in my childhood!" It came to her at all hours, whether alone or in company, and not only at home, but elsewhere, and even when travelling, assisting her when in danger; it sometimes floated in the air, spake to her in its own language, which somehow, she says, she understood, and could speak, too; and it was once seen by another person. He bade her call him *Immanuel.* She earnestly begged him to show himself to her husband, but he alleged that it would make him ill, and cause his death. On asking him *wherefore*, he answered, "Few persons are able to see such things."

Her two children, one six years old, and the other younger, saw this figure as well as herself.

Schubert, in his "Geschichte der Seele," relates that the ecclesiastical councillor Schwartz, of Heidelberg, when about twelve years of age, and at a time that he was learning the Greek language, but knew very little about it, dreamed that his grandmother, a very pious woman, to whom he had been much attached, appeared to him, and unfolded a parchment inscribed with Greek characters which foretold the fortunes of his future life. He read it off with as much facility as if it had been in German, but being dissatisfied with some particulars of the prediction, he begged they might be changed. His grandmother answered him in Greek, whereupon he awoke, remembering the dream, but, in spite of all the efforts to arrest them, he was unable to recall the particulars the parchment had contained. The answer of his grandmother, however, he was able to grasp before it had fled his memory, and he wrote down the words; but the meaning of them he could not discover without the assistance of his grammar and lexicon. Being interpreted, they proved to be these: "As it is prophesied to me, so I prophesy to thee!" He had written the words in a volume of Gessner's works, being the first thing he laid his hand on; and he often philosophized on them in later days, when they chanced to meet his eye. How, he says, should he have been able to read and produce that in his sleep, which, in his waking state, he would have been quite incapable of? "Even long after, when I left school," he adds, "I could scarcely have put together such a sentence; and it is extremely remarkable that the feminine form was observed in conformity with the sex of the speaker." The words were these: Ταῦτα Χρησμῳδηθεῖσα Χρησμῳδέω σοι.

Grotius relates, that when Mr. de Saumaise was councillor of the parliament at Dijon, a person, who knew not a word of Greek, brought him a paper on which was written some words in that language, but not in the character. He said that a voice had uttered them to him in the night, and that he had written them down, imitating the sound as well as he could. Mons de Saumaise made out that the signification of the words was, "Begone! do you not see that death impends?" Without comprehending what danger was predicted, the person obeyed the mandate and departed. On that night the house that he had been lodging in fell to the ground.

The difficulty in these two cases is equally great, apply to it whatever explanation we may; for even if the admonitions proceeded from some friendly guardian, as we might be inclined to conclude, it is not easy to conceive why they should have been communicated in a language the persons did not understand.

After the death of Dante, it was discovered that the thirteenth canto of the "Paradiso" was missing; great search was made for it, but in vain; and to the regret of everybody concerned, it was at length concluded that it had either never been written, or had been destroyed. The quest was therefore given up, and some months had elapsed, when Pietro Allighieri, his son, dreamed that his father had appeared to him and told him that if he removed a certain panel near the window of the room in which he had been accustomed to write, the thirteenth canto would be found. Pietro told his dream, and was laughed at, of course; however, as the canto did not turn up, it was thought as well to examine the spot indicated in the dream. The panel was removed, and there lay the missing canto behind it; much mildewed, but, fortunately, still legible.

If it be true that the dead do return sometimes to solve our perplexities, here was not an unworthy occasion for the exercise of such a power. We can imagine the spirit of the great poet still clinging to the memory of his august work, immortal as himself—the record of those high thoughts which can never die.

There are numerous curious accounts extant of persons being awakened by the calling of a voice which announced some impending danger to them. Three boys are sleeping in the wing of a castle, and the eldest is awakened by what appears to him to be the voice of his father calling him by name. He rises and hastens to his parent's chamber, situated in another part of the building, where he finds his father asleep, who, on being awakened, assures him that he had not called him, and the boy returns to bed. But he is scarcely asleep, before the circumstance recurs, and he goes again to his father with the same result. A third time he falls asleep, and a third time he is aroused by the voice, too distinctly heard for him to doubt his senses; and now, alarmed at he knows not what, he rises and takes his brothers with him to his father's chamber; and while they are discussing the singularity of the circumstance, a crash is heard, and that wing of the castle in which the boys slept falls to the ground. This incident excited so much attention in Germany that it was recorded in a ballad.

It is related by Amyraldus, that Monsieur Calignan, chancellor of Navarre, dreamed three successive times in one night, at Berne, that a voice called to him and bade him quit the place, as the plague would soon break out in that town; that, in consequence, he removed his family, and the result justified his flight.

A German physician relates, that a patient of his told him, that he dreamed repeatedly, one night, that a voice bade him go to his hop-garden, as there were thieves there. He resisted the injunction some time, till at length he was told that if he delayed any longer he would lose all his produce. Thus urged, he went at last, and arrived just in time to see the thieves, loaded with sacks, making away from the opposite side of the hop-ground.

A Madame Von Militz found herself under the necessity of parting with a property which had long been in her family. When the bargain was concluded, and she was preparing to remove, she solicited permission of the new proprietor to carry away with her some little relic as a memento of former days—a request which he uncivilly denied. On one of the nights that preceded her departure from the home of her ancestors, she dreamed that a voice spoke to her, and bade her go to the cellar and open a certain part of the wall, where she would find something that nobody would dispute with her. Impressed with her dream, she sent for a bricklayer, who, after long seeking, discovered a place which appeared less solid than the rest. A hole was made, and in a niche was found a goblet, which contained something that looked like a pot pourri. On shaking out the contents, there lay at the bottom a small ring, on which was engraven the name *Anna Von Militz*.

A friend of mine, Mr. Charles Kirkpatrick Sharpe, has some coins that were found exactly in the same manner. The child of a Mr. Christison, in whose house his father was lodging, in the year 1781, dreamed that there was a treasure hid in the cellar. Her father had no faith in the dream; but Mr. Sharpe had the curiosity to have the place dug up, and a copper pot was found, full of coins.

A very singular circumstance was related to me by Mr. J——, as having occurred not long since to himself. A tonic had been prescribed to him by his physician, for some slight derangement of the system, and as there was no good chemist in the village he inhabited, he was in the habit of walking to a town about five miles off, to get the bottle filled as occasion required. One night, that he had been to M—— for this purpose, and had obtained his last supply, for he was now recovered, and about to discontinue the medicine, a voice seemed to warn him that some great danger was impending, his life was in jeopardy; then he heard, but not with his outward ear, a beautiful prayer. "It was not myself that prayed," he said, "the prayer was far beyond anything I am capable of composing — it spoke of me in the third person, always as *he;* and supplicated that for the sake of my widowed mother this calamity might be averted. My father had been dead some months. I was sensible of all this, yet I can not say whether I was asleep or awake. When I rose in the morning, the whole was present to my mind, although I had slept soundly in the interval; I felt, however, as if there was some mitigation of the calamity, though what the danger was with which I was threatened, I had no notion. When I was dressed, I prepared to take my medicine, but on lifting the bottle, I fancied that the color was not the same as usual. I looked again, and hesitated, and finally, instead of taking two tablespoonfuls, which was my accustomed dose, I took but one. Fortunate it was that I did so; the apothecary had made a mistake; the drug was poison; I was seized with a violent vomiting, and other alarming symptoms, from which I was with difficulty recovered. Had I taken the two spoonfuls, I should, probably, not have survived to tell the tale."

The manner in which I happened to obtain these particulars is not uninteresting. I was spending the evening with Mr. Wordsworth, at Ridal, when he mentioned to me that a stranger, who had called on him that morning, had quoted two lines from his poem of "Laodamia," which, he said, to him had a peculiar interest. They were these: —

"The invisible world with thee hath sympathized;
Be thy affections raised and solemnized."

"I do not know what he alludes to," said Mr. Wordsworth; "but he gave me to understand that these lines had a deep meaning for him, and that he had himself been the subject of such a sympathy."

Upon this, I sought the stranger, whose address the poet gave me, and thus learned the above particulars from himself. His very natural persuasion was, that the interceding spirit was his father. He described the prayer as one of earnest anguish.

One of the most remarkable instances of warning that has come to my knowledge, is that of Mr. M——, of Kingsborough. This gentleman, being on a voyage to America, dreamed, one night, that a little old man came into his cabin and said, "Get up! Your life is in danger!" Upon which, Mr. M—— awoke; but considering it to be only a dream, he soon composed himself to sleep again. The dream, however, if such it were, recurred, and the old man urged him still more strongly to get up directly; but he still persuaded himself it was only a dream; and after listening a few minutes, and hearing nothing to alarm him, he turned round and addressed himself once more to sleep. But now the old man appeared again, and angrily bade him rise instantly, and take his gun and ammunition with him, for he had not a moment to lose. The injunction was now so distinct that Mr. M—— felt he could no longer resist it; so he hastily dressed himself, took his gun, and ascended to the deck, where he had scarcely arrived, when the ship struck on a rock, which he and several others contrived to reach. The place, however, was uninhabited, and but for his gun, they would never have been able to provide themselves with food till a vessel arrived to their relief.

Now these can scarcely be looked upon as instances of clear-seeing, or of second-sight in sleep, which, in Denmark, is called *first-seeing*, I believe; for in neither case did the sleeper perceive the danger, much less the nature of it. If, therefore, we refuse to attribute them to some external protecting influence, they resolve themselves into cases of vague presentiment; but it must then be admitted that the mode of the manifestation is very extraordinary; so extraordinary, indeed, that we fall into fully as great a difficulty as that offered by the supposition of a guardian spirit.

An American clergyman told me that an old woman, with whom he was acquainted, who had two sons, heard a voice say to her in the night, "John's dead!" This was her eldest son. Shortly afterward, the news of his death arriving, she said to the person who communicated the intelligence to her, "If John's dead, then I know that David is dead, too, for the same voice has since told me so;" and the event proved that the information, whence ever it came, was correct.

Not many years since, Captain S—— was passing a night at the Manse of Strachur, in Argyleshire, then occupied by a relation of his own; shortly after he retired, the bed-curtains were opened, and somebody looked in upon him. Supposing it to be some inmate of the house, who was not aware that the bed was occupied, he took no notice of the circumstance, till it being two or three times repeated, he at length said, "What do you want? Why do you disturb me in this manner?"

"I come," replied a voice, "to tell you, that this day twelvemonth you will be with your father!"

After this, Captain S—— was no more disturbed. In the morning, he related the circumstance to his host, though, being an entire disbeliever in all such phenomena, without attaching any importance to the warning.

In the natural course of events, and quite irrespective of this visitation, on that day twelvemonth he was again at the Manse of Strachur, on his way to the north, for which purpose it was necessary that he should cross the ferry to Craigie. The day was, however, so exceedingly stormy, that his friend begged him not to go; but he pleaded his business, adding that he was determined not to be withheld from his intention by the ghost, and, although the minister delayed his departure, by engaging him in a game of backgammon, he at length started up, declaring he could stay no longer. They, therefore, proceeded to the water, but they found the boat moored to the side of the lake, and the boatman assured them that it would be impossible to cross. Captain S——, however, insisted, and, as the old man was firm in his refusal, he became somewhat irritated, and laid his cane lightly across his shoulders.

"It ill becomes you, sir," said the ferryman, "to strike an old man like me; but, since you will have your way, you must; I can not go with you, but my son will; but you will never reach the other side; he will be drowned, and you too.

The boat was then set afloat, and Captain S——, together with his horse and servant, and the ferryman's son, embarked in it.

The distance was not great, but the storm was tremendous; and, after having with great difficulty got half way across the lake, it was found impossible to proceed. The danger of tacking was, of course, considerable; but, since they could not advance, there was no alternative but to turn back, and it was resolved to attempt it. The manœuvre, however, failed; the boat capsized, and they were all precipitated into the water.

"You keep hold of the horse—I can swim," said Captain S—— to his servant, when he saw what was about to happen.

Being an excellent swimmer, and the distance from the shore inconsiderable, he hoped to save himself, but he had on a heavy top-coat, with boots and spurs. The coat he contrived to take off in the water, and then struck out with confidence; but, alas! the coat had got entangled with one of the spurs, and, as he swam, it clung to him, getting heavier and heavier as it became saturated with water, ever dragging him beneath the stream. He, however, reached the shore, where his anxious friend still stood watching the event; and, as the latter bent over him, he was just able to make a gesture with his hand, which seemed to say, "You see, it was to be!" and then expired.

The boatman was also drowned; but, by the aid of the horse, the servant escaped.

As I do not wish to startle my readers, nor draw too suddenly on their faith, I have commenced with this class of phenomena, which it must be admitted are sufficiently strange, and, if true, must also be admitted to be well worthy of attention. No doubt these cases, and still more those to which I shall next proceed, give a painful shock to the received notions of polished and educated society in general—especially in this country, where the analytical or scientifical psychology of the eighteenth century has almost superseded the study of synthetic or philosophical psychology. It has become a custom to look at all the phenomena regarding man in a purely physiological point of view; for although it is admitted that he has a mind, and although there is such a science as metaphysics, the existence of what we call *mind* is never considered but as connected with the body. 'We know that body can exist without mind; for, not to speak of certain living conditions, the body subsists without mind when the spirit has fled; albeit, without the living principle it can subsist but for a short period, except under particular circumstances; but we seem to have forgotten that mind, though dependent upon body as long as the connection between them continues, can yet subsist without it. There have indeed been philosophers, purely materialistic, who have denied this, but they are not many; and not only the whole Christian world, but all who believe in a future state, must perforce admit it; for even those who hold that most unsatisfactory doctrine that there will be neither memory nor consciousness till a second incorporation takes place, will not deny that the mind, however in a state of abeyance and unable to manifest itself, must still subsist as an inherent property of man's immortal part. Even if, as some philosophers believe, the spirit, when freed from the body by death, returns to the Deity and is reabsorbed in the being of God, not to become again a separate entity until reincorporated, still what we call mind can not be disunited from it. And when once we have begun to conceive of mind, and consequently of perception, as separated from and independent of bodily organs, it will not be very difficult to apprehend that those bodily organs must circumscribe and limit the view of the spiritual in-dweller, which must otherwise be necessarily perceptive of spirit like itself, though perhaps unperceptive of material objects and obstructions.

"It is perfectly evident to me," said Socrates, in his last moments, "that, to see clearly, we must detach ourselves from the body, and perceive by the soul alone. Not while we live, but when we die, will that wisdom which we desire and love be first revealed to us; it must be then, or never, that we shall attain to true understanding and knowledge, since by means of the body we never can. But if, during life, we would make the nearest approaches possible to its possession, it must be by divorcing ourselves as much as in us lies from the flesh and its nature." In their spiritual views and apprehension of the nature of man, how these old heathens shame us!

The Scriptures teach us that God chose to reveal himself to his people chiefly in dreams, and we are entitled to conclude that the reason of this was, that the spirit was then more free to the reception of spiritual influences and impressions; and the class of dreams to which I next proceed seem to be best explained by this hypothesis. It is also to be remarked that the awe or fear which pervades a mortal at the mere conception of being brought into relation with a spirit, has no place in sleep, whether natural or magnetic. There is no fear then, no surprise; we seem to meet on an equality—is it not that we meet spirit to spirit? Is it not that our spirit being then released from the trammels—the dark chamber of the flesh—it does enjoy a temporary equality? Is not that true, that some German psychologist has said—"*The magnetic man is a spirit!*"

There are numerous instances to be met with of persons receiving information in their sleep, which either is, or seems to be, communicated by their departed friends. The approach of danger, the period of the sleeper's death, or of that of some persons beloved, has been frequently made known in this form of dream.

Dr. Binns quotes, from Cardanus, the case of Johannes Maria Maurosenus, a Venetian senator, who, while governor of Dalmatia, saw in a dream one of his brothers, to whom he was much attached: the brother embraced him and bade him farewell, because he was going into the other world. Maurosenus having followed him a long way weeping, awoke in tears, and expressed much anxiety respecting this brother. Shortly afterward he received tidings from Venice that this Domatus, of whom he had dreamed, had died on the night and at the hour of the dream, of a pestilential fever, which had carried him off in three days.

On the night of the 21st of June, in the year 1813, a lady, residing in the north of England, dreamed that her brother, who was then with his regiment in Spain, appeared to her, saying, "Mary, I die this day at Vittoria!"

Vittoria was a town which, previous to the famous battle, was not generally known even by name in this country, and this dreamer, among others, had never heard of it; but, on rising, she eagerly resorted to a gazetteer for the purpose of ascertaining if such a place existed. On finding that it was so, she immediately ordered her horses, and drove to the house of a sister, some eight or nine miles off, and her first words on entering the room were, "Have you heard anything of John?"—"No," replied the second sister, "but I know he is dead! He appeared to me last night, in a dream, and told me that he was killed at Vittoria. I have been looking into the gazetteer and the atlas, and I find there is such a place, and I am sure that he is dead!" And so it proved: the young man died that day at Vittoria, and, I believe, on the field of battle. If so, it is worthy of observation that the communication was not made till the sisters slept.

A similar case to this is that of Miss D——, of G——, who one night dreamed that she was walking about the washing-greens, when a figure approached, which she recognised as that of a beloved brother who was at that time with the British army in America. It gradually faded away into a kind of anatomy, holding up its hands, through which the light could be perceived, and asking for clothes to dress a body for the grave. The dream recurred more than once in the same night, and, apprehending some misfortune, Miss D—— noted down the date of the occurrence. In due course of post, the news arrived that this brother had been killed at the battle of Bunker's hill. Miss D——, who died only within the last few years, though unwilling to speak of the circumstance, never refused to testify to it as a fact.

Here, supposing this to be a real apparition, we see an instance of that desire for decent obsequies so constantly attributed by the ancients to the souls of the dead.

When the German poet Collin died at Vienna, a person named Hartmann, who was his friend, found himself very much distressed by the loss of a hundred and twenty florins, which he had paid for the poet, under a promise of reimbursement. As this sum formed a large portion of his whole possessions, the circumstance was occasioning him considerable anxiety, when he dreamed one night that his deceased friend appeared to him, and bade him immediately set two florins on No. 11, on the first calling of the little lottery, or loto, then about to be drawn. He was bade to confine his venture to two florins, neither less nor more; and to communicate this information to nobody. Hartmann availed himself of the hint, and obtained a prize of a hundred and thirty florins.

Since we look upon lotteries, in this country, as an immoral species of gambling, it may be raised as an objection to this dream, that such intelligence was an unworthy mission for a spirit, supposing the communication to have been actually made by Collin. But, in the first place, we have only to do with facts, and not with their propriety or impropriety, according to our notions; and, by-and-by, I shall endeavor to show that such discrepancies possibly arise from the very erroneous notions commonly entertained of the state of those who have disappeared from the terrestrial life.

Simonides the poet, arriving at the seashore with the intention of embarking on board a vessel on the ensuing day, found an unburied body, which he immediately desired should be decently interred. On the same night, this deceased person appeared to him, and bade him by no means go to sea, as he had proposed. Simonides obeyed the injunction, and beheld the vessel founder, as he stood on the shore. He raised a monument on the spot to the memory of his preserver, which is said still to exist, on which are engraven some lines, to the effect that it was dedicated by Simonides, the poet of Cheos, in gratitude to the dead who had preserved him from death.

A much-esteemed secretary died a few years since, in the

house of Mr. R—— von N——. About eight weeks afterward, Mr. R—— himself being ill, his daughter dreamed that the house-bell rang, and that, on looking out, she perceived the secretary at the door. Having admitted him, and inquired what he was come for, he answered, "To fetch somebody." Upon which, alarmed for her father, she exclaimed, "I hope not my father!" He shook his head solemnly, in a manner that implied it was not the old man he had come for, and turned away toward a guest-chamber, at that time vacant, and there disappeared at the door. The father recovered, and the lady left home for a few days, on a visit. On her return, she found her brother had arrived in the interval to pay a visit to his parents, and was lying sick in that room, where he died.

I will here mention a curious circumstance regarding Mr. H——, the gentleman alluded to in a former page, who, being at the seaside, saw, in a dream, the danger that awaited his son when he went to bathe. This gentleman has frequently, on waking, felt a consciousness that he had been conversing with certain persons of his acquaintance—and, indeed, with some of whom he knew little—and has afterward, not without a feeling of awe, learned that these persons had died during the hours of his sleep.

Do not such circumstances entitle us to entertain the idea that I have suggested above, namely, that in sleep the spirit is free to see, and to know, and to communicate with spirit, although the memory of this knowledge is rarely carried into the waking state?

The story of the two Arcadians, who travelled together to Megara, though reprinted in other works, I can not omit here. One of these established himself, on the night of their arrival, at the house of a friend, while the other sought shelter in a public lodging-house for strangers. During the night, the latter appeared to the former, in a dream, and besought him to come to his assistance, as his villanous host was about to take his life, and only the most speedy aid could save him. The dreamer started from his sleep, and his first movement was to obey the summons, but, reflecting that it was only a dream, he presently lay down, and composed himself again to rest. But now his friend appeared before him a second time, disfigured by blood and wounds, conjuring him, since he had not listened to his first entreaties, that he would, at least, avenge his death. His host, he said, had murdered him, and was, at that moment, depositing his body in a dung-cart, for the purpose of conveying it out of the town. The dreamer was thoroughly alarmed, arose, and hastened to the gates of the city, where he found, waiting to pass out, exactly such a vehicle as his friend had described. A search being instituted, the body was found underneath the manure; and the host was consequently seized, and delivered over to the chastisement of the law.

"Who shall venture to assert," says Dr. Ennemoser, "that this communing with the dead in sleep is merely a subjective phenomenon, and that the presence of these apparitions is a pure illusion?"

A circumstance fully as remarkable as any recorded, occurred at Odessa, in the year 1842. An old blind man, named Michel, had for many years been accustomed to get his living by seating himself every morning on a beam in one of the timber-yards, with a wooden bowl at his feet, into which the passengers cast their alms. This long-continued practice had made him well known to the inhabitants, and, as he was believed to have been formerly a soldier, his blindness was attributed to the numerous wounds he had received in battle. For his own part, he spoke little, and never contradicted this opinion.

One night, Michel, by some accident, fell in with a little girl of ten years old, named Powleska, who was friendless, and on the verge of perishing with cold and hunger. The old man took her home, and adopted her; and, from that time, instead of sitting in the timber-yards, he went about the streets in her company, asking alms at the doors of the houses. The child called him *father*, and they were extremely happy together But when they had pursued this mode of life for about five years, a misfortune befell them. A theft having been committed in a house which they had visited in the morning, Powleska was suspected and arrested, and the blind man was left once more alone. But, instead of resuming his former habits, he now disappeared altogether; and this circumstance causing the suspicion to extend to him, the girl was brought before the magistrate to be interrogated with regard to his probable place of concealment.

"Do you know where Michel is?" said the magistrate.

"He is dead!" replied she, shedding a torrent of tears.

As the girl had been shut up for three days, without any means of obtaining information from without, this answer, together with her unfeigned distress, naturally excited considerable surprise.

"Who told you he was dead?" they inquired.

"Nobody!"

"Then how can you know it?"

"I saw him killed!"

"But you have not been out of the prison?"

"But I saw it, nevertheless!"

"But how was that possible? Explain what you mean!"

"I can not. All I can say is, that I saw him killed."

"When was he killed, and how?"

"It was the night I was arrested."

"That can not be: he was alive when you were seized!"

"Yes, he was; he was killed an hour after that. They stabbed him with a knife."

"Where were you then?"

"I can't tell; but I saw it."

The confidence with which the girl asserted what seemed to her hearers impossible and absurd, disposed them to imagine that she was either really insane, or pretending to be so. So, leaving Michel aside, they proceeded to interrogate her about the robbery, asking her if she was guilty.

"Oh, no!" she answered.

"Then how came the property to be found about you?"

"I don't know: I saw nothing but the murder."

"But there are no grounds for supposing Michel is dead: his body has not been found."

"It is in the aqueduct."

"And do you know who slew him?"

"Yes—it is a woman. Michel was walking very slowly, after I was taken from him. A woman came behind him with a large kitchen-knife; but he heard her, and turned round: and then the woman flung a piece of gray stuff over his head, and struck him repeatedly with the knife; the gray stuff was much stained with the blood. Michel fell at the eighth blow, and the woman dragged the body to the aqueduct and let it fall in without ever lifting the stuff which stuck to his face."

As it was easy to verify these latter assertions, they despatched people to the spot; and there the body was found, with the piece of stuff over his head, exactly as she described. But when they asked her how she knew all this, she could only answer, "I don't know."

"But you know who killed him?"

"Not exactly: it is the same woman that put out his eyes; but, perhaps, he will tell me her name to-night; and if he does, I will tell it to you."

"Whom do you mean by *he?*"

"Why, Michel, to be sure!"

During the whole of the following night, without allowing her to suspect their intention, they watched her; and it was observed that she never lay down, but sat upon the bed in a sort of lethargic slumber. Her body was quite motionless, except at intervals, when this repose was interrupted by violent nervous shocks, which pervaded her whole frame. On the ensuing day, the moment she was brought before the judge, she declared that she was now able to tell them the name of the assassin.

"But stay," said the magistrate: "did Michel never tell you, when he was alive, how he lost his sight?"

"No—but the morning before I was arrested, he promised me to do so; and that was the cause of his death."

"How could that be?"

"Last night, Michel came to me, and he pointed to the man hidden behind the scaffolding on which he and I had been sitting. He showed me the man listening to us, when he said, 'I'll tell you all about that to-night;' and then the man——"

"Do you know the name of this man?"

"It is *Luck*. He went afterward to a broad street that leads down to the harbor, and he entered the third house on the right——"

"What is the name of the street?"

"I don't know: but the house is one story lower than the adjoining ones. Luck told Catherine what he had heard, and she proposed to him to assassinate Michel; but he refused, saying, 'It was bad enough to have burnt out his eyes fifteen years before, while he was asleep at your door, and to have kidnapped him into the country.' Then I went in to ask charity, and Catherine put a piece of plate into my pocket, that I might be arrested; then she hid herself behind the aqueduct to wait for Michel, and she killed him."

"But, since you say all this, why did you keep the plate—why didn't you give information?"

"But I didn't see it then. Michel showed it me last night."

"But what should induce Catherine to do this?"

"Michel was her husband, and she had forsaken him to come to Odessa and marry again. One night, fifteen years ago, she saw Michel, who had come to seek her. She slipped hastily into her house, and Michel, who thought she had not seen him, lay down at her door to watch; but he fell asleep, and then Luck burnt out his eyes, and carried him to a distance."

"And is it Michel who has told you this?"

"Yes: he came, very pale, and covered with blood; and he took me by the hand and showed me all this with his fingers."

Upon this, Luck and Catherine were arrested; and it was ascertained that she had actually been married to Michel in the year 1819, at Kherson. They at first denied the accusation, but Powleska insisted, and they subsequently confessed the crime. When they communicated the circumstances of the confession to Powleska, she said, "I was told it last night."

This affair naturally excited great interest, and people all round the neighborhood hastened into the city to learn the sentence.

CHAPTER VI.

DOUBLE-DREAMING AND TRANCE.

AMONG the phenomena of the dream-life which we have to consider, that of double-dreaming forms a very curious department. A somewhat natural introduction to this subject may be found in the cases above recorded, of Professor Herder and Mr. S——, of Edinburgh, who appear, in their sleep, to have received so lively an impression of those earnest wishes of their dying friends to see them, that they found themselves irresistibly impelled to obey the spiritual summons. These two cases occurred to men engaged in active daily life, and in normal physical conditions, on which account I particularly refer to them here, although many similar ones might be adduced.

With respect to this subject of double-dreaming, Dr. Ennemoser thinks that it is not so difficult to explain as might appear on a first view, since he considers that there exists an indisputable sympathy between certain organisms, especially where connected by relationship or by affection, which may be sufficient to account for the supervention of simultaneous thoughts, dreams, or presentiments; and I have met with some cases where the magnetiser and his patient have been the subjects of this phenomenon. With respect to the power asserted to have been frequently exercised by causing or suggesting dreams by an operator at a distance from the sleeper, Dr. E. considers the two parties to stand in a positive and negative relation to each other; the antagonistic power of the sleeper being = 0, he becomes a perfectly passive recipient of the influence exerted by his positive *half*, if I may use the expression; for, where such a polarity is established, the two beings seem to be almost blended into one; while Dr. Passavent observes, that we can not pronounce what may be the limits of the nervous force, which certainly is not bounded by the termination of its material conductors.

I have yet, myself, met with no instance of dream compelling by a person at a distance; but Dr. Ennemoser says that Agrippa von Nettesheim asserts that this can assuredly be done, and also that the abbot Trithemius and others possessed the power. In modern times, Wesermaun, in Dusseldorf, pretended to the same faculty, and affirms that he had frequently exercised it.

All such phenomena, Dr. Passavent attributes to the interaction of imponderables—or of one universal imponderable under different manifestations—which acts not only within the organism, but beyond it, independently of all material obstacles; just as a sympathy appears between one organ and another, unobstructed by the intervening ones; and he instances the sympathy which exists between the mother and the fœtus, as an example of this sort of double life, and standing as midway between the sympathy between two organs in the same body and that between two separate bodies, each having its own life, and its life also in and for another, as parts of one whole. The sympathy between a bird and the eggs it sits upon, is of the same kind; many instances having been observed, wherein eggs, taken from one bird and placed under another, have produced a brood feathered like the foster instead of the real parent.

Thus, this vital force may extend dynamically the circle of its influence, till, under favorable circumstances, it may act on other organisms, making their organs its own.

I need scarcely remind my readers of the extraordinary sympathies manifested by the Siamese twins, Chang and Eng. I never saw them myself; and, for the benefit of others in the same sitnation, I quote the following particulars from Dr. Passavent: "They were united by a membrane which extended from the breast-bone to the navel; but, in other respects, were not different from their countrymen in general. They were exceedingly alike, only that Eng was rather the more robust of the two. Their pulsations were not always coincident.

They were active and agile, and fond of bodily exercises; their intellects were well developed, and their tones of voice and accent were precisely the same. As they never conversed together, they had nearly forgotten their native tongue. If one was addressed, they both answered. They played some games of skill, but never with each other; as that, they said, would have been like the right hand playing with the left. They read the same book at the same time, and sang together in unison. In America they had a fever, which ran precisely a similar course with each. Their hunger, thirst, sleeping, and waking, were alway coincident, and their tastes and inclinations were identical. Their movements were so simultaneous, that it was impossible to distinguish with which the impulse had originated; they appeared to have but one will. The idea of being separated by an operation was abhorrent to them; and they consider themselves much happier in their duality than are the individuals who look upon them with pity."

This admirable sympathy, although necessarily in an inferior degree, is generally manifested, more or less, between all persons twin-born. Dr. Passavent and other authorities mention several instances of this kind, in which, although at some distance from each other, the same malady appeared simultaneously in both, and ran precisely a similar course. A very affecting instance of this sort of sympathy was exhibited, not very long ago, by a young lady, twin-born, who was suddenly seized with an unaccountable horror, followed by a strange convulsion, which the doctor, who was hastily called in, said exactly resembled the struggles and sufferings of a person drowning. In process of time, the news arrived that her twin-brother, then abroad, had been drowned precisely at that period.

It is probably a link of the same kind that is established between the magnetiser and his patient, of which, besides those recorded in various works on the subject, some curious instances have come to my knowledge, such as uncontrollable impulses to go to sleep, or to perform certain actions, in subservience to the will of the distant operator. Mr. W—— W——, a gentleman well known in the north of England, related to me that he had been cured, by magnetism, of a very distressing malady. During part of the process of cure, after the *rapport* had been well established, the operations were carried on while he was at Malvern, and his magnetiser at Cheltenham, under which circumstances the existence of this extraordinary dependence was frequently exhibited in a manner that left no possibility of doubt. On one occasion, I remember that Mr. W—— W—— being in the magnetic sleep, he suddenly started from his seat, clasping his hands as if startled, and presently afterward burst into a violent fit of laughter. As, on waking, he could give no account of these impulses, his family wrote to the magnetiser to inquire if he had sought to excite any particular manifestations in his patient, as the sleep had been somewhat disturbed. The answer was, that no such intention had been entertained, but that the disturbance might possibly have arisen from one to which he had himself been subjected. "While my mind was concentrated on you," said he, "I was suddenly so much startled by a violent knock at the door, that I actually jumped off my seat, clasping my hands with affright. I had a hearty laugh at my own folly, but am sorry if you were made uncomfortable by it."

I have met with some accounts of a sympathy of this kind existing between young children and their parents, so that the former have exhibited great distress and terror at the moment that death or danger have supervened to the latter; but it would require a great number of instances to establish this particular fact, and separate it from cases of accidental coincidence. Dr. Passavent, however, admits the phenomena.

I shall return to these mysterious influences by-and-by; but to revert, in the meanwhile, to the subject of double dreams, I will relate one that occurred to two ladies, a mother and daughter, the latter of whom related it to me. They were sleeping in the same bed at Cheltenham, when the mother, Mrs. C——, dreamed that her brother-in-law, then in Ireland, had sent for her; that she entered his room, and saw him in bed, apparently dying. He requested her to kiss him, but, owing to his livid appearance, she shrank from doing so, and awoke with the horror of the scene upon her. The daughter awoke at the same moment, saying, "Oh, I have had such a frightful dream!" "Oh, so have I!" returned the mother; "I have been dreaming of my brother-in-law!"—"My dream was about him, too," added Miss C——. "I thought I was sitting in the drawing-room, and that he came in wearing a shroud, trimmed with black ribands, and, approaching me, he said: 'My dear niece, your mother has refused to kiss me, but I am sure you will not be so unkind!'"

As these ladies were not in habits of regular correspondence with their relative, they knew that the earliest intelligence likely to reach them, if he were actually dead, would be by means of the Irish papers; and they waited anxiously for the following Wednesday, which was the day these journals were received in Cheltenham. When that morning arrived, Miss C—— hastened at an early hour to the reading-room, and there she learned what the dreams had led them to expect: their friend was dead; and they afterward ascertained that his decease had taken place on that night. They moreover observed, that neither one nor the other of them had been speaking or thinking of this gentleman for some time previous to the occurrence of the dreams; nor had they any reason whatever for uneasiness with regard to him. It is a remarkable peculiarity in this case, that the dream of the daughter appears to be a continuation of that of the mother. In the one, he is seen alive; in the other, the shroud and black ribands seem to indicate that he is dead, and he complains of the refusal to give him a farewell kiss.

One is almost inevitably led here to the conclusion that the thoughts and wishes of the dying man were influencing the sleepers, or that the released spirit was hovering near them.

Pomponius Mela relates, that a certain people in the interior of Africa lay themselves down to sleep on the graves of their forefathers, and believe the dreams that ensue to be the unerring counsel of the dead.

The following dream, from St. Austin, is quoted by Dr. Binns: Præstantius desired from a certain philosopher the solution of a doubt, which the latter refused to give him; but, on the following night, the philosopher appeared at his bedside and told him what he desired to know. On being asked, the next day, why he had chosen that hour for his visit, he answered: 'I came not to you truly, but in my dream I appeared to you to do so.' In this case, however, only one of the parties seems to have been asleep, for Præstantius says that he was awake; and it is perhaps rather an example of another kind of phenomena, similar to the instance recorded of himself by the late Joseph Wilkins, a dissenting minister, who says that, being one night asleep, he dreamed that he was travelling to London, and that, as it would not be much out of his way, he would go by Gloucestershire and call upon his friends. Accordingly he arrived at his father's house, but, finding the front door closed, he went round to the back and there entered. The family, however, being already in bed, he ascended the stairs and entered his father's bedchamber. Him he found asleep; but to his mother, who was awake, he said, as he walked round to her side of the bed, 'Mother, I am going a long journey, and am come to bid you good-by;' to which she answered, 'Oh, dear son, thee art dead!' Though struck with the distinctness of the dream, Mr. Wilkins attached no importance to it, till, to his surprise, a letter arrived from his father, addressed to himself, if alive—or, if not, to his surviving friends—begging earnestly for immediate intelligence, since they were under great apprehensions that their son was either dead, or in danger of death; for that, on such a night (naming that on which the above dream had occurred), he, the father, being asleep, and Mrs. Wilkins awake, she had distinctly heard somebody try to open the fore door, which being fast, the person had gone round to the back and there entered. She had perfectly recognised the footstep to be that of her son, who had ascended the stairs, and entering the bedchamber, had said to her, 'Mother, I am going a long journey, and am come to bid you good-by;' whereupon she had answered, 'Oh, dear son, thee art dead!' Much alarmed, she had awakened her husband and related what had occurred, assuring him that it was not a dream, for that she had not been asleep at all. Mr. Wilkins mentions that this curious circumstance took place in the year 1754, when he was living at Ottery; and that he had frequently discussed the subject with his mother, on whom the impression made was even stronger than on himself. Neither death nor anything else remarkable ensued."

A somewhat similar instance to this, which I also quote from Dr. Binns, is that of a gentleman who dreamed that he was pushing violently against the door of a certain room, in a house with which he was well acquainted; while the people in that room were, at the same time, actually alarmed by a violent pushing against the door, which it required their utmost force effectually to resist. As soon as the attempt to burst open the door had ceased, the house was searched, but nothing discovered to account for the disturbance.

These examples are extremely curious, and they conduct us by a natural transition to another department of this mysterious subject.

There must be few persons who have not heard, among their friends and acquaintance, instances of what is called a *wraith;* that is, that in the moment of death, a person is seen in a place where *bodily* he is not. I believe the Scotch use this term also in the same sense as the Irish word *fetch;* which is a person's double seen at some indefinite period previous to his death, of which such an appearance is generally supposed to be a prognostic. The Germans express the same thing by the word *döppelganger*.

With respect to the appearance of wraiths, at the moment of death, the instances to be met with are so numerous and well-authenticated, that I generally find the most skeptical people unable to deny that some such phenomenon exists, although they evade, without I think, diminishing the difficulty, by pronouncing it to be of a subjective, and not of an objective, nature; that is, that the image of the dying person is, by some unknown operation, presented to the imagination of the seer, without the existence of any real outstanding figure, from which it is reflected; which reduces such instances so nearly to the class of mere sensuous illusion, that it seems difficult to draw the distinction. The distinction those theorists wish to imply, however, is that the latter are purely subjective and self-originating, while the others have an external cause, although not an external visible object—the image seen being protruded by the imagination of the seer, in consequence of an unconscious intuition of the death of the person whose wraith is perceived.

Instances of this kind of phenomenon have been common in all ages of the world, insomuch that Lucretius, who did not believe in the immortality of the soul, and was yet unable to deny the facts, suggested the strange theory that the superficial surfaces of all bodies were continually flying off, like the coats of an onion, which accounted for the appearance of wraiths, ghosts, doubles, &c.; and a more modern author, Gaffarillus, suggests that corrupting bodies send forth vapors, which being compressed by the cold night air, appear visible to the eye in the forms of men.

It will not be out of place, here, to mention the circumstance recorded in Professor Gregory's "Abstract of Baron von Reichenbach's Researches in Magnetism," regarding a person called Billing, who acted in the capacity of amanuensis to the blind poet Pfeffel, at Colmar. Having treated of various experiments, by which it was ascertained that certain sensitive persons were not only able to detect electric influences of which others were unconscious, but could also perceive, emanating from the wires and magnets, flames which were invisible to people in general; "the baron," according to Dr. Gregory, "proceeded to a useful application of the results, which is, he says, so much the more welcome, as it utterly eradicates one of the chief foundations of superstition, that worst enemy to the develment of human enlightenment and liberty. A singular occurrence, which took place at Colmar, in the garden of the poet Pfeffel, has been made generally known by various writings. The following are the essential facts. The poet, being blind, had employed a young clergyman, of the evangelical church, as amanuensis. Pfeffel, when he walked out, was supported and led by this young man, whose name was Billing. As they walked in the garden, at some distance from the town, Pfeffel observed, that as often as they passed over a particular spot, the arm of Billing trembled, and he betrayed uneasiness. On being questioned, the young man reluctantly confessed, that as often as he passed over that spot, certain feelings attacked him, which he could not control, and which he knew well, as he always experienced the same, in passing over any place where human bodies lay buried. He added, that at night, when he came near such places, he saw supernatural appearances. Pfeffel, with the view of curing the youth of what he looked on as fancy, went that night with him to the garden. As they approached the spot in the dark, Billing perceived a feeble light, and when still nearer, he saw a luminous ghostlike figure floating over the spot. This he described as a female form, with one arm laid across the body, the other hanging down, floating in the upright posture, but tranquil, the feet only a hand-breadth or two above the soil. Pfeffel went alone, as the young man declined to follow him, up to the place where the figure was said to be, and struck about in all directions with his stick, besides running actually through the shadow; but the figure was not more affected than a flame would have been; the luminous form, according to Billing always returned to its original position after these experiments. Many things were tried during several months, and numerous companies of people were brought to the spot, but the matter remained the same, and the ghost-seer adhered to his serious assertion, and to the opinion founded on it, that some individual lay buried there. At last, Pfeffel had the place dug up. At a considerable depth was found a firm layer of white lime, of the length and breadth of a grave, and of considerable thickness, and when this had been broken into, there were found the bones of a human being. It was evident that some one had been buried in the place, and covered with a thick layer of lime (quicklime), as is generally done in times of pestilence, of earthquakes, and other similar events. The bones were removed, the pit filled up, the lime scattered abroad, and the surface again made smooth. When Billing was now brought back to the place, the phenomena did not return, and the nocturnal spirit had for ever disappeared.

"It is hardly necessary to point out to the reader what view the author takes of this story, which excited much attention in Germany, because it came from the most truthful man alive, and theologians and psychologists gave to it sundry terrific meanings. It obviously falls into the province of chemical action, and thus meets with a simple and clear explanation from natural and physical causes. A corpse is a field for abundant chemical changes, decompositions, fermentation, putrefaction, gasification, and general play of affinities. A stratum of quick-lime, in a narrow pit, unites its powerful affinities to those of the organic matters, and gives rise to a long-continued working of the whole. Rain-water filters through and contributes to the action: the lime on the outside of the mass first falls to a fine powder, and afterward, with more water, forms lumps which are very slowly penetrated by the air. Slaked lime prepared for building, but not used, on account of some cause connected with a warlike state of society some centuries since, has been found in subterraneous holes or pits, in the ruins of old castles; and the mass, except on the outside, was so unaltered that it has been used for modern buildings. It is evident, therefore, that in such circumstances there must be a very slow and long-continued chemical action, partly owing to the slow penetration of the mass of lime by the external carbonic acid, partly to the change going on in the remains of animal matter, at all events as long as any is left. In the above case, this must have gone on in Pfeffel's garden, and, as we know that chemical action is invariably associated with light, visible to the sensitive, this must have been the origin of the luminous appearance, which again must have continued until the mutual affinities of the organic remains, the lime, the air, and water, had finally come to a state of chemical rest or equilibrium. As soon, therefore, as a sensitive person, although otherwise quite healthy, came that way, and entered into the sphere of the force in action, he must feel, by day, like Mdlle. Maix, the sensations so often described, and see by night, like Mdlle. Reichel, the luminous appearance. Ignorance, fear, and superstition, would dress up the feebly shining, vaporous light into a human form, and furnish it with human limbs and members; just as we can at pleasure fancy every cloud in the sky to represent a man or a demon.

"The wish to strike a fatal blow at the monster superstition, which, at no distant period, poured out upon European society from a similar source, such inexpressible misery, when, in trials for witchcraft, not hundreds, not thousands, but hundreds of thousands of innocent human beings perished miserably, either on the scaffold, at the stake, or by the effects of torture—this desire induced the author to try the experiment of bringing, if possible, a highly-sensitive patient by night to a churchyard. It appeared possible that such a person might see, over graves in which mouldering bodies lie, something similar to that which Billing had seen. Mdlle. Reichel had the courage, rare in her sex, to gratify this wish of the author. On two very dark nights she allowed herself to be taken from the castle of Reisenberg, where she was living with the author's family, to the neighboring churchyard of Grunzing. The result justified his anticipation in the most beautiful manner. She very soon saw a light, and observed on one of the graves, along its length, a delicate, breathing flame: she also saw the same thing, only weaker on the second grave. But she saw neither witches nor ghosts; she described the fiery appearances as a shining vapor, one to two spans high, extending as far as the grave, and floating near its surface. Some time afterward she was taken to two large cemeteries near Vienna, where several burials occur daily, and graves lie about by thousands. Here she saw numerous graves provided with similar lights. Wherever she looked, she saw luminous masses scattered about. But this appearance was most vivid over the newest graves, while in the oldest it could not be perceived. She described the appearance less as a clear flame than as a dense, vaporous mass of fire, intermediate between fog and flame. On many graves the flames were four feet high, so that when she stood on them, it surrounded her up to the neck. If she thrust her hand into it, it was like putting it into a dense, fiery cloud. She betrayed no uneasiness, because she had all her life been accustomed to such emanations, and had seen the same, in the author's experiments, often produced by natural causes.

"Many ghost-stories will now find their natural explanation. We can also see that it was not altogether erroneous, when old women declared that all had not the gift to see the departed wandering about their graves; for it must have always been the sensitive alone who were able to perceive the light given out by the chemical action going on in the corpse. The author has thus, he hopes, succeeded in tearing down one of the most impenetrable barriers erected by dark ignorance and superstitious folly against the progress of natural truth."

"(The reader will at once apply the above most remarkable experiments to the explanation of corpse-lights in churchyards, which were often visible to the gifted alone—to those who had the second-sight, for example. Many nervous or hysterical females must often have been alarmed by white, faintly-luminous objects in dark churchyards, to which objects fear has given a defined form. In this, as well as in numerous other points, which will force themselves on the attention of the careful reader of both works, Baron Reichenbach's experiments illustrate the experiences of the Seeress of Prevorst.—W. G.)"*

That the flames here described may have originated in chemical action, is an opinion I have no intention of disputing; the fact may possibly be so; such a phenomenon has frequently been observed hovering over coffins and decomposing flesh: but I confess I can not perceive the slightest grounds for the assertion that it was the ignorance, fear, and superstition, of Billing, who was an evangelical clergyman, that caused him to dress up this vaporous light in a human form and supply it with members, &c. In the first place, I see no proof adduced that Billing was either ignorant or superstitious, or even afraid—the feelings he complained of appearing to be rather physical than moral; and it must be a weak person indeed, who, in company with another, could be excited to such a freak of the imagination. It is easily comprehensible that that which appeared

* This very curious work I have translated from the German. Published by Moore, London.—C. C. Also republished in this country.—AM. ED.

only a luminous vapor by day, might, when reflected on a darker atmosphere, present a defined form; and the suggestion of this possibility might lead to some curious speculations with regard to a mystery called the PALINGANESIA, said to have been practised by some of the chemists and alchemists of the sixteenth century.

Gaffarillus, in his book, entitled "*Curiosités Inouïes*," published in 1650, when speaking on the subject of talismans, signatures, &c., observes that, since in many instances the plants used for these purposes were reduced to ashes, and no longer retained their form, their efficacy, which depended on their figure, should inevitably be destroyed; but this, he says, is not the case, since, by an admirable potency existing in nature, the form, though invisible, is still retained in the ashes. This, he observes, may appear strange to those who have never attended to the subject; but he asserts that an account of the experiment will be found in the works of Mr. Du Chesne, one of the best chemists of the period, who had been shown, by a Polish physician at Cracow, certain vials containing ashes, which, when duly heated, exhibited the forms of various plants. A small obscure cloud was first observed, which gradually took on a defined form, and presented to the eye a rose, or whatever plant or flower the ashes consisted of. Mr. Du Chesne, however, had never been able to repeat the experiment, though he had made several unsuccessful attempts to do so; but at length he succeeded, by accident, in the following manner: Having for some purpose extracted the salts from some burnt nettles, and having left the ley outside the house all night, to cool, in the morning he found it frozen; and, to his surprise, the form and figure of the nettles were so exactly represented on the ice, that the living plant could not be more perfect. Delighted at this discovery, he summoned Mr. De Luynes, parliamentary councillor, to behold this curiosity; whence, he says, they both concluded that, when a body dies, its form or figure still resides in its ashes.

Kircher, Vallemont, Digby, and others, are said to have practised this art of resuscitating the forms of plants from their ashes and at the meeting of naturalists at Stuttgard, in 1834, a Swiss savant seems to have revived the subject, and given a receipt for the experiment, extracted from a work by Oetinger, called "Thoughts on the Birth and Generation of Things."—"The earthly husk," says Oetinger, "remains in the retort, while the volatile essence ascends, like a spirit, perfect in form, but void of substance."

But Oetinger also records another discovery of this description, which, he says, he fell upon unawares. A woman having brought him a large bunch of balm, he laid it under the tiles, which were yet warm with the summer's heat, where it dried in the shade. But, it being in the month of September, the cold soon came, and contracted the leaves, without expelling the volatile salts. They lay there till the following June, when he chopped up the balm, put it into a glass retort, poured rain-water upon it, and placed a receiver above. He afterward heated it till the water boiled, and then increased the heat—whereupon there appeared on the water a coat of yellow oil, about the thickness of the back of a knife, and this oil shaped itself into the forms of innumerable balm-leaves, which did not run one into another, but remained perfectly distinct and defined, and exhibited all the marks that are seen in the leaves of the plant. Oetinger says he kept the fluid some time, and showed it to a number of people. At length, wishing to throw it away, he shook it, and the leaves ran into one another with the disturbance of the oil, but resumed their distinct shape again as soon as it was at rest, the fluid form retaining the perfect signature.

Now, how far these experiments are really practicable, I can not say; their not being repeated, or not being repeated successfully, is no very decided argument against their possibility, as all persons acquainted with the annals of chemistry well know; but there is certainly a curious coincidence between these details and the experience of Billing, where it is to be observed that, according to his account—and what right have we to dispute it?—the figure, after being disturbed by Pfeffel, always resumed its original form. The same peculiarity has been observed with respect to some apparitions, where the spectator has been bold enough to try the experiment. In a letter to Dr. Bentley, from the Rev. Thomas Wilkins, curate of Warblington, in Hampshire, written in the year 1695, wherein he gives an account of an apparition which haunted the parsonage-house, and which he himself and several other persons had seen, he particularly mentions that, thinking it might be some fellow hid in the room, he put his arm out to feel it, and his hand seemingly went through the body of it, and felt no manner of substance, until it reached the wall. "Then I drew back my hand, but still the apparition was in the same place."

Yet this spectre did not appear above or near a grave, but moved from place to place, and gave considerable annoyance to the inhabitants of the rectory.

With respect to the lights over the graves, sufficing to account for the persuasion regarding what are called *corpse-candles*, they certainly, up to a certain point, afford a very satisfactory explanation, but that explanation does not comprehend the whole of the mystery; for most of those persons who have professed to see corpse-candles, have also asserted that they were not always stationary over the graves, but sometimes moved from place to place, as in the following instance, related to me by a gentleman who assured me that he received the account from the person who witnessed the phenomenon. Now, this last fact—I mean the locomotion of the lights—will, of course, be disputed; but so was their existence: yet they exist, for all that, and may travel from place to place, for anything we know to the contrary.

The story related to me, or a similar instance, is, I think, mentioned by Mrs. Grant; but it was to the effect that a minister, newly inducted in his curé, was standing one evening leaning over the wall of the churchyard which adjoined the manse, when he observed a light hovering over a particular spot. Supposing it to be somebody with a lantern, he opened the wicket and went forward to ascertain who it might be; but before he reached the spot, the light moved onward; and he followed, but could see nobody. It did not rise far from the ground, but advanced rapidly across the road, entered a wood, and ascended a hill, till it at length disappeared at the door of a farmhouse. Unable to comprehend of what nature this light could be, the minister was deliberating whether to make inquiries at the house or return, when it appeared again, seeming to come out of the house, accompanied by another, passed him, and, going over the same ground, they both disappeared on the spot where he had first observed the phenomenon. He left a mark on the grave by which he might recognise it, and the next day inquired of the sexton whose it was. The man said it belonged to a family that lived up the hill (indicating the house the light had stopped at), named M'D——, but that it was a considerable time since any one had been buried there. The minister was extremely surprised to learn, in the course of the day, that a child of that family had died of scarlet fever on the preceding evening.

With respect to the class of phenomena accompanied by this phosphorescent light, I shall have more to say by-and-by. The above will appear a very incredible story to many people, and there was a time that it would have appeared equally so to myself; but I have met with so much strange corroborative evidence, that I no longer feel myself entitled to reject it. I asked the gentleman who told me the story, whether he believed it; he said that he could not believe in anything of the sort. I then inquired if he would accept the testimony of that minister on any other question, and he answered, "Most assuredly." As, however, I shall have occasion to recur to this subject in a subsequent chapter, I will leave it aside for the present, and relate some of the facts which led me to the consideration of the above theories and experiments.

Dr. S—— relates that a Madame T——, in Prussia, dreamed, on the 16th of March, 1832, that the door opened, and her godfather, Mr. D——, who was much attached to her, entered the room, dressed as he usually was when prepared for church on Sundays; and that, knowing him to be in bad health, she asked him what he was doing abroad at such an early hour, and whether he was quite well again. Whereupon, he answered that he was; and, being about to undertake a very long journey, he had come to bid her farewell, and to intrust her with a commission, which was, that she would deliver a letter he had written to his wife; but accompanying it with an injunction that she (the wife) was not to open it till that day four years, when he would return himself, precisely at five o'clock in the morning, to fetch the answer, till which period he charged her not to break the seal. He then handed her a letter, sealed with black, the writing on which shone through the paper, so that she (the dreamer) was able to perceive that it contained an announcement to Mrs. D——, the wife, with whom, on account of the levity of her character, he had long lived unhappily, that she would die at that time four years.

At this moment, the sleeper was awakened by what appeared to her a pressure of the hand; and, feeling an entire conviction that this was something more than an ordinary dream, she was not surprised to learn that her god-father was dead. She related the dream to Madame D——, omitting, however, to mention the announcement contained in the letter, which she thought the dream plainly indicated was not to be communicated. The widow laughed at the story, soon resumed her gay life, and married again. In the winter of 1835–'6, however, she was attacked by an intermittent fever, on which occasion Dr. S—— was summoned to attend her. After various vicissitudes, she finally sunk; and, on the 16th of March, 1836, exactly at five o'clock in the morning, she suddenly started up in her bed, and, fixing her eyes apparently on some one she saw standing at the foot, she exclaimed: "What are you come for? God be gracious to me! I never believed it!" She then sank back, closed her eyes, which she never opened again, and, in a quarter of an hour afterward, expired very calmly.

A friend of mine, Mrs. M——, a native of the West Indies, was at Blair Logie at the period of the death of Dr. Abercrombie, in Edinburgh, with whom she was extremely intimate. Dr. A. died quite suddenly, without any previous indisposition, just as he was about to go out in his carriage, at 11 o'clock on a Thursday morning. On the night between the Thursday and

Friday, Mrs. M—— dreamed that she saw the family of Dr. A. all dressed in white, dancing a solemn funereal dance; upon which she awoke, wondering that she should have dreamed a thing so incongruous, since it was contrary to their custom to dance on any occasion. Immediately afterward, while speaking to her maid who had come to call her, she saw Dr. Abercrombie against the wall, with his jaw fallen, and a livid countenance, mournfully shaking his head as he looked at her. She passed the day in great uneasiness, and wrote to inquire for the doctor, relating what had happened, and expressing her certainty that he was dead; the letter was seen by several persons in Edinburgh on the day of its arrival.

The two following cases seem rather to belong to what is called, in the east, *second hearing*,—although sympathy was probably the exciting cause of the phenomena. A lady and gentleman in Berwickshire were awakened one night by a loud cry, which they both immediately recognised to proceed from the voice of their son, who was then absent and at a considerable distance. Tidings subsequently reached them, that exactly at that period their son had fallen overboard and was drowned. On another occasion, in Perthshire, a person aroused her husband one night, saying that their son was drowned, for she had been awakened by the splash. Her presentiment also proved too well founded, the young man having fallen from the mast-head of the ship. In both cases, we may naturally conclude that the thoughts of the young men, at the moment of the accident, would rush homeward; and, admitting Dr. Ennemoser's theory of polarity, the passive sleepers became the recipients of the force. I confess, however, that the opinions of another section of philosophers appear to me to be more germain to the matter; although, to many persons, they will doubtless be difficult of acceptance, from their appertaining to those views commonly called mystical.

These psychologists then believe, as did Socrates and Plato, and others of the ancients, that in certain conditions of the body, which conditions may arise naturally, or be produced artificially, the links which unite it with the spirit may be more or less loosened; and that the latter may thus be temporarily disjoined from the former, and so enjoy a foretaste of its future destiny. In the lowest or first degree of this disunion, we are awake, though scarcely conscious, while the imagination is vivified to an extraordinary amount, and our fancy supplies images almost as lively as the realities. This probably is the temporary condition of inspired poets and eminent discoverers.

Sleep is considered another stage of this disjunction; and the question has ever been raised whether, when the body is in profound sleep, the spirit is not altogether free and living in another world, while the organic life proceeds as usual, and sustains the temple till the return of its inhabitant. Without at present attempting to support or refute this doctrine, I will only observe, that once admitting the possibility of the disunion, all consideration of *time* must be set aside as irrelevant to the question; for spirit, freed from matter, must move with the rapidity of thought;—in short, *a spirit must be where its thoughts and affections are.*

It is the opinion of these psychologists, however, that in the normal and healthy condition of man, the union of body, soul, and spirit, is most complete, and that all the degrees of disunion in the waking state are degrees of morbid derangement. Hence it is that somnambulists and clairvoyants are chiefly to be found among sickly women. There have been persons who have appeared to possess a power which they could exert at will, whereby they withdrew from their bodies, these remaining during the absence of the spirit in a state of catalepsy, scarcely if at all to be distinguished from death.

I say *withdrew from their bodies*, assuming that to be the explanation of the mystery; for, of course, it is but an assumption. Epimenides is recorded to have possessed this faculty; and Hermotinus, of Clazomenes, is said to have wandered, in spirit, over the world, while his body lay apparently dead. At length his wife, taking advantage of this absence of his soul, burned his body and thus intercepted its return: so say Lucien and Pliny the elder;—and Varro relates, that the eldest of two brothers, named Corfidius, being supposed to die, his will was opened and preparations were made for his funeral by the other brother, who was declared his heir. In the meantime, however, Corfidius revived, and told the astonished attendants, whom he summoned by clapping his hands, that he had just come from his younger brother, who had committed his daughter to his care, and informed him where he had buried some gold, requesting that the funeral preparations he had made might be converted to his own use. Immediately afterward, the news arrived that the younger brother was unexpectedly deceased, and the gold was found at the place indicated. The last appears to have been a case of natural trance; but the two most remarkable instances of voluntary trance I have met with in modern times is that of Colonel Townshend, and the dervish who allowed himself to be buried. With regard to the former, he could, to all appearance, die whenever he pleased; his heart ceased to beat; there was no perceptible respiration; and his whole frame became cold and rigid as death itself; the features being shrunk and colorless, and the eyes glazed and ghastly. He would continue in this state for several hours and then gradually revive; but the revival does not appear to have been an effort of will—or rather, we are not informed whether it was so or not. Neither are we told whether he brought any recollections back with him, nor how this strange faculty was first developed or discovered—all very important points, and well worthy of investigation.*

* Since the above was penned, I find from the account of Dr. Cheyne, who attended him, that Colonel Townshend's own way of describing the phenomenon to which he was subject, was, that he "could die, or expire, when he pleased; and yet, by an effort or *somehow*, he could come to life again." He performed the experiment in the presence of three medical men, one of whom kept his hand on his heart, another held his wrist, and the third placed a looking-glass before his lips; and they found that all traces of respiration and pulsation gradually ceased, insomuch that, after consulting about his condition for some time, they were leaving the room, persuaded that he was really dead, when signs of life appeared and he slowly revived. He did not die while repeating this experiment, as has been sometimes stated.

This reviving "by an effort or somehow," seems to be better explained by the hypothesis I have suggested, than by any other—namely, that, as in the case of Mr. Holloway (mentioned on page 120), his spirit, or soul, was released from his body, but a sufficient *rapport* was maintained to reunite them.

With respect to the dervish, or fakeer, an account of his singular faculty was, I believe, first presented to the public in the Calcutta papers about nine or ten years ago. He had then frequently exhibited it for the satisfaction of the natives; but subsequently he was put to the proof by some of the European officers and residents. Captain Wade, political agent at Loodhiana, was present when he was disinterred, ten months after he had been buried by General Ventura, in presence of the maharajah and many of his principal sirdars.

It appears that the man previously prepared himself by some processes, which, he says, temporarily annihilate the powers of digestion, so that milk received into the stomach undergoes no change. He next forces all the breath in his body into his brain, which becomes very hot, upon which the lungs collapse, and the heart ceases to beat. He then stops up, with wax, every aperture of the body through which air could enter, except the mouth, but the tongue is so turned back as to close the gullet, upon which a state of insensibility ensues. He is then stripped and put into a linen bag; and, on the occasion in question, this bag was sealed with Runjeet Sing's own seal. It was then placed in a deal box, which was also locked and sealed, and the box being buried in a vault, the earth was thrown over it and trod down, after which a crop of barley was sown on the spot, and sentries placed to watch it. The maharajah, however, was so skeptical, that, in spite of all these precautions, he had him, twice in the course of the ten months, dug up and examined, and each time he was found to be exactly in the same state as when they had shut him up.

When he is disinterred, the first step toward his recovery is to turn back his tongue, which is found quite stiff, and requires for some time to be retained in its proper position by the finger; warm water is poured upon him, and his eyes and lips moistened with ghee, or oil. His recovery is much more rapid than might be expected, and he is soon able to recognise the bystanders, and converse. He says, that, during this state of trance, his dreams are ravishing, and that it is very painful to be awakened; but I do not know that he has ever disclosed any of his experiences. His only apprehension seems to be, lest he should be attacked by insects, to avoid which accident the box is slung to the ceiling. The interval seems to be passed in a complete state of hibernation; and when he is taken up, no pulse is perceptible, and his eyes are glazed like those of a corpse.

He subsequently refused to submit to the conditions proposed by some English officers, and thus incurred their suspicions, that the whole thing was an imposition; but the experiment has been too often repeated by people very well capable of judging, and under too stringent precautions, to allow of this mode of escaping the difficulty. The man assumes to be *holy*, and is very probably a worthless fellow, but that does not affect the question one way or the other. Indian princes do not permit themselves to be imposed on with impunity; and, as Runjeet Sing would not value the man's life at a pin's point, he would neglect no means of debarring him all access to food or air.

In the above quoted cases, except in those of Corfidius and Hermotinus, the absence of the spirit is alone suggested to the spectator by the condition of the body; since the memory of one state does not appear to have been carried into the other — if the spirit wandered into other regions it brings no tidings back; but we have many cases recorded where this deficient evidence seems to be supplied. The magicians and soothsayers of the northern countries, by narcotics, and other means, produce a cataleptic state of the body, resembling death, when their prophetic faculty is to be exercised; and although we know that an alloy of imposition is generally mixed up with these exhibitions, still it is past a doubt, that a state of what we call clear-seeing is thus induced; and that on awaking, they bring tidings from various parts of the world of actions then performing and events occurring, which subsequent investigations have verified

One of the most remarkable cases of this kind, is that recorded by Jung Stilling, of a man, who about the year 1740, resided in the neighborhood of Philadelphia, in the United States. His habits were retired, and he spoke little; he was grave, benevolent, and pious, and nothing was known against his character, except that he had the reputation of possessing some secrets that were not altogether *lawful*. Many extraordinary stories were told of him, and among the rest, the following: The wife of a ship-captain, whose husband was on a voyage to Europe and Africa, and from whom she had been long without tidings, overwhelmed with anxiety for his safety, was induced to address herself to this person. Having listened to her story, he begged her to excuse him for awhile, when he would bring her the intelligence she required. He then passed into an inner room, and she sat herself down to wait; but his absence continuing longer than she expected, she became impatient, thinking he had forgotten her; and so softly approaching the door, she peeped through some aperture, and to her surprise, beheld him lying on a sofa, as motionless as if he was dead. She of course, did not think it advisable to disturb him, but waited his return, when he told her that her husband had not been able to write to her for such and such reasons; but that he was then in a coffeehouse in London, and would shortly be home again. Accordingly, he arrived, and as the lady learned from him that the causes of his unusual silence had been precisely those alleged by the man, she felt extremely desirous of ascertaining the truth of the rest of the information; and in this she was gratified; for he no sooner set his eyes on the magician than he said that he had seen him before, on a certain day, in a coffeehouse in London; and that he had told him his wife was extremely uneasy about him; and that he, the captain, had thereon mentioned how he had been prevented writing; adding that he was on the eve of embarking for America. He had then lost sight of the stranger among the throng, and knew nothing more about him.

I have no authority for this story, but that of Jung Stilling; and if it stood alone, it might appear very incredible; but it is supported by so many parallel examples of information given by people in somnambulic states, that we are not entitled to reject it on the score of impossibility.

The late Mr. John Holloway, of the bank of England, brother to the engraver of that name, related of himself that being one night in bed with his wife and unable to sleep, he had fixed his eyes and thoughts with uncommon intensity on a beautiful star that was shining in at the window, when he suddenly found his spirit released from his body and soaring into that bright sphere. But, instantly seized with anxiety for the anguish of his wife, if she discovered his body apparently dead beside her, he returned, and re-entered it with *difficulty* (hence, perhaps, the violent convulsions with which some somnambules of the highest order are awakened). He described that returning, was returning to darkness; and that while the spirit was free, he was *alternately in the light or the dark, accordingly as his thoughts were with his wife or with the star.* He said that he always avoided anything that could produce a repetition of this accident, the consequences of it being very distressing.

We know that by intense contemplation of this sort, the dervishes produce a state of ecstasy, in which they pretend to be transported to other spheres; and not only the seeress of Prevorst, but many other persons in a highly magnetic state, have asserted the same thing of themselves; and certainly the singular conformity of the intelligence they bring is not a little remarkable.

Dr. Kerner relates of his somnambule, Frederica Hauffe, that one day, at Weinsberg, she exclaimed in her sleep, "Oh! God!" She immediately awoke, as if aroused by the exclamation, and said that she seemed to have heard two voices proceeding from herself. At this time her father was lying dead in his coffin, at Oberstenfeld, and Dr. Fohr, the physician, who had attended him in his illness, was sitting with another person in an adjoining room, with the door open, when he heard the exclamation "Oh, God!" so distinctly, that, feeling certain there was nobody there, he hastened to the coffin, whence the sound had appeared to proceed, thinking that Mr. W——'s death had only been apparent, and that he was reviving. The other person, who was an uncle of Frederica, had heard nothing. No person was discovered from whom the exclamation could have proceeded, and the circumstance remained a mystery till an explanation ensued. Plutarch relates, that a certain man, called Thespesius, having fallen from a great height, was taken up apparently dead from the shock, although no external wound was to be discovered. On the third day after the accident, however, when they were about to bury him, he unexpectedly revived; and it was afterward observed, to the surprise of all who knew him, that, from being a vicious reprobate, he became one of the most virtuous of men. On being interrogated with respect to the cause of the change, he related that, during the period of his bodily insensibility, it appeared to him that he was dead, and that he had been first plunged into the depths of an ocean, out of which, however he soon emerged, and then, at one view, the whole of space was disclosed to him. Everything appeared in a different aspect, and the dimensions of the planetary bodies, and the intervals between them, were tremendous, while his spirit seemed to float in a sea of light, like a ship in calm waters. He also described many other things that he had seen. He said that the souls of the dead, on quitting the body, appeared like a bubble of light, out of which a human form was quickly evolved. That of these, some shot away at once in a direct line, with great rapidity, while others, on the contrary, seemed unable to find their due course, and continued to hover about, going hither and thither, till at length they also darted away in one direction or another. He recognised few of these persons he saw, but those whom he did, and sought to address, appeared as if they were stunned and amazed, and avoided him with terror. Their voices were indistinct, and seemed to be uttering vague lamentings. There were others, also, who floated farther from the earth, who looked bright, and were gracious; these avoided the approach of the last. In short, the demeanor and appearance of these spirits manifested clearly their degrees of joy or grief. Thespesius was then informed by one of them, that he was not dead, but that he had been permitted to come there by a Divine decree, and that his soul, which was yet attached to his body, as by an anchor, would return to it again. Thespesius then observed that he was different to the dead by whom he was surrounded, and this observation seemed to restore him to his recollection. They were transparent, and environed by a radiance, but he seemed to trail after him a dark ray, or line of shadow. These spirits also presented very different aspects; some were entirely pervaded by a mild, clear radiance, like that of the full moon; through others there appeared faint streaks, that diminished this splendor; while others, on the contrary, were distinguished by spots, or stripes of black, or of a dark color, like the marks on the skin of a viper.

There is a circumstance which I can not help here mentioning in connection with this history of Thespesius, which on first reading struck me very forcibly.

About three years ago, I had several opportunities of seeing two young girls, then under the care of a Mr. A——, of Edinburgh, who hoped, chiefly by means of magnetism, to restore them to sight. One was a maid-servant afflicted with amaurosis, whom he had taken into his house from a charitable desire to be of use to her; the other, who had been blind from her childhood, was a young lady in better circumstances, the daughter of respectable tradespeople in the north of England. The girl with amaurosis was restored to sight, and the other was so far benefited that she could distinguish houses, trees, carriages, &c., and at length, though obscurely, the features of a person near her. At this period of the cure she was, unhappily, removed, and may possibly have relapsed into her former state. My reason, however, for alluding to these young women on this occasion is, that they were in the habit of saying, when in the magnetic state—for they were both, more or less, *clairvoyantes*—that the people whom Dr. A—— was magnetizing, in the same room, presented very different appearances. Some of them they described as looking bright, while others were, in different degrees, streaked with black.

One or two they mentioned over whom there seemed to hang a sort of cloud, like a ragged veil of darkness. They also said, though this was before any tidings of Baron von Reichenbach's discoveries had reached this country, that they saw light streaming from the fingers of Mr. A—— when he magnetized them; and that sometimes his whole person seemed to them radiant. Now, I am positively certain that neither Mr. A—— nor these girls had ever heard of this story of Thespesius; neither had I, at that time; and I confess, when I did meet with it I was a good deal struck by the coincidence. These young people said that it was the "goodness or badness," meaning the moral state, of the persons that was thus indicated. Now, surely, this concurrence between the man mentioned by Plutarch, and these two girls—one of whom had no education whatever, and the other very little—is worthy of some regard.

I once asked a young person in a highly clairvoyant state, whether she ever "saw the spirits of them that had passed away;" for so *she* designated the dead, never using the word *death* herself, in any of its forms. She answered me that she did.

"Then where are they?" I inquired.

"Some are waiting, and some are gone on before."

"Can you speak to them?" I asked.

"No," she replied, "there is no meddling nor direction."

In her waking state she would have been quite incapable of these answers; and that "some are waiting and some gone on before," seems to be much in accordance with the vision of Thespesius.

Dr. Passavent mentions a peasant-boy who, after a short but painful illness, apparently died, his body being perfectly stiff. He, however, revived, complaining bitterly of being called back to life. He said he had been in a delightful place, and seen his deceased relations. There was a great exaltation of the faculties after this; and having been before rather stupid, he now, while his body lay stiff and immoveable and his eyes closed, prayed and discoursed with eloquence. He continued in this state for seven weeks, but finally recovered.

In the year 1733, Johann Schwerzeger fell into a similar state of trance, after an illness, but revived. He said he had seen his whole life, and every sin he had committed, even those he had quite forgotten—everything had been as present to him as when it happened. He also lamented being recalled from the happiness he was about to enter into; but said that he had only two days to spend in this valley of tears, during which time he wished everybody that would, should come and listen to what he had to tell them. His before sunken eyes now looked bright, his face had the bloom of youth, and he discoursed so eloquently, that the minister said they had exchanged offices, and the sick man had become his teacher. He died at the time he had foretold.

The most frightful cases of trance recorded are those in which the patient retains entire consciousness, although utterly unable to exhibit any evidence of life; and it is dreadful to think how many persons may have been actually buried, hearing every nail that was screwed into their own coffin, and as perfectly aware of the whole ceremony as those who followed them to the grave.

Dr. Binns mentions a girl, at Canton, who lay in this state, hearing every word that was said around her, but utterly unable to move a finger. She tried to cry out, but could not, and supposed that she was really dead. The horror of finding herself about to be buried at length caused a perspiration to appear on her skin, and she finally revived. She described that she felt that her soul had no power to act upon her body, and that it seemed to be *in her body and out of it, at the same time!*

Now, this is very much what the somnambulists say: their soul is out of the body, but is still so far in rapport with it, that it does not leave it entirely. Probably magnetism would be the best means of reviving a person from this state.

The custom of burying people before there are unmistakable signs of death, is a very condemnable one. A Mr. M'G—— fell into a trance, some few years since, and remained insensible for five days, his mother being meanwhile quite shocked that the physician would not allow him to be buried. He had afterward a recurrence of the malady, which continued seven days.

A Mr. S——, who had been some time out of the country, died, apparently, two days after his return. As he had eaten of a pudding which his stepmother had made for his dinner with her own hands, people took into their heads she had poisoned him; and, the grave being opened for purposes of investigation, the body was found lying on its face.

One of the most frightful cases extant is that of Dr. Walker, of Dublin, who had so strong a presentiment on this subject, that he had actually written a treatise against the Irish customs of hasty burial. He himself subsequently died, as was believed, of a fever. His decease took place in the night, and on the following day he was interred. At this time, Mrs. Bellamy, the once-celebrated actress, was in Ireland; and as she had promised him, in the course of conversation, that she would take care he should not be laid in the earth till unequivocal signs of dissolution had appeared, she no sooner heard of what had happened than she took measures to have the grave reopened; but it was, unfortunately, too late; Dr. Walker had evidently revived, and had turned upon his side; but life was now quite extinct.

The case related by Lady Fanshawe, of her mother, is very remarkable, from the confirmation furnished by the event of her death. "My mother, being sick of a fever," says Lady Fanshawe, in her memoirs, "her friends and servants thought her deceased, and she lay in that state for two days and a night; but Mr. Winslow, coming to comfort my father, went into my mother's room, and, looking earnestly in her face, said, 'She was so handsome, and looked so lovely, that he could not think her dead;' and, suddenly taking a lancet out of his pocket, he cut the sole of her foot, which bled. Upon this, he immediately caused her to be removed to the bed again, and to be rubbed, and such means used that she came to life, and, opening her eyes, saw two of her kinswomen standing by her (Lady Knollys and Lady Russell), both with great wide sleeves, as the fashion then was; and she said, 'Did you not promise me fifteen years, and are you come again already?'—which they, not understanding, bade her keep her spirits quiet in that great weakness wherein she was; but, some hours after, she desired my father and Dr. Howlesworth might be left alone with her, to whom she said: 'I will acquaint you, that, during my trance, I was in great grief, but in a place I could neither distinguish nor describe; but the sense of leaving my girl, who is dearer to me than all my children, remained a trouble upon my spirits. Suddenly I saw two by me, clothed in long white garments, and methought I fell down upon my face in the dust, and they asked me why I was so troubled in so great happiness. I replied, "Oh, let me have the same grant given to Hezekiah, that I may live fifteen years to see my daughter a woman!"—to which they answered, "It is done!"—and then at that instant I awoke out of my trance!' And Dr. Howlesworth did affirm that the day she died made just fifteen years from that time."

I have met with a somewhat similar case to this, which occurred to the mother of a very respectable person now living in Edinburgh. She having been ill, was supposed to be dead, and preparations were making for her funeral, when one of her fingers was seen to move, and restoratives being applied, she revived. As soon as she could speak, she said she had been at the gates of heaven, where she saw some going in, but that they told her she was not ready. Among those who had passed her, and been admitted, she said *she had seen Mr. So-and-so, the baker*, and the remarkable thing was, that during the time she had been in the trance, this man had died.

On the 10th of January, 1717, Mr. John Gardner, a minister, at Elgin, fell into a trance, and, being to all appearance dead, he was put into a coffin, and on the second day was carried to the grave. But, fortunately, a noise being heard, the coffin was opened, and he was found alive and taken home again, where, according to the record, "he related many strange and amazing things which he had seen in the other world."

Not to mention somnambules, there are numerous other cases recorded of persons who have said, on awaking from a trance, that they had been in the other world; though frequently the freed spirit—supposing that to be the interpretation of the mystery—seems busied with the affairs of the earth, and brings tidings from distant places, as in the case of the American above mentioned. Perhaps, in these latter cases, the disunion is less complete. Dr. Werner relates of his somnambule, that it was after those attacks of catalepsy, in which her body had lain stiff and cold, that she used to say she had been wandering away through other spheres. Where the catalepsy is spontaneous and involuntary, and resembles death so nearly as not to be distinguished from it, we may naturally conclude, if we admit this hypothesis at all, that the seeing of the spirit would be clear in proportion to its disentanglement from the flesh.

I have spoken above of dream compelling or suggesting, and I have heard of persons who have a power of directing their own dreams to any particular subject.

This faculty may be in some degree analogous to that of the American, and a few somnambulic persons, who appear to carry the recollections of one state into the other. The effects produced by the witch-potions seem to have been somewhat similar, inasmuch as they dreamed what they wished or expected to dream. Jung Stilling mentions that a woman gave in evidence, on a witch-trial, that having visited the so-called witch, she had found her concocting a potion over the fire, of which she had advised her (the visiter) to drink, assuring her that she would then accompany her to the Sàbbath. The woman said, lest she should give offence, she had put the vessel to her lips, but had not drunk of it. The witch, however, swallowed the whole, and immediately afterward sunk down upon the hearth in a profound sleep, where she had left her. When she went to see her on the following day, she declared she had been to the Brocken.

Paolo Minucci relates that a woman accused of sorcery, being brought before a certain magistrate at Florence, she not only confessed her guilt, but she declared that, provided they would let her return home and anoint herself, she would attend the Sâbbath that very night. The magistrate, a man more enlightened than the generality of his contemporaries, consented. The woman went home, used her unguent, and fell immediately into a profound sleep; whereupon they tied her to the bed, and tested the reality of the sleep by burns, blows, and pricking her with sharp instruments. When she awoke on the following day, she related that she had attended the Sâbbath.

I could quote several similar facts; and Gassendi actually endeavored to undeceive some peasants who believed themselves witches, by composing an ointment that produced the same effects as their own magical applications.

In the year 1545, André Laguna, physician to Pope Julius

III., anointed a patient of his, who was suffering from frenzy and sleeplessness, with an unguent found in the house of a sorcerer, who had been arrested. The patient slept for thirty-six hours consecutively, and when, with much difficulty, she was awakened, she complained that they had torn her from the most ravishing delights—delights which seem to have rivalled the heaven of the Mohammedan. According to Llorente, the women who were dedicated to the service of the mother of the gods, heard continually the sounds of flutes and tambourines, beheld the joyous dances of the fauns and satyrs, and tasted of intoxicating pleasures, doubtless from a similar cause.

It is difficult to imagine that all the unfortunate wretches who suffered death at the stake in the middle ages, for having attended the unholy assemblies they described, had no faith in their own stories; yet, in spite of the unwearied vigilance of public authorities and private malignity, no such assemblage was ever detected. How, then, are we to account for the pertinacity of their confessions, but by supposing them the victims of some extraordinary delusion? In a paper addressed to the Inquisition, by Llorente, he does not scruple to assert that the crimes imputed to and confessed by witches have most frequently no existence but in their dreams, and that their dreams are produced by the drugs with which they anointed themselves.

The recipes for these compositions, which had descended traditionally from age to age, have been lost since witchcraft went out of fashion, and modern science has no time to investigate secrets which appear to be more curious than profitable; but in the profound sleep produced by these applications, it is not easy to say what phenomena may have occurred to justify, or, at least, account for, their self-accusations.

CHAPTER VII.

WRAITHS.

Such instances as that of Lady Fanshawe, and other similar ones, certainly seem to favor the hypothesis that the spirit is freed from the body when the latter becomes no longer a fit habitation for it. It does so when actual death supervenes, and the reason of its departure we may naturally conclude to be, that the body has ceased to be available for its manifestations; and in these cases, which seem so nearly allied to death, that frequently there would actually be no revival but for the exertions used, it does not seem very difficult to conceive that this separation may take place. When we are standing by a deathbed, all we see is the death of the body—of the going forth of the spirit we see nothing: so, in cases of apparent death, it may depart and return, while we are aware of nothing but the reanimation of the organism. Certain it is, that the Scriptures countenance this view of the case in several instances; thus, Luke says, viii. 34: "And he put them all out, and took her by the hand, and called, saying, 'Maid, arise!' And her spirit came again, and she arose straightway," &c., &c.

Dr. Wigan observes, when speaking of the effects of temporary pressure on the brain, that the mind is not annihilated, because, if the pressure is timely removed, it is restored, though, if continued too long, the body will be resolved into its primary elements: and he compares the human organism to a watch, which we can either stop or set going at will—which watch, he says, will also be gradually resolved into its original elements by chemical action; and he adds that, to ask where the mind is, during the interruption, is like asking where the motion of the watch is. I think a wind-instrument would be a better simile, for the motion of the watch is purely mechanical. It requires no informing, intelligent spirit to breathe into its apertures, and make it the vehicle of the harshest discords, or of the most eloquent discourses. "The divinely mysterious essence, which we call the soul," he adds, "is not, then, the mind, from which it must be carefully distinguished, if we would hope to make any progress in mental philosophy. Where the soul resides during the suspension of the mental powers by asphyxia, I know not, any more than I know where it resided before it was united with that specific compound of bones, muscles, and nerve."

By a temporary pressure on the brain, the mind is certainly not annihilated, but its manifestations by means of the brain are suspended—the source of these manifestations being the soul, or anima, in which dwells the life, fitting the temple for its divine inhabitant, the spirit. The connection of the soul and the body is probably a much more intimate one than that of the latter with the spirit,—though the soul, as well as the spirit, is immortal, and survives when the body dies. Somnambulic persons seem to intimate that the soul of the fleshly body becomes hereafter the body of the spirit, as if the *imago* or *idolon* were the soul.

Dr. Wigan and indeed psychologists in general do not appear to recognise the old distinction between the pneuma, or anima, and the psyches—the soul and the spirit; and, indeed, the Scriptures occasionally seem to use the terms indifferently. But still there are passages enough which mark the distinction; as where St. Paul speaks of a "living soul and a quickening spirit:" 1 Cor. xv. 45;—again, 1 Thess. v. 23: "I pray God your whole spirit, and soul, and body," &c.;—and also Heb. iv. 12, where he speaks of the sword of God "dividing asunder the soul and spirit." In Genesis, chap. ii., we are told that "man became a living soul;" but it is distinctly said, 1 Cor. xii., that the gifts of prophecy, the discerning of spirits, &c., &c., belong to the spirit. Then, with regard to the possibility of the spirit absenting itself from the body, St. Paul says, in referring to his own vision—2 Cor. xii.—"I knew a man in

Christ, about fourteen years ago (whether in the body, I can not tell; or out of the body, I can not tell: God knoweth); such a one caught up to the third heaven:" and we are told, also, that to be "absent from the body is to be present with the Lord;" and that when we are "at home in the body we are absent from the Lord." We are told, also, "the spirit returns to God, who gave it;" but it depends on ourselves whether or not our souls shall perish. We must suppose, however, that even in the worst cases, some remnant of this divine spirit remains with the soul as long as the latter is not utterly perverted and rendered incapable of salvation.

St. John also says, that when he prophesied, he was in the *spirit;* but it was the "*souls of the slain*" that he saw, and that "cried with a loud voice," &c., &c.; *souls*, here, being probably used in the sense of individuals,—as we say, so many "souls perished by shipwreck," &c.

In the *Revue de Paris*, 29th July, 1838, it is related that a child *saw* the soul of a woman, who was lying insensible in a magnetic crisis in which death nearly ensued, depart out of her; and I find recorded in another work that a somnambule, who was brought to give advice to a patient, said: "It is too late—her soul is leaving her: I see the vital flame quitting her brain."

From some of the cases I have above related, we are led to the conclusion that in certain conditions of the body, the spirit, in a manner unknown to us, resumes a portion of its freedom, and is enabled to exercise more or less of its inherent properties. It is somewhat released from those inexorable conditions of time and space which bound and limit its powers, while in close connection with matter, and it communes with other spirits who are also liberated. How far this liberation (if such it be), or reintegration of natural attributes, may take place in ordinary sleep, we can only conclude from examples. In prophetic dreams, and in those instances of information apparently received from the dead, this condition seems to occur; as also in such cases as that of the gentleman mentioned in a former chapter, who has several times been conscious, on awaking, that he had been conversing with some one, whom he has been subsequently startled to hear had died at that period, and this is a man apparently in excellent health, endowed with a vigorous understanding, and immersed in active business.

In the story of the American, quoted in a former chapter from Jung Stilling, there was one point which I forebore to comment on at the moment, but to which I must now revert: this is the assertion that the voyager had seen the man, and even conversed with him, in the coffeehouse in London whence the desired intelligence was brought. Now, this single case, standing alone, would amount to nothing, although Jung Stilling, who was one of the most conscientious of men, declares himself to have been quite satisfied with the authority on which he relates it; but, strange to say—for undoubtedly the thing *is* very strange—there are numerous similar instances recorded; and it seems to have been believed in all ages of the world, that people were sometimes seen where bodily they were not—seen, not by sleepers alone, but by persons in a perfect state of vigilance; and that this phenomenon, though more frequently occurring at the moment that the individual seen is at the point of death, does occasionally occur at indefinite periods anterior to the catastrophe, and sometimes where no such catastrophe is impending. In some of these cases, an earnest desire seems to be the cause of the phenomenon. It is not very long since a very estimable lady, who was dying in the Mediterranean, expressed herself perfectly ready to meet death, if she could but once more behold her children, who were in England. She soon afterward fell into a comatose state, and the persons surrounding her were doubtful whether she had not already breathed her last; at all events, they did not expect her to revive. She did so, however, and now cheerfully announced that, having seen her children, she was ready to depart. During the interval that she lay in this state, her family saw her in England, and were thus aware of her death before the intelligence reached them. As it is a subject, I understand, they are unwilling to speak of, I do not know precisely under what circumstances she was seen;—but this is an exactly analogous case to that already recorded of Maria Goffe, of Rochester, who, when dying away from home, expressed precisely the same feelings. She said she could not die happy till she had seen her children. By-and-by she fell into a state of coma, which left them uncertain whether she was dead or alive. Her eyes were open and fixed, her jaw fallen, and there was no perceptible respiration. When she revived, she told her mother, who attended her, that she had been home and seen her children; which the other said was impossible, since she had been lying there in bed the whole time. "Yes," replied the dying woman, "but I was there in my sleep." A widow woman, called Alexander, who had the care of these children, declared herself ready to take oath upon the sacrament, that, during this period, she had seen the form of Maria Goffe come out of the room where the oldest child slept, and approach the bed where she herself lay with the younger beside her. The figure had stood there nearly a quarter of an hour, as far as she she could judge; and she remarked that the eyes and the mouth moved, though she heard no sound. She declared herself to have been perfectly awake, and that, as it was the longest night in the year, it was quite light. She sat up in bed, and while she was looking on the figure the clock on the bridge struck two. She then adjured the form in the name of God, whereupon it moved. She immediately arose and followed it, but could not tell what had become of it. She then became alarmed, and throwing on her clothes, went out and walked on the quay, returning to the house ever and anon to look at the children. At five o'clock she knocked at a neighbor's door, but they would not let her in. At six she knocked again and was then admitted, and related to them what she had seen, which they, of course, endeavored to persuade her was a dream or an illusion. She declared herself, however, to have been perfectly awake, and said that if she had ever seen Maria Goffe in her life she had seen her that night.

The following story has been currently related in Rome, and is already in print. I take it from a German work, and I do not know how far its authenticity can be established. It is to the effect that two friends having agreed to attend confession together, one of them went at the appointed time to the Abbate B——, and made his confession; after which the priest commenced the usual admonition, in the midst of which he suddenly ceased speaking. After waiting a short time, the penitent stepped forward and perceived him lying in the confessional in a state of insensibility. Aid was summoned and means used to restore him, which were for some time ineffectual; at length, when he opened his eyes, he bade the penitent recite a prayer for his friend, who had just expired. This proved to be the case, on inquiry; and when the young man, who had naturally hastened to his friend's house, expressed a hope that he had not died without the last offices of the church, he was told in amazement, that the Abbate B—— had arrived just as he was in *extremis*, and had remained with him till he died.

These appearances seem to have taken place when the corporeal condition of the person seen elsewhere, permits us to conceive the possibility of the spirit's having withdrawn from the body; but the question then naturally arises, what is it that was seen; and I confess, that of all the difficulties that surround the subject, I have undertaken to treat of, this seems to me the greatest; for we can not suppose that a spirit can be visible to the human eye, and both in the above instances and several others I have to narrate, there is nothing that can lead us to the conclusion, that the persons who saw the wraith or double, were in any other than a normal state; the figure, in short, seems to have been perceived through their external organs of sense. Before I discuss this question, however, any further, I will relate some instances of a similar kind, only with this difference, that the wraith appearing as nearly as could be ascertained at the moment of death, it remains uncertain whether it was seen before or after the dissolution had taken place. As in both these cases above related and those that follow, the material body was visible in one place, while the wraith was visible in another, they appear to be strictly analogous; especially, as in both class of examples, the body itself was either dead or in a state that closely resembled death.

Instances of people being seen at a distance from the spot on which they are dying, are so numerous, that in this department I have positively an *embarras de richesse*, and find it difficult to make a selection; more especially as there is in each case little to relate, the whole phenomenon being comprised in the fact of the form being observed and the chief variations consisting in this, that the seer, or seers, frequently entertain no suspicion that what they have seen is any other than a form of flesh and blood; while on other occasions the assurance that the person is far away, or some peculiarity connected with the appearance itself, produces the immediate conviction that the shape is not corporeal.

Mrs. K——, the sister of Provost B——, of Aberdeen, was sitting one day with her husband, Dr. K——, in the parlor of the manse, when she suddedly said, "Oh! there's my brother come! he has just passed the window," and, followed by her husband, she hastened to the door to meet the visiter. He was however not there. "He is gone round to the back door," said she; and thither they went; but neither was he there, nor had the servants seen anything of him. Dr. K—— said she must be mistaken, but she laughed at the idea; her brother had passed the window and looked in; he must have gone somewhere, and would doubtless be back directly. But he came not; and the intelligence shortly arrived from St. Andrew's, that at that precise time, as nearly as they could compare circumstances, he had died quite suddenly at his own place of residence. I have heard this story from connections of the family, and also from an eminent professor of Glasgow, who told me that he had once asked Dr. K——, whether he believed in these appearances. "I can not choose but believe," returned Dr. K——, and then he accounted for his conviction by narrating the above particulars.

Lord and Lady M—— were residing on their estate in Ireland: Lord M—— had gone out shooting in the morning, and was not expected to return till toward dinner-time. In the course of the afternoon, Lady M—— and a friend were walking on the terrace that forms a promenade in front of the castle, when she said, "Oh, there is M—— returning!" whereupon she called to him to join them. He, however, took no notice, but walked on before them, till they saw him enter the house, whither they followed him;—but he was not to be found: and before they had recovered their surprise at his sudden disappearance, he was brought home dead, having been killed by his own gun. It is a curious fact, in this case, that while the ladies were walking behind the figure on the terrace, Lady M—— called the attention of her companion to the shooting-jacket, observing that it was a convenient one, and that she had the credit of having contrived it for him herself.

A person in Edinburgh, busied about her daily work, saw a woman enter her house, with whom she was on such ill terms that she could not but be surprised at the visit; but while she was expecting an explanation, and under the influence of her resentment avoiding to look at her, she found she was gone. She remained quite unable to account for the visit, and, as she said, "was wondering what had brought her there," when she heard that the woman had expired at that precise time.

Madame O—— B—— was engaged to marry an officer who was with his regiment in India; and, wishing to live in privacy till the union took place, she retired to the country and boarded with some ladies of her acquaintance, awaiting his return. She at length heard that he had obtained an appointment, which, by improving his prospects, had removed some difficulties out of the way of the marriage, and that he was immediately coming home. A short time after the arrival of this intelligence, this lady, and one of those with whom she was residing, were walking over a bridge, when the friend said, alluding to an officer she saw on the other side of the way, "What an extraordinary expression of face!" But, without pausing to answer, Madame O—— B—— darted across the road to meet the stranger—but he was gone: where? they could not conceive. They ran to the toll-keepers at the ends of the bridge, to inquire if they had observed such a person, but they had not. Alarmed and perplexed—for it was her intended husband that she had seen—Madame O—— B—— returned home; and in due time the packet which should have brought himself, brought the sad tidings of his unexpected death.

Madame O—— B—— never recovered the shock, and died herself of a broken heart not long afterward.

Mr. H——, an eminent artist, was walking arm in arm with a friend in Edinburgh, when he suddenly left him, saying, "Oh, there's my brother!" He had seen him with the most entire distinctness; but was confounded by losing sight of him, without being able to ascertain whither he had vanished. News came, ere long, that at that precise period his brother had died.

Mrs. T——, sitting in her drawing-room, saw her nephew, then at Cambridge, pass across the adjoining room. She started up to meet him, and, not finding him, summoned the servants to ask where he was. They, however, had not seen him, and declared he could not be there; while she as positively declared he was. The young man had died at Cambridge quite unexpectedly.

A Scotch minister went to visit a friend who was dangerously ill. After sitting with the invalid for some time, he left him to take some rest, and went below. He had been reading in the library some little time, when, on looking up, he saw the sick man standing at the door. "God bless me!" he cried, starting up, "how can you be so imprudent?" The figure disappeared; and, hastening up stairs, he found his friend had expired.

Three young men at Cambridge had been out hunting, and afterward dined together in the apartments of one of them. After dinner, two of the party, fatigued with their morning's exercise, fell asleep, while the third, a Mr. M——, remained awake. Presently the door opened, and a gentleman entered and placed himself behind the sleeping owner of the rooms, and, after standing there a minute, proceeded to the gyp-room—a small inner chamber, from which there was no egress. Mr. M—— waited a little while, expecting the stranger would come out again; but, as he did not, he awoke his host, saying, "There's somebody gone into your room: I don't know who it can be."

The young man rose and looked into the gyp-room; but, there being nobody there, he naturally accused Mr. M—— of dreaming; but the other assured him he had not been asleep. He then described the stranger—an elderly man, &c., dressed like a country squire, with gaiters on, &c. "Why that's my father," said the host, and he immediately made inquiry, thinking it possible the old gentleman had slipped out unobserved by Mr. M——. He was not, however, to be heard of; and the post shortly brought a letter announcing that he had died at the time he had been seen in his son's chamber at Cambridge.

Mr. C—— F—— and some young ladies, not long ago, were standing together looking in at a shop window at Brighton,—when he suddenly darted across the way, and they saw him hurrying along the street, apparently in pursuit of somebody. After waiting a little while, as he did not return, they went home without him; and, when he was come, they of course arraigned him for his want of gallantry.

"I beg your pardon," said he; "but I saw an acquaintance of mine that owes me money, and I wanted to get hold of him."

"And did you?" inquired the ladies.

"No," returned he; "I kept sight of him some time; but I suddenly missed him—I can't think how."

No more was thought of the matter; but, by the next morning's post, Mr. C—— F—— received a letter enclosing a draft, from the father of the young man he had seen, saying that his son had just expired, and that one of his last requests had been that he would pay Mr. C—— F—— the money that he owed him.

Two young ladies, staying at the Queen's Ferry, arose one morning early to bathe; as they descended the stairs, they each exclaimed: "There's my uncle!" They had seen him standing by the clock. He died at that time.

Very lately, a gentleman living in Edinburgh, while sitting with his wife, suddenly arose from his seat and advanced toward the door with his hand extended, as if about to welcome a visiter. On his wife's inquiring what he was about, he answered that he had seen so-and-so enter the room. She had seen nobody. A day or two afterward, the post brought a letter announcing the death of the person seen.

A regiment, not very long since, stationed at New Orleans, had a temporary mess-room erected, at one end of which was a door for the officers, and at the other, a door and a space railed off for the messman. One day, two of the officers were playing at chess, or draughts, one sitting with his face toward the centre of the room, the other with his back to it. "Bless me! why, surely that is your brother!" exclaimed the former to the latter, who looked eagerly round, his brother being then, as he believed, in England. By this time the figure, having passed the spot where the officers were sitting, presented only his back to them. "No," replied the second, "that is not my brother's regiment; that's the uniform of the rifle-brigade. By heavens! it *is* my brother, though," he added, starting up and eagerly pursuing the stranger, who at that moment turned his head and looked at him, and then, somehow, strangely disappeared among the people standing at the messman's end of the room. Supposing he had gone out that way, the brother pursued him, but he was not to be found; neither had the messman, nor anybody there, observed him. The young man died at that time in England, having just exchanged into the rifle-brigade.

I could fill pages with similar instances, not to mention those recorded in other collections and in history. The case of Lord Balcarres is perhaps worth alluding to, from its being so perfectly well established. Nobody has ever disputed the truth of it, only they get out of the difficulty by saying that it was a spectral illusion! Lord Balcarres was in confinement in the castle of Edinburgh, under suspicion of Jacobitism, when one morning, while lying in bed, the curtains were drawn aside by his friend, Viscount Dundee, who looked upon him steadfastly, leaned for some time on the mantel-piece, and then walked out of the room. Lord Balcarres, not supposing that what he saw was a spectre, called to Dundee to come back and speak to him, but he was gone; and shortly afterward the news came that he had fallen about that same hour at Killicranky.

Finally, I have met with three instances of persons who are so much the subjects of this phenomenon, that they see the wraiths of most people that die belonging to them, and frequently of those who are merely acquaintance. They see the person as if he were alive, and unless they know him positively to be elsewhere, they have no suspicion but that it is himself, in the flesh, that is before them, till the sudden disappearance of the figure brings the conviction. Sometimes, as in the case of Mr. C—— F——, above alluded to, no suspicion arises till the news of the death arrives; and they mention, without reserve, that they have met so and so, but he did not stop to speak, and so forth.

On other occasions, however, the circumstances of the appearance are such that the seer is instantly aware of its nature. In the first place, the time and locality may produce the conviction.

Mrs. J—— wakes her husband in the night, and tells him she has just seen her father pass through the room—she being in the West Indies and her father in England. He died that night. Lord T—— being at sea, on his way to Calcutta, saw his wife enter his cabin.

Mrs. Mac——, of Skye, went from Lynedale, where she resided, to pay a visit in Perthshire. During her absence there was a ball given at Lynedale, and when it was over, three young ladies, two of them her daughters, assembled in their bedroom to talk over the evening's amusement. Suddenly, one of them cried, "O God! my mother." They all saw her pass across the room toward a chest of drawers, where she vanished. They immediately told their friends what they had seen, and afterward learned that the lady died that night.

Lord M—— being from home, saw Lady M——, whom he had left two days before, perfectly well, standing at the foot of his bed; aware of the nature of the appearance, but wishing to satisfy himself that it was not a mere spectral illusion, he called his servant, who slept in the dressing-room, and said, "John, who 's that?" "It 's my lady!" replied the man. Lady M—— had been seized with inflammation, and died after a few hours' illness. This circumstance awakened so much interest at the time, that, as I am informed by one of the family, George the Third was not satisfied without hearing the particulars from Lord M—— and from the servant also.

But, besides time and locality, there are very frequently other circumstances accompanying the appearance, which not only show the form to be spectral, but also make known to the seer the nature of the death that has taken place.

A lady, with whose family I am acquainted, had a son abroad. One night she was lying in bed, with a door open which led into an adjoining room, where there was a fire. She had not been asleep, when she saw her son cross this adjoining room and approach the fire, over which he leaned, as if very cold. She saw that he was shivering and dripping wet. She immediately exclaimed, "That 's my G——!" The figure turned its face round, looked at her sadly, and disappeared. That same night the young man was drowned.

Mr. P——, the American manager, in one of his voyages to England, being in bed one night, between sleeping and waking, was disturbed by somebody coming into his cabin, dripping with water. He concluded that the person had fallen overboard, and asked him why he came there to disturb him, when there were plenty of other places for him to go to. The man muttered something indistinctly, and Mr. P—— then perceived that it was his own brother. This roused him completely, and feeling quite certain that somebody had been there, he got out of bed to feel if the carpet was wet on the spot where his brother stood. It was not, however; and when he questioned his shipmates, the following morning, they assured him that nobody had been overboard, nor had anybody been in his cabin. Upon this, he noted down the date and the particulars of the event, and, on his arrival at Liverpool, sent the paper sealed to a friend in London, desiring it might not be opened till he wrote again. The Indian post, in due time, brought the intelligence that on that night Mr. P——'s brother was drowned.

A similar case to this is that of Captain Kidd, which Lord Byron used to say he heard from the captain himself. He was one night awakened in his hammock, by feeling something heavy lying upon him. He opened his eyes, and saw, or thought he saw, by the indistinct light in the cabin, his brother, in uniform, lying across the bed. Concluding that this was only an illusion arising out of some foregone dream, he closed his eyes again to sleep; but again he felt the weight, and there was the form still lying across the bed. He now stretched out his hand, and felt the uniform, which was quite wet. Alarmed, he called out for somebody to come to him; and, as one of the officers entered, the figure disappeared. He afterward learned that his brother was drowned on that night in the Indian ocean.

Ben Jonson told Drummond, of Hawthornden, that, being at Sir Robert Cotton's house, in the country, with old Cambden, he saw, in a vision, his eldest son, then a child at London, appear to him with a mark of a bloody cross on his forehead; at which, amazed, he prayed to God; and, in the morning, mentioned the circumstance to Mr. Cambden, who persuaded him it was fancy. In the meantime, came letters announcing that the boy had died of the plague. The custom of indicating an infected house by a red cross is here suggested, the cross apparently symbolizing the manner of the death.

Mr. S—— C——, a gentleman of fortune, had a son in India. One fine, calm summer's morning, in the year 1780, he and his wife were sitting at breakfast, when she arose and went to the window; upon which, turning his eyes in the same direction, he started up and followed her, saying, "My dear, do you see that?"—"Surely," she replied, "it is our son. Let us go to him!" As she was very much agitated, however, he begged her to sit down and recover herself; and when they looked again, the figure was gone. The appearance was that of their son, precisely as they had last seen him. They took note of the hour, and afterward learned that he had died in India at that period.

A lady, with whose family I am acquainted, was sitting with her son, named Andrew, when she suddenly exclaimed that she had seen him pass the window, in a white mantle. As the window was high from the ground, and overhung a precipice, no one could have passed; else, she said, "Had there been a path, and he not beside her at the moment, she should have thought he had walked by on stilts." Three days afterward, Andrew was seized with a fever which he had caught from visiting some sick neighbors, and expired after a short illness.

In 1807, when several people were killed in consequence of a false alarm of fire, at Sadler's Wells, a woman named Price, in giving her evidence at the inquest, said that her little girl had gone into the kitchen about half-past ten o'clock, and was surprised to see her brother there, whom she supposed to be at the theatre. She spoke to him, whereupon he disappeared. The child immediately told her mother, who, alarmed, set off to the theatre, and found the boy dead.

In the year 1813, a young lady in Berlin, whose intended husband was with the army at Dusseldorf, heard some one knock at the door of her chamber, and her lover entered in a white *negligé*, stained with blood. Thinking that this vision proceeded from some disorder in herself, she arose and quitted the room, to call a servant; who not being at hand, she returned, and found the figure there still. She now became much alarmed, and having mentioned the circumstance to her father, inquiries were made of some prisoners that were marching through the town, and it was ascertained that the young man had been wounded, and carried to the house of Dr. Ehrlick, in Leipsic, with great hopes of recovery. It afterward proved, however, that he had died at that period, and that his last thoughts were with her. This lady earnestly wished and prayed for another such visit, but she never saw him again.

In the same year, a woman in Bavaria, who had a brother with the army in Russia, was one day at field-work, on the skirts of a forest, and everything quiet around her, when she repeatedly felt herself hit by small stones, though, on looking round, she could see nobody. At length, supposing it was some jest, she threw down her implements, and stepped into the wood whence they had proceeded, when she saw a headless figure, in a soldier's mantle, leaning against a tree. Afraid to approach, she summoned some laborers from a neighboring field, who also saw it; but on going up to it, it disappeared. The woman declared her conviction that the circumstance indicated her brother's death; and it was afterward ascertained that he had, on that day, fallen in a trench.

Some few years ago, a Mrs. H——, residing in Limerick, had a servant whom she much esteemed, called Nelly Hanlon. Nelly was a very steady person, who seldom asked for a holyday, and consequently Mrs. H—— was the less disposed to refuse her when she requested a day's leave of absence for the purpose of attending a fair that was to take place a few miles off. The petition was therefore favorably heard; but when Mr. H—— came home and was informed of Nelly's proposed excursion, he said she could not be spared, as he had invited some people to dinner for that day, and he had nobody he could trust with the keys of the cellar except Nelly, adding that it was not likely his business would allow him to get home time enough to bring up the wine himself.

Unwilling, however, after giving her consent, to disappoint the girl, Mrs. H—— said that she would herself undertake the cellar department on the day in question; so when the wished-for morning arrived, Nelly departed in great spirits, having faithfully promised to return that night, if possible, or, at the latest, the following morning.

The day passed as usual, and nothing was thought about Nelly, till the time arrived for fetching up the wine, when Mrs. H—— proceeded to the cellar-stairs with the key, followed by a servant carrying a bottle-basket. She had, however, scarcely begun to descend, when she uttered a loud scream and dropped down in a state of insensibility. She was carried up stairs and laid upon the bed, while, to the amazement of the other servants, the girl who had accompanied her said that they had seen Nelly Hanlon, dripping with water, standing at the bottom of the stairs. Mr. H—— being sent for, or coming home at the moment, this story was repeated to him, whereupon he reproved the woman for her folly; and, proper restoratives being applied, Mrs. H—— at length began to revive. As she opened her eyes, she heaved a deep sigh, saying, "Oh, Nelly Hanlon!" and as soon as she was sufficiently recovered to speak, she corroborated what the girl had said: she had seen Nelly at the foot of the stairs, dripping as if she had just come out of the water. Mr. H—— used his utmost efforts to persuade his wife out of what he looked upon to be an illusion; but in vain. "Nelly," said he, "will come home by-and-by and laugh at you;" while she, on the contrary, felt sure that Nelly was dead.

The night came, and the morning came, but there was no Nelly. When two or three days had passed, inquiries were made; and it was ascertained that she had been seen at the fair, and started to return home in the evening; but from that moment all traces of her were lost till her body was ultimately found in the river. How she came by her death was never known.

Now, in most of these cases which I have above detailed, the person was seen where his dying thoughts might naturally be supposed to have flown, and the visit seems to have been made either immediately before or immediately after the dissolution of the body: in either case, we may imagine that the final parting of the spirit had taken place, even if the organic life was not quite extinct.

I have met with some cases in which we are not left in any doubt with respect to the last wishes of the dying person. For example: a lady, with whom I am acquainted, was on her way to India; when near the end of her voyage, she was one night awakened by a rustling in her cabin, and a consciousness that there was something hovering about her. She sat up, and saw a bluish, cloudy form moving away; but persuading herself it must be fancy, she addressed herself again to sleep; but as soon as she lay down, she both heard and felt the same thing: it seemed to her as if this cloudy form hung over and enveloped her. Overcome with horror, she screamed. The cloud then moved away, assuming distinctly a human shape. The people about her naturally persuaded her that she had been dreaming; and she wished to think so; but when she arrived in India, the first thing she heard was, that a very particular friend had come down to Calcutta to be ready to receive her on her landing, but that he had been taken ill and died, saying he only wished to live to see his old friend once more. He had expired on the night she saw the shadowy form in her room.

A very frightful instance of this kind of phenomenon is related by Dr. H. Werner, of Baron Emilius von O——. This young man had been sent to prosecute his studies in Paris; but, forming some bad connections, he became dissipated, and neglected them. His father's counsels were unheeded, and his letters remained unanswered. One day the young baron was sitting alone on a seat, in the Bois de Boulogne, and had fallen somewhat into a revery, when, on raising his eyes, he saw his father's form before him. Believing it to be a mere spectral illusion, he struck at the shadow with his riding-whip, upon which it disappeared. The next day brought him a letter, urging his return home instantly, if he wished to see his parent alive. He went, but found the old man already in his grave. The person who had been about him said that he had been quite conscious, and had a great longing to see his son; he had, indeed, exhibited one symptom of delirium, which was, that after expressing this desire, he had suddenly exclaimed, "My God! he is striking at me with his riding-whip!" and immediately expired.

In this case, the condition of the dying man resembles that of a somnambulist, in which the patient describes what he sees taking place at a distance; and the archives of magnetism furnish some instances, especially that of Auguste Müller, of Carlsruhe, in which, by the force of will, the sleeper has not only been able to bring intelligence from a distance, but also, like the American magician, to make himself visible. The faculties of prophecy and clear or far seeing, frequently disclosed by dying persons, is fully acknowledged by Dr. Abercrombie and other physiologists.

Mr. F—— saw a female relative, one night, by his bedside. Thinking it was a trick of some one to frighten him, he strnck at the figure; whereon she said: "What have I done? I know I should have told it you before." This lady was dying at a distance, earnestly desiring to speak to Mr. F—— before she departed.

I will conclude this chapter with the following extract from "Lockhart's Life of Scott:"—

"WALTER SCOTT *to* DANIEL TERRY, *April* 30, 1818. *(The new house at Abbotsford being then in progress,* SCOTT *living in an older part, close adjoining.)*

"'..... The exposed state of my house has led to a mysterious disturbance. The night before last we were awakened by a violent noise, like drawing heavy boards along the new part of the house. I fancied something had fallen, and thought no more about it. This was about *two* in the morning. Last night, at the same witching hour, the very same noise occurred. Mrs. Scott, as you know, is rather timbersome; so up I got, with Beardie's broadsword under my arm—

"Bolt upright,
And ready to fight."

But nothing was out of order, neither can I discover what occasioned the disturbance.'"

Mr. Lockhart adds: "On the morning that Mr. Terry received the foregoing letter, in London, Mr. William Erskine was breakfasting with him, and the chief subject of their conversation was the sudden death of George Bullock, which had occurred on the same night, and, as nearly as they could ascertain, at the very hour when Scott was roused from his sleep by the 'mysterious disturbance' here described. This coincidence, when Scott received Erskine's minute detail of what had happened in Tenterdon street (that is, the death of Bullock, who had the charge of furnishing the new rooms at Abbotsford), made a much stronger impression on his mind than might be gathered from the tone of an ensuing communication."

It appears that Bullock had been at Abbotsford, and made himself a great favorite with old and young. Scott, a week or two afterward, wrote thus to Terry: "Were you not struck with the fantastical coincidence of our nocturnal disturbances at Abbotsford, with the melancholy event that followed? I protest to you, the noise resembled half a dozen men hard at work, putting up boards and furniture; and nothing can be more certain than that there was nobody on the premises at the time. With a few additional touches, the story would figure in Glanville or Aubrey's collection. In the meantime, you may set it down with poor Dubisson's warnings, as a remarkable coincidence coming under your own observation."

CHAPTER VIII.

DÖPPELGANGERS, OR DOUBLES.

In the instances detailed in the last chapter, the apparition has shown itself, as nearly as could be discovered, at the moment of dissolution; but there are many cases in which the wraith is seen at an indefinite period before or after the catastrophe. Of these I could quote a great number; but as they generally resolve themselves into simply seeing a person where they were not, and death ensuing very shortly afterward, a few will suffice.

There is a very remarkable story of this kind, related by Macnish, which he calls "a case of hallucination, arising without the individual being conscious of any physical cause by which it might be occasioned." If this case stood alone, strange as it is, I should think so too: but when similar instances abound, as they do, I can not bring myself to dispose of it so easily. The story is as follows: Mr. H—— was one day walking along the street, apparently in perfect health, when he saw, or supposed he saw, his acquaintance, Mr. C——, walking before him. He called to him aloud; but he did not seem to hear him, and continued moving on. Mr. H—— then quickened his pace for the purpose of overtaking him; but the other increased his, also, as if to keep ahead of his pursuer, and proceeded at such a rate that Mr. H—— found it impossible to make up to him. This continued for some time, till, on Mr.

C——'s reaching a gate, he opened it and passed in, slamming it violently in Mr. H——'s face. Confounded at such treatment from a friend, the latter instantly opened the gate, and looked down the long lane into which it led, where, to his astonishment, no one was to be seen. Determined to unravel the mystery, he then went to Mr. C——'s house, and his surprise was great to hear that he was confined to his bed, and had been so for several days. A week or two afterward, these gentlemen met at the house of a common friend, when Mr. H—— related the circumstance, jocularly telling Mr. C—— that, as he had seen his wraith, he of course could not live long. The person addressed laughed heartily, as did the rest of the party; but, in a few days, Mr. C—— was attacked with putrid sore throat and died; and within a short period of his death, Mr. H—— was also in the grave.

This is a very striking case; the hastening on, and the actually opening and shutting the gate, evincing not only *will* but *power* to produce mechanical effects, at a time the person was bodily elsewhere. It is true he was ill, and it is highly probable was at the time asleep. The showing himself to Mr. H——, who was so soon to follow him to the grave, is another peculiarity which appears frequently to attend these cases, and which seems like what was in old English, and is still in Scotch, called a *tryst*—an appointment to meet again between those spirits, so soon to be free. Supposing Mr. C—— to have been asleep, he was possibly, in that state, aware of what impended over both.

There is a still more remarkable case given by Mr. Barham in his reminiscences. I have no other authority for it: but he relates, as a fact, that a respectable young woman was awaked, one night, by hearing somebody in her room, and that on looking up she saw a young man to whom she was engaged. Extremely offended by such an intrusion, she bade him instantly depart, if he wished her ever to speak to him again. Whereupon he bade her not be frightened, but said he was come to tell her that he was to die that day six weeks,—and then disappeared. Having ascertained that the young man himself could not possibly have been in her room, she was naturally much alarmed, and, her evident depression leading to some inquiries, she communicated what had occurred to the family with whom she lived—I think as dairy-maid; but I quote from memory. They attached little importance to what seemed so improbable, more especially as the young man continued in perfectly good health, and entirely ignorant of this prediction, which his mistress had the prudence to conceal from him. When the fatal day arrived, these ladies saw the girl looking very cheerful, as they were going for their morning's ride, and observed to each other that the prophecy did not seem likely to be fulfilled; but when they returned, they saw her running up the avenue toward the house in great agitation, and learned that her lover was either dead or dying, from an accident.

The only key I can suggest as the explanation of such a phenomenon as this, is, that the young man in his sleep was aware of the fate that awaited him,—and that while the body lay in his bed, in a state approaching to trance or catalepsy, the freed spirit—free as the spirits of the actual dead—went forth to tell the tale to the mistress of his soul.

Franz von Baader says, in a letter to Dr. Kerner, that Eckartshausen, shortly before his death, assured him that he possessed the power of making a person's double or wraith appear, while his body lay elsewhere in a state of trance or catalepsy. He added that the experiment might be dangerous, if care were not taken to prevent intercepting the rapport of the ethereal form with the material one.

A lady, an entire disbeliever in these spiritual phenomena, was one day walking in her own garden with her husband, who was indisposed, leaning on her arm, when seeing a man with his back toward them, and a spade in his hand, digging, she exclaimed, "Look there! who's that?" "Where?" said her companion; and at that moment the figure leaning on the spade turned round and looked at her, sadly shaking its head, and she saw it was her husband. She avoided an explanation, by pretending she had made a mistake. Three days afterward the gentleman died,—leaving her entirely converted to a belief she had previously scoffed at.

Here, again, the foreknowledge and evident design, as well as the power of manifesting it, are extremely curious—more especially as the antitype of the figure was neither in a trance nor asleep, but perfectly conscious, walking and talking. If any particular purpose were to be gained by the information indicated, the solution might be less difficult. One object, it is true, may have been, and indeed was attained, namely, the change in the opinions of the wife; and it is impossible to say what influence such a conversion may have had on her after-life.

It must be admitted that these cases are very perplexing. We might, indeed, get rid of them by denying them; but the instances are too numerous, and the phenomenon has been too well known in all ages, to be set aside so easily. In the above examples, the apparition, or wraith, has been in some way connected with the death of the person whose visionary likeness is seen; and, in most of these instances, the earnest longing to behold those beloved seems to have been the means of effecting the object. The mystery of death is to us so awful and impenetrable, and we know so little of the mode in which the spiritual and the corporeal are united and kept together during the continuance of life, or what condition may ensue when this connection is about to be dissolved, that while we look with wonder upon such phenomena as those above alluded to, we yet find very few persons who are disposed to reject them as utterly apocryphal. They feel that in that department, already so mysterious, there may exist a greater mystery still; and the very terror with which the thoughts of present death inspires most minds, deters people from treating this class of facts with that scornful skepticism with which many approximate ones are denied and laughed at. Nevertheless, if we suppose the person to have been dead, though it be but an inappreciable instant of time before he appears, the appearance comes under the denomination of what is commonly called a ghost; for whether the spirit has been parted from the body one second or fifty years, ought to make no difference in our appreciation of the fact, nor is the difficulty less in one case than the other.

I mention this because I have met with, and do meet with,

people constantly, who admit this class of facts, while they declare they can not believe in ghosts; the instances, they say, of people being seen at a distance at the period of their death, are too numerous to permit of the fact being denied. In granting it, however, they seem to me to grant everything. If, as I have said above, the person be dead, the form seen is a ghost or spectre, whether he has been dead a second or a century; if he be alive, the difficulty is certainly not diminished; on the contrary, it appears to me to be considerably augmented; and it is to this perplexing class of facts that I shall next proceed, namely, those in which the person is not only alive, as in some of the cases above related, but where the phenomenon seems to occur without any reference to the death of the subject, present or prospective.

In either case, we are forced to conclude that the thing seen is the same; the questions are, what is it that we see, and how does it render itself visible? and, still more difficult to answer, appears the question, of how it can communicate intelligence, or exert a mechanical force. As, however, this investigation will be more in its place when I have reached that department of my subject commonly called ghosts, I will defer it for the present, and merely confine myself to that of doubles, or döppelgangers, as the Germans denominate the appearance of a person out of his body.

In treating of the case of Auguste Muller, a remarkable somnambule, who possessed the power of appearing elsewhere, while his body lay cold and stiff in his bed, Professor Keiser, who attended him, says, that the phenomenon, as regards the seer, must be looked upon as purely subjective—that is, that there was no outstanding form of Auguste Muller visible to the sensuous organs, but that the magnetic influence of the somnambule, by the force of his will, acted on the imagination of the seer, and called up the image which he believed he saw. But then, allowing this to be possible, as Dr. Werner says, how are we to account for those numerous cases in which there is no somnambule concerned in the matter, and no especial rapport, that we are aware of, established between the parties?

And yet these latter cases are much the most frequent; for, although I have met with numerous instances recorded by the German physiologists, of what is called far-working on the part of the somnambules, this power of appearing out of the body seems to be a very rare one. Many persons will be surprised at these allusions to a kind of magnetic phenomena, of which, in this country, so little is known or believed; but the physiologists and psychologists of Germany have been studying this subject for the last fifty years, and the volumes filled with their theoretical views and records of cases, are numerous beyond anything the English public has an idea of.

The only other theory I have met with, which pretends to explain the mode of this double appearance, is that of the spirit leaving the body, as we have supposed it to do in cases of dreams and catalepsy; in which instances the nerve-spirit, which seems to be the archæus or astral spirit of the ancient philosophers, has the power of projecting a visible body out of the imponderable matter of the atmosphere. According to this theory, this nerve-spirit, which seems to be an embodiment of—or rather, a body constructed out of the nervous fluid, or ether—in short, the spiritual body of St. Paul, is the bond of union between the body and the soul, or spirit; and has the plastic force of raising up an aerial form. Being the highest organic power, it can not by any other, physical or chemical, be destroyed; and when the body is cast off, it follows the soul; and as, during life, it is the means by which the soul acts upon the body, and is thus enabled to communicate with the external world, so when the spirit is disembodied, it is through this nerve-spirit that it can make itself visible, and even exercise mechanical powers.

It is certain, that not only somnambules, but sick persons, are occasionally sensible of a feeling that seems to lend some countenance to this latter theory.

The girl at Canton, for example, mentioned in a former chapter, as well as many somnambulic patients, declare, while their bodies are lying stiff and cold, that they see it, as if out of it; and, in some instances, they describe particulars of its appearance, which they could not see in the ordinary way. There are also numerous cases of sick persons seeing themselves double, where no tendency to delirium or spectral illusion has been observed. These are, in this country, always placed under the latter category; but I find various instances recorded by the German physiologists, where this appearance has been seen by others, and even by children, at the same that it was *felt* by the invalid. In one of these cases, I find the sick person saying, "I can not think how I am lying. It seems to me that I am divided and lying in two places at once." It is remarkable, that a friend of my own, during an illness in the autumn of 1845, expressed precisely the same feeling; we, however, saw nothing of this second *ego;* but it must be remembered, that the seeing of these things, as I have said in a former chapter, probably depends on a peculiar faculty or condition of the seer. The servant of Elisha was not blind, but yet he could not see what his master saw, till his eyes were opened—that is, till he was rendered capable of perceiving spiritual objects.

When Peter was released from prison by the angel—and it is not amiss here to remark, that even he "wist not that it was true which was done by the angel, but thought he saw a vision," that is, he did not believe his senses, but supposed himself the victim of a spectral illusion—but when he was released, and went and knocked at the door of the gate, where many of his friends were assembled, they, not conceiving it possible he could have escaped, said, when the girl who had opened the door insisted that he was there, "It is his angel." What did they mean by this? The expression is not *an* angel, but *his* angel. Now, it is not a little remarkable, that in the East, to this day, a double, or döppelganger, is called a man's angel, or messenger. As we can not suppose that this term was used otherwise than seriously by the disciples that were gathered together in Mark's house, for they were in trouble about Peter, and, when he arrived, were engaged in prayer, we are entitled to believe they alluded to some recognised phenomenon. They knew, either that the likeness of a man—his spiritual self—sometimes appeared where bodily he was not; and that this *imago* or *idolon* was capable of exerting a mechanical force, or else that other spirits sometimes assumed a mortal form, or they would not have supposed it to be Peter's angel that had *knocked* at the gate.

Dr. Ennemoser, who always leans to the physical rather than the psychical explanation of a phenomenon, says, that the faculty of self-seeing, which is analogous to seeing another person's double, is to be considered an illusion; but that this imago of another seen at a distance, at the moment of death, must be supposed to have an objective reality. But if we are capable of thus perceiving the imago of another person, I can not comprehend why we may not see our own; unless, indeed, the former was never perceived but when the body of the person seen was in a state of insensibility; but this does not always seem to be a necessary condition, as will appear by some examples I am about to detail. The faculty of perceiving the object, Dr. Ennemoser considers analogous to that of second sight, and thinks it may be evolved by local, as well as idiosyncratical conditions. The difficulty arising from the fact that some persons are in the habit of seeing the wraiths of their friends and relations, must be explained by his hypothesis. The spirit, as soon as liberated from the body, is adapted for communion with *all* spirits, embodied or otherwise; but all embodied spirits are not prepared for communion with it.

A Mr. R——, a gentleman who has attracted public attention by some scientific discoveries, had had a fit of illness at Rotterdam. He was in a state of convalescence, but was still so far taking care of himself as to spend part of the day in bed, when, as he was lying there one morning, the door opened, and there entered in tears, a lady with whom he was intimately acquainted, but whom he believed to be in England. She walked hastily to the side of his bed, wrung her hands, evincing by her gestures extreme anguish of mind, and before he could sufficiently recover his surprise to inquire the cause of her distress and sudden appearance, she was gone. She did not disappear, but walked out of the room again, and Mr. R—— immediately summoned the servants of the hotel, for the purpose of making inquiries about the English lady—when she came, what had happened to her, and where she had gone to, on quitting his room? The people declared there was no such person there; he insisted there was, but they at length convinced him that they, at least, knew nothing about her. When his physician visited him, he naturally expressed the great perplexity into which he had been thrown by this circumstance; and, as the doctor could find no symptoms about his patient that could warrant a suspicion of spectral illusion, they made a note of the date and hour of the occurrence, and Mr. R—— took the earliest opportunity of ascertaining if anything had happened to the lady in question. Nothing had happened to herself, but at that precise period her son had expired, and she was actually in the state of distress in which Mr. R—— beheld her. It would be extremely interesting to know whether her thoughts had been intensely directed to Mr. R—— at the moment; but that is a point which I have not been able to ascertain. At all events the impelling cause of the form projected, be the mode of it what it may, appears to have been violent emotion. The following circumstance, which is forwarded to me by the gentleman to whom it occurred, appears to have the same origin:—

"On the evening of the 12th of March, 1792," says Mr. H——, an artist, and a man of science, "I had been reading in the 'Philosophical Transactions,' and retired to my room somewhat fatigued, but not inclined to sleep. It was a bright moonlight night and I had extinguished my candle and was sitting on the side of the bed, deliberately taking off my clothes, when I was amazed to behold the visible appearance of my half-uncle, Mr. R. Robertson, standing before me; and, at the same instant, I heard the words, '*Twice will be sufficient!*' The face was so distinct that I actually saw the pock-pits. His dress seemed to be made of a strong twilled sort of sackcloth, and of the same dingy color. It was more like a woman's dress than a man's—resembling a petticoat, the neck-band close to the chin, and the garment covering the whole person, so that I saw neither hands nor feet. While the figure stood there, I twisted my fingers till they cracked, that I might be sure I was awake.

"On the following morning, I inquired if anybody had heard lately of Mr. R., and was well laughed at when I confessed the origin of my inquiry. I confess I thought he was dead; but when my grandfather heard the story, he said that the dress I described, resembled the strait-jacket Mr. R. had been put in formerly, under an attack of insanity. Subsequently, we learned that on the night, and at the very hour I had seen him, he had attempted suicide, and been actually put into a strait-jacket.

"He afterward recovered, and went to Egypt with Sir Ralph Abercrombie. Some people laugh at this story, and maintain that it was a delusion of the imagination; but surely this is blinking the question! Why should my imagination create such an image, while my mind was entirely engrossed with a mathematical problem?"

The words "*Twice will be sufficient.*" probably embodied the thought, uttered or not, of the maniac, under the influence of his emotion—two blows or two stabs would be sufficient for his purpose.

Dr. Kerner relates a case of a Dr. John B——, who was studying medicine in Paris, seeing his mother one night, shortly after he had got into bed, and before he had put out his light. She was dressed after a fashion in which he had never seen her; but she vanished,—and thus, aware of the nature of the appearance, he became much alarmed, and wrote home to inquire after her health. The answer he received was that she was extremely unwell, having been under the most intense anxiety on his account, from hearing that several medical students in Paris had been arrested as resurrectionists; and, knowing his passion for anatomical investigations, she had apprehended he might be among the number. The letter concluded with an earnest request that he would pay her a visit. He did so; and his surprise was so great on meeting her, to perceive that she was dressed exactly as he had seen her in his room at Paris, that he could not at first embrace her, and was obliged to explain the cause of his astonishment and repugnance.

An analogous case to these is that of Dr. Donne,—which is

already mentioned in so many publications, that I should not allude to it here but for the purpose of showing that these examples belong to a *class* of facts, and that it is not to be supposed that similarity argues identity, or that one and the same story is reproduced with new names and localities. I mention this because, when circumstances of this kind are related, I sometimes hear people say, "Oh, I have heard that story before, but it was said to have happened to Mr. So-and-so, or at such a place; the truth being, that these things happen in all places and to a great variety of people.

Dr. Donne was with the embassy in Paris, where he had been but a short time, when his friend Mr. Roberts, entering the *salon*, found him in a state of considerable agitation. As soon as he was sufficiently recovered to speak, he said that his wife had passed twice through the room with a dead child in her arms. An express was immediately despatched to England to inquire for the lady, and the intelligence returned was that, after much suffering, she had been delivered of a dead infant. The delivery had taken place at the time that her husband had seen her in Paris. Nobody has ever disputed Dr. Donne's assertion that he saw his wife: but, as usual, the case is crammed into the theory of spectral illusions. They say Dr. Donne was naturally very anxious about his wife's approaching confinement, of which he must have been aware, and that his excited imagination did all the rest. In the first place, I do not find it recorded that he was suffering any particular anxiety on the subject; and, even if he were, the coincidences in time and in the circumstance of the dead child remain unexplained. Neither are we led to believe that the doctor was unwell, or living the kind of life that is apt to breed thick-coming fancies. He was attached to the embassy in the gay city of Paris; he had just been taking luncheon with others of the *suite*, and had been left alone but a short time, when he was found in the state of amazement above described. If such extraordinary cases of spectral illusion as this, and many others I am recording, can suddenly arise in constitutions apparently healthy, it is certainly high time that the medical world reconsider the subject, and give us some more comprehensible theory of it; if they are not cases of spectral illusion, but are to be explained under that vague and abused term *imagination*, let us be told something more about imagination—a service which those who consider the word sufficient to account for these strange phenomena, must of course be qualified to perform. If, however, both these hypotheses—for they are but simple hypotheses, unsupported by any proof whatever, only, being delivered with an air of authority in a rationalistic age, they have been allowed to pass unquestioned—if, however, they are not found sufficient to satisfy a vast number of minds, which I know to be the case, I think the inquiry I am instituting can not be wholly useless or unacceptable, let it lead us where it may. The *truth* is all I seek; and I think there is a very important truth to be deduced from the further investigation of this subject in its various relations—in short, a truth of paramount importance to all others; one which contains evidence of a fact in which we are more deeply concerned than in any other, and which, if well established, brings demonstration to confirm intuition and tradition. I am very well aware of all the difficulties in the way—difficulties internal and external,—many inherent to the subject itself, and others extraneous but inseparable from it; and I am very far from supposing that my book is to settle the question even with a single mind. All I hope or expect is to show that the question is not disposed of yet, either by the rationalists or the physiologists, and that it is still an open one; and all I desire is to arouse inquiry and curiosity, and that thus some mind, better qualified than mine to follow out the investigation, may be incited to undertake it.

Dr. Kerner mentions the case of a lady named Dillenius, who was awakened one night by her son, a child six years of age; her sister-in-law, who slept in the same room, also awoke at the same time, and all three saw Madame Dillenius enter the room, attired in a black dress, which she had lately bought. The sister said, "I see you double! you are in bed, and yet you are walking about the room." They were both extremely alarmed, while the figure stood between the doors in a melancholy attitude with the head leaning on the hand. The child—who also saw it, but seems not to have been terrified—jumped out of bed, and running to the figure, put his hand through it as he attempted to push it, exclaiming, "Go away, you black woman." The form, however, remained as before; and the child, becoming alarmed, sprung into bed again. Madame Dillenius expected that the appearance foreboded her own death; but that did not ensue. A serious accident immediately afterward occurred to her husband, and she fancied there might be some connection between the two events.

This is one of those cases which, from their extremely perplexing nature, have induced some psychologists to seek an explanation in the hypothesis that other spirits may for some purpose, or under certain conditions, assume the form of a person with a view to giving an intimation or impression, which the gulf separating the material from the spiritual world renders it difficult to convey. As regards such instances as that of Madame Dillenius, however, we are at a loss to discover any motive—unless, indeed, it be sympathy—for such an exertion of power, supposing it to be possessed. But in the famous case of Catherine of Russia, who is said, while lying in bed, to have been seen by the ladies to enter the throne-room, and, being informed of the circumstance, went herself and saw the figure seated on the throne, and bade her guards fire on it, we may conceive it possible that her guardian-spirit, if such she had, might adopt this mode of warning her to prepare for a change, which, after such a life as hers, we are entitled to conclude she was not very fit to encounter.

There are numerous examples of similar phenomena to be met with. Professor Stilling relates that he heard from the son of a Madame M——, that his mother, having sent her maid up stairs on an errand, the woman came running down in a great fright, saying that her mistress was sitting above, in her arm-chair, looking precisely as she had left her below. The lady went up stairs, and saw herself as described by the woman, very shortly after which she died.

Dr. Werner relates that a jeweller at Ludwigsburg, named

Ratzel, when in perfect health, one evening, on turning the corner of a street, met his own form, face to face. The figure seemed as real and lifelike as himself; and he was so close as to look into its very eyes. He was seized with terror, and it vanished. He related the circumstance to several people, and endeavored to laugh, but, nevertheless, it was evident he was painfully impressed with it. Shortly afterward, as he was passing through a forest, he fell in with some wood-cutters, who asked him to lend a hand to the ropes with which they were pulling down an oak-tree. He did so, and was killed by its fall.

Becker, professor of mathematics at Rostock, having fallen into argument with some friends regarding a disputed point of theology, on going to his library to fetch a book which he wished to refer to, saw himself sitting at the table in the seat he usually occupied. He approached the figure, which appeared to be reading, and, looking over its shoulder, he observed that the book open before it was a bible, and that, with one of the fingers of the right hand, it pointed to the passage—"Make ready thy house, for thou must die!" He returned to the company, and related what he had seen, and, in spite of all their arguments to the contrary, remained fully persuaded that his death was at hand. He took leave of his friends, and expired on the following day, at six o'clock in the evening. He had already attained a considerable age.

Those who would not believe in the appearance, said he had died of the fright; but, whether he did so or not, the circumstance is sufficiently remarkable: and, if this were a real, outstanding apparition, it would go strongly to support the hypothesis alluded to above, while, if it were a spectral illusion, it is certainly an infinitely strange one.

As I am aware how difficult it is, except where the appearance is seen by more persons than one, to distinguish cases of actual self-seeing from those of spectral illusion, I do not linger longer in this department; but, returning to the analogous subject of *döppelgangers*, I will relate a few curious instances of this kind of phenomena:—

Stilling relates that a government-officer, of the name of Triplin, in Weimar, on going to his office to fetch a paper of importance, saw his own likeness sitting there, with the deed before him. Alarmed, he returned home, and desired his maid to go there and fetch the paper she would find on the table. The maid saw the same form, and imagined that her master had gone by another road, and got there before her. His mind seems to have preceded his body.

The landrichter, or sheriff, F——, in Frankfort, sent his secretary on an errand. Presently afterward, the secretary re-entered the room, and laid hold of a book. His master asked him what had brought him back, whereupon the figure vanished, and the book fell to the ground. It was a volume of Linnæus. In the evening, when the secretary returned, and was interrogated with regard to his expedition, he said that he had fallen into an eager dispute with an acquaintance, as he went along, about some botanical question, and had ardently wished he had had his Linnæus with him to refer to.

Dr. Werner relates that Professor Happach had an elderly maid-servant, who was in the habit of coming every morning to call him, and on entering the room, which he generally heard her do, she usually looked at a clock which stood under the mirror. One morning, she entered so softly, that, though he saw her, he did not hear her foot. She went, as was her custom, to the clock, and came to his bedside, but suddenly turned round and left the room. He called after her, but she not answering, he jumped out of bed and pursued her. He could not see her, however, till he reached her room, where he found her fast asleep in bed. Subsequently, the same thing occurred frequently with this woman.

An exactly parallel case was related to me, as occurring to himself, by a publisher in Edinburgh. His housekeeper was in the habit of calling him every morning. On one occasion, being perfectly awake, he saw her enter, walk to the window, and go out again without speaking. Being in the habit of fastening his door, he supposed he had omitted to do so; but presently afterward he heard her knocking to come in, and he found the door was still locked She assured him she had not been there before. He was in perfectly good health at the time this happened.

Only a few nights since, a lady, with whom I am intimately acquainted, was in bed, and had not been to sleep, when she saw one of her daughters, who slept in an upper room, and who had retired to rest some time before, standing at the foot of her bed. "H——," she said, "what is the matter? what are you come for?" The daughter did not answer, but moved away. The mother jumped out of bed, but not seeing her, got in again: but the figure was still there. Perfectly satisfied it was really her daughter, she spoke to her, asking if anything had happened; but again the figure moved silently away, and again the mother jumped out of bed, and actually went part of the way up stairs: and this occurred a third time! The daughter was during the whole of this time asleep in her bed, and the lady herself is quite in her usual state of health—not robust, but not by any means sickly, nor in the slightest degree hysterical or nervous; yet she is perfectly convinced that she saw the figure of her daughter on that occasion, though quite unable to account for the circumstance. Probably the daughter was dreaming of the mother.

Edward Stern, author of some German works, had a friend who was frequently seen *out of the body*, as the Germans term it; and the father of that person was so much the subject of this phenomenon, that he was frequently observed to enter his house while he was yet working in the fields! His wife used to say to him, "Why, papa, you came home before;" and he would answer, "I dare say, I was so anxious to get away earlier, but it was impossible!"

The cook in a convent of nuns, at Ebersdorf, was frequently seen picking herbs in the garden, when she was in the kitchen and much in need of them.

A Danish physician, whose name Dr. Werner does not mention, is said to have been frequently seen entering a patient's room, and on being spoken to, the figure would disappear, with a sigh. This used to occur when he had made an appointment which he was prevented keeping, and was rendered uneasy by the failure. The hearing of it, however, occasioned him such an unpleasant sensation, that he requested his patients never to tell him when it happened.

A president of the supreme court, in Ulm, named Pfizer, attests the truth of the following case: A gentleman, holding an official situation, had a son at Gottingen, who wrote home to his father, requesting him to send him, without delay, a certain book, which he required to aid him in preparing a dissertation he was engaged in. The father answered that he had sought but could not find the work in question. Shortly afterward, the latter had been taking a book from his shelves, when, on turning round, he beheld, to his amazement, his son just in the act of stretching up his hand toward one on a high shelf in another part of the room. "Hallo!" he exclaimed, supposing it to be the young man himself, but the figure disappeared; and, on examining the shelf, the father found there the book that was required, which he immediately forwarded to Gottingen; but before it could arrive there, he received a letter from his son, describing the exact spot where it was to be found.

A case of what is called spectral illusion is mentioned by Dr. Paterson, which appears to me to belong to the class of phenomena I am treating of. One Sunday evening, Miss N—— was left at home, the sole inmate of the house, not being permitted to accompany her family to church on account of her delicate state of health. Her father was an infirm old man, who seldom went from home, and she was not aware whether, on this occasion, he had gone out with the rest or not. By-and-by, there came on a severe storm of thunder, lightning, and rain, and Miss N—— is described as becoming very uneasy about her father. Under the influence of this feeling, Dr. Paterson says she went into the back room, where he usually sat, and there saw him in his arm-chair. Not doubting but it was himself, she advanced and laid her hand upon his shoulder, but her hand encountered vacancy; and, alarmed, she retired. As she quitted the room, however, she looked back, and there still sat the figure. Not being a believer in what is called the "supernatural," Miss N—— resolved to overcome her apprehensions, and return into the room, which she did, and saw the figure as before. For the space of fully half an hour she went in and out of the room in this manner, before it disappeared. She did not see it vanish, but the fifth time she returned, it was gone.

Dr. Paterson vouches for the truth of this story, and no doubt of its being a mere illusion occurs to him, though the lady had never before or since, as she assured him, been troubled with the malady. It seems to me much more likely that, when the storm came on, the thoughts of the old man would be intensely drawn homeward: he would naturally wish himself in his comfortable arm-chair, and, knowing his young daughter to be alone, he would inevitably feel some anxiety about her too. There was a mutual projection of their spirits toward each other; and the one that was most easily freed from its bonds, was seen where in the spirit it actually was; for, as I have said above, a spirit out of the flesh, to whom space is annihilated, must be where its thoughts and affections are, for its thoughts and affections are *itself.*

I observe that Sir David Brewster and others, who have written on this subject, and who represent all these phenomena as images projected on the retina from the brain, dwell much on the fact that they are seen alike, whether the eye be closed or open. There are, however, two answers to be made to this argument: first, that even if it were so, the proof would not be decisive, since it is generally with closed eyes that somnambulic persons see, whether natural somnambules or magnetic patients; and, secondly, I find in some instances, which appear to me to be genuine cases of an objective appearance, that where the experiment has been tried, the figure is not seen when the eyes are closed.

The author of a work entitled "An Inquiry into the Nature of Ghosts," who adopts the illusion theory, relates the following story, as one he can vouch for, though not permitted to give the names of the parties:—

"Miss ——, at the age of seven years, being in a field not far from her father's house, in the parish of Kirklinton, in Cumberland, saw what she thought was her father in the field, at a time that he was in bed, from which he had not been removed for a considerable period. There were in the field also, at the same moment, George Little, and John, his fellow-servant. One of these cried out, 'Go to your father, miss!' She turned round, and the figure had disappeared. On returning home, she said, 'Where is my father?' The mother answered, 'In bed, to be sure, child!'—out of which he had not been."

I quote this case, because the figure was seen by two persons. I could mention several similar instances, but when only seen by one, they are, of course, open to another explanation.

Goethe (whose family, by-the-way, were ghost-seers) relates that as he was once in an uneasy state of mind, riding along the footpath toward Drusenheim, he saw, "not with the eyes of his body, but with those of his spirit," himself on horseback coming toward him, in a dress that he then did not possess. It was gray, and trimmed with gold. The figure disappeared; but eight years afterward he found himself, quite accidentally, on that spot, on horseback, and in precisely that attire. This seems to have been a case of second-sight.

The story of Byron's being seen in London when he was lying in a fever at Patras, is well known; but may possibly have arisen from some extraordinary personal resemblance, though so firm was the conviction of its being his actual self, that a bet of a hundred guineas was offered on it.

Some time ago, the "Dublin University Magazine" related a case—I know not on what authority—as having occurred at Rome, to the effect that a gentleman had, one night on going home to his lodging, thrown his servant into great amazement, the man exclaiming, "Good Lord, sir, you came home before!" He declared that he had let his master into the house, attended him up stairs, and, I think, undressed him, and seen him get into bed. When they went to the room, they found no clothes; but the bed appeared to have been lain in, and there was a strange mark upon the ceiling, as if from the passage of an electrical fluid. The only thing the young man could remember, whereby to account for this extraordinary circumstance, was, that while abroad, and in company, he had been overcome with ennui, fallen into a deep revery, and had for a time forgotten that he was not at home.

When I read this story, though I have learned from experience to be very cautious how I pronounce that impossible which I know nothing about, I confess it somewhat exceeded my receptive capacity, but I have since heard of a similar instance, so well authenticated, that my incredulity is shaken.

Dr. Kerner relates that a canon of a catholic cathedral, of somewhat dissipated habits, on coming home one evening, saw a light in his bedroom. When the maid opened the door, she started back with surprise, while he inquired why she had left a candle burning up stairs; upon which she declared that he had come home just before, and gone to his room, and she had been wondering at his unusual silence. On ascending to his chamber, he saw himself sitting in the arm-chair. The figure rose, passed him, and went out at the room-door. He was extremely alarmed, expecting his death was at hand. He, however, lived many years afterward, but the influence on his moral character was very beneficial.

Not long since, a professor, I think of theology, at a college at Berlin, addressed his class, saying, that, instead of his usual lecture, he should relate to them a circumstance which, the preceding evening, had occurred to himself, believing the effects would be no less salutary.

He then told them that, as he was going home the last evening, he had seen his own imago, or double, on the other side of the street. He looked away, and tried to avoid it, but, finding it still accompanied him, he took a short cut home, in hopes of getting rid of it, wherein he succeeded, till he came opposite his own house, when he saw it at the door.

It rang, the maid opened, it entered, she handed it a candle, and, as the professor stood in amazement, on the other side of the street, he saw the light passing the windows, as it wound its way up to his own chamber. He then crossed over and rang; the servant was naturally dreadfully alarmed on seeing him, but, without waiting to explain, he ascended the stairs. Just as he reached his own chamber, he heard a loud crash, and, on opening the door, they found no one there, but the ceiling had fallen in, and his life was thus saved. The servant corroborated this statement to the students; and a minister, now attached to one of the Scotch churches, was present when the professor told his tale. Without admitting the doctrine of protecting spirits, it is difficult to account for these latter circumstances.

. A very interesting case of an apparent friendly intervention occurred to the celebrated Dr. A—— T——, of Edinburgh. He was sitting up late one night, reading in his study, when he heard a foot in the passage, and knowing the family were, or ought to be, all in bed, he rose and looked out to ascertain who it was, but, seeing nobody, he sat down again. Presently, the sound recurred, and he was sure there was somebody, though he could not see him. The foot, however, evidently ascended the stairs, and he followed it, till it led him to the nursery-door, which he opened, and found the furniture was on fire; and thus, but for this kind office of his good angel, his children would have been burned in their beds.

The most extraordinary history of this sort, however, with which I am acquainted, is the following, the facts of which are perfectly authentic: —

Some seventy or eighty years since, the apprentice, or assistant, of a respectable surgeon in Glasgow, was known to have had an illicit connection with a servant-girl, who somewhat suddenly disappeared. No suspicion, however, seems to have been entertained of foul play. It appears rather to have been supposed that she had retired for the purpose of being confined, and, consequently, no inquiries were made about her.

Glasgow was, at that period, a very different place to what it is at present, in more respects than one; and, among its peculiarities, was the extraordinary strictness with which the observance of the sabbath was enforced, insomuch, that nobody was permitted to show themselves in the streets or public walks during the hours dedicated to the church services; and there were actually inspectors appointed to see that this regulation was observed, and to take down the names of defaulters.

At one extremity of the city, there is some open ground, of rather considerable extent, on the north side of the river, called "The Green," where people sometimes resort for air and exercise; and where lovers not unfrequently retire to enjoy as much solitude as the proximity to so large a town can afford.

One Sunday morning, the inspectors of public piety above alluded to having traversed the city, and extended their perquisitions as far as the lower extremity of the Green, where it was bounded by a wall, observed a young man lying on the grass, whom they immediately recognised to be the surgeon's assistant. They, of course, inquired why he was not at church, and proceeded to register his name in their books, but, instead of attempting to make any excuse for his offence, he only rose from the ground, saying, "I am a miserable man; look in the water!" He then immediately crossed a stile, which divided the wall, and led to a path extending along the side of the river toward the Rutherglen road. They saw him cross the stile, but, not comprehending the significance of his words, instead of observing him further, they naturally directed their attention to the water, where they presently perceived the body of a woman. Having with some difficulty dragged it ashore, they immediately proceeded to carry it into the town, assisted by several other persons, who by this time had joined them. It was now about one o'clock, and, as they passed through the streets, they were obstructed by the congregation that was issuing from one of the principal places of worship; and, as they stood up for a moment, to let them pass, they saw the surgeon's assistant issue from the church door. As it was quite possible for him to have gone round some other way, and got there before them, they were not much surprised. He did not approach them, but mingled with the crowd, while they proceeded on their way.

On examination, the woman proved to be the missing servant-girl. She was pregnant, and had evidently been murdered with a surgeon's instrument, which was found entangled among her clothes. Upon this, in consequence of his known connection with her, and his implied self-accusation to the inspectors, the young man was apprehended on suspicion of being the guilty party, and tried upon the circuit. He was the last person seen in her company, immediately previous to her disappearance; and there was, altogether, such strong presumptive evidence against him, as corroborated by what occurred on the green would have justified a verdict of guilty. But, strange to say, this last most important item in the evidence failed, and he established an incontrovertible *alibi;* it being proved, beyond all possibility of doubt, that he had been in church from the beginning of the service to the end of it. He was, therefore, acquitted; while the public were left in the greatest perplexity, to account as they could for this extraordinary discrepancy. The young man was well known to the inspectors, and it was in broad daylight that they had met him and placed his name in their books. Neither, it must be remembered, were they seeking for him, nor thinking of him, nor of the woman, about whom there existed neither curiosity nor suspicion. Least of all, would they have sought her where she was, but for the hint given to them.

The interest excited, at the time, was very great; but no natural explanation of the mystery has ever been suggested.

CHAPTER IX.

APPARITIONS.

The number of stories on record, which seem to support the views I have suggested in my last chapter, is, I fancy, little suspected by people in general; and still less is it imagined that similar occurrences are yet frequently taking place. I had, indeed, myself no idea of either one circumstance or the other, till my attention being accidentally turned in this direction, I was led into inquiries, the result of which has extremely surprised me. I do not mean to imply that all my acquaintance are ghost-seers, or that these things happen every day; but the amount of what I do mean, is this: first, that besides the numerous instances of such phenomena alluded to in history, which have been treated as fables by those who profess to believe the rest of the narratives, though the whole rests upon the same foundation, that is, tradition and hearsay; besides these, there exists in one form or another, hundreds and hundreds of recorded cases, in all countries, and in all languages, exhibiting that degree of similarity which mark them as belonging to a class of facts, many of these being of a nature which seems to preclude the possibility of bringing them under the theory of spectral illusions; and, secondly, that I scarcely meet any one man or woman, who, if I can induce them to believe I will not publish their names, and am not going to laugh at them, is not prepared to tell me of some occurrence of the sort, as having happened to themselves, their family, or their friends. I admit that in many instances they terminate their narration, by saying, that they think it must have been an illusion, *because* they can not bring themselves to believe in ghosts; not unfrequently adding, that they *wish* to think so; since to think otherwise would make them uncomfortable. I confess, however, that this seems to me a very unwise, as well as a very unsafe way of treating the matter. Believing the appearance to be an illusion, *because* they can not bring themselves to believe in ghosts, simply amounts to saying, "I don't believe, because I don't believe;" and is an argument of no effect, except to invalidate their capacity for judging the question, at all; but the second reason for not believing, namely, that they do not wish to do so, has not only the same disadvantage, but is liable to much more serious objections; for it is our duty to ascertain the truth in an affair that concerns every soul of us so deeply; and to shrink from looking at it, lest it should disclose something we do not like, is an expedient as childish as it is desperate.

In reviewing my late novel of "Lilly Dawson," where I announce the present work, I observe that while some of the reviewers scout the very idea of anybody's believing in ghosts, others, less rash, while they admit that it is a subject we know nothing about, object to further investigation, on account of the terrors and uncomfortable feelings that will be engendered. Now, certainly, if it were a matter in which we had no personal concern, and which belonged merely to the region of speculative curiosity, everybody would be perfectly justified in following their inclinations with regard to it; there would be no reason for frightening themselves, if they did not like it; but, since it is perfectly certain that the fate of these poor ghosts, be what it may, will be ours some day—perhaps before another year or another week has passed over our heads—to shut our eyes to the truth, because it may perchance occasion us some uncomfortable feelings, is surely a strange mixture of contemptible cowardice and daring temerity. If it be true that, by some law of nature, departed souls occasionally revisit the earth, we may be quite certain that it was intended we should know it, and that the law is to some good end; for no law of God can be purposeless or mischievous; and is it conceivable that we should say we will not know it, because it is disagreeable to us? Is not this very like saying, "Let us eat, drink, and be merry, for to-morrow we die!" and yet refusing to inquire what is to become of us when we do die? refusing to avail ourselves of that demonstrative proof which God has mercifully placed within our reach? And, with all this obstinacy, people do not get rid of the apprehension; they go on struggling against it and keeping it down by argument and reason; but there are very few persons indeed, men or women, who, when placed in a situation calculated to suggest the idea, do not feel the intuitive conviction striving within them. In the ordinary circumstances of life, nobody suffers from this terror; in the extraordinary ones, I find the professed disbelievers not much better off than the believers. Not long ago, I heard a lady expressing the great alarm she should have felt, had she been exposed to spend a whole night on Ben Lomond, as Margaret Fuller, the American authoress, did lately; "for," said she, "though I don't believe in ghosts, I should have been dreadfully afraid of seeing one then!"

Moreover, though I do not suppose that man, in his normal state, could ever encounter an incorporeal spirit without considerable awe, I am inclined to think that the extreme terror the idea inspires arises from bad training. The ignorant frighten children with ghosts, and the better educated assure them there is no such thing. Our understanding may believe the latter, but our instincts believe the former; so that, out of this education, we retain the terror, and just belief enough to make it very troublesome whenever we are placed in circumstances that awaken it. Now, perhaps, if the thing were differently managed, the result might be different. Suppose the subject were duly investigated, and it were ascertained that the views which I and many others are disposed to entertain with regard to it are correct,—and suppose, then, children were calmly told that it is not impossible but that, on some occasion, they may see a departed friend again—that the laws of nature, established by an allwise Providence, admit of the dead sometimes revisiting the earth, doubtless for the benevolent purpose of keeping alive in us our faith in a future state—that death is merely a transition to another life, which it depends on ourselves to make happy or otherwise—and that while those spirits which appear bright and blessed may well be objects of our envy, the others should excite only our intense compassion: I am persuaded that a child so educated would feel no terror at the sight of an apparition, more especially as there very rarely appears to be anything terrific in the aspect of these forms; they generally come in their "habits as they lived," and appear so much like the living person in the flesh, that where they are not known to be already dead, they are frequently mistaken for them. There are exceptions to this rule,—but the forms in themselves rarely exhibit anything to create alarm.

As a proof that a child would not naturally be terrified at the sight of an apparition, I will adduce the following instance, the authenticity of which I can vouch for:—

A lady with her child embarked on board a vessel at Jamaica, for the purpose of visiting her friends in England, leaving her husband behind her quite well. It was a sailing packet; and they had been some time at sea, when one evening, while the child was kneeling before her saying his prayers previous to going to rest, he suddenly said: "Mamma, papa!" "Nonsense, my dear!" the mother answered, "you know your papa is not here!"—"He is indeed, mamma," returned the child, he is looking at us now." Nor could she convince him to the contrary. When she went on deck, she mentioned the circumstance to the captain, who thought it so strange, that he said he would note down the date of the occurrence. The lady begged him not to do so, saying it was attaching a significance to it which would make her miserable. He did it, however; and, shortly after her arrival in England, she learned that her husband had died exactly at that period.

I have met with other instances in which children have seen apparitions without exhibiting any alarm; and in the case of Fredericka Hauffe, the infant in her arms was frequently observed to point smilingly to those which she herself said she saw. In the above related case, we find a valuable example of an apparition which we can not believe to have been a mere subjective phenomenon, being seen by one person and not by another. The receptivity of the child may have been greater, or the rapport between it and its father stronger; but this occurrence inevitably leads us to suggest, how often our departed friends may be near us, and we not see them!

A Mr. B——, with whom I am acquainted, informed me that, some years ago, he lost two children. There was an interval of two years between their deaths; and about as long a period had elapsed since the decease of the second, when the circumstance I am about to relate took place. It may be conceived that at that distance of time, however vivid the impression had been at first, it had considerably faded from the mind of a man engaged in business; and he assures me that, on the night this event occurred, he was not thinking of the children at all; he was, moreover, perfectly well, and had neither eaten nor drank anything unusual, nor abstained from eating or drinking anything to which he was accustomed. He was therefore in his normal state; when shortly after he had lain down in bed, and before he had fallen asleep, he heard the voice of one of the children say: "Papa—papa!"

"Do you hear that?" he said to his wife, who lay beside him—"I hear Archy calling me, as plain as ever I heard him in my life!"

"Nonsense!" returned the lady; "you are fancying it."

But presently he again heard "Papa, papa!" and now both voices spoke. Upon which—exclaiming, "I can stand this no longer"—he started up, and, drawing back the curtains, saw both children in their night-dresses, standing near the bed. He immediately jumped out; whereupon they retreated slowly, and with their faces toward him, to the window, where they disappeared. He says that the circumstance made a great impression upon him at the time; and, indeed, that it was one that could never be effaced; but he did not know what to think of it, not believing in ghosts, and therefore concluded it must have been some extraordinary spectral illusion, especially as his wife heard nothing. It may have been so; but that circumstance by no means proves it.

From these varying degrees of susceptibility, or affinity, there seems to arise another consequence, namely, that more than one person may see the same object, and yet see it differently, and I mention this particularly, because it is one of the objections that unreflecting persons make to phenomena of this kind, second sight especially. In the remarkable instance which is recorded to have occurred at Ripley, in the year 1812, to which I shall allude more particularly in a future chapter, much stress was laid on the fact, that the first seer said, "Look at those beasts!" While the second answered, they were "not beasts, but men." In a former chapter, I mentioned the case of a lady, on board a ship, seeing and feeling a sort of blue cloud hanging over her, which afterward, as it retired, assumed a human form, though still appearing a vapory substance. Now, possibly, had her receptivity, or the rapport, been greater, she might have seen the distinct image of her dying friend. I have met with several instances of these cloudy figures being seen, as if the spirit had built itself up a form of atmospheric air; and it is remarkable, that when other persons perceived the apparitions that frequented the Seeress of Prevorst, some saw those as cloudy forms, which she saw distinctly attired in the costume they wore when alive; and thus, on some occasions, apparitions are represented as being transparent, while on others they have not been distinguishable from the real corporeal body. All these discrepancies, and others, to be hereafter alluded to, are doubtless only absurd to our ignorance; they are the results of physical laws, as absolute, though not so easily ascertained, as those by which the most ordinary phenomena around us are found explicable.

With respect to these cloudy forms, I have met with four instances lately, two occurring to ladies, and two to gentlemen; the one a minister, and the other a man engaged in business; and although I am quite aware that these cases are not easily to be distinguished from those of spectral illusion, yet I do not think them so myself; and as they occurred to persons in their normal state of health, who never before or since experienced anything of the kind, and who could find nothing in their own circumstances to account for its happening then, I shall mention them. In the instances of the gentlemen and one of the ladies, they were suddenly awakened, they could not tell by what, and perceived bending over them a cloudy form, which immediately retreated slowly to the other end of the room, and disappeared. In the fourth case, which occurred to an intimate friend of my own, she had not been asleep; but having been the last person up in the house, had just stepped into the bed, where her sister had already been some time asleep. She was perfectly awake, when her attention was attracted by hearing the clink of glass, and, on looking up, she saw a figure standing on the hearth, which was exactly opposite her side of the bed, and as there was water and a tumbler there, she concluded that her sister had stepped out at the bottom, unperceived by her, and was drinking. While she was carelessly observing the figure, it moved toward the bed, and laid a heavy hand upon her, pressing her arm in a manner that gave her pain. "Oh, Maria, don't!" she exclaimed; but as the form retreated, and she lost sight of it, a strange feeling crept over her, and she stretched out her hand to ascertain if her sister was beside her. She was, and asleep; but this movement awoke her, and she found the other now in considerable agitation. She, of course, tried to persuade her that it was a dream, or night-mare, as did the family the next day; but she was quite clear in her mind at the time, as she then assured me, that it was neither one nor the other; though now, at the distance of a year from the occurrence, she is very desirous of putting that construction upon it. As somebody will be ready to suggest that this was a freak played by one of the family, I can only answer that that is an explanation that no one who is acquainted with all the circumstances, could admit; added to which, the figure did not disappear in the direction of the door, but in quite an opposite one.

A very singular thing happened to the accomplished authoress of "Letters from the Baltic," on which my readers may put what interpretation they please, but I give it here as a pendant to the last story. The night before she left Petersburgh she passed in the house of a friend. The room appropriated to her use was a large dining-room, in which a temporary bed was placed, and a folding screen was so arranged as to give an air of comfort to the nook where the bed stood. She went to bed, and to sleep, and no one who knows her can suspect her of seeing spectral illusions, or being incapable of distinguishing her own condition when she saw anything whatever. As she was to commence her journey on the following day, she had given orders to be called at an early hour, and, accordingly, she found herself awakened toward morning by an old woman in a complete Russian costume, who looked at her, nodding and smiling, and intimating, as she supposed, that it was time to rise. Feeling, however, very sleepy, and very unwilling to do so, she took her watch from behind her pillow, and, looking at it, perceived that it was only four o'clock. As, from the costume of the old woman, she knew her to be a Russian, and therefore not likely to understand any language she could speak, she shook her head, and pointed to the watch, giving her to understand that it was too early. The woman looked at her, and nodded, and then retreated, while the traveller lay down again and soon fell asleep. By-and-by, she was awakened by a knock at the door and the voice of the maid whom she had desired to call her. She bade her come in, but, the door being locked on the inside, she had to get out of bed to admit her. It now occurred to her to wonder how the old woman had entered, but, taking it for granted that there was some other mode of ingress she did not trouble herself about it, but dressed, and descended to breakfast. Of course, the inquiry usually addressed to a stranger was made—they hoped she had slept well! "Perfectly," she said, "only that one of their good people had been somewhat over anxious to get her up in the morning;" and she then mentioned the old woman's visit, but to her surprise, they declared they had no such person in the family. "It must have been some old nurse, or laundress, or something of that sort," she suggested. "Impossible!" they answered; "you must have dreamed the whole thing; we have no old woman in the house; nobody wearing that costume; and nobody could have got in, since the door must have been fastened long after that!" And these assertions the servants fully confirmed; added to which, I should observe, that the house, like foreign houses in general, consisted of a flat, or floor, shut in by a door, which separated it entirely from the rest of the building, and, being high up from the street, nobody could even have gained access by a window. The lady now beginning to get somewhat puzzled, inquired if there were any second entrance into the room; but, to her surprise, she heard there was not; and she then mentioned that she had locked the door on going to bed, and had found it locked in the morning. The thing has ever remained utterly inexplicable, and the family, who were much more amazed by it than she was, would willingly believe it to have been a dream; but, whatever the interpretation of it may be, she feels quite certain that that is not the true one.

I make no comments on the above case, though a very inexplicable one; and I scarcely know whether to mention any of those well-established tales, which appear to be certainly as satisfactorily attested as any circumstance which is usually taken simply on report. I allude particularly to the stories of General Wynyard; Lord Tyrone and Lady Beresford; the case which took place at Havant, in Hampshire, and which is related in a letter from Mr. Caswell the mathematician to Dr. Bentley; that which occurred in Cornwall, as narrated by the Rev. Mr. Ruddle, one of the prebendaries of Exeter, whose assistance and advice were asked, and who himself had two interviews with the spirit; and many others, which are already published in different works; especially in a little book entitled "Accredited Ghost-Stories." I may, however, mention that, with respect to those of Lady Beresford and General Wynyard, the families of the parties have always maintained their entire belief in the circumstances; as do the family of Lady Betty Cobb, who took the riband from Lady Beresford's arm, after she was dead—she having always worn it since her interview with the apparition, in order to conceal the mark he had left by touching her.

There have been many attempts to explain away the story of Lord Littleton's warning, although the evidence for it certainly satisfied the family, as we learn from Dr. Johnson, who said, in regard to it, that it was the most extraordinary thing that had happened in his day, and that he heard it from the lips of Lord Westcote, the uncle of Lord Littleton.

There is a sequel, however, to this story, which is extremely well authenticated, though much less generally known. It appears that Mr. Miles Peter Andrews, the intimate friend of Lord Littleton, was at his house, at Dartford, when Lord L. died at Pitt-place, Epsom, thirty miles off. Mr. Andrews' house was full of company, and he expected Lord Littleton, whom he had left in his usual state of health, to join him the next day, which was Sunday.

Mr. Andrews himself feeling rather indisposed on the Saturday evening, retired early to bed, and requested Mrs. Pigou, one of his guests, to do the honors of his supper-table. He admitted (for he is himself the authority for the story) that he fell into a feverish sleep on going to bed, but was awakened between eleven and twelve by somebody opening his curtains, which proved to be Lord Littleton, in a night-gown and cap, which Mr. Andrews recognised. Lord Littleton spoke, saying that he was come to tell him *all was over*. It appears that Lord Littleton was fond of practical joking, and as Mr. Andrews entertained no doubt whatever of his visiter being Lord Littleton himself, in the body, he supposed that this was one of his tricks; and, stretching his arm out of bed, he took hold of his slippers, the nearest thing he could get at, and threw them at him, whereupon the figure retreated to a dressing-room, which had no ingress or egress except through the bed-chamber. Upon this, Mr. Andrews jumped out of bed to follow him, intending to chastise him further, but he could find nobody in either of the rooms, although the door was locked on the inside; so he rang his bell, and inquired who had seen Lord Littleton. Nobody had seen him; but, though how he had got in or out of the room remained an enigma, Mr. Andrews asserted that he was certainly there; and, angry at the supposed trick, he ordered that they should give him no bed, but let him go and sleep at the inn. Lord Littleton, however, appeared no more, and Mr. Andrews went to sleep, not entertaining the slightest suspicion that he had seen an apparition.

It happened that, on the following morning, Mrs. Pigou had occasion to go at an early hour to London, and great was her astonishment to learn that Lord Littleton had died on the preceding night. She immediately despatched an express to Dartford with the news, upon the receipt of which, Mr. Andrews, then quite well, and remembering perfectly all that had happened, swooned away. He could not understand it, but it had a most serious effect upon him, and, to use his own expression, he was not his own man again for three years.

There are various authorities for this story, the correctness of which is vouched for by some members of Mrs. Pigou's family, with whom I am acquainted, who have frequently heard the circumstances detailed by herself, and who assure me it was always believed by the family. I really, therefore, do not see what grounds we have for doubting either of these facts. Lord Westcote, on whose word Dr. Johnson founded his belief of Lord Littleton's warning, was a man of strong sense; and that the story was not looked upon lightly by the family, is proved by the fact that the dowager Lady Littleton had a picture—which was seen by Sir Nathaniel Wraxhall in her house in Portugal street, as mentioned in his memoirs—wherein the event was commemorated. His lordship is in bed; the dove appears at the window; and a female figure stands at the foot of the couch, announcing to the unhappy profligate his approaching dissolution. That he mentioned the warning to his valet, and some other persons, and that he talked of *jockeying* the ghost by surviving the time named, is certain; as also that he died with his watch in his hand, precisely at the appointed period! Mr. Andrews says that he was subject to fits of strangulation, from a swelling in the throat, which might have killed him at any moment; but his decease having proceeded from a natural and obvious cause, does not interfere one way or the other with the validity of the prediction, which simply foretold his death at a particular period, not that there was to be anything preternatural in the manner of it.

As I find so many people willing to believe in wraiths, who can not believe in ghosts—that is, they are overpowered by the numerous examples, and the weight of evidence for the first—it would be desirable if we could ascertain whether these wraiths are seen before the death occurs or after it; but, though the day is recorded, and seems always to be the one on which the death took place, and the hour about the same, minutes are not sufficiently observed to enable us to answer that question. It would be an interesting one, because the argument advanced by those who believe that the dead never are seen, is, that it is the strong will and desire of the expiring person which enables him so to act on the nervous system of his distant friend, that the imagination of the latter projects the form, and sees it as if objectively. By *imagination* I do not simply mean to convey the common notion implied by that much-abused word, which is only *fancy*, but the *constructive* imagination, which is a much higher function, and which, inasmuch as man is made in the likeness of God, bears a distant relation to that sublime power by which the Creator projects, creates, and upholds, his universe; while the far-working of the departing spirit seems to consist in the strong will to do, reinforced by the strong faith that it can be done. We have rarely the strong will, and still more rarely the strong faith, without which the will remains ineffective. In the following case, which is perfectly authentic, the apparition of Major R—— was seen several hours after his death had occurred.

In the year 1785, some cadets were ordered to proceed from Madras to join their regiments up the country. A considerable part of the journey was to be made in a barge, and they were under the conduct of a senior officer, Major R——. In order to relieve the monotony of the voyage, this gentleman proposed, one day, that they should make a shooting excursion inland, and walk round to meet the boat at a point agreed on, which, owing to the windings of the river, it would not reach till evening. They accordingly took their guns, and as they had to cross a swamp, Major R——, who was well acquainted with the country, put on a heavy pair of top-boots, which, together with an odd limp he had in his gait, rendered him distinguishable from the rest of the party at a considerable distance. When they reached the jungle, they found there was a wide ditch to leap, which all succeeded in doing except the major, who being less young active, jumped short of the requisite distance; and although he scrambled up unhurt, he found his gun so crammed full of wet sand that it would be useless till thoroughly cleansed. He therefore bade them walk on, saying he would follow; and taking off his hat, he sat down in the shade, where they left him. When they had been beating about for game some time, they began to wonder why the major did not come on, and they shouted to let him know whereabouts they were; but there was no answer, and hour after hour passed without his appearance, till at length they began to feel somewhat uneasy.

Thus the day wore away, and they found themselves approaching the rendezvous. The boat was in sight, and they were walking down to it, wondering how their friend could have missed them, when suddenly, to their great joy, they saw him before them, making toward the barge. He was without his hat or gun, limping hastily along in his top-boots, and did not appear to observe them. They shouted after him, but as he did not look round, they began to run, in order to overtake him; and, indeed, fast as he went, they did gain considerably upon him. Still he reached the boat first, crossing the plank which the boatmen had placed ready for the gentlemen they saw approaching. He ran down the companion-stairs, and they after him; but inexpressible was their surprise when they could not find him below! They ascended again, and inquired of the boatmen what had become of him; but they declared he had not come on board, and that nobody had crossed the plank till the young men themselves had done so.

Confounded and amazed at what appeared so inexplicable, and doubly anxious about their friend, they immediately resolved to retrace their steps in search of him; and, accompanied by some Indians who knew the jungle, they made their way back to the spot where they had left him. Thence somo footmarks enabled them to trace him, till, at a very short distance from the ditch, they found his hat and his gun. Just then the Indians called out to them to beware, for that there was a sunken well thereabouts, into which they might fall. An apprehension naturally seized them that this might have been the fate of their friend; and on examining the edge, they saw a mark as of a heel slipping up. Upon this, one of the Indians consented to go down, having a rope with which they had provided themselves tied round his waist; for, aware of the existence of the wells, the natives suspected what had actually occurred, namely, that the unfortunate gentleman had slipped into one of these traps, which, being overgrown with brambles, were not discernible by the eye. With the assistance of the Indian, the body was brought up and carried back to the boat, amid the deep regrets of the party, with whom he had been a great favorite. They proceeded with it to the next station, where an inquiry was instituted as to the manner of his death, but of course there was nothing more to be elicited.

I give this story as related by one of the parties present, and there is no doubt of its perfect authenticity. He says he can in no way account for the mystery—he can only relate the fact;

and not one, but the whole *five* cadets, saw him as distinctly as they saw each other. It was evident, from the spot where the body was found, which was not many hundred yards from the well, that the accident must have occurred very shortly after they left him. When the young men reached the boat, Major R—— must have been, for some seven or eight hours, a denizen of the other world, yet he kept the rendezvous!

There was a similar occurrence in Devonshire, some years back, which happened to the well-known Dr. Hawker, who, one night in the street, observed an old woman pass him, to whom he was in the habit of giving a weekly charity. Immediately after she had passed, he felt somebody pull his coat, and on looking round saw it was her, whereupon he put his hand in his pocket to seek for a sixpence, but on turning to give it to her she was gone. He thought nothing about it; but when he got home, he inquired if she had had her money that week,—when, to his amazement, he heard she was dead, but his family had forgotten to mention the circumstance. I have met with two curious cases, occurring in Edinburgh, of late years; in one, a young man and his sister were in their kitchen, warming themselves over the fire before they retired to bed, when, on raising their eyes, they both saw a female figure, dressed in white, standing in the door-way and looking at them; she was leaning against one of the door-posts. Miss E——, the young lady, screamed; whereupon the figure advanced, crossed the kitchen toward a closet, and disappeared. There was no egress at the closet: and as they lived in a flat, and the door was closed for the night, a stranger could neither have entered the house nor got out of it. In the other instance, there were two houses on one flat, the doors opposite each other. In one of the houses there resided a person with her two daughters, grown-up women: in the other lived a shoemaker and his wife. The latter died, and it was said her husband had ill-treated her and worried her out of the world. He was a drunken, dissipated man, and used to be out till a late hour most nights, while this poor woman sat up for him, and when she heard a voice on the stairs, or a bell, she used often to come out and look over to see if it were her husband returned. One night, when she had been dead some weeks, the two young women were ascending the stairs to their own door, when, to their amazement, they both saw her standing at the top, looking over as she used to do in her lifetime. At the same moment their mother opened the door and saw the figure also; the girls rushed past, overcome with terror, and one if not both fainted as soon as they got into the door. The youngest fell on her face in the passage.

Another case, which occurred in this town, I mention—although I know it is liable to be called a spectral illusion—because it bears a remarkable similarity to one which took place in America. A respectable woman lost her father, for whom she had a great affection; she was of a serious turn, and much attached to the tenets of her church, in which particulars she thought her father had been deficient. She was therefore very unhappy about him, fearing that he had not died in a proper state of mind. A considerable time had elapsed since his death, but her distrust of his condition was still causing her uneasiness; when one day, while she was sitting at her work, she felt something touch her shoulder, and on looking round she perceived her father, who bade her cease to grieve about him, as he was not unhappy. From that moment she became perfectly resigned and cheerful. The American case—I have omitted to write down the name of the place, and forget it—was that of a mother and son. She was also a highly respectable person, and was described to me as perfectly trustworthy by one who knew her. She was a widow, and had one son, to whom she was extremely attached. He however disappeared one day, and she never could learn what had become of him; she always said that if she did but know his fate she should be happier. At length, when he had been dead a considerable time, her attention was one day, while reading, attracted by a slight noise, which induced her to look round, and she saw her son, dripping with water, and with a sad expression of countenance. The features, however, presently relaxed, and they assumed a more pleasing aspect before he disappeared. From that time she ceased to grieve, and it was subsequently ascertained that the young man had run away to sea; but no more was known of him. Certain it was, however, that she attributed her recovered tranquillity to having seen her son as above narrated.

A lady with whom I am acquainted was one day, when a girl, standing at the top of the stairs, with two others, discussing their games, when they each suddenly exclaimed: "Who's that?" There was a fourth among them—a girl in a checked pinafore; but she was gone again. They had all seen her. One day a younger brother, in the same house, was playing with a whip, when he suddenly laughed at something, and cried "Take that;" and described having seen the same girl. This led to some inquiry, and it was said that such a girl as they described had lived in that house, and had died from the bite of a mad dog; or, rather, had been smothered between two feather-beds: but whether that was actually done, or was only a report, I can not say. Supposing this to have been no illusion, and I really can not see how it could be one, the memory of past sports and pleasures seems to have so survived as to have attracted the young soul, prematurely cut off, to the spot where the same sports and pleasures were being enjoyed by the living.

A maid-servant in one of the midland counties of England, being up early one morning, heard her name called in a voice that seemed to be her brother's, a sailor then at sea; and running up, she found him standing in the hall; he said he was come from afar, and was going again, and mentioned some other things; when her mistress, hearing voices, called to know who she was talking to: she said it was her brother from sea. After speaking to her for some time, she suddenly lost sight of him, and found herself alone. Amazed and puzzled, she told her mistress what had happened, who being led thus to suspect the kind of visiter it was, looked out of the window to ascertain if there were any marks of footsteps, the ground being covered with snow. There were, however, none,—and it was therefore clear that nobody could have entered the house. Intelligence afterward arrived of the young man's death.

This last is a case of wraith, but a more complicated one, from the circumstance of speech being superadded. But this is not by any means an isolated particular; there are many such. The author of the book called "Accredited Ghost Stories"—whose name I at this moment forget, and I have not the book at hand—gives, on his own authority, the following circumstance, professing to be acquainted with the parties. A company were visiting York cathedral, when a gentleman and lady, who had detached themselves from the rest, observed an officer wearing a naval uniform approaching them; he walked quickly, saying to the lady, as he passed, "There *is* another world." The gentleman, seeing her greatly agitated, pursued the stranger, but lost sight of him, and nobody had seen such a person but themselves. On returning to his companion, she told him that it was her brother, who was then abroad with his ship, and with whom she had frequently held discussions as to whether there was or was not a future life. The news of the young man's death shortly reached the family. In this case the brother must have been dead; the spirit must have passed out of this world into that other, the existence of which he came to certify. This is one of those cases which—happening not long ago—leads one especially to regret the want of moral courage which prevents people giving up their names and avowing their experience. The author of the abovementioned book, from which I borrow this story, says that the sheet had gone to the press with the real names of the parties attached, but that he was requested to withdraw them, as it would be painful to the family. My view of this case is so different, that, had it occurred to myself, I should have felt it my imperative duty to make it known and give every satisfaction to inquirers.

Some years ago, during the war, when Sir Robert H. E—— was in the Netherlands, he happened to be quartered with two other officers, one of whom was despatched into Holland on an expedition. One night, during his absence, Sir R. H. E—— awoke, and, to his great surprise, saw this absent friend sitting on the bed which he used to occupy, with a wound in his breast. Sir Robert immediately awoke his companion, who saw the spectre also. The latter then addressed them, saying that he had been that day killed in a skirmish, and that he had died in great anxiety about his family, wherefore he had come to communicate that there was a deed of much consequence to them deposited in the hands of a certain lawyer in London, whose name and address he mentioned, adding that this man's honesty was not to be altogether relied on. He therefore requested that, on their return to England, they would go to his house and demand the deed, but that, if he denied the possession of it, they were to seek it in a certain drawer in his office, which he described to them. The circumstance impressed them very much at the time, but a long time had elapsed ere they reached England, during which period they had gone through so many adventures and seen so many friends fall around them, that this impression was considerably weakened, insomuch that each went to his own home and his own pursuits without thinking of fulfilling the commission they had undertaken. Some time afterward, however, it happened that they both met in London, and they then resolved to seek the street that had been named to them, and ascertain if such a man lived there. They found him, requested an interview, and demanded the deed, the possession of which he denied; but their eyes were upon the drawer that had been described to them, where they asserted it to be, and being there discovered, it was delivered into their hands. Here, also, the soul had parted from the body, while the memory of the past and an anxiety for the worldly prosperity, of those left behind, survived; and we thus see that the condition of mind in which this person had died, remained unchanged. He was not indifferent to the worldly prosperity of his relatives, and he found his own state rendered unhappy by the fear that they might suffer from the dishonesty of his agent. It may here be naturally objected that hundreds of much-loved widows and orphans have been ruined by dishonest trustees and agents, where no ghost came back to instruct them in the means of obviating the misfortune. This is, no doubt, a very legitimate objection, and one which it is very difficult to answer. I must, however, repeat what I said before, nature is full of exceptional cases, while we know very little of the laws which regulate these exceptions; but we may see a very good reason for the fact that such communications *are* the exception, and not the rule; for if they were the latter, the whole economy of this earthly life would be overturned, and its affairs must necessarily be conducted in a totally different manner to that which prevails at present. What the effects of such an arrangement of nature would be, had it pleased God to make it, he alone knows; but certain it is, that man's freedom, as a moral agent, would be in a great degree abrogated, were the barriers that impede our intercourse with the spiritual world removed.

It may be answered, that this is an argument which may be directed against the fact of such appearances being permitted at all; but that is a fallacious objection. Earthquakes and hurricanes are occasionally permitted, which overthrow the work of man's hands for centuries; but if these convulsions of nature were of every-day occurrence, nobody would think it worth their while to build a house or cultivate the earth, and the world would be a wreck and a wilderness. The apparitions that do appear, are not without their use to those who believe in them; while there is too great an uncertainty attending the subject, generally to allow of its ever being taken into consideration in mundane affairs.

The old, so called, superstition of the people, that a person's "dying with something on his mind" is one of the frequent causes of these revisitings, seems, like most other of their superstitions, to be founded on experience. I meet with many cases in which some apparently trivial anxiety, or some frustrated communication, prevents the uneasy spirit flinging off the bonds that bind it to the earth. I could quote many examples characterized by this feature, but will confine myself to two or three.

Jung Stilling gives a very curious one, which occurred in the year 1746, and for the authenticity of which he vouches. A gentleman of the name of Dorrien, of most excellent character and amiable disposition, who was tutor in the Carolina Colleges, at Brunswick, died there in that year; and immediately previous to his death he sent to request an interview with another tutor, of the name of Hofer, with whom he had lived on terms of friendship. Hofer obeyed the summons, but came too late, the dying man was already in the last agonies. After a short time, rumors began to circulate that Herr Dorrien had been seen by different persons about the college; but as it was with the pupils that these rumors originated, they were supposed to be mere fancies, and no attention whatever was paid to them. At length, however, in the month of October, three months after the decease of Herr Dorrien, a circumstance occurred that excited considerable amazement among the professors. It formed part of the duty of Hofer to go through the college every night, between the hours of eleven and twelve, for the purpose of ascertaining that all the scholars were in bed, and that nothing irregular was going on among them. On the night in question, on entering one of the ante-rooms in the execution of this duty, he saw, to his great amazement, Herr Dorrien, seated, in the dressing-gown and white cap he was accustomed to wear, and holding the latter with his right hand, in such a manner as to conceal the upper part of the face; from the eyes to the chin, however, it was distinctly visible. This unexpected sight naturally startled Hofer, but, summoning resolution, he advanced into the young men's chamber, and, having ascertained that all was in order, closed the door; he then turned his eyes again toward the spectre, and there it sat as before, whereupon he went up to it, and stretched out his arm toward it; but he was now seized with such a feeling of indescribable horror, that he could scarcely withdraw his hand, which became swollen to a degree that for some months he had no use of it. On the following day he related this circumstance to the professor of mathematics, Oeder, who of course treated the thing as a spectral illusion. He, however, consented to accompany Hofer on his rounds the ensuing night, satisfied that he should be able either to convince him it was a mere phantasm, or else a spectre of flesh and blood that was playing him a trick. They accordingly went at the usual hour, but no sooner had the professor set his foot in that same room, than he exclaimed, "By

Heavens! it is Dorrien himself!" Hofer, in the meantime, proceeded into the chamber as before, in the pursuance of his duties, and, on his return, they both contemplated the figure for some time; neither of them had, however, the courage to address or approach it, and finally quitted the room, very much impressed, and perfectly convinced that they had seen Dorrien.

This incident soon got spread abroad, and many people came in hopes of satisfying their own eyes of the fact, but their pains were fruitless; and even Professor Oeder, who had made up his mind to speak to the apparition, sought it repeatedly in the same place in vain. At length, he gave it up, and ceased to think of it, saying, "I have sought the ghost long enough; if he has anything to say, he must now seek me." About a fortnight after this, he was suddenly awakened, between three and four o'clock in the morning, by something moving in his chamber, and on opening his eyes, he beheld a shadowy form, having the same appearance as the spectre, standing in front of a press which was not more than two steps from his bed. He raised himself, and contemplated the figure, the features of which he saw distinctly for some minutes, till it disappeared. On the following night he was awakened in the same manner, and saw the figure as before, with the addition that there was a sound proceeded from the door of the press, as if somebody was leaning against it. The spectre also stayed longer this time, and Professor Oeder, no doubt frightened and angry, addressing it as an evil spirit, bade it begone, whereon it made gestures with its head and hands that alarmed him so much, that he adjured it in the name of God to leave him, which it did. Eight days now elapsed without any further disturbance, but, after that period, the visits of the spirit were resumed, and he was awakened by it repeatedly about three in the morning, when it would advance from the press to the bed, and, hang its head over him in a manner so annoying, that he started up and struck at it, whereupon it would retire, but presently advance again. Perceiving now, that the countenance was rather placid and friendly than otherwise, the professor at length addressed it, and, having reason to believe that Dorrien had left some debts unpaid, he asked him if that were the case, upon which the spectre retreated some steps, and seemed to place itself in an attitude of attention. Oeder reiterated the inquiry, whereupon the figure drew its hand across its mouth, in which the professor now observed a short pipe. "Is it to the barber you are in debt?" he inquired. The spectre slowly shook its head. "Is it to the tobacconist, then?" asked he, the question being suggested by the pipe. Hereupon the form retreated, and disappeared. On the following day, Oeder narrated what had occurred to Councillor Erath, one of the curators of the college, and also to the sister of the deceased, and arrangements were made for discharging the debt. Professor Seidler, of the same college, now proposed to pass the night with Oeder, for the purpose of observing if the ghost came again, which it did about five o'clock, and awoke Oeder as usual, who awoke his companion, but just then the form disappeared, and Seidler said he only saw something white. They then both disposed themselves to sleep, but presently Seidler was aroused by Oeder's starting up and striking out, while he cried, with a voice expressive of rage and horror, "Begone! You have tormented me long enough! If you want anything of me, say what it is, or give me an intelligible sign, and come here no more!"

Seidler heard all this, though he saw nothing; but as soon as Oeder was somewhat appeased, he told him that the figure had returned, and not only approached the bed, but stretched itself upon it. After this, Oeder burned a light, and had some one in the room every night. He gained this advantage by the light, that he saw nothing; but about four o'clock, he was generally awakened by noises in his room, and other symptoms that satisfied him the ghost was there. At length, however, this annoyance ceased also; and trusting that his unwelcome guest had taken his leave, he dismissed his bedfellow, and dispensed with his light. Two nights passed quietly over; on the third, however, the spectre returned; but very perceptibly darker. It now presented another sign, or symbol, which seemed to represent a picture, with a hole in the middle, through which it thrust its head. Oeder was now so little alarmed, that he bade it express its wishes more clearly, or approach nearer. To these requisitions the apparition shook its head, and then vanished. This strange phenomenon recurred several times, and even in the presence of another curator of the college; but it was with considerable difficulty they discovered what the symbol was meant to convey. They at length, however, found that Dorrien just before his illness, had obtained, on trial, several pictures for a magic lantern, which had never been returned to their owner. This was now done, and from that time the apparition was neither seen nor heard again. Professor Oeder made no secret of these circumstances; he related them publicly in court and college; he wrote the account to several eminent persons, and declared himself ready to attest the facts upon his oath.

Stilling, who relates this story, has been called superstitious; he may be so; but his piety and his honesty are above suspicion; he says the facts are well known, and that he can vouch for their authenticity; and as he must have been a contemporary of the parties concerned, he had, doubtless, good opportunities of ascertaining what foundation there was for the story. It is certainly a very extraordinary one, and the demeanor of the spirit as little like what we should have naturally apprehended as possible; but, as I have said before, we have no right to pronounce any opinion on this subject, except from experience, and there are two arguments to be advanced in favor of this narration; the one being, that I can not imagine anybody setting about to invent a ghost-story, would have introduced circumstances so apparently improbable and inappropriate; and the other consisting in the fact, that I have met with numerous relations, coming from very opposite quarters, which seem to corroborate the one in question.

With respect to the cause of the spectre's appearance, Jung Stilling, I think, reasonably enough, suggests, that the poor man had intended to commission Hofer to settle these little affairs for him, but that delaying this duty too long, his mind had been oppressed by the recollection of them in his last moments—he had carried his care with him, and it bound him to the earth.

Wherefore, considering how many persons die with duties unperformed, this anxiety to repair the neglect, is not more frequently manifested, we do not know; some reasons we have already suggested as possible; there may be others of which we can form no idea, any more than we can solve the question, why in some cases communication and even speech seems easy, while in this instance, the spirit was only able to convey its wishes by gestures and symbols. Its addressing itself to Oeder instead of Hofer, probably arose from its finding communication with him less difficult; the swelling of Hofer's arm indicating that his physical nature was not adapted for this spiritual intercourse. With respect to Oeder's expedient of burning a light in his room, in order to prevent his seeing this shadowy form, we can comprehend, that the figure would be discerned more easily on the dark ground of comparative obscurity, and that clear light would render it invisible. Dr. Kerner mentions, on one occasion, that while sitting in an adjoining room, with the door open, he had seen a shadowy figure, to whom his patient was speaking, standing beside her bed; and catching up a candle, he had rushed toward it; but as soon as he thus illuminated the chamber, he could no longer distinguish it.

The ineffective and awkward attempts of this apparition to make itself understood, are not easily to be reconciled to our ideas of a spirit, while, at the same time, that which it could do, and that which it could not—the powers it possessed and those it wanted—tend to throw some light on its condition. As regards space, we may suppose that, in this instance, what St. Martin said of ghosts in general, may be applicable: "*Je ne crois pas aux revenants, mais je croix aux restants;*" that is, he did not believe that spirits who had once quitted the earth returned to it, but he believed that some did not quit it, and thus, as the somnambule mentioned in a former chapter said to me, "Some are waiting and some are gone on before."

Dorrien's uneasiness and worldly care chained him to the earth, and he was a *restant*—but, being a spirit, he was inevitably inducted into some of the inherent properties of spirit;

matter to him was no impediment, neither doors nor walls could keep him out; he had the intuitive perception of whom he could most easily communicate with, or he was brought into rapport with Oeder by the latter's seeking him; and he could either so act on Oeder's constructive imagination as to enable it to project his own figure, with the short pipe and the pictures, or he could, by the magical power of his will, build up these images out of the constituents of the atmosphere. The last seems the most probable, because, had the rapport with Oeder, or Oeder's receptivity, been sufficient to enable the spirit to act potently upon him, it would have been also able to infuse into his mind the wishes it desired to convey, even without speech, for speech, as a means of communication between spirits, must be quite unnecessary. Even in spite of these dense bodies of ours, we have great difficulty in concealing our thoughts from each other; and the somnambule reads the thoughts of not only his magnetizer, but of others with whom he is placed in rapport. In cases where speech appears to be used by a spirit, it is frequently not audible speech, but only this transference of thought, which appears to be speech from the manner in which the thought is borne in and enters the mind of the receiver; but it is not through his ears, but through his universal supplementary sense, that he receives it; and it is no more like what we mean by *hearing*, than is the seeing of a *clairvoyant*, or a spirit, like our seeing by means of our bodily organs. In those cases where the speech is audible to other persons, we must suppose that the magical will of the spirit can, by means of the atmosphere, simulate these sounds as it can simulate others, of which I shall have to treat by-and-by. It is remarkable that, in some instances, this magical power seems to extend so far as to represent to the eye of the seer a form apparently so real, solid, and lifelike, that it is not recognisable from the living man; while in other cases the production of a shadowy figure seems to be the limit of its agency, whether limited by its own faculty or the receptivity of its subject: but we must be quite sure that the form is, in either instance, equally ethereal or immaterial. And it will not be out of place here to refer to the standing joke of the skeptics, about ghosts appearing in coats and waistcoats. Bentham thought he had settled the question for ever by that objection; and I have heard it since frequently advanced by very acute persons; but, properly considered, it has not the least validity.

Whether or not the soul on leaving its earthly tabernacle finds itself at once clothed with that spiritual body which St. Paul refers to, is what we can not know, though it seems highly probable; but if it be so, we must be sure that this body resembles in its nature that fluent, subtle kind of matter, called by us imponderables, which are capable of penetrating all substances; and unless there be no visible body at all, but only the will of a disembodied spirit acting upon one yet in the flesh (in which case it were as easy to impress the imagination with a clothed figure as an unclothed one), we must conclude that this ethereal flexible form, whether permanent or temporary, may be held together and retain its shape by the volition of the spirit, as our bodies are held together by the principle of life that is in them; and we see in various instances, where the spectator has been bold enough to try the experiment, that though the shadowy body was pervious to any substance passed through it, its integrity was only momentarily interrupted, and it immediately recovered its previous shape.

Now, as a spirit—provided there be no especial law to the contrary, partial or universal, absolute or otherwise, governing the spiritual world—must be where its thoughts and wishes are, just as we should be at the place we intently think of, or desire, if our solid bodies did not impede us, so must a spirit appear as it is, or as it *conceives* of itself. Morally, it can only conceive of itself as it is, good or bad, light or dark; but it may conceive of itself clothed as well as unclothed; and if it can conceive of its former body, it can equally conceive of its former habiliments, and so represent them by its power of will to the eye, or present them to the constructive imagination of the seer: and it will be able to do this with a degree of distinctness proportioned to the receptivity of the latter, or to the intensity of the rapport which exists between them. Now, considered in this way, the appearance of a spirit "in its habit as it lived" is no more extraordinary than the appearance of a spirit at all, and it adds no complexity to the phenomenon. If it appears at all in a recognisable form, it must come naked or clothed: the former, to say the least of it, would be much more frightful and shocking; and if it be clothed, I do not see what right we have to expect it shall be in a fancy costume, conformable to our ideas (which are no ideas at all) of the other world; nor why, if it be endowed with the memory of the past, it should not be natural to suppose it would assume the external aspect it wore during its earthly pilgrimage. Certain it is, whether consistent with our notions or not, all tradition seems to show that this is the appearance they assume; and the very fact that on the first view of the case, and until the question is philosophically considered, the addition of a suit of clothes to the phenomenon not only renders its acceptance much more difficult, but throws an air of absurdity and improbability on the whole subject, furnishes a very strong argument in favor of the persuasion that this notion has been founded on experience, and is not the result of either fancy or gratuitous invention.

The idea of spirits appearing like angels, with wings, &c., seems to be drawn from these relations in the Bible, when messengers were sent from God to man; but those departed spirits are not angels, though probably destined in the course of ages to become so: in the meantime, their moral state continues as when they quitted the body, and their memories and affections are with the earth—and so, earthly they appear, more or less. We meet with some instances in which bright spirits have been seen—protecting spirits, for example, who have shaken off their earth entirely, clinging to it yet but by some holy affection or mission of mercy—and these appear, not with wings, which whenever seen are merely symbolical, for we can not imagine they are necessary to the motion of a spirit, but clothed in robes of light. Such appearances, however, seem much more rare than the others.

It will seem to many persons very inconsistent with their ideas of the dignity of a spirit that they should appear and act in the manner I have described, and shall describe further; and I have heard it objected that we can not suppose God would permit the dead to return merely to frighten the living, and that it is showing him little reverence to imagine he would suffer them to come on such trifling errands, or demean themselves in so undignified a fashion. But God permits men of all degrees of wickedness, and of every kind of absurdity, to exist, and to harass and disturb the earth, while they expose themselves to its obloquy or its ridicule.

Now, as I have observed in a former chapter, there is nothing more perplexing to us in regarding man as a responsible being, than the degree to which we have reason to believe his moral nature is influenced by his physical organization; but leaving this difficult question to be decided (if ever it can be decided in this world) by wiser heads than mine, there is one thing of which we may rest perfectly assured, namely, that let the fault of an impure, or vicious, or even merely sensuous life, lie where it will—whether it be the wicked spirit within, or the ill-organized body without, or a *tertium quid* of both combined—still the soul that has been a party to this earthly career, must be soiled and deteriorated by its familiarity with evil; and there seems much reason to believe that the dissolution of the connection between the soul and body produces far less change in the former than has been commonly supposed. People generally think—if they think on the subject at all—that as soon as they are dead, if they have lived tolerably virtuous lives, or indeed been free from any great crimes, they will immediately find themselves provided with wings, and straightway fly up to some delightful place, which they call heaven, forgetting how unfit they are for heavenly fellowship; and although I can not help thinking that the Almighty has mercifully permitted occasional relaxations of the boundaries that separate the dead from the living, for the purpose of showing us our error, we are determined not to avail ourselves of the advantage. I do not mean that these spirits—these *revenants* or *restants*—are special messengers sent to warn us: I only mean that their occasionally "revisiting the glimpses of the moon" form the exceptional cases in a great general law of nature which divides the spiritual from the material world; and that, in framing this law, these exceptions may have been designed for our benefit.

There are several stories extant in the English, and a vast number in the German records, which, supposing them to be well founded—and I repeat, that for many of them we have just as good evidence as for anything else we believe as hearsay or tradition—would go to confirm the fact that the spirits of the dead are sometimes disturbed by what appear to us very trifling cares. I give the following case from Dr. Kerner, who says it was related to him by a very respectable man, on whose word he can entirely rely:—

"I was," said Mr. St. S——, of S——, "the son of a man who had no fortune but his business, in which he was ultimately successful. At first, however, his means being narrow, he was perhaps too anxious and inclined to parsimony; so that when my mother, careful housewife as she was, asked him for money, the demand generally led to a quarrel. This occasioned her great uneasiness, and having mentioned this characteristic of her husband to her father, the old man advised her to get a second key made to the money-chest, unknown to her husband, considering this expedient allowable and even preferable to the destruction of their conjugal felicity, and feeling satisfied that she would make no ill use of the power possessed. My mother followed his advice, very much to the advantage of all parties; and nobody suspected the existence of this second key except myself, whom she had admitted into her confidence.

"Two-and-twenty years my parents lived happily together, when I, being at the time about eighteen hours' journey from home, received a letter from my father informing me that she was ill—that he hoped for her speedy amendment—but that if she grew worse he would send a horse to fetch me home to see her. I was extremely busy at that time, and therefore waited for further intelligence; and as several days elapsed without any reaching me, I trusted my mother was convalescent. One night, feeling myself unwell, I had lain down on the bed with my clothes on to take a little rest. It was between

11 and 12 o'clock, and I had not been asleep, when some one knocked at the door, and my mother entered, dressed as she usually was. She saluted me, and said: 'We shall see each other no more in this world: but I have an injunction to give you. I have given that key to R—— (naming a servant we then had), and she will remit it to you. Keep it carefully, or throw it into the water, but never let your father see it—it would trouble him. Farewell, and walk virtuously through life.' And with these words she turned and quitted the room by the door, as she had entered it. I immediately arose, called up my people, expressed my apprehension that my mother was dead, and, without further delay, started for home. As I approached the house, R——, the maid, came out and informed me that my mother had expired between the hours of 11 and 12 on the preceding night. As there was another person present at the moment, she said nothing further to me, but she took an early opportunity of remitting me the key, saying that my mother had given it to her just before she expired, desiring her to place it in my hands, with an injunction that I should keep it carefully, or fling it into the water, so that my father might never know anything about it. I took the key, kept it for some years, and at length threw it into the Lahne."

I am aware that it may be objected by those who believe in wraiths, but in no other kind of apparition, that this phenomenon occurred before the death of the lady, and that it was produced by her energetie anxiety with regard to the key. It may be so, or it may not; but, at all events, we see in this case how a comparatively trifling uneasiness may disturb a dying person, and how, therefore—if memory remains to them—they may carry it with them, and seek, by such means as they have, to obtain relief from it.

A remarkable instance of anxiety for the welfare of those left behind, is exhibited in the following story, which I received from a member of the family concerned: Mrs. R——, a lady very well connected, lost her husband when in the prime of life, and found herself with fourteen children, unprovided for.

The overwhelming nature of the calamity depressed her energies to such a degree as to render her incapable of those exertions which could alone redeem them from ruin. The flood of misfortune seemed too strong for her, and she yielded to it without resistance. She had thus given way to despondency some time, when one day, as she was sitting alone, the door opened, and her mother, who had been a considerable time dead, entered the room and addressed her, reproving her for this weak indulgence of useless sorrow, and bidding her exert herself for the sake of her children. From that period she threw off the depression, set actively to work to promote the fortunes of her family, and succeeded so well that they ultimately emerged from all their difficulties. I asked the gentleman who related this circumstance to me whether he believed it. He answered, that he could only assure me that she herself affirmed the fact, and that she avowedly attributed the sudden change in her character and conduct to this cause;—for his own part, he did not know what to say, finding it difficult to believe in the possibility of such a visit from the dead.

A somewhat similar instance is related by Dr. Kerner, which he says he received from the party himself, a man of sense and probity. This gentleman, Mr. F——, at an early age lost his mother. Two-and-twenty years afterward he formed an attachment to a young person, whose hand he resolved to ask in marriage. Having one evening seated himself at his desk, for the purpose of writing his proposal, he was amazed, on accidentally lifting his eyes from the paper, to see his mother, looking exactly as if alive, seated opposite to him, while she, raising her finger with a warning gesture, said: "Do not that thing!" Not the least alarmed, Mr. F—— started up to approach her, whereupon she disappeared. Being very much attached to the lady, however, he did not feel disposed to follow her counsel; but having read the letter to his father, who highly approved of the match and laughed at the ghost, he returned to his chamber to seal it; when, while he was adding the superscription, she again appeared as before and reiterated her injunction. But love conquered; the letter was despatched, the marriage ensued, and, after ten years of strife and unhappiness, was dissolved by a judicial process.

A remarkable circumstance occurred about forty years ago, in the family of Dr. Paulus, at Stuttgard. The wife of the head of the family having died, they, with some of their connections, were sitting at table a few days afterward, in the room adjoining that in which the corpse lay; suddenly the door of the latter apartment opened, and the figure of the mother clad in white robes entered, and, saluting them as she passed, walked slowly and noiselessly through the room, and then disappeared again through the door by which she had entered. The whole company saw the apparition; but the father, who was at that time quite in health, died eight days afterward.

Madame R—— had promised an old wood-cutter—who had a particular horror of dying in the poor-house, because he knew his body would be given to the surgeons—that she would take care to see him properly interred. The old man lived some years afterward, and she had quite lost sight of him, and indeed forgotten the circumstance, when she was one night awakened by the sound of some one cutting wood in her bed-chamber; and so perfect was the imitation, that she heard every log flung aside as separated. She started up, exclaiming, "The old man must be dead!" and so it proved,—his last anxiety having been that Madame R—— should remember her promise.

That our interest in whatever has much concerned us in this life accompanies us beyond the grave, seems to be proved by many stories I meet with, and the following is of undoubted authenticity: Some years ago, a music-master died at Erfert at the age of seventy. He was a miser, and had never looked with very friendly eyes on Professor Rinck, the composer, who he knew was likely to succeed to his classes. The old man had lived and died in an apartment adjoining the class-room; and the first day that Rinck entered on his office, while the scholars were singing *Aus der tiefe ruf ich dich*, which is a paraphrase of the *De profundis*, he thought he saw, through a hole or bull's eye in the door, something moving about the inner chamber. As the room was void of every kind of furniture, and nobody could possibly be in it, Rinck looked more fixedly, when he distinctly saw a shadow, whose movements were accompanied by a strange rustling sound. Perplexed at the circumstance, he told his pupils that on the following day he should require them to repeat the same choral. They did so; and while they were singing, Rinck saw a person walking backward and forward in the next room, who frequently approached the hole in the door. Very much struck with so extraordinary a circumstance, Rinck had the choral repeated on the ensuing day,—and this time his suspicions were fully confirmed; the old man, his predecessor, approaching the door, and gazing steadfastly into the class-room. "His face," said Rinck—in relating the story to Dr. Mainzer, who has obligingly furnished it to me as entered in his journal at the time—"was of an ashy-gray. The apparition," he added, "never more appeared to me, although I frequently had the choral repeated."

"I am no believer in ghost-stories," he added, "nor in the least superstitious; nevertheless, I can not help admitting that I have seen this: it is impossible for me ever to doubt or to deny that which I know I saw."

CHAPTER X.

THE FUTURE THAT AWAITS US.

In all ages of the world, and in all parts of it, mankind have earnestly desired to learn the fate that awaited them when they had "shuffled off this mortal coil;" and those pretending to be their instructors have built up different systems which have stood in the stead of knowledge, and more or less satisfied the bulk of the people. The interest on this subject is, at the present period, in the most highly civilized portions of the globe, less than it has been at any preceding one. The great proportion of us live for this world alone, and think very little of the next: we are in too great a hurry of pleasure or business to bestow any time on a subject of which we have such vague notions—notions so vague, that, in short, we can scarcely by any effort of the imagination bring the idea home to ourselves; and when we are about to die, we are seldom in a situation to do more than resign ourselves to what is inevitable, and blindly meet our fate; while, on the other hand, what is generally called the religious world is so engrossed by its struggles for power and money, or by its sectarian disputes and enmities, and so narrowed and circumscribed by dogmatic orthodoxies, that it has neither inclination nor liberty to turn back or look around, and endeavor to gather up from past records and present observation such hints as are now and again dropped in our path, to give us an intimation of what the truth may be. The rationalistic age, too, out of which we are only just emerging, and which succeeded one of gross superstition, having settled, beyond appeal, that there never was such a thing as a ghost—that the dead never do come back to tell us the secrets of their prison-house, and that nobody believes such idle tales but children and old women—seemed to have shut the door against the only channel through which any information could be sought. Revelation tells us very little on this subject—reason can tell us nothing; and if Nature is equally silent, or if we are to be deterred from questioning her from the fear of ridicule, there is certainly no resource left us but to rest contented in our ignorance, and each wait till the awful secret is disclosed to ourselves.

A great many things have been pronounced untrue and absurd, and even impossible, by the highest authorities of the age in which they lived, which have afterward, and indeed within a very short period, been found to be both possible and true. I confess myself, for one, to have no respect whatever for these dogmatic denials and affirmations, and I am quite of opinion that vulgar incredulity is a much more contemptible thing than vulgar credulity. We know very little of what *is*, and still less of what may be; and till a thing has been proved, by induction, logically impossible, we have no right whatever to pronounce that it is so. As I have said before, *à priori* conclusions are perfectly worthless; and the sort of investigation that is bestowed upon subjects of the class of which I am treating, something worse—inasmuch as they deceive the timid and the ignorant, and that very numerous class which pins its faith on authority and never ventures to think for itself, by an assumption of wisdom and knowledge, which, if examined and analyzed, would very frequently prove to be nothing more respectable than obstinate prejudice and rash assertion.

For my own part, I repeat, I insist upon nothing. The opinions I have formed, from the evidence collected, may be quite erroneous; if so, as I seek only the truth, I shall be glad to be undeceived, and shall be quite ready to accept a better explanation of these facts, whenever it is offered to me: but it is in vain to tell me that this explanation is to be found in what is called imagination, or in a morbid state of the nerves, or an unusual excitement of the organs of color and form, or in imposture; or in all these together. The existence of all such sources of error and delusion I am far from denying, but I find instances that it is quite impossible to reduce under any one of those categories, as we at present understand them. The multiplicity of these instances, too—for, not to mention the large number that are never made known or carefully concealed, if I were to avail myself liberally of cases already recorded in various works, many of which I know, and many others I hear of as existing, but which I can not conveniently get access to, I might fill volumes (German literature abounds in them)—the number of the examples, I repeat, even on the supposition that they are not facts, would of itself form the subject of a very curious physiological or psychological inquiry. If so many people in respectable situations of life, and in apparently a normal state of health, are capable of either such gross impostures, or the subjects of such extraordinary spectral illusions, it would certainly be extremely satisfactory to learn something of the conditions that induce these phenomena in such abundance; and all I expect from my book at present is, to induce a suspicion that we are not quite so wise as we think ourselves; and that it might be worth while to inquire a little seriously into reports, which may perchance turn out to have a deeper interest for us than all those various questions, public and private, put together, with which we are daily agitating ourselves.

I have alluded, in an earlier part of this work, to the belief entertained by the ancients that the souls of men, on being disengaged from the bodies, passed into a middle state, called Hades, in which their portions seemed to be neither that of complete happiness nor of insupportable misery. They retained their personality, their human form, their memory of the past, and their interest in those that had been dear to them on earth. Communications were occasionally made by the dead to the living: they mourned over their duties neglected and their errors committed; many of their mortal feelings, passions, and propensities, seemed to survive; and they sometimes sought to repair, through the instrumentality of the living, the injuries they had formerly inflicted. In short, death was merely a transition from one condition of life to another; but in this latter state, although we do not see them condemned to undergo any torments, we perceive that they are not happy. There are, indeed, compartments in this dark region: there is Tartarus for the wicked, and the Elysian fields for the good, but they are comparatively thinly peopled. It is in the mid region that these pale shades abound, consistently with the fact that here on earth, moral as well as intellectual mediocrity is the rule, and extremes of good or evil the exceptions.

With regard to the opinion entertained of a future state by the Hebrews, the Old Testament gives us very little information; but what glimpses we do obtain of it appear to exhibit notions analogous to those of the heathen nations, inasmuch as that the personality and the form seem to be retained, and the possibility of these departed spirits revisiting the earth and holding commune with the living is admitted. The request of the rich man, also, that Lazarus might be sent to warn his brethren, yet alive, of his own miserable condition, testifies to the existence of these opinions; and it is worthy of remark that the favor is denied, not because its performance is impossible, but because the mission would be unavailing — a prediction which, it appears to me, time has singularly justified.

Altogether, the notion that in the state entered upon after we leave this world, the personality and form are retained, that these shades sometimes revisit the earth, and that the memory of the past still survives, seems to be universal; for it is found to exist among all people, savage and civilized: and if not founded on observation and experience, it becomes difficult to account for such unanimity on a subject which I think, speculatively considered, would not have been productive of such results; and one proof of this is, that those who reject such testimony and tradition as we have in regard to it, and rely only on their own understandings, appear to be pretty uniformly led to form opposite conclusions. They can not discern the mode of such a phenomenon; it is open to all sorts of scientific objections, and the *cui bono* sticks in their teeth.

This position being admitted, as I think it must be, we have but one resource left, whereby to account for the universality of this persuasion — which is, that in all periods and places, both mankind and womankind, as well in health as in sickness, have been liable to a series of spectral illusions of a most extraordinary and complicated nature, and bearing such a remarkable similarity to each other in regard to the objects supposed to be seen or heard, that they have been universally led to the same erroneous interpretation of the phenomenon. It is manifestly not impossible that this may be the case; and if it be so, it becomes the business of physiologists to inquire into the matter, and give us some account of it. In the meantime, we may be permitted to take the other view of the question, and examine what probabilities seem to be in its favor.

When the body is about to die, that which can not die, and which, to spare words, I will call THE SOUL, departs from it — whither? We do not know: but, in the first place, we have no reason to believe that the space destined for its habitation is far removed from the earth, since, knowing nothing about it, we are equally entitled to suppose the contrary; and, in the next, that which we call distance is a condition that merely regards material objects, and of which a spirit is quite independent, just as our thoughts are, which can travel from here to China, and back again, in a second of time.

Well, then, supposing this being to exist somewhere—and it is not unreasonable to suppose that the souls of the inhabitants of each planet continue to hover within the sphere of that planet, to which, for anything we can tell, they may be attached by a magnetic attraction—supposing it to find itself in space, free of the body, endowed with the memory of the past, and consequently with a consciousness of its own deserts, able to perceive that which we do not ordinarily perceive, namely, those who have passed into a similar state with itself—will it not naturally seek its place among those spirits which most resemble itself, and with whom, therefore, it must have the most affinity? On earth, the good seek the good, and the wicked the wicked: and the axiom that "like associates with like," we can not doubt will be as true hereafter as now. "In my Father's house there are many mansions," and our intuitive sense of what is fit and just must needs assure us that this is so. There are too many degrees of moral worth and of moral unworth among mankind, to permit of our supposing that justice could be satisfied by an abrupt division into two opposite classes. On the contrary, there must be infinite shades of desert; and, as we must consider that that which a spirit enters into on leaving the body is not so much a *place* as a *condition*, so there must be as many degrees of happiness or suffering as there are individuals, each carrying with him his own heaven or hell. For it is a vulgar notion to imagine that heaven and hell are *places;* they are states; and it is in ourselves we must look for both. When we leave the body, we carry them with us: "As the tree falls, so it shall lie." The soul which here has wallowed in wickedness or been sunk in sensuality, will not be suddenly purified by the death of the body: its moral condition remains what its earthly sojourn has trained it to, but its means of indulging its propensities are lost. If it has had no godly aspirations here, it will not be drawn to God there; and if it has so bound itself to the body that it has known no happiness but that to which the body ministered, it will be incapable of happiness when deprived of that enjoyment. Here we see at once what a variety of conditions must necessarily ensue—how many comparatively negative states there must be between those of positive happiness or positive misery!

We may thus conceive how a soul, on entering upon this new condition, must find its own place or state; if its thoughts and aspirations here have been heavenward, and its pursuits noble, its conditions will be heavenly. The contemplation of God's works, seen not as by our mortal eyes, but in their beauty and their truth and ever-glowing sentiments of love and gratitude—and, for aught we know, good offices to souls in need—would constitute a suitable heaven or happiness for such a being; an incapacity for such pleasures, and the absence of all others, would constitute a negative state, in which the chief suffering would consist in mournful regrets and a vague longing for something better, which the untrained soul, that never lifted itself from the earth, knows not how to seek; while malignant passions and unquenchable desires would constitute the appropriate hell of the wicked; for we must remember, that although a spirit is independent of those physical laws which are the conditions of matter, the moral law, which is indestructible, belongs peculiarly to it—that is, to the spirit—and is inseparable from it.

We must next remember, that this earthly body we inhabit is more or less a mask, by means of which we conceal from each other those thoughts which, if constantly exposed, would unfit us for living in community; but when we die, this mask falls away, and the truth shows nakedly: there is no more disguise; we appear as we are—spirits of light, or spirits of darkness;—and there can be no difficulty, I should think, in conceiving this, since we know that even our present opaque and comparatively inflexible features, in spite of all efforts to the contrary, will be the index of the mind; and that the expression of the face is gradually moulded to the fashion of the thoughts. How much more must this be the case with the fluent and diaphanous body which we expect is to succeed the fleshly one!

Thus, I think, we have arrived at forming some conception of the state that awaits us hereafter: the indestructible moral law fixes our place or condition; affinity governs our associations; and the mask under which we conceal ourselves having fallen away, we appear to each other as we are;—and I must here observe, that in this last circumstance must be comprised one very important element of happiness or misery; for the love of the pure spirits for each other will be for ever excited, by simply beholding that beauty and brightness which will be the inalienable expression of their goodness;—while the reverse will be the case with the spirits of darkness; for no one loves wickedness, in either themselves or others, however we may practise it. We must also understand, that the words "dark" and "light"—which, in this world of appearance, we use metaphorically to express good and evil—must be understood literally when speaking of that other world where everything will be seen as it is. Goodness is truth, and truth is light—and wickedness is falsehood, and falsehood is darkness; and so it will be seen to be. Those who have not the light of truth to guide them, will wander darkly through this valley of the shadow of death; those in whom the light of goodness shines will dwell in the light, which is inherent in themselves. The former will be in the kingdom of darkness—the latter in the kingdom of light. All the records existing of the blessed spirits that have appeared, ancient or modern, exhibit them as robed in light, while their anger or sorrow is symbolized by their darkness. Now, there appears to me nothing incomprehensible in this view of the future; on the contrary, it is the only one which I ever found myself capable of conceiving or reconciling with the justice and mercy of our Creator. He does not punish us—we punish ourselves: we have built up a heaven or a hell to our own liking, and we carry it with us. The fire that for ever burns without consuming, is the fiery evil in which we have chosen our part; and the heaven in which we shall dwell, will be the heavenly peace which will dwell in us. We are our own judges and our own chastisers. And here I must say a few words on the subject of that apparently (to us) preternatural memory which is developed under certain circumstances, and to which I alluded in a former chapter. Every one will have heard that persons who have been drowned and recovered, have had—in what would have been their last moments, if no means had been used to revive them—a strange vision of the past, in which their whole life seemed to float before them in review; and I have heard of the same phenomenon taking place, in moments of impending death, in other forms. Now, as it is not during the struggle for life, but immediately before insensibility ensues, that this vision occurs, it must be the act of a moment; and this renders incomprehensible to us what is said by the seeress of Prevorst, and other somnambules of the highest order, namely, that the instant the soul is freed from the body, it sees its whole earthly career in a single sign: it knows that it is good or evil, and pronounces its own sentence. The extraordinary memory occasionally exhibited in sickness, where the link between the soul and the body is probably loosened, shows us an adumbration of this faculty.

But this self-pronounced sentence we are led to hope is not final; nor does it seem consistent with the love and mercy of God that it should be so. There must be few, indeed, who leave this earth fit for heaven; for, although the immediate frame of mind in which dissolution takes place is probably very important, it is surely a pernicious error, encouraged by jail chaplains and philanthropists, that a late repentance and a few parting prayers can purify a soul sullied by years of wickedness. Would we at once receive such a one into our intimate communion and love? Should we not require time for the stains of vice to be washed away and habits of virtue to be formed? Assuredly we should! And how can we imagine that the purity of heaven is to be sullied by that approximation which the purity of earth would forbid? It would be cruel to say, and irrational to think, that this late repentance is of no avail; it is doubtless so far of avail, that the straining upward and the heavenly aspirations of the parting soul are carried with it, so that when it is free, instead of choosing the darkness it will flee to as much light as is in itself, and be ready, through the mercy of God and the ministering of brighter spirits, to receive more. But in this case, as also in the innumerable instances of those who die in what may be called a negative state, the advance must be progressive; though, wherever the desire exists, I must believe that this advance is possible. If not, wherefore did Christ, after being "put to death in the flesh," go and "preach to the spirits in prison"? It would have been a mockery to preach salvation to those who had no hope; nor would they, having no hope, have listened to the preacher.

I think these views are at once cheering, encouraging, and beautiful; and I can not but believe, that were they more generally entertained and more intimately conceived, they would be very beneficial in their effects. As I have said before, the extremely vague notions people have of a future life prevent the possibility of its exercising any great influence upon the present. The picture, on one side, is too revolting and inconsistent with our ideas of Divine goodness to be deliberately accepted; while, with regard to the other, our feelings somewhat resemble those of a little girl I once knew, who, being told by her mother what was to be the reward of goodness if she were so happy as to reach heaven, put her finger in her eye and began to cry, exclaiming, "Oh, mamma, how tired I shall be singing!"

The question which will now naturally arise, and which I am bound to answer, is, How have these views been formed? and what is the authority for them? And the answer I have to make will startle many minds when I say, that they have been gathered from two sources; first and chiefly from the state in which those spirits appear to be, and sometimes avow themselves to be, who, after quitting the earth, return to it and make themselves visible to the living; and, secondly, from the revelations of numerous somnambules of the highest order, which entirely conform in all cases, not only with the revelations of the dead, but with each other. I do not mean to imply, when I say this, that I consider the question finally settled as to whether somnambules are really clear-seers or only visionaries; nor that I have by any means established the fact that the dead do sometimes actually return; but I am obliged to beg the question for the moment, since, whether these sources be pure or impure, it is from them the information has been collected. It is true that these views are extremely conformable with those entertained by Plato and his school of philosophers, and also with those of the mystics of a later age; but the latter certainly, and the former probably, built up their systems on the same foundation; and I am very far from using the term *mystics* in the opprobious, or at least contemptuous, tone in which it has of late years been uttered in this country; for, although abounding in errors, as regarded the concrete, and although their want of an inductive *methodology* led them constantly astray in the region of the real, they were sublime teachers in that of the ideal; and they seem to have been endowed with a wonderful insight into this veiled department of our nature.

It may be here objected, that we only admire their insight, because, being in entire ignorance of the subject of it, we accept raving for revelation; and that no weight can be attached to the conformity of later disclosures with theirs, since they have no doubt been founded upon them. As to the ignorance, it is admitted; and, simply looking at their views, as they stand, they have nothing to support them but their sublimity and consistency; but, as regards the value of the evidence afforded by conformity, it rests on very different grounds; for the reporters from whom we collect our intelligence are, with very few exceptions, those of whom we may safely predicate, that they were wholly unacquainted with the systems promulgated by the Platonic philosophers, or the mystics either, nor, in most instances, had ever heard of their names; for, as regards that peculiar somnambulic state which is here referred to, the subjects of it appear to be generally very young people of either sex, and chiefly girls; and, as regards ghost-seeing, although this phenomenon seems to have no connection with the age of the seer, yet it is not usually from the learned or the cultivated that we collect our cases, inasmuch as the apprehension of ridicule on the one hand, and the fast hold the doctrine of spectral illusions has taken of them on the other, prevent their believing in their own senses, or producing any evidence they might have to furnish.

And here will be offered another subtle objection, namely, that the testimony of such witnesses as I have above described is perfectly worthless; but this I deny. The somnambulic states I allude to, are such as have been developed, not artificially, but naturally; and often, under very extraordinary nervous diseases, accompanied with catalepsy, and various symptoms far beyond feigning. Such cases are rare, and, in this country, seem to have been very little observed, for doubtless they must occur, and when they do occur they are very carefully concealed by the families of the patient, and not followed up or investigated as a psychological phenomenon by the physician; for it is to be observed that, without questioning, no revelations are made; they are not, as far as I know, ever spontaneous. I have heard of two such cases in this country, both occurring in the higher classes, and both patients being young ladies; but, although surprising phenomena were exhibited, interrogation was not permitted, and the particulars were never allowed to transpire.

No doubt there are examples of error and examples of imposture, so there are in everything where room is to be found for them; and I am quite aware of the propensity of hysterical patients to deceive, but it is for the judicious observers to examine the genuineness of each particular instance; and it is perfectly certain and well established by the German physiologists and psychologists, who have carefully studied the subject, that there are many above all suspicion. Provided, then, that the case be genuine, it remains to be determined how much value is to be attached to the revelations, for they may be quite honestly delivered, and yet be utterly worthless—the mere ravings of a disordered brain; and it is here that conformity becomes important, for I can not admit the objection that the simple circumstance of the patients' being diseased invalidates their evidence so entirely as to annul even the value of their unanimity, because, although it is not logically impossible that a certain state of nervous derangement should occasion all somnambules, of the class in question, to make similar answers, when interrogated regarding a subject of which, in their normal condition, they know nothing, and on which they have never reflected, and that these answers should be not only consistent, but disclosing far more elevated views than are evolved by minds of a very superior order which *have* reflected on it very deeply — I say, although this is not logically impossible, it will assuredly be found, by most persons, an hypothesis of much more difficult acceptance than the one I propose; namely, that whatever be the cause of the effect, these patients are in a state of clear-seeing, wherein they have "more than mortal knowledge;" that is, more knowledge than mortals possess in their normal condition: and it must not be forgotten, that we have some facts confessed by all experienced physicians and physiologists, even in this country, proving that there are states of disease in which preternatural faculties have been developed, such as no theory has yet satisfactorily accounted for.

But Dr. Passavent, who has written a very philosophical work on the subject of vital magnetism and clear-seeing, asserts, that it is an error to imagine that the ecstatic condition is merely the product of disease. He says, that it has sometimes exhibited itself in persons of very vigorous constitutions, instancing Joan of Arc, a woman, whom historians have little understood, and whose memory Voltaire's detestable poem has ridiculed and degraded, but who was, nevertheless, a great psychological phenomenon.

The circumstance, too, that phenomena of this kind are more frequently developed in women than in men, and that they are merely the consequence of her greater nervous irritability, has been made another objection to them — an objection, however, which Dr. Passavent considers founded on ignorance of the essential difference between the sexes, which is not merely a physical but a psychological one. Man is more productive than receptive. In a state of perfectibility, both attributes would be equally developed in him; but in this terrestrial life, only imperfect phases of the entire sum of the soul's faculties are so. Mankind are but children, male or female, young or old; of man, in his totality, we have but faint adumbrations, here and there.

Thus the ecstatic woman will be more frequently a seer, instinctive and intuitive; man, a doer and a worker; and as all genius is a degree of ecstasy or clear-seeing, we perceive the reason wherefore in man it is more productive than in woman, and that our greatest poets and artists, in all kinds, are of the former sex, and even the most remarkable women produce but little in science or art; while on the other hand, the feminine instinct, and tact, and intuitive seeing of truth, are frequently more sure than the ripe and deliberate judgment of man; and it is hence that solitude and such conditions as develop the passive or receptive at the expense of the active, tend to produce this state, and to assimilate the man more to the nature of the woman; while in her they intensify these distinguishing characteristics; and this is also the reason that simple and childlike people and races are the most frequent subjects of these phenomena.

It is only necessary to read Mozart's account of his own moments of inspiration, to comprehend not only the similarity, but the positive identity, of the ecstatic state with the state of genius in activity. "When all goes well with me," he says—"when I am in a carriage, or walking, or when I can not sleep at night, the thoughts come streaming in upon me most fluently: whence, or how, is more than I can tell. What comes, I hum to myself as it proceeds. Then follow the counterpoint and the clang of the different instruments; and, if I am not disturbed, my soul is fixed, and the thing grows greater, and broader, and clearer; and I have it all in my head, even when the piece is a long one; and I see it like a beautiful picture—not hearing the different parts in succession as they must be played, but the whole at once. That is the delight! The composing and the making is like a beautiful and vivid dream; but this hearing of it is the best of all."

What is this but clear-seeing, backward and forward, the past and the future? The one faculty is not a whit more surprising and incomprehensible than the other, to those who possess neither; only we see the material product of one, and therefore believe in it. But, as Passavent justly observes, these coruscations belong not to genius exclusively—they are latent in all men. In the highly-gifted this divine spark becomes a flame to light the world withal; but even in the coarsest and least-developed organizations, it may and does momentarily break forth. The germ of the highest spiritual life is in the rudest, according to its degree, as well as in the highest form of man we have yet seen;—he is but a more imperfect type of the race, in whom this spiritual germ has not unfolded itself.

Then, with respect to our second source of information, I am quite aware that it is equally difficult to establish its validity; but there are a few arguments in our favor here, too. In the first place, as Dr. Johnson says, though all reason is against us, all tradition is for us; and this conformity of tradition is surely of some weight, since I think it would be difficult to find any parallel instance of a universal tradition that was entirely without a foundation in truth; for with respect to witchcraft, the belief in which is equally universal, we now know that the phenomena were generally facts, although the interpretations put upon them were fables. It may certainly be objected that this universal belief in ghosts only arises from the universal prevalence of spectral illusions; but if so, as I have before observed, these spectral illusions become a subject of very curious inquiry; for, in the first place, they frequently occur under circumstances the least likely to induce them, and to people whom we should least expect to find the victims of them; and, in the second, there is a most remarkable conformity here, too, not only between the individual cases occurring among all classes of persons, who had never exhibited the slightest tendency to nervous derangement or somnambulism, but also between these and the revelations of the somnambules. In short, it seems to me that life is reduced to a mere phantasmagoria, if spectral illusions are so prevalent, so complicated in their nature, and so delusive as they must be if all the instances of ghost-seeing that come before us are to be referred to that theory. How numerous these are, I confess myself not to have had the least idea, till my attention was directed to the inquiry; and that these instances have been equally frequent in all periods and places we can not doubt, from the variety of persons that have given in their adhesion, or at least that have admitted, as Addison did, that he could not refuse the universal testimony in favor of the reappearance of the dead, strengthened by that of many credible persons with whom he was acquainted. Indeed, the testimony in favor of the facts has been at all periods too strong to be wholly rejected; so that even the materialists, like Lucretius and the elder Pliny, find themselves obliged to acknowledge them; while, on the other hand, the extravagant admissions that are demanded of us by those who endeavor to explain them away, prove that their disbelief rests on no more solid foundation than their own prejudices. I acknowledge all the difficulty of establishing the facts — such difficulties as indeed encompass few other branches of inquiry; but I maintain that the position of the opponents is still worse, although, by their high tone and contemptuous laugh, they assume to have taken up one that, being fortified by reason, is quite impregnable, forgetting that the wisdom of man is pre-eminently "foolishness before God," when it wanders into this region of unknown things; — forgetting, also, that they are just serving this branch of inquiry, as their predecessors, whom they laughed at, did physiology; concocting their systems out of their own brains, instead of the responses of nature — and with still more rashness and presumption, this department of her kingdom being more inaccessible, more incapable of demonstration, and more entirely beyond our control; for these spirits will not "come when we do call them;" — and I confess it often surprises me to hear the very shallow nonsense that very clever men talk upon the subject, and the inefficient arguments they use to disprove what they know nothing about. I am quite conscious that the facts I shall adduce are open to controversy: I can bring forward no evidence that will satisfy a scientific mind; but neither are my opponents a whit better fortified. All I do hope to establish is, not a proof, but a presumption; and the conviction I desire to awaken in people's minds is, not that these things *are* so, but that they *may be* so, and that it is well worth our while to inquire whether they are or not.

It will be seen that these views of a future state are extremely similar to those of Isaac Taylor, as suggested in his physical theory of another life—at least, as far as he has entered upon the subject;—and it is natural that they should be so, because he seems also to have been a convert to the opinion that "the dead do sometimes break through the boundaries that hem in the ethereal crowds; and if so, as if by trespass, may in single instances infringe upon the ground of common corporeal life."

Let us now fancy this dispossessed soul entering on its new career, amazed, and no more able than when it was in the body to accommodate itself at once to conditions of existence for which it was unprepared. If its aspirations had previously been heavenward, these conditions would not be altogether new, and it would speedily find itself at home in a sphere in which it had dwelt before; for, as I have formerly said, a spirit must be where its thoughts and affections are, and the soul, whose thoughts and affections had been directed to heaven, would only awaken after death into a more perfect and unclouded heaven. But imagine the contrary of all this. Conceive what this awakening must be to an earth-bound spirit—to one altogether unprepared for its new home—carrying no light within it—floating in the dim obscure—clinging to the earth, where all its affections were garnered up: for where its treasure is, there shall it be also. It will find its condition evil, more or less, according to the degree of its moral light or darkness, and in proportion to the amount of the darkness will be its incapacity to seek for light. Now, there seems nothing offensive to our notions of the Divine goodness in this conception of what awaits us when the body dies. It appears to me, on the contrary, to offer a more comprehensible and coherent view than any other that has been presented to me; yet the state I have depicted is very much the hades of the Greeks and Romans. It is the middle state, on which all souls enter—a state in which there are many mansions; that is, there are innumerable states—probably not permanent, but ever progressive or retrograde; for we can not conceive of any moral state being permanent, since we know perfectly well that ours is never so; it is always advancing or retroceding. When we are not improving, we are deteriorating; and so it must necessarily be with us hereafter.

Now, if we admit the probability of this middle state, we have removed one of the great objections which are made to the belief in the reappearance of the dead: namely, that the blest are too happy to return to the earth, and that the wicked have it not in their power to do so. This difficulty arises, however, very much from the material ideas entertained of heaven and hell—the notion that they are places instead of states. I am told that the Greek word *hades* is derived from *aides, invisible;* and that the Hebrew word *scheôl*, which has the same signification, also implies a state, not a place, since it may be interpreted into *desiring, longing, asking, praying.* These words in the Septuagint are translated *grave, death*, and *hell;* but previously to the Reformation they seem to have borne their original meaning—that is, the state into which the soul entered at the death of the body. It was probably to get rid of the purgatory of the Roman Church, which had doubtless become the source of many absurd notions and corrupt practices, that the doctrine of a middle state or hades was set aside: besides which, the honest desire for reformation, in all reforming churches, being alloyed by the *odium theologicum*, the purifying besom is apt to take too discursive a sweep, exercising less modesty and discrimination than might be desirable, and thus not uncommonly wiping away truth and falsehood together.

Dismissing the idea, therefore, that heaven and hell are places in which the soul is imprisoned, whether in bliss or wo, and supposing that, by a magnetic relation, it may remain connected with the sphere to which it previously belonged, we may easily conceive that, if it have the memory of the past, the more entirely sensuous its life in the body may have been, the closer it will cling to the scene of its former joys; or even if its sojourn on earth were not a period of joy, but the contrary, still, if it have no heavenward aspirations, it will find itself, if not in actual wo, yet aimless, objectless, and out of a congenial element. It has no longer the organs whereby it perceived, communicated with, and enjoyed, the material world and its pleasures. The joys of heaven are not its joys; we might as well expect a hardened prisoner in Newgate, associating with others as hardened as himself, to melt into ecstatic delight at the idea of that which he can not apprehend! How helpless and inefficient such a condition seems! and how natural it is to us to imagine that, under such circumstances, there might be awakened a considerable desire to manifest itself to those yet living in the flesh, if such a manifestation be possible! And what right have we, in direct contradiction to all tradition, to assert that it is not? We may raise up a variety of objections from physical science, but we can not be sure that these are applicable to the case; and of the laws of spirit we know very little, since we are only acquainted with it as circumscribed, confined, and impeded, in its operations, by the body; and whenever such abnormal states occur as enable it to act with any degree of independence, man, under the dominion of his all-sufficient reason, denies and disowns the facts.

That the manifestation of a spirit to the living, whether seen or heard, is an exception, and not the rule, is evident; for, supposing the desire to exist at all, it must exist in millions and millions of instances which never take effect. The circumstances must therefore no doubt be very peculiar, as regards both parties in which such a manifestation is possible. What these are, we have very little means of knowing; but, as far as we do know, we are led to conclude that a certain magnetic rapport or polarity constitutes this condition, while, at the same time, as regards the seer, there must be what the prophet called the "opening of the eye," which may perhaps signify the seeing of the spirit without the aid of the bodily organ—a condition which may temporarily occur to any one under we know not what influence, but which seems, to a certain degree, hereditary in some families.

The following passage is quoted from Sir William Hamilton's edition of Dr. Reid's works, published in 1846:—

"No man can show it to be impossible to the Supreme Being to have given us the power of perceiving external objects, without any such organs"—that is, our organs of sense. "We have reason to believe that when we put off these bodies, and all the organs belonging to them, our perceptive powers shall rather be improved than destroyed or impaired. We have reason to believe that the Supreme Being perceives everything in a much more perfect manner than we do, without bodily organs. We have reason to believe that there are other created beings endowed with powers of perception more perfect and more extensive than ours, without any such organs as we find necessary;" and Sir William Hamilton adds the following note:—

"However astonishing, it is now proved beyond all rational doubt that in certain abnormal states of the nervous organism, perceptions are possible through other than the ordinary channels of the sense."

Of the existence of this faculty in nature, any one, who chooses, may satisfy himself by a very moderate degree of trouble, provided he undertake the investigation honestly; and this being granted, another objection, if not altogether removed, is considerably weakened. I allude to the fact that, in numerous reported cases of ghost-seeing, the forms were visible to only one person, even though others were present, which, of course, rendered them undistinguishable from cases of spectral illusion, and indeed unless some additional evidence be afforded, they must remain so still, only we have gained thus much, that this objection is no longer unanswerable; for whether the phenomenon is to be referred to a mutual rapport, or to the opening of the spiritual eye, we comprehend how one may see what others do not. But really, if the seeing depended upon ordinary vision, I can not perceive that the difficulty is insurmountable; for we perfectly well know that some people are endowed with an acuteness of sense, or power of perception, which is utterly incomprehensible to others; for, without entering into the disputed region of clear-seeing, everybody must have met with instances of those strange antipathies to certain objects, accompanied by an extraordinary capacity for perceiving their presence, which remain utterly unexplained. Not to speak of cats and hares, where some electrical effects might be conceived, I lately heard of a gentleman who fainted if he were introduced into a room where there was a raspberry tart; and that there have been persons endowed with a faculty for discovering the proximity of water and metals, even without the aid of the divining rod—which latter marvel seems to be now clearly established as an electrical phenomenon—will scarcely admit of further doubt.

A very eminent person, with whom I am acquainted, possessing extremely acute olfactory powers, is the subject of one single exception. He is insensible to the odor of a beanfield, however potent: but it would surely be very absurd in him to deny that the beanfield emits an odor, and the evidence of the majority against him is too strong to admit of his doing so.

Now, we have only the evidence of a minority with regard to the existence of certain faculties not generally developed, but surely it argues great presumption to dispute their possibility. We might, I think, with more appearance of reason, insist upon it that my friend *must* be mistaken, and that he does smell the beanfield, for we have the majority against him there most decidedly. The difference is, that nobody cares whether the odor of the beanfield is perceptible or not: but if the same gentleman asserted that he had seen a ghost, beyond all doubt his word would be disputed.

Though we do not know what the conditions are that develop the faculty of what St. Paul calls the discerning of spirits, there is reason to believe that the approach of death is one. I have heard of too many instances of this kind, where the departing person has been in the entire possession of his or her faculties, to doubt that in our last moments we are frequently visited by those who have gone before us; and it being admitted by all physiologists that preternatural faculties are sometimes exhibited at this period, we can have no right to say that "the discerning of spirits" is not one of them.

There is an interesting story recorded by Beaumont, in his "World of Spirits," and quoted by Dr. Hibbert with the remark that no reasonable doubt can be placed on the authenticity of the narrative, as it was drawn up by the bishop of Gloucester from the recital of the young lady's father; and I mention it here, not for any singularity attending it, but first, because its authenticity is admitted, and next, on account of the manner in which—so much being granted—the fact is attempted to be explained away:—

"Sir Charles Lee, by his first lady, had only one daughter, of which she died in childbirth; and when she was dead, her sister, the Lady Everard, desired to have the education of the child, and she was very well educated till she was marriageable, and a match was concluded for her with Sir W. Parkins, but was then prevented in an extraordinary manner. Upon a Thursday night, she thinking she saw a light in her chamber after she was in bed, knocked for her maid, who presently came to her, and she asked why she left a candle burning in her room. The maid answered that she had left none, and that there was none but what she had brought with her at that time. 'Then,' she said, 'it must be the fire;' but that, her maid told her, was quite out, adding she believed it was only a dream, whereupon Miss Lee answered that it might be so, and composed herself again to sleep. But, about two of the clock, she was awakened again, and saw the apparition of a little woman between her curtains and her pillow, who told her she was her mother, that she was happy, and that, by twelve of the clock that day, she should be with her. Whereupon, she knocked again for her maid, called for her clothes, and when she was dressed, went into her closet, and came not out again till nine, and then brought out with her a letter, sealed, to her father, carried it to her aunt, the Lady Everard, told her what had happened, and desired that as soon as she was dead it might be sent to him. The lady thought she was suddenly fallen mad, and therefore sent presently away to Chelmsford for a physician and surgeon, who both came immediately, but the physician could discern no indication of what the lady imagined, or of any indisposition of her body; notwithstanding, the lady would needs have her let blood, which was done accordingly: and when the young woman had patiently let them do what they would with her, she desired that the chaplain might be called to read prayers; and when the prayers were ended, she took her guitar and psalm-book, and sat down upon a chair without arms, and played and sung so melodiously and admirably, that her music-master, who was then there, admired at it. And near the stroke of twelve, she rose and sat herself down in a great chair with arms, and presently fetching a strong breathing or two, she immediately expired, and was so suddenly cold as was much wondered at by the physician and surgeon. She died at Waltham, in Essex, three miles from Chelmsford, and the letter was sent to Sir Charles, at his house in Warwickshire; but he was so afflicted at the death of his daughter, that he came not till she was buried: but when he came, he caused her to be taken up, and to be buried with her mother, at Edmonton, as she desired in her letter."

This circumstance occurred in the year 1662, and is, as Dr. Hibbert observes, "one of the most interesting ghost-stories on record:" yet he insists on placing it under the category of spectral illusions, upon the plea that, let the physician (whose skill he arraigns) say what he would, her death within so short a period proves that she must have been indisposed at the time she saw the vision, and that probably "the languishing female herself might have unintentionally contributed to the more strict verification of the ghost's prediction," concluding with these words: "All that can be said of it is, that the coincidence was a *fortunate one;* for, without it, the story would probably never have met with a recorder," &c., &c.

Now, I ask if this is a fair way of treating any fact, transmitted to us on authority which the objector himself admits to be perfectly satisfactory — more especially as the assistants on the occasion appear to have been quite as unwilling to believe in the *supernatural* interpretation of it as Dr. Hibbert could have been himself, had he been present; for what more could he have done than conclude the young lady to be mad, and bled her?—a line of practice which is precisely what would be followed at the present time, and which proves that they were very well aware of the sensuous illusions produced by a disordered state of the nervous system; and with respect to his conclusion that the "languishing female" contributed to the verification of the prediction, we are entitled to ask, where is the proof that she was languishing? A very clever watchmaker once told me that a watch may go perfectly well for years, and at length stop suddenly, in consequence of an organic defect in its construction, which only becomes perceptible, even to the eye of a watchmaker, when this effect takes place; and we do know that many persons have suddenly fallen dead immediately after declaring themselves in the best possible health: and we have therefore no right to dispute what the narrator implies, namely, that there were no sensible indications of the impending catastrophe.

There was either some organic defect or derangement in this lady's physical economy, which rendered her death inevitable at the hour of noon, on that particular Thursday, or there was not. If there was, and her certain death was impending at that hour, how came she acquainted with the fact? Surely it is a monstrous assumption to say that it was "a fortunate coincidence," when no reason whatever is given us for concluding that she felt otherwise than perfectly well! If, on the contrary, we are to take refuge in the supposition that there was no death impending, and that she only died of the fright, how came she —feeling perfectly well, and, in this case, we have a right to conclude *being* perfectly well—to be the subject of such an extraordinary spectral illusion? And if such spectral illusions can occur to people in a good normal state of health, does it not become very desirable to give us some clearer theory of them than we have at present?

But there is a third presumption to which the skeptical may have recourse, in order to get rid of this well-established, and therefore very troublesome fact, namely, that Miss Lee *was* ill, although unconscious of it herself, and indicating no symptoms that could guide her physician to an enlightened diagnosis; and that the proof of this is to be found in the occurrence of the spectral illusion; and that this spectral illusion so impressed her that it occasioned the precise fulfilment of the imaginary prediction — an hypothesis which appears to me to be pressing very hard on the spectral illusion; for it is first called upon to establish the fact of an existing indisposition of no slight character, of which neither patient nor physician was aware, and it is next required to kill the lady with unerring certainty, at the hour appointed, she being, according to the only authority we have for the story, in a perfectly calm and composed state of mind! for there is nothing to be discerned in the description of her demeanor but an entire and willing submission to the announced decree, accompanied by that pleasing exaltation, which appears to me perfectly natural under the circumstances; and I do not think that anything we know of human vitality can justify us in believing that life can be so easily extinguished. But to such straits people are reduced, who write with a predetermination to place their facts on a Procrustean bed till they have fitted them into their own cherished theory.

In the above-recorded case of Miss Lee, the motive for the visit is a sufficient one; but one of the commonest objections to such narrations, is the insignificance of the motive when any communication is made, or there being apparently no motive at all, when none is made. Where any previous attachment has subsisted, we need seek no further for an impelling cause; but in other cases this impelling cause must probably be sought in the earthly rapport still subsisting and the urgent desire of the spirit to manifest itself and establish a communication where its thoughts and affections still reside; and we must consider that, provided there be no law of God prohibiting its revisiting the earth, which law would of course supersede all other laws, then, as I have before observed, where its thoughts and affections are it must be also. What is it but our heavy material bodies that prevents us from being where our thoughts are? But the being near us, and the manifesting itself to us, are two very different things, the latter evidently depending on conditions we do not yet understand.

As I am not writing a book on vital magnetism, and there are so many already accessible to everybody who chooses to be informed on it, I shall not here enter into the subject of *magnetic rapport*, it being, I believe, now generally admitted, except by the most obstinate skeptics, that such a relation can be established between two human beings. In what this relation consists, is a more difficult question, but the most rational view appears to be that of a magnetic polarity, which is attempted to be explained by two theories—the dynamical and the ethereal, the one viewing the phenomena as simply the result of the transmission of forces, the other hypothetizing an ether which pervades all space and penetrates all substance, maintaining the connection between body and soul, and between matter and spirit. To most minds this latter hypothesis will be the most comprehensible; on which account, since the result would be the same in either case, we may adopt for the moment; and there will then be less difficulty in conceiving that the influence or ether of every being or thing, animate or inanimate, must extend beyond the periphery of its own terminations: and that this must be eminently the case where there is animal life, the nerves forming the readiest conductors for this supposed imponderable. The proofs of the existence of this ether are said to be manifold, and more especially to be found in the circumstances that every created thing sheds an atmosphere around it, after its kind; this atmosphere becoming, under certain conditions, perceptible or even visible, as in the instances of electric fish, &c., the fascinations of serpents, the influence of human beings upon plants, and *vice versa;* and finally, the phenomena of animal magnetism, and the undoubted fact, to which I myself can bear witness, that the most ignorant girls, when in a state of somnambulism, have been known to declare that they saw their magnetiser surrounded by a halo of light; and it is doubtless this halo of light, that, from their being strongly magnetic men, has frequently been observed to surround the heads of saints and eminently holy persons: the temperament that produced the internal fervor, causing the visible manifestation of it. By means of this ether, or force, a never-ceasing motion and an intercommunication are sustained between all created things, and between created things and their Creator, who sustains them and creates them ever anew, by the constant exertion of his Divine will, of which this is the messenger and the agent as it is between our will and our own bodies; and without this sustaining will, so exerted, the whole would fall away, dissolve, and die; for it is the life of the universe. That all inanimate objects emit an influence, greater or less, extending beyond their own peripheries, is established by their effects on various susceptible individuals, as well as on somnambules; and thus there exist a universal polarity and rapport, which are however stronger between certain organisms; and every being stands in a varying relation of positive and negative to every other.

With regard to these theories, however, where there is so much obscurity even in the language, I do not wish to insist; more especially as I am fully aware that this subject may be discussed in a manner much môre congruous with the dynamical spirit of the philosophy of this century: but, in the meanwhile, as either of the causes alluded to is capable of producing the effects, we adopt the hypothesis of an all-pervading ether as the one most easily conceived.

Admitting this, then, to be the case, we begin to have some notion of the *modus operandi* by which a spirit may manifest itself to us, whether to our internal universal sense, or even to our sensuous organs; and we also find one stumbling-block removed out of our way, namely, that it shall be visible or even audible to one person and not to another, or at one time and not at another; for by means of this ether, or force, we are in communication with all spirit, as well as with all matter; and since it is the vehicle of will, a strong exertion of will may reinforce its influence to a degree far beyond our ordinary conceptions: but man is not acquainted with his own power, and has, consequently, no faith in his own will: nor is it probably the design of Providence, in ordinary cases, that he should. He can not therefore exert it; if he could, he "might remove mountains." Even as it is, we know something of the power of will in its effect on other organisms, as exhibited by certain strong-willed individuals; also in popular movements; and more manifestly in the influence and far-working of the magnetizer on his patient. The power of will, like the seeing of the spirit, is latent in our nature, to be developed in God's own time; but meanwhile, slight examples are found, shooting up here and there, to keep alive in man the consciousness that he is a spirit, and give evidence of his Divine origin.

What especial laws may appertain to this supersensuous domain of nature, of course we can not know, and it is therefore impossible for us to pronounce how far a spirit is free, or not free, at all times to manifest itself; and we can, therefore, at present, advance no reason for these manifestations not being the rule instead of the exception. The law which restrains more frequent intercourse may, for anything we know to the contrary, have its relaxations and its limitations, founded in nature; and a rapport with, or the power of acting on, particular individuals, may arise from causes of which we are equally ignorant. Undoubtedly, the receptivity of the corporeal being is one of the necessary conditions, while, on the part of the incorporeal, the will is at once the cause and the agent that produces the effect; while attachment, whether to individuals or to the lost joys of this world, is the motive. The happy spirits in whom this latter impulse is weak, and who would float away into the glorious light of the pure moral law, would have little temptation to return, and at least would only be brought back by their holy affections, or desire to serve mankind. The less happy, clinging to their dear corporeal life, would hover nearer to the earth; and I do question much whether the often-ridiculed idea of the mystics, that there is a moral *weight*, as well as a moral *darkness*, be not founded in truth. We know very well that even these substantial bodies of ours are, to our own sensations (and, very possibly, if the thing could be tested, would prove to be in fact), lighter or heavier, according to the lightness or heaviness of the spirit—terms used figuratively, but perhaps capable of a literal interpretation; and thus the common idea of *up* and *down*, as applied to heaven or hell, is founded in truth, though not mathematically correct, we familiarly using the words *up* and *down* to express *farther* or *nearer*, as regards the planet on which we live.

Experience seems to justify this view of the case; for, supposing the phenomena I am treating of to be facts, and not spectral illusions, all tradition shows that the spirits most frequently manifested to man have been evidently not in a state of bliss; while, when bright ones appeared it has been to serve him; and hence the old persuasion, that they were chiefly the wicked that haunted the earth, and hence, also, the foundation for the belief that not only the murderer but the murdered returned to vex the living, and the just view, that in taking away life the injury is not confined to the body, but extends to the surprised and angry soul, which is—

> "Cut off, even in the blossom of its sin,
> Unhouselled, disappointed, unaneled;
> No reckoning made, but sent to its account
> With all its imperfections on its head."

It seems also to be gathered from experience, that those whose lives have been rendered wretched, "rest not in their graves;" at least, several accounts I have met with, as well as tradition, countenance this view; and this may originate in the fact that cruelty and ill-usage frequently produce very pernicious effects on the mind of the sufferer, in many instances inspiring, not resignation or a pious desire for death, but resentment, and an eager longing for a fair share of earthly enjoyment. Supposing, also, the feelings and prejudices of the earthly life to accompany this dispossessed soul—for, though the liberation from the body inducts it into certain privileges inherent in spirit, its moral qualities remain as they were ("as the tree falls, so it shall lie")—supposing, therefore, that these feelings, and prejudices, and recollections, of its past life, are carried with it, we see at once why the discontented spirits of the heathen world could not rest till their bodies had obtained sepulture, why the buried money should torment the soul of the miser, and why the religious opinions, whatever they may have been, believed in the flesh, seem to survive with the spirit. There are two remarkable exceptions, however, and these are precisely such as might be expected. Those who, during their corporeal life, have not believed in a future state, return to warn their friends against the same error. "There is another world!" said the brother of the young lady who appeared to her in the cathedral of York, on the day he was drowned; and there are several similar instances recorded. The belief that this life "is the be-all and the end-all here," is a mistake that death must instantly rectify. The other exception I allude to is, that that toleration, of which, unfortunately, we see much less than is desirable in this world, seems happily to prevail in the next; for, among the numerous narrations I meet with, in which the dead have returned to ask the prayers or the services of the living, they do not seem, as will be seen by-and-by, to apply by any means exclusively to members of their own church. The *attrait* which seems to guide their selection of individuals is evidently not of a polemical nature. The pure worship of God, and the inexorable moral law, are what seem to prevail in the other world, and not the dogmatic theology which makes so much of the misery of this.

There is a fundamental truth in all religions: the real end of all is morality, however the means may be mistaken, and however corrupt, selfish, ambitious, and sectarian, the mass of their teachers may and generally do become; while the effect of prayer—in whatever form, or to whatever ideal of the Deity it may be offered, provided that offering be honestly and earnestly made—is precisely the same to the supplicant and in its results.

I have reserved the following story, which is not a fiction, but the relation of an undoubted and well-attested fact, till the present chapter, as being particularly applicable to this branch of my subject:—

Some ninety years ago, there flourished in Glasgow a club of young men, which, from the extreme profligacy of its members, and the licentiousness of their orgies, was commonly called the "Hell-Club!" Besides their nightly or weekly meetings, they held one grand annual saturnalia, in which each tried to excel the other in drunkenness and blasphemy; and on these occasions there was no star among them whose lurid light was more conspicuous than that of young Mr. Archibald B——, who, endowed with brilliant talents and a handsome person, had held out great promise in his boyhood, and raised hopes, which had been completely frustrated by his subsequent reckless dissipations.

One morning, after returning from this annual festival, Mr. Archibald B—— having retired to bed, dreamed the following dream:—

He fancied that he himself was mounted on a favorite black horse, that he always rode, and that he was proceeding toward his own house—then a country-seat embowered by trees, and situated upon a hill, now entirely built over, and forming part of the city—when a stranger, whom the darkness of night prevented his distinctly discerning, suddenly seized his horse's rein, saying, "You must go with me!"

"And who are you?" exclaimed the young man, with a volley of oaths, while he struggled to free himself.

"That you will see by-and-by!" returned the other, in a tone that excited unaccountable terror in the youth, who, plunging his spurs into his horse, attempted to fly. But in vain: however fast the animal flew, the stranger was still beside him, till at length, in his desperate efforts to escape, the rider was thrown; but instead of being dashed to the earth, as he expected, he found himself falling—falling—falling still, as if sinking into the bowels of the earth.

At length, a period being put to this mysterious descent, he found breath to inquire of his companion, who was still beside him, whither they were going: "Where am I? where are you taking me?" he exclaimed.

"To hell!" replied the stranger, and immediately interminable echoes repeated the fearful sound, "To hell!—to hell!—to hell!"

At length a light appeared, which soon increased to a blaze;

but, instead of the cries, and groans, and lamentings, which the terrified traveller expected, nothing met his ear but sounds of music, mirth, and jollity; and he found himself at the entrance of a superb building, far exceeding any he had seen constructed by human hands. Within, too, what a scene! No amusement, employment, or pursuit of man on earth, but was here being carried on with a vehemence that excited his unutterable amazement. "There the young and lovely still swam through the mazes of the giddy dance! There the panting steed still bore his brutal rider through the excitements of the goaded race! There, over the midnight bowl, the intemperate still drawled out the wanton song or maudlin blasphemy! The gambler plied for ever his endless game, and the slaves of Mammon toiled through eternity their bitter task; while all the magnificence of earth paled before that which now met his view!"

He soon perceived that he was among old acquaintances, whom he knew to be dead, and each he observed was pursuing the object, whatever it was, that had formerly engrossed him; when, finding himself relieved of the presence of his unwelcome conductor, he ventured to address his former friend Mrs. D——, whom he saw sitting, as had been her wont on earth, absorbed at loo, requesting her to rest from the game, and introduce him to the pleasures of the place, which appeared to him to be very unlike what he had expected, and, indeed, an extremely agreeable one. But, with a cry of agony, she answered that there was no rest in hell; that they must ever toil on at those very pleasures: and innumerable voices echoed through the interminable vaults, "There is no rest in hell!"—while, throwing open their vests, each disclosed in his bosom an ever-burning flame! These, they said, were the pleasures of hell: their choice on earth was now their inevitable doom! In the midst of the horror this scene inspired, his conductor returned, and at his earnest entreaty, restored him again to earth; but, as he quitted him, he said, "Remember!—in a year and a day we meet again!"

At this crisis of his dream, the sleeper awoke, feverish and ill; and, whether from the effect of his dream, or of his preceding orgies, he was so unwell as to be obliged to keep his bed for several days, during which period he had time for many serious reflections, which terminated in a resolution to abandon the club and his licentious companions altogether.

He was no sooner well, however, than they flocked around him, bent on recovering so valuable a member of their society; and having wrung from him a confession of the cause of his defection, which, as may be supposed, appeared to them eminently ridiculous, they soon contrived to make him ashamed of his good resolutions. He joined them again, resumed his former course of life, and when the annual saturnalia came round, he found himself with his glass in his hand at the table—when the president, rising to make the accustomed speech, began with saying, "Gentlemen, this being leap-year, it is a year and a day since our last anniversary," &c., &c. The words struck upon the young man's ear like a knell; but, ashamed to expose his weakness to the jeers of his companions, he sat out the feast, plying himself with wine even more liberally than usual, in order to drown his intrusive thoughts; till, in the gloom of a winter's morning, he mounted his horse to ride home. Some hours afterward, the horse was found, with his saddle and bridle on, quietly grazing by the roadside, about half way between the city and Mr. B——'s house; while, a few yards off, lay the corpse of his master!

Now, as I have said in introducing this story, it is no fiction: the circumstance happened as here related. An account of it was published at the time, but the copies were bought up by the family. Two or three, however, were preserved, and the narrative has been reprinted.

The dream is evidently of a symbolical character, and accords in a very remarkable degree with the conclusions to be drawn from the sources I have above indicated. The interpretation seems to be, that the evil passions and criminal pursuits which have been indulged in here, become our curse hereafter. I do not mean to imply that the ordinary amusements of life are criminal—far from it. There is no harm in dancing, nor in playing at loo either; but if people make these things the whole business of their lives, and think of nothing else, cultivating no higher tastes, nor forming no higher aspirations, what sort of preparation are they making for another world? I can hardly imagine that anybody would wish to be doing these things to all eternity, the more especially that it is most frequently *ennui* that drives their votaries into excesses, even here; but if they have allowed their minds to be entirely absorbed in such frivolities and trivialities, surely they can not expect that God will, by a miracle, suddenly obliterate these tastes and inclinations, and inspire them with others better suited to their new condition! It was their business to do that for themselves, while here; and such a process of preparation is not in the slightest degree inconsistent with the enjoyment of all manner of harmless pleasures; on the contrary, it gives the greatest zest to them; for a life, in which there is nothing serious—in which all is play and diversion—is, beyond doubt, next to a life of active, persevering wickedness, the saddest thing under the sun! But let everybody remember that we see in nature no violent transitions; everything advances by almost insensible steps—at least everything that is to endure: and therefore to expect that because they have quitted their fleshly bodies, which they always knew were but a temporary appurtenance, doomed to perish and decay, they themselves are to undergo a sudden and miraculous conversion and purification, which is to elevate them into fit companions for the angels of heaven, and the blessed that have passed away, is surely one of the most inconsistent, unreasonable, and pernicious errors, that mankind ever indulged in!

CHAPTER XI.

THE POWER OF WILL.

The power, be it what it may, whether of dressing up an ethereal visible form, or of acting on the constructive imagination of the seer, which would enable a spirit to appear "in his habit as he lived," would also enable him to present any other object to the eye of the seer, or himself in any shape, or fulfilling any function he willed; and we thus find in various instances, especially those recorded in the Seeress of Prevorst, that this is the case. We not only see changes of dress, but we see books, pens, writing materials, &c., in their hands; and we find a great variety of sounds imitated—which sounds are frequently heard, not only by those who have the faculty of "discerning of spirits," as St. Paul says, but also by every other person on the spot, for the hearing these sounds does not seem to depend on any particular faculty on the part of the auditor, except it be in the case of speech. The hearing the speech of a spirit, on the contrary, appears in most instances to be dependent on the same conditions as the seeing it, which may possibly arise from there being, in fact, no *audible* voice at all, but the same sort of spiritual communication which exists between a magnetizer and his patient, wherein the sense is conveyed without words.

This imitating of sounds I shall give several instances of in a future chapter. It is one way in which a death is frequently indicated. I could quote a number of examples of this description, but shall confine myself to two or three.

Mrs. D——, being one night in her kitchen, preparing to go to bed, after the house was shut up and the rest of the family retired, was startled by hearing a foot coming along the passage, which she recognised distinctly to be that of her father, who she was quite certain was not in the house. It advanced to the kitchen-door, and she waited with alarm to see if the door was to open; but it did not, and she heard nothing more. On the following day, she found that her father had died at that time; and it was from her niece I heard the circumstance.

A Mr. J—— S——, belonging to a highly respectable family, with whom I am acquainted, having been for some time in declining health, was sent abroad for change of air. During his absence, one of his sisters, having been lately confined, an old servant of the family was sitting half asleep in an arm-chair, in a room adjoining that in which the lady slept, when she was startled by hearing the foot of Mr. J—— S—— ascending the stairs. It was easily recognisable, for, owing to his constant confinement to the house, in consequence of his infirm health, his shoes were always so dry that their creaking was heard from one end of the house to the other. So far surprised out of her recollection as to forget he was not in the country, the good woman started up, and, rushing out with her candle in her hand, to light him, she followed the steps up to Mr. J—— S——'s own bed-chamber, never discovering that he was not preceding her till she reached the door. She then returned, quite amazed, and having mentioned the occurrence to her mistress, they noted the date; and it was afterward ascertained that the young man had died at Lisbon on that night.

Mrs. F—— tells me that, being one morning, at eleven o'clock, engaged in her bedroom, she suddenly heard a strange, indescribable, sweet, but unearthly sound, which apparently proceeded from a large open box which stood near her. She was seized with an awe and a horror which there seemed nothing to justify, and fled up stairs to mention the circumstance, which she could not banish from her mind. At that precise day and hour, eleven o'clock, her brother was drowned. The news reached her two days afterward.

Instances of this kind are so well known that it is unnecessary to multiply them further. With respect to the mode of producing these sounds, however, I should be glad to say something more definite if I could; but, from the circumstance of their being heard not only by one person, who might be supposed to be *en rapport*, or whose constructive imagination might be acted upon, but by any one who happens to be within hearing, we are led to conclude that the sounds are really reverberating through the atmosphere. In the strange cases recorded in "The Seeress of Prevorst," although the apparitions were visible only to certain persons, the sounds they made were audible to all; and the seeress says they are produced by means of the nervo-spirit, which I conclude is the spiritual body of St. Paul and the atmosphere, as we produce sound by means of our *material* body and the atmosphere.

In this plastic power of the spirit to present to the eye of the seer whatever object it wills, we find the explanation of such stories as the famous one of Ficinus and Mercatus, related by Baronius in his annals. These two illustrious friends, Michael Mercatus and Marcellinus Ficinus, after a long discourse on the nature of the soul, had agreed that, if possible, whichever died first should return to visit the other. Some time afterward, while Mercatus was engaged in study at an early hour in the morning, he suddenly heard the noise of a horse galloping in the street, which presently stopped at his door, and the voice of his friend Ficinus exclaimed: "Oh, Michael! oh, Michael! *vera sunt illa!*—those things are true!" Whereupon Mercatus hastily opened his window and espied his friend Ficinus on a white steed. He called after him, but he galloped away out of his sight. On sending to Florence to inquire for Ficinus, he learned that he had died about that hour he called to him. From this period to that of his death, Mercatus abandoned all profane studies, and addicted himself wholly to divinity. Baronius lived in the sixteenth century; and even Dr. Ferrier and the spectral illusionists admit that the authenticity of this story can not be disputed, although they still claim it for their own.

Not very many years ago, Mr. C——, a staid citizen of Edinburgh—whose son told me the story—was one day riding gently up Corstorphina hill, in the neighborhood of the city, when he observed an intimate friend of his own, on horseback also, immediately behind him; so he slackened his pace to give him an opportunity of joining company. Finding he did not come up so quickly as he should, he looked round again, and was astonished at no longer seeing him, since there was no side road into which he could have disappeared. He returned home, perplexed at the oddness of the circumstance, when the first thing he learned was that during his absence this friend had been killed, by his horse falling, in Candlemaker's row.

I have heard of another circumstance, which occurred some years ago in Yorkshire, where, I think, a farmer's wife was seen to ride into a farm-yard on horseback, but could not be afterward found, or the thing accounted for, till it was ascertained that she had died at that period.

There are very extraordinary stories extant in all countries, of persons being annoyed by appearances in the shape of different animals, which one would certainly be much disposed to give over altogether to the illusionists; though, at the same time, it is very difficult to reduce some of the circumstances under that theory—especially one mentioned page 307 of my "Translation of the Seeress of Prevorst." If they are not illusions, they are phenomena, to be attributed either to this plastic power, or to that magico-magnetic influence in which the belief in lycanthropy and other strange transformations have originated. The multitudes of unaccountable stories of this description recorded in the witch trials, have long furnished a subject of perplexity to everybody who was sufficiently just to human nature to conclude, that there must have been some strange mystery at the bottom of an infatuation that prevailed so universally, and in which so many sensible, honest, and well-meaning persons were involved. Till of late years, when some of the arcana of animal or vital magnetism have been disclosed to us, it was impossible for us to conceive by what means such strange conceptions could prevail; but since we now know, and many of us have witnessed, that all the senses of a patient are frequently in such subjection to his magnetiser, that they may be made to convey any impressions to the brain that magnetiser wills, we can without much difficulty conceive how this belief in the power of transformation took its rise; and we also know how a magician could render himself visible or invisible at pleasure. I have seen the sight or hearing of a patient taken away, and restored by Mr. Spencer Hall in a manner that could leave no doubt on the mind of the beholder—the evident paralysis of the eye of the patient testifying to the fact. Monsieur Eusèbe Salverte, the most determined of rationalistic skeptics, admits that we have numerous testimonies to the existence of an art, which he confesses himself at some loss to explain, although the opposite quarters from which the accounts of it reach us, render it difficult to imagine that the historians have copied each other. The various transformations of the gods into eagles, bulls, &c., have been set down as mere mythological fables; but they appear to have been founded on an art, known in all quarters of the world, which enabled the magician to take on a form that was not his own, so as to deceive his nearest and dearest friends. In the history of Gengis Khan, there is mention of a city which he conquered—"in which dwelt," says Suidas, "certain men, who possessed the secret of surrounding themselves with deceptive appearances, insomuch that they were able to represent themselves to the eyes of people quite different to what they really were." Saxo Grammaticus, in speaking of the traditions connected with the religion of Odin, says that "the magi were very expert in the art of deceiving the eyes, being able to assume, and even to enable others to assume, the forms of various objects, and to conceal their real aspects under the most attractive appearances."

John of Salisbury, who seems to have drawn his information from sources now lost, says that "Mercury, the most expert of magicians, had the art of fascinating the eyes of men to such a degree as to render people invisible, or make them appear in forms quite different to what they really bore. We also learn from an eye-witness that Simon, the magician, possessed the secret of making another person resemble him so perfectly that every eye was deceived. Pomponius Mela affirms that the druidesses of the island of Sena could transform themselves into any animal they chose, and Proteus has become a proverb by his numerous metamorphoses.

Then, to turn to another age and another hemisphere, we find Joseph Acosta, who resided a long time in Peru, assuring us that there existed at that period magicians who had the power of assuming any form they chose. He relates that the predecessor of Montezuma, having sent to arrest a certain chief, the latter successively transformed himself into an eagle, a tiger, and an immense serpent; and so eluded the envoys, till, having consented to obey the king's mandate, he was carried to court and instantly executed.

The same perplexing exploits are confidently attributed to the magicians of the West Indies; and there were two men eminent among the natives, the one called Gomez and the other Gonzalez, who possessed this art in an eminent degree; but both fell victims to the practice of it, being shot during the period of their apparent transformations.

It is also recorded that Nanuk, the founder of the Sikhs—who are not properly a nation, but a religious sect—was violently opposed by the Hindoo zealots; and at one period of his career, when he visited Vatala, the Yogiswaras—who were recluses, that, by means of corporeal mortifications, were supposed to have acquired command over the powers of nature—were so enraged against him, that they strove to terrify him by their enchantments, assuming the shapes of tigers and serpents. But they could not succeed, for Nanuk appears to have been a real philosopher, who taught a pure theism, and inculcated universal peace and toleration. His tenets, like the tenets of the founders of all religions, have been since corrupted by his followers. We can scarcely avoid concluding that the power by which these feats were performed is of the same nature as that by which a magnetiser persuades his patient that the water he drinks is beer, or the beer wine; and the analogy between it and that by which I have supposed a spirit to present himself, with such accompaniments as he desires, to the eye of a spectator, is evident. In those instances where female figures are seen with children in their arm, the appearance of the child we must suppose to be produced in this manner.

Spirits of darkness, however, can not, as I have before observed, appear as spirits of light; the moral nature can not be disguised. On one occasion, when Frederica Hauffe asked a spirit if he could appear in what form he pleased, he answered "No"—that if he had lived as a brute, he should appear as a brute: "as our dispositions are, so we appear to you."

This plastic power is exhibited in those instances I have related, where the figure appeared dripping with water, indicating the kind of death that had been suffered; and also in such cases as that of Sir Robert H. E——, where the apparition showed a wound in his breast. There are a vast number of similar ones on record in all countries;—but I will here mention one which I received from the lips of a member of the family concerned, wherein one of the trivial actions of life was curiously represented.

Miss L—— lived in the country with her three brothers, to whom she was much attached, as they were to her. These young men, who amused themselves all the morning with their out-door pursuits, were in the habit of coming to her apartment most days before dinner, and conversing with her till they were summoned to the dining-room. One day, when two of them had joined her as usual, and they were chatting cheerfully over the fire, the door opened, and the third came in, crossed the room, entered an adjoining one, took off his boots, and then, instead of sitting down beside them as usual, passed again through the room, went out, leaving the door open, and they saw him ascend the stairs toward his own chamber, whither they concluded he was gone to change his dress. These proceedings had been observed by the whole party: they saw him enter—saw him take off his boots—saw him ascend the stairs, —continuing the conversation, without the slightest suspicion of anything extraordinary. Presently afterward the dinner was announced; and as this young man did not make his appearance, the servant was desired to let him know they were waiting for him. The servant answered that he had not come in yet; but, being told that he would find him in his bedroom, he went up stairs to call him. He was, however, not there nor in the house; nor were his boots to be found where he had been seen to take them off. While they were yet wondering what could have become of him, a neighbor arrived to break the news to the family that their beloved brother had been killed while hunting, and that the only wish he expressed was that he could live to see his sister once more.

I observed in a former chapter, while speaking of wraiths, now very desirable it would be to ascertain whether the phenomenon takes place before or after the dissolution of the bond between soul and body: I have since received the most entire satisfaction on that head, so far as the establishing the fact that it does sometimes occur after the dissolution. Three cases have been presented to me, from the most undoubted authority, in which the wraith was seen at intervals varying from one to three days after the decease of the person whose image it was; very much complicating the difficulty of that theory which considers these phenomena the result of an interaction, wherein the vital principle of one person is able to influence another within its sphere, and thus make the organs of that other the subjects of its will—a magical power, by the way, which far exceeds that which we possess over our own organs. There is here, however, where death has taken place, no living organism to produce the effect, and the phenomenon becomes, therefore, purely subjective—a mere spectral illusion, attended by a coincidence, or else the influence is that of the disembodied spirit; and those who will take the trouble of investigating this subject will find that the number of these coincidences would violate any theory of probabilities, to a degree that precludes the acceptance of that explanation. I do not see, therefore, on what we are to fall back, except it be the willing agency of the released spirit, unless we suppose that the operation of the will of the dying person travelled so slowly, that it did not take effect till a day or two after it was exerted—an hypothesis too extravagant to be admitted.

Dr. Passavent, whose very philosophical work on this occult

department of nature is well worth attention, considers the fact of these appearances far too well established to be disputed; and he enters into some curious disquisitions with regard to what the Germans call *far-working*, or the power of acting on bodies at a distance without any sensible conductor, instancing the case of a gymnotus, which was kept alive for four months in Stockholm, and which, when urged by hunger, could kill fish at a distance without contact, adding that it rarely miscalculated the amount of the shock necessary to its purpose. These and all such effects are attributed by this school of physiologists to the supposed imponderable—the nervous ether I have elsewhere mentioned—which Dr. Passavent conceives, in cases of somnambulism, certain sicknesses, and the approach of death, to be less closely united to its material conductors, the nerves, and therefore capable of being more or less detached, and acting at a distance, especially on those with whom relationship, friendship, or love, establishes a rapport, or polarity; and he observes that intervening substances or distance can no more impede this agency than they do the agency of mineral magnetism. And he considers that we must here seek for the explanation of those curious so-called coincidences of pictures falling, and clocks and watches stopping, at the moment of a death, which we frequently find recorded.

With respect to the wraiths, he observes that the more the ether is freed, as by trance or the immediate approach of death, the more easily the soul sets itself in rapport with distant persons; and that thus it either acts magically, so that the seer perceives the real actual body of the person that is acting upon him, or else that he sees the ethereal body, which presents the perfect form of the fleshly one, and which, while the organic life proceeds, can be momentarily detached and appear elsewhere; and this ethereal body he holds to be the fundamental form, of which the external body is only the copy, or husk.

I confess, I much prefer this theory of Dr. Passavent's, which seems to me to go very much to the root of the matter. We have here the "spiritual body" of St. Paul, and the "nerve-spirit" of the somnambulists, and their magical effects are scarcely more extraordinary, if properly considered, than their agency on our own *material* bodies. It is this ethereal body which obeys the intelligent spirit within, and which is the intermediate agent between the spirit and the fleshly body. We here find the explanation of wraiths, while persons are in trance, or deep sleep, or comatose, this ethereal body can be detached and appear elsewhere; and I think there can be no great difficulty for those who can follow us so far, to go a little further, and admit that this ethereal body must be indestructible, and survive the death of the material one; and that it may, therefore, not only become visible to us under given circumstances, but that it may, also, produce effects bearing some similarity to those it was formerly capable of, since, in acting on our bodies during life, it is already acting on a material substance in a manner so incomprehensible to us, that we might well apply the word *magical* when speaking of it, were it not that custom has familiarized us to the marvel.

It is to be observed, that this idea of a spiritual body is one that pervaded all Christendom in the earlier and purer ages of Christianity, before priestcraft—and by priestcraft I mean the priestcraft of all denominations—had overshadowed and obscured, by its various sectarian heresies, the pure teaching of Jesus Christ.

Dr. Ennemoser mentions a curious instance of this *actio in distans*, or far-working. It appears that Van Helmont having asserted that it was possible for a man to extinguish the life of an animal by the eye alone (*oculis intentis*), Rousseau, the naturalist, repeated the experiment, when in the East, and in this manner killed several toads; but on a subsequent occasion, while trying the same experiment at Lyons, the animal, on finding it could not escape, fixed its eyes immovably on him, so that he fell into a fainting fit, and was thought to be dead. He was restored by means of theriacum and viper powder—a truly homeopathic remedy! However, we here probably see the origin of the universal popular persuasion, that there is some mysterious property in the eye of a toad; and also of the, so called, superstition of the *evil eye*.

A very remarkable circumstance occurred some years ago, at Kirkaldy, when a person, for whose truth and respectability I can vouch, was living in the family of a Colonel M——, at that place. The house they inhabited was at one extremity of the town, and stood in a sort of paddock. One evening when Colonel M—— had dined out, and there was nobody at home but Mrs. M——, her son (a boy about twelve years old), and Ann the, maid (my informant), Mrs. M—— called the latter, and directed her attention to a soldier, who was walking backward and forward in the drying ground, behind the house, where some linen was hanging on the lines. She said she wondered what he could be doing there, and bade Ann fetch in the linen, lest he should purloin any of it. The girl, fearing he might be some ill-disposed person, felt afraid; Mrs. M——, however, promising to watch from the window, that nothing happened to her, she went; but still apprehensive of the man's intentions, she turned her back toward him, and hastily pulling down the linen, she carried it into the house; he continuing his walk the while, as before, taking no notice of her whatever. Ere long the colonel returned, and Mrs. M—— lost no time in taking him to the window to look at the man, saying she could not conceive what he could mean by walking backward and forward there all that time; whereupon Ann added, jestingly, "I think it 's a ghost, for my part!" Colonel M—— said "he would soon see that," and calling a large dog that was lying in the room, and accompanied by the little boy, who begged to be permitted to go also, he stepped out and approached the stranger; when, to his surprise, the dog, which was an animal of high courage, instantly flew back, and sprung through the glass-door, which the colonel had closed behind him, shivering the panes all around.

The colonel, meantime, advanced and challenged the man, repeatedly, without obtaining any answer or notice whatever, till, at length, getting irritated, he raised a weapon with which he had armed himself, telling him he "must speak or take the consequences," when, just as he was preparing to strike, lo! there was nobody there! The soldier had disappeared, and the child sunk senseless to the ground. Colonel M—— lifted the boy in his arms, and as he brought him into the house, he said to the girl, "You are right, Ann; it *was* a ghost!" He was exceedingly impressed with this circumstance, and much regretted his own behavior, and also the having taken the child with him, which he thought had probably prevented some communication that was intended. In order to repair, if possible, these errors, he went out every night, and walked on that spot for some time, in hopes the apparition would return. At length he said that he had seen and conversed with it; but the purport of the conversation he would never communicate to any human being, not even to his wife. The effect of this occurrence on his own character was perceptible to everybody that knew him. He became grave and thoughtful, and appeared like one who had passed through some strange experience. The above-named Ann H——, from whom I have the account, is now a middle-aged woman. When the circumstance occurred, she was about twenty years of age. She belongs to a highly-respectable family, and is, and always has been, a person of unimpeachable character and veracity.

In this instance, as in several others I meet with, the animal had a consciousness of the nature of the appearance, while the persons around him had no suspicion of anything unusual. In the following singular case we must conclude that attachment counteracted this instinctive apprehension. A farmer in Argyleshire lost his wife, and a few weeks after her decease, as he and his son were crossing a moor, they saw her sitting on a stone, with their house-dog lying at her feet, exactly as he used to do when she was alive. As they approached the spot the woman vanished, and supposing the dog must be equally visionary, they expected to see him vanish, also; when, to their surprise, he rose and joined them, and they found it was actually the very animal of flesh and blood. As the place was at least three miles from any house, they could not conceive what could have taken him there. It was, probably, the influence of her will.

The power of *will* is a phenomenon that has been observed

in all ages of the world, though of late years much less than at an earlier period; and, as it was then more frequently exerted for evil than good, it was looked upon as a branch of the art of black magic, while the philosophy of it being unknown, the devil was supposed to be the real agent, and the witch, or wizard, only his instrument. The profound belief in the existence of this art is testified by the twelve tables of Rome, as well as by the books of Moses, and those of Plato, &c. It is extremely absurd to suppose that all these statutes were enacted to suppress a crime which never existed: and, with regard to these witches and wizards, we must remember, as Dr. Ennemoser justly remarks, that the force of will has no relation to the strength or weakness of the body: witness the extraordinary feats occasionally performed by feeble persons under excitement, &c.; and, although these witches and wizards were frequently weak, decrepit people, they either believed in their own arts, or else that they had a friend or coadjutor in the devil, who was able and willing to aid them. They, therefore, did not doubt their own power, and they had the one great requisite, *faith.* To *will and to believe,* was the explanation given by the Marquis de Puységur of the cures he performed; and this unconsciously becomes the recipe of all such men as Greatrix, the Shepherd of Dresden, and many other wonder-workers, and hence we see why it is usually the humble, the simple and the child-like, the solitary, the recluse, nay, the ignorant, who exhibit traces of these occult faculties; for he who can not believe can not *will,* and the skepticism of the intellect disables the magician; and hence we say, also, wherefore, in certain parts of the world and in certain periods of its history, these powers and practices have prevailed. They were believed in because they existed; and they existed because they were believed in. There was a continued interaction of cause and effect—of faith and works. People who look superficially at these things, delight in saying that the more the witches were persecuted the more they abounded; and that when the persecution ceased we heard no more of them. Naturally, the more they were persecuted the more they believed in witchcraft and in themselves; when persecution ceased, and men in authority declared that there was no such thing as witchcraft or witches, they lost their faith, and with it that little sovereignty over nature that that faith had conquered.

Here we also see an explanation of the power attributed to blessings and curses. The Word of God is creative, and man is the child of God, made in his image; who never outgrows his childhood, and is often most a child when he thinks himself the wisest, for "the wisdom of this world," we can not too often repeat, "is foolishness before God"—and being a child, his faculties are feeble in proportion; but though limited in amount, they are divine in kind, and are latent in all of us; still shooting up here and there, to amaze and perplex the wise, and make merry the foolish, who have nearly all alike forgotten their origin, and disowned their birthright.

CHAPTER XII.

TROUBLED SPIRITS.

A VERY curious circumstance, illustrative of the power of will, was lately narrated to me by a Greek gentleman, to whose uncle it occurred. His uncle, Mr. M——, was some years ago travelling in Magnesia with a friend, when they arrived one evening at a caravanserai, where they found themselves unprovided with anything to eat. It was therefore agreed that one should go forth and endeavor to procure food; and the friend offering to undertake the office, Mr. M—— stretched himself on the floor to repose. Some time had elapsed, and his friend had not yet returned, when his attention was attracted by a whispering in the room. He looked up, but saw nobody, though still the whispering continued, seeming to go round by the wall. At length it approached him; but though he felt a burning sensation on his cheek, and heard the whispering distinctly, he could not catch the words. Presently he heard the footsteps of his friend, and thought he was returning; but though they appeared to come quite close to him, and it was perfectly light, he still saw nobody. Then he felt a strange sensation—an irresistible impulse to rise: he felt himself *drawn up*, across the room, out of the door, down the stairs—he must go, he could not help it—to the gate of the caravanserai, a little farther; and there he found the dead body of his friend, who had been suddenly assailed and cut down by robbers, unhappily too plenty in the neighborhood at that period.

We here see the desire of the spirit to communicate his fate to the survivor; the imperfection of the rapport, or the receptivity, which prevented a more direct intercourse; and the exertion of a magnetic influence, which Mr. M—— could not resist, precisely similar to that of a living magnetizer over his patient.

There is a story extant in various English collections, the circumstances of which are said to have occurred about the middle of the last century, and which I shall here mention, on account of its similarity to the one that follows it.

Dr. Bretton, who was, late in life, appointed rector of Ludgate, lived previously in Herefordshire, where he married the daughter of Dr. Santer, a woman of great piety and virtue. This lady died; and one day, as a former servant of hers—to whom she had been attached, and who had since married—was nursing her child in her own cottage, the door opened, and a lady entered so exactly resembling the late Mrs. Bretton in dress and appearance, that she exclaimed: "If my mistress were not dead, I should think you were she!" Whereupon the apparition told her that she was, and requested her to go with her, as she had business of importance to communicate. Alice objected, being very much frightened, and entreated her to address herself rather to Dr. Bretton; but Mrs. B. answered that *she had endeavored to do so, and had been several times in his room for that purpose, but he was still asleep, and she had no power to do more toward awakening him than once uncover his feet.* Alice then pleaded that she had nobody to leave with her child; but Mrs. B. promising that the child should sleep till her return, she at length obeyed the summons; and having accompanied the apparition into a large field, the latter bade her observe how much she measured off with her feet, and, having taken a considerable compass, she bade her go and tell her brother that all that portion had been wrongfully taken from the poor by their father, and that he must restore it to them, adding that she was the more concerned about it, since her name had been used in the transaction. Alice then asking how she should satisfy the gentleman of the truth of her mission, Mrs. B. mentioned to her some circumstance known only to herself and this brother; she then entered into much discourse with the woman, and gave her a great deal of good advice, remaining till, hearing the sound of horse-bells, she said: "Alice, I must be seen by none but yourself," and then disappeared. Whereupon Alice proceeded to Dr. Bretton, who admitted that he had actually heard some one walking about his room, in a way he could not account for. On mentioning the thing to the brother, he laughed heartily, till Alice communicated the secret which constituted her credentials, upon which he changed his tone, and declared himself ready to make the required restitution.

Dr. Bretton seems to have made no secret of this story, but to have related it to various persons; and I think it is somewhat in its favor, that it exhibits a remarkable instance of the various degrees of receptivity of different individuals, where there was no suspicion of the cause, nor any attempt made to explain why Mrs. Bretton could not communicate her wishes to her husband as easily as to Alice. The promising that the child should sleep, was promising no more than many a magnetiser could fulfil. There are several curious stories extant, of lame and suffering persons suddenly recovering, who attributed their restoration to the visit of an apparition which had stroked their limbs, &c.; and these are the more curious from the fact that they occurred before Mesmer's time, when people in general knew nothing of vital magnetism. Dr. Binns quotes the case of a person named Jacob Olaffson, a resident in some small island subject to Denmark, who, after lying very ill for a fortnight, was found quite well, which he accounted for by saying that a person in shining clothes had come to him in the night and stroked him with his hand, whereupon he was presently healed. But the stroking is not always necessary, since we know that the eye and the will can produce the same effect.

The other case to which I alluded, as similar to that of Mrs. Bretton, occurred in Germany, and is related by Dr. Kerner.

The late Mr. L—— St. ——, he says, quitted this world with an excellent reputation, being at the time superintendent of an institution for the relief of the poor in B——. His son inherited his property, and, in acknowledgment of the faithful services of his father's old housekeeper, he took her into his family and established her in a country house, a few miles from

B——, which formed part of his inheritance. She had been settled there but a short time, when she was awakened in the night, she knew not how, and saw a tall, haggard-looking man in her room, who was rendered visible to her by a light that seemed to issue from himself. She drew the bedclothes over her head; but, as this apparition appeared to her repeatedly, she became so much alarmed that she mentioned it to her master, begging permission to resign her situation. He however laughed at her—told her it must be all imagination—and promised to sleep in the adjoining apartment, in order that she might call him whenever this terror seized her. He did so; but, when the spectre returned, she was so much oppressed with horror that she found it impossible to raise her voice. Her master then advised her to inquire the motive of its visits. This she did: whereupon, it beckoned her to follow, which, after some struggles, she summoned resolution to do. It then led the way down some steps to a passage, where it pointed out to her a concealed closet, which it signified to her, by signs, she should open. She represented that she had no key: whereupon, it described to her, in sufficiently articulate words, where she would find one. She procured the key, and, on opening the closet, found a small parcel, which the spirit desired her to remit to the governor of the institution for the poor, at B——, with the injunction that the contents should be applied to the benefit of the inmates,—this restitution being the only means whereby he could obtain rest and peace in the other world. Having mentioned these circumstances to her master, who bade her do what she had been desired, she took the parcel to the governor and delivered it, without communicating by what means it had come into her hands. Her name was entered in their books and she was dismissed; but, after she was gone, they discovered to their surprise that the packet contained an order for thirty thousand florins, of which the late Mr. St. —— —— had defrauded the institution and converted to his own use.

Mr. St. ——, jr., was now called upon to pay the money, which he refusing to do, the affair was at length referred to the authorities; and the housekeeper being arrested, he and she were confronted in the court, where she detailed the circumstances by which the parcel had come into her possession. Mr. St. —— denied the possibility of the thing, declaring the whole must be, for some purpose or other, an invention of her own. Suddenly, while making this defence, he felt a blow upon his shoulder, which caused him to start and look round, and at the same moment the housekeeper exclaimed: "See! there he stands, now—there is the ghost!" None perceived the figure excepting the woman herself and Mr. St. ——; but everybody present heard the following words: "My son, repair the injustice I have committed, that I may be at peace!" The money was paid; and Mr. St. —— was so much affected by this painful event, that he was seized with a severe illness, from which he with difficulty recovered.

Dr. Kerner says that these circumstances occurred in the year 1816, and created a considerable sensation at the time, though, at the earnest request of the family of Mr. St. ——, there was an attempt made to hush them up; adding, that in the month of October, 1819, he was himself assured by a very respectable citizen of B——, that it was universally known in the town that the ghost of the late superintendent had appeared to the housekeeper, and pointed out to her where she would find the packet; that she had consulted the minister of her parish, who bade her deliver it as directed; that she had been subsequently arrested, and the affair brought before the authorities, where, while making his defence, Mr. St. —— had received a blow from an invisible hand; and that Mr. St. —— was so much affected by these circumstances, which got abroad in spite of the efforts to suppress them, that he did not long survive the event.

Grose, the antiquary, makes himself very merry with the observation that ghosts do not go about their business like other people; and that in cases of murder, instead of going to the nearest justice of peace, or to the nearest relation of the deceased, a ghost addresses itself to somebody who had nothing to do with the matter, or hovers about the grave where its body is deposited. "The same circuitous mode is pursued," he says, "with respect to redressing injured orphans or widows; where it seems as if the shortest and most certain way would be to go and haunt the person guilty of the injustice, till he were terrified into restitution." We find the same sort of strictures made on the story of the ghost of Sir George Villiers, which—instead of going directly to his son, the duke of Buckingham, to warn him of his danger—addressed himself to an inferior person; while the warning was, after all, inefficacious, as the duke would not take counsel;—but surely such strictures are as absurd as the conduct of the ghost: at least I think there can be nothing more absurd than pretending to prescribe laws to nature, and judging of what we know so little about.

The proceedings of the ghost in the following case will doubtless be equally displeasing to the critics. The account is extracted verbatim from a work published by the Bannatyñe Club, and is entitled, "Authentic Account of the Appearance of a Ghost in Queen Ann's County, Maryland, United States of North America, proved in the following remarkable trial, from attested notes taken in court at the time by one of the counsel."

It appears that Thomas Harris had made some alteration in the disposal of his property, immediately previous to his death; and that the family disputed tho will and raised up difficulties likely to be injurious to his children.

"William Brigs said, that he was forty-three years of age; that Thomas Harris died in September, in the year 1790. In the March following he was riding near the place where Thomas Harris was buried, on a horse formerly belonging to Thomas Harris. After crossing a small branch, his horse began to walk on very fast. It was between the hours of eight and nine o'clock in the morning. He was alone: it was a clear day. He entered a lane adjoining to the field where Thomas Harris was buried. His horse suddenly wheeled in a panel of the fence, looked over the fence into the field where Thomas Harris was buried, and neighed very loud. Witness then saw Thomas Harris coming toward him, in the same apparel he had last seen him in in his lifetime; he had on a sky-blue coat. Just before he came to the fence, he varied to the right and vanished; his horse immediately took the road. Thomas Harris came within two panels of the fence to him; he did not see his features, nor speak to him. He was acquainted with Thomas Harris when a boy, and there had always been a great intimacy between them. He thinks the horse knew Thomas Harris, because of his neighing, pricking up his ears, and looking over the fence.

"About the first of June following, he was ploughing in his own field, about three miles from where Thomas Harris was buried. About dusk Thomas Harris came alongside of him, and walked with him about two hnndred yards. He was dressed as when first seen. He made a halt about two steps from him. J. Bailey who was ploughing along with him, came driving up, and he lost sight of the ghost. He was much alarmed: not a word was spoken. The young man Bailey did not see him; he did not tell Bailey of it. There was no motion of any particular part: he vanished. It preyed upon his mind so as to affect his health. He was with Thomas Harris when he died, but had no particular conversation with him. Some time after, he was lying in bed, about eleven and twelve o'clock at night, when he heard Thomas Harris groan; it was like the groan he gave a few minutes before he expired: Mrs. Brigs, his wife, heard the groan. She got up and searched the house: he did not, because he knew the groan to be from Thomas Harris. Some time after, when in bed, and a great fire-light in the room, he saw a shadow on the wall, and at the same time he felt a great weight upon him. Some time after, when in bed and asleep, he felt a stroke between his eyes, which blackened them both: his wife was in bed with him, and two young men were in the room. The blow awaked him, and all in the room were asleep; is certain no one in the room struck him: the blow swelled his nose. About the middle of August he was alone, coming from Hickey Collins's, after dark, about one hour in the night, when Thomas Harris appeared, dressed as he had seen him when going down to the meeting-house branch, three miles and a half from the graveyard of Thomas Harris. It was starlight. He extended his arms over his shoulders. Does not know how long he remained in this situation. He was much alarmed. Thomas Harris disappeared. Nothing was said. He felt no weight on his shoulders. He went back to Collins's, and got a young man to go with him. After he got home he mentioned it to the young man. He had, before this, told James Harris he had seen his brother's ghost.

"In October, about twilight in the morning, he saw Thomas Harris about one hundred yards from the house of the witness; his head was leaned to one side; same apparel as before; his face was toward him; he walked fast and disappeared: there was nothing between them to obstruct the view; he was about fifty yards from him, and alone; he had no conception why Thomas Harris appeared to him. On the same day, about eight o'clock in the morning, he was handing up blades to John Bailey, who was stacking them; he saw Thomas Harris come along the garden fence, dressed as before; he vanished, and always to the east; was within fifteen feet of him; Bailey did not see him. An hour and a half afterward, in the same place, he again appeared, coming as before; came up to the fence; leaned on it within ten feet of the witness, who called to Bailey to look there (pointing toward Thomas Harris). Bailey asked what was there. Don't you see Harris? Does not recollect what Bailey said. Witness advanced toward Harris. One or the other spoke as witness got over the fence on the same panel that Thomas Harris was leaning on. They walked off together about five hundred yards; a conversation took place as they walked; he has not the conversation on his memory. He could not understand Thomas Harris, his voice was so low. He asked Thomas Harris a question, and he forbid him. Witness then asked, 'Why not go to your brother, instead of me?' Thomas Harris said, 'Ask me no questions.' Witness told him his will was doubted. Thomas Harris told him to ask his brother if he did not remember the conversation which passed between them on the east side of the wheat-stacks, the day he was taken with his death-sickness; that he then declared that he wished all his property kept together by James Harris, until his children arrived at age, then the whole should be sold and divided among his children; and, should it be immediately sold, as expressed in his will, that the property would be most wanting to his children while minors, therefore he had changed his will, and said that witness should see him again. He then told witness to turn, and disappeared. He did not speak to him with the same voice as in his lifetime. He was not daunted while with Thomas Harris, but much afterward. Witness then went to James Harris and told him that he had seen his brother three times that day. Related the conversation he had with him. Asked James Harris if he remembered the conversation between him and his brother, at the wheat-stack; he said he did; then told him what had passed. Said he would fulfil his brother's will. He was satisfied that witness had seen his brother, for that no other person knew the conversation. On the same evening, returning home about an hour before sunset, Thomas Harris appeared to him, and came alongside of him. Witness told him that his brother said he would fulfil his will. No more conversation on this subject. He disappeared. He had further conversation with Thomas Harris, but not on this subject. He was always dressed in the same manner. He had never related to any person the last conversation, and never would.

"Bailey, who was sworn in the cause, declared that as he and Brigs were stacking blades, as related by Brigs, he called to witness and said, 'Look there! Do you not see Thomas Harris?' Witness said, 'No.' Brigs got over the fence, and walked some distance—appeared by his action to be in deep conversation with some person. Witness saw no one.

"The counsel was extremely anxious to hear from Mr. Brigs the whole of the conversation of the ghost, and on his cross-examination took every means, without effect, to obtain it. They represented to him, as a religious man, he was bound to disclose the whole truth. He appeared agitated when applied to, declaring nothing short of life should make him reveal the whole conversation, and, claiming the protection of the court, that he had declared all he knew relative to the case.

"The court overruled the question of the counsel. Hon. James Tilgman, judge.

"His excellency Robert Wright, late governor of Maryland, and the Hon. Joseph H. Nicholson, afterward judge of one of the courts in Maryland, were the counsel for the plaintiff.

"John Scott and Richard T. Earl, Esqs., were counsel for the defendant."

Here, as in the case of Col. M——, mentioned in a former chapter, and some others I have met with, we find disclosures made that were held sacred.

Dr. Kerner relates the following singular story, which he declares himself to have received from the most satisfactory authority. Agnes B——, being at the time eighteen years of age, was living as servant in a small inn at Undenheim, her native place. The host and hostess were quiet old people, who generally went to bed about eight o'clock, while she and the boy, the only other servant, were expected to sit up till ten, when they had to shut up the house and retire to bed also. One evening, as the host was sitting on a bench before the door, there came a beggar, requesting a night's lodging. The host, however, refused, and bade him seek what he wanted in the village; whereon the man went away.

At the usual hour the old people went to bed; and the two servants, having closed the shutters, and indulged in a little gossip with the watchman, were about to follow their example, when the beggar came round the corner of the neighboring street, and earnestly entreated them to give him a lodging for the night, since he could find nobody that would take him in. At first the young people refused, saying they dared not, without their master's leave; but at length the entreaties of the man prevailed, and they consented to let him sleep in the barn, on condition that, when they called him in the morning, he would immediately depart. At three o'clock they rose, and when the boy entered the barn, to his dismay, he found that the old man had expired in the night. They were now much perplexed with the apprehension of their master's displeasure; so, after some consultation, they agreed that the lad should convey the body out of the barn, and lay it in a dry ditch that was near at hand, where it would be found by the laborers, and excite no question, as they would naturally conclude he had laid himself down there to die.

This was done, the man was discovered and buried, and they thought themselves well rid of the whole affair; but, on the following night, the girl was awakened by the beggar, whom she saw standing at her bedside. He looked at her, and then quitted the room by the door. "Glad was I," she says, "when the day broke; but I was scarcely out of my room when the boy came to me, trembling and pale, and, before I could say a word to him of what I had seen, he told me that the beggar had been to his room in the night, had looked at him, and then gone away. He said he was dressed as when we had seen him alive, only he looked blacker, which I also had observed."

Still afraid of incurring blame, they told nobody, although the apparition returned to them every night; and although they found removing to the other bedchambers did not relieve them from his visits. But the effects of this persecution became so visible on both, that much curiosity was awakened in the village with respect to the cause of the alteration observed in them; and at length the boy's mother went to the minister, requesting him to interrogate her son, and endeavor to discover what was preying on his mind. To him the boy disclosed their secret; and this minister, who was a protestant, having listened with attention to the story, advised him, when next he went to Mayence, to market, to call on Father Joseph, of the Franciscan convent, and relate the circumstance to him. This advice was followed; and Father Joseph, assuring the lad that the ghost could do him no harm, recommended him to ask him, in the name of God, what he desired. The boy did so; whereupon the apparition answered, "Ye are children of mercy, but I am a child of evil; in the barn, under the straw, you will find my money. Take it; it is yours." In the morning, the boy found the money accordingly, in an old stocking hid under the straw; but having a natural horror of it, they took it to their minister, who advised them to divide it into three parts, giving one to the

Franciscan convent at Mayence, another to the reformed church in the village, and the other third to that to which they themselves belonged, which was of the Lutheran persuasion. This they did, and were no more troubled with the beggar. With respect to the minister who gave them this good advice, I can only say, all honor be to him! I wish there were many more such! The circumstance occurred in the year 1750, and is related by the daughter of Agnes B——, who declared that she had frequently heard it from her mother.

The circumstance of this apparition looking darker than the man had done when alive, is significant of his condition, and confirms what I have said above, namely, that the moral state of the disembodied soul can no longer be concealed as it was in the flesh, but that as he is, he must necessarily appear.

There is an old saying, that we should never lie down to rest at enmity with any human being; and the story of the ghost of the Princess Anna of Saxony, who appeared to Duke Christian of Saxe-Eisenburg, is strongly confirmatory of the wisdom of this axiom.

Duke Christian was sitting one morning in his study, when he was surprised by a knock at his door—an unusual circumstance, since the guards as well as the people in waiting were always in the ante-room. He, however, cried, "Come in!" when there entered, to his amazement, a lady in an ancient costume, who, in answer to his inquiries, told him that she was no evil spirit, and would do him no harm; but that she was one of his ancestors, and had been the wife of Duke John Casimer, of Saxe-Coburg. She then related that she and her husband had not been on good terms at the period of their deaths, and that, although she had sought a reconciliation, he had been inexorable; pursuing her with unmitigated hatred, and injuring her by unjust suspicions; and that, consequently, although *she* was happy, *he* was still wandering in cold and darkness, between time and eternity. She had, however, long known that one of their descendants was destined to effect this reconciliation for them, and they were rejoiced to find the time for it had at length arrived. She then gave the duke eight days to consider if he were willing to perform this good office, and disappeared; whereupon he consulted a clergyman, in whom he had great confidence, who, after finding the ghost's communication verified, by a reference to the annals of the family, advised him to comply with her request.

As the duke had yet some difficulty in believing it was really a ghost he had seen, he took care to have his door well watched; she, however, entered at the appointed time, unseen by the attendants, and, having received the duke's promise, she told him she would return with her husband on the following night; for that, though she could come by day, he could not; that then, having heard the circumstances, the duke must arbitrate between them, and then unite their hands, and bless them. The door was still watched, but nevertheless the apparitions both came, the Duke Casimer in full royal costume, but of a livid paleness; and when the wife had told her story, he told his. Duke Christian decided for the lady, in which judgment Duke Casimer fully acquiesced. Christian then took the ice-cold hand of Casimer and laid it in that of his wife, which felt of a natural heat. They then prayed and sang together, and the apparitions disappeared, having foretold that Duke Christian would ere long be with them. The family records showed that these people had lived about one hundred years before Duke Christian's time, who himself died in 1707, two years after these visits of his ancestors. He desired to be buried in quick-lime —it is supposed from an idea that it might prevent his ghost walking the earth.

The costume in which they appeared was precisely that they had worn when alive, as was ascertained by a reference to their portraits.

The expression that her husband was *wandering in cold and darkness, between time and eternity*, is here very worthy of observation, as are the circumstances that his hand was cold, while hers was warm; and also, the greater privilege she seemed to enjoy. The hands of the unhappy spirits appear, I think, invariably to communicate a sensation of cold.

I have heard of three instances of persons now alive, who

declare that they hold continual intercourse with their deceased partners. One of these is a naval officer, whom the anthor of a book lately published, called "The Unseen World," appears to be acquainted with. The second is a professor in a college in America, a man of eminence and learning, and full of activity and energy — yet he assured a friend of mine that he receives constant visits from his departed wife, which afford him great satisfaction. The third example is a lady in this country. She is united to a second husband, has been extremely happy in both marriages, and declares that she receives frequent visits from her first. Oberlin, the good pastor of *Ban de la Roche*, asserted the same thing of himself. His wife came to him frequently after her death; was seen by the rest of his household, as well as himself; and warned him beforehand of many events that occurred.

Mrs. Mathews relates in the memoirs of her husband, that he was one night in bed and unable to sleep, from the excitement that continues some time after acting, when, hearing a rustling by the side of the bed, he looked out, and saw his first wife, who was then dead, standing by the bedside, dressed as when alive. She smiled, and bent forward as if to take his hand; but in his alarm he threw himself out on the floor to avoid the contact, and was found by the landlord in a fit. On the same night, and at the same hour, the present Mrs. Mathews, who was far away from him, received a similar visit from her predecessor, whom she had known when alive. She was quite awake, and in her terror seized the bell-rope to summon assistance, which gave way, and she fell with it in her hand to the ground.

Professor Barthe, who visited Oberlin in 1824, says, that while he spoke of his intercourse with the spiritual world as familiarly as of the daily visits of his parishioners, he was at the same time perfectly free from fanaticism, and eagerly alive to all the concerns of this earthly existence. He asserted, what I find many somnambules and deceased persons also assert, that everything on earth is but a copy, of which the antitype is to be found in the other.

He said to his visiter, that he might as well attempt to persuade him that that was not a table before them, as that he did not hold communication with the other world. "I give you credit for being honest when you assure me that you never saw anything of the kind," said he; "give me the same credit when I assure you that I do."

With respect to the faculty of ghost-seeing, he said, it depends on several circumstances, external and internal. People who live in the bustle and glare of the world seldom see them, while those who live in still, solitary, thinly-inhabited places, like the mountainous districts of various countries, do. So if I go into the forest by night, I see the phosphoric light of a piece of rotten wood; but if I go by day I can not see it; yet it is still there. Again, there must be a rapport. A tender mother is awakened by the faintest cry of her infant, while the maid slumbers on and never hears it; and if I thrust a needle among a parcel of wood-shavings, and hold a magnet over them, the needle is stirred while the shavings are quite unmoved. There must be a particular aptitude; what it consists in I do not know; for of my people, many of whom are ghost-seers, some are weak and sickly, others vigorous and strong. Here are several pieces of flint: I can see no difference in them; yet some have so much iron in them that they easily become magnetic; others have little or none. So it is with the faculty of ghost-seeing. People may laugh as they will, but the thing is a fact, nevertheless.

The visits of his wife continued for nine years after her death, and then ceased.

At length she sent him a message, through another deceased person, to say that she was now elevated to a higher state, and could therefore no longer revisit the earth.

Never was there a purer spirit, nor a more beloved human being, than Oberlin. When first he was appointed to the curé of Ban de la Roche, and found his people talking so familiarly of the reappearance of the dead, he reproved them and preached against the superstition; nor was he convinced, till after the death of his wife. She had, however, previously received a visit from her deceased sister, the wife of Professor Oberlin, of

Strasburg, who had warned her of her approaching death, for which she immediately set about preparing, making extra clothing for her children, and even laying in provision for the funeral feast. She then took leave of her husband and family, and went quietly to bed. On the following morning she died; and Oberlin never heard of the warning she had received, till she disclosed it to him in her spectral visitations.

In narrating the following story, I am not permitted to give the names of the place or parties, nor the number of the regiment, with all of which, however, I am acquainted. The account was taken down by one of the officers, with whose family I am also acquainted; and the circumstance occurred within the last ten years.

"About the month of August," says Captain E——, "my attention was requested by the schoolmaster-sergeant, a man of considerable worth, and highly esteemed by the whole corps, to an event which had occurred in the garrison hospital. Having heard his recital, which, from the serious earnestness with which he made it, challenged attention, I resolved to investigate the matter; and, having communicated the circumstances to a friend, we both repaired to the hospital for the purpose of inquiry.

"There were two patients to be examined—both men of good character, and neither of them suffering from any disorder affecting the brain; the one was under treatment for consumptive symptoms, and the other for an ulcerated leg: and they were both in the prime of life.

"Having received a confirmation of the schoolmaster's statement from the hospital-sergeant, also a very respectable and trustworthy man, I sent for the patient principally concerned, and desired him to state what he had seen and heard, warning him, at the same time, that it was my intention to take down his deposition, and that it behooved him to be very careful, as possibly serious steps might be taken for the purpose of discovering whether an imposition had been practised in the wards of the hospital—a crime for which, he was well aware, a very severe penalty would be inflicted. He then proceeded to relate the circumstances, which I took down in the presence of Mr. B—— and the hospital-sergeant, as follows:—

"'It was last Tuesday night, somewhere between eleven and twelve, when all of us were in bed, and all lights out except the rush-light that was allowed for the man with the fever, when I was awoke by feeling a weight upon my feet, and at the same moment, as I was drawing up my legs, Private W——, who lies in the cot opposite mine, called out, "I say, Q——, there's somebody sitting upon your legs!"—and as I looked to the bottom of my bed, I saw some one get up from it, and then come round and stand over me, in the passage between my cot and the next. I felt somewhat alarmed, for the last few nights the ward had been disturbed by sounds as of a heavy foot walking up and down; and as nobody could be seen, it was beginning to be supposed among us that it was haunted, and fancying this that came up to my bed's head might be the ghost, I called out, "Who are you, and what do you want?"

"'The figure then, leaning with one hand on the wall, over my head, and stooping down, said, in my ear, "I am Mrs. M——;" and I could then distinguish that she was dressed in a flannel gown, edged with black riband, exactly similar to a set of grave-clothes in which I had assisted to clothe her corpse, when her death took place a year previously.

"'The voice, however, was not like Mrs. M——'s, nor like anybody else's, yet it was very distinct, and seemed somehow to sing through my head. I could see nothing of a face beyond a darkish color about the head, and it appeared to me that I could see through her body against the window-glasses.

"'Although I felt very uncomfortable, I asked her what she wanted. She replied, "I am Mrs. M——, and I wish you to write to him that was my husband, and tell him . . . . ."

"'I am not, sir,' said Corporal Q——, 'at liberty to mention to anybody what she told me, except to her husband. He is at the dépôt in Ireland, and I have written and told him. She made me promise not to tell any one else. After I had promised secrecy, she told me something of a matter that convinced me I was talking to a spirit, for it related to what only I and

Mrs. M—— knew, and no one living could know anything whatever of the matter; and if I was now speaking my last words on earth, I say solemnly that it was Mrs. M——'s spirit that spoke to me then, and no one else. After promising that if I complied with her request, she would not trouble me or the ward again, she went from my bed toward the fireplace, and with her hands she kept feeling about the wall over the mantel-piece. After a while, she came toward me again; and while my eyes were upon her, she somehow disappeared from my sight altogether, and I was left alone.

"'It was then that I felt faint-like, and a cold sweat broke out over me; but I did not faint, and after a time I got better, and gradually I went off to sleep.

"'The men in the ward said, next day, that Mrs. M—— had come to speak to me about purgatory, because she had been a Roman catholic, and we had often had arguments on religion: but what she told me had no reference to such subjects, but to a matter only she and I knew of.'

"After closely cross-questioning Corporal Q——, and endeavoring without success to reason him out of his belief in the ghostly character of his visiter, I read over to him what I had written, and then, dismissing him, sent for the other patient.

"After cautioning him, as I had done the first, I proceeded to take down his statement, which was made with every appearance of good faith and sincerity:—

"'I was lying awake,' said he, 'last Tuesday night, when I saw some one sitting on Corporal Q——'s bed. There was so little light in the ward, that I could not make out who it was, and the figure looked so strange that I got alarmed, and felt quite sick. I called out to Corporal Q—— that there was somebody sitting upon his bed, and then the figure got up; and as I did not know but it might be coming to me, I got so much alarmed, that being but weakly' (this was the consumptive man), 'I fell back, and I believe I fainted away. When I got round again, I saw the figure standing and apparently talking to the corporal, placing one hand against the wall and stooping down. I could not, however, hear any voice; and being still much alarmed, I put my head under the clothes for a considerable time. When I looked up again I could only see Corporal Q——, sitting up in bed alone, and he said he had seen a ghost; and I told him I had also seen it. After a time he got up and gave me a drink of water, for I was very faint. Some of the other patients being disturbed by our talking, they bade us be quiet, and after some time I got to sleep. The ward has not been disturbed since.'

"The man was then cross-questioned; but his testimony remaining quite unshaken, he was dismissed, and the hospital-sergeant was interrogated with regard to the possibility of a trick having been practised. He asserted, however, that this was impossible; and, certainly, from my own knowledge of the hospital regulations, and the habits of the patients, I should say that a practical joke of this nature was too serious a thing to have been attempted by anybody, especially as there were patients in the ward very ill at the time, and one very near his end. The punishment would have been extremely severe, and discovery almost certain, since everybody would have been adverse to the delinquent.

"The investigation that ensued was a very brief one, it being found that there was nothing more to be elicited; and the affair terminated with the supposition that the two men had been dreaming. Nevertheless, six months afterward, on being interrogated, their evidence and their conviction were as clear as at first, and they declared themselves ready at any time to repeat their statement upon oath."

Supposing this case to be as the men believed it, there are several things worthy of observation. In the first place, the ghost is guilty of that inconsistency so offensive to Francis Grose and many others. Instead of telling her secret to her husband, she commissions the corporal to tell it him, and it is not till a year after her departure from this life that she does even that; and she is heard in the ward two or three nights before she is visible. We are therefore constrained to suppose that, like Mrs. Bretton, she could not communicate with her husband, and that, till that Tuesday night, the necessary conditions for attaining her object, as regarded the corporal, were wanting. It is also remarkable that, although the latter heard her speak distinctly, and spoke to her, the other man heard no voice, which renders it probable that she had at length been able to produce that impression upon him which a magnetizer does on his somnambule, enabling each to understand the other by a transference of thought, which was undistinguishable to the corporal from speech, as it is frequently to the somnambule. The imitating the actions of life by leaning against the wall and feeling about the mantel-piece, are very unlike what a person would have done who was endeavoring to impose on the man; and equally unlike what they would have reported, had the thing been an invention of their own.

Among the established jests on the subject of ghosts, their sudden vanishing is a very fruitful one; but, I think, if we examine this question, we shall find that there is nothing comical in the matter except the ignorance or want of reflection of the jesters.

In the first place, as I have before observed, a spirit must be where its thoughts and affections are, for they are itself; *our* spirits are where our thoughts and affections are, although our solid bodies remain stationary: and no one will suppose that walls or doors, or material obstacles of any kind, could exclude a spirit any more than they can exclude our thoughts.

But, then, there is the visible body of the spirit—what is that, and how does it retain its shape?—for we know that there is a law (discovered by Dalton) that two masses of gaseous matter can not remain in contact, but they will immediately proceed to diffuse themselves into one another; and accordingly, it may be advanced that a gaseous corporeity in the atmosphere is an impossibility, because it could not retain its form, but would inevitably be dissolved away, and blend with the surrounding air. But precisely the same objection might be made by a chemist to the possibility of our fleshly bodies retaining their integrity and compactness: for the human body, taken as a whole, is known to be an impossible chemical compound, except for the vitality which upholds it; and no sooner is life withdrawn from it, than it crumbles into putrescence; and it is undeniable that the aeriform body would be an impossible mechanical phenomenon, but for the vitality which, we are entitled to suppose, may uphold it. But, just as the state or condition of organization protects the fleshly body from the natural reactions which would destroy it, so may an analogous condition of organization protect a spiritual ethereal body from the destructive influence of the mutual interdiffusion of gases.

Thus, supposing this aeriform body to be a permanent appurtenance of the spirit, we see how it may subsist and retain its integrity; and it would be as reasonable to hope to exclude the electric fluid by walls or doors as to exclude by them this subtle, fluent form. If, on the contrary, the shape be only one constructed out of the atmosphere by an act of will, the same act of will, which is a vital force, will preserve it entire, until, the will being withdrawn, it dissolves away. In either case, the moment the will or thought of the spirit is elsewhere, it is gone — it has vanished.

For those who prefer the other hypothesis — namely, that there is no outstanding shape at all, but that the will of the spirit, acting on the constructive imagination of the seer, enables him to conceive the form, as the spirit itself conceives of it — there can be no difficulty in understanding that the becoming invisible will depend merely on a similar act of will.

CHAPTER XIII.

HAUNTED HOUSES.

Everybody has heard of haunted houses; and there is no country, and scarcely any place, in which something of the sort is not known or talked of; and I suppose there is no one who, in the course of their travels, has not seen very respectable, good-looking houses shut up and uninhabited, because they had this evil reputation assigned to them. I have seen several such, for my own part; and it is remarkable that this *mala fama* does not always, by any means, attach itself to buildings one would imagine most obnoxious to such a suspicion. For example, I never heard of a ghost being seen or heard in Haddon hall, the most ghostly of houses; nor in many other antique, mysterious-looking buildings, where one might expect them, while sometimes a house of a very prosaic aspect remains uninhabited, and is ultimately allowed to fall to ruin, for no other reason, we are told, than that nobody can live in it. I remember, in my childhood, such a house in Kent—I think it was on the road between Maidstone and Tunbridge—which had this reputation. There was nothing dismal about it: it was neither large nor old, and it stood on the borders of a well-frequented road; yet I was assured it had stood empty for years; and as long as I lived in that part of the country it never had an inhabitant, and I believe was finally pulled down—and all for no other reason than that it was haunted, and nobody could live in it. I have frequently heard of people, while travelling on the continent, getting into houses at a rent so low as to surprise them, and I have, moreover, frequently heard of very strange things occurring while they were there. I remember, for instance, a family of the name of S—— S——, who obtained a very handsome house at a most agreeably cheap rate, somewhere on the coast of Italy—I think it was at Mola de Gaeta. They lived very comfortably in it till one day, while Mrs. S—— S—— was sitting in the drawing-room, which opened into a balcony overhanging the sea, she saw a lady dressed in white pass along before the windows, which were all closed. Concluding it was one of her daughters, who had been accidentally shut out, she arose and opened the window, to allow her to enter; but on looking out, to her amazement there was nobody there, although there was no possible escape from the balcony unless by jumping into the sea! On mentioning this circumstance to somebody in the neighborhood, they were told that "that was the reason they had the house so cheap: nobody liked to live in it."

I have heard of several houses, even in populous cities, to which some strange circumstance of this sort is attached—some in London even, and some in this city and neighborhood; and, what is more, unaccountable things actually do happen to those who inhabit them. Doors are strangely opened and shut, a rustling of silk, and sometimes a whispering, and frequently footsteps, are heard. There is a house in Ayrshire to which this sort of thing has been attached for years, insomuch that it was finally abandoned to an old man and woman, who said that they were so used to it that they did not mind it. A distinguished authoress told me that some time ago she passed a night at the house of an acquaintance, in one of the midland counties of England. She and her sister occupied the same room, and in the night they heard some one ascending the stairs. The foot came distinctly to the door, then turned away, ascended the next flight, and they heard it overhead. In the morning, on being asked if they had slept well, they mentioned this circumstance. "That is what everybody hears who sleeps in that room," said the lady of the house. "Many a time I have, when sleeping there, drawn up the night-bolt, persuaded that the nurse was bringing the baby to me; but there was nobody to be seen. We have taken every pains to ascertain what it is, but in vain; and are now so used to it, that we have ceased to care about the matter."

I know of two or three other houses in this city, and one in the neighborhood, in which circumstances of this nature are transpiring, or have transpired very lately; but people hush them up, from the fear of being laughed at, and also from an apprehension of injuring the character of a house; on which account, I do not dwell on the particulars. But there was, some time since, a *fama* of this kind attached to a house in St. J—— street, some of the details of which became very public. It had stood empty a long time, in consequence of the annoyances to which the inhabitants had been subjected. There was one room, particularly, which nobody could occupy without disturbance. On one occasion, a youth who had been abroad a considerable time, either in the army or navy, was put there to sleep on his arrival, since, knowing nothing of these reports, it was hoped his rest might not be interrupted. In the morning, however, he complained of the dreadful time he had had, with people looking in at him between the curtains of his bed all night—avowing his resolution to terminate his visit that same day, as he would not sleep there any more. After this period, the house stood empty again for a considerable time, but was at length taken and workmen sent in to repair it. One day, when the men were away at dinner, the master tradesman took the key and went to inspect progress, and, having examined the lower rooms, he was ascending the stairs, when he heard a man's foot behind him. He looked round, but there was nobody there, and he moved on again; still there was somebody following, and he stopped and looked over the rails; but there was no one to be seen. So, although feeling rather queer, he advanced into the drawing-room, where a fire had been lighted; and, wishing to combat the uncomfortable sensation that was creeping over him, he took hold of a chair, and drawing it resolutely along the floor, he slammed it down upon the hearth with some force and seated himself in it; when, to his amazement, the action, in all its particulars of sound, was immediately repeated by his unseen companion, who seemed to seat himself beside him on a chair as invisible as himself. Horror-struck, the worthy builder started up and rushed out of the house.

There is a house in S—— street, in London, which, having stood empty a good while, was at length taken by Lord B——. The family were annoyed by several unpleasant occurrences, and by the sound of footseps, which were often audible, especially in Lady B——'s bedroom—who, though she could not see the form, was occasionally conscious of its immediate proximity.

Some time since, a gentleman having established himself in a lodging in London, felt, the first night he slept there, that the clothes were being dragged off his bed. He fancied he had done it himself in his sleep, and pulled them on again;—but it happens repeatedly: he gets out of bed each time—can find nobody, no string, no possible explanation—nor can obtain any from the people of the house, who only seem distressed and annoyed. On mentioning it to some one in the neighborhood, he is informed that the same thing has occurred to several preceding occupants of the lodging, which, of course, he left.

The circumstances that happened at New House, in Hampshire—as detailed by Mr. Barham in the third volume of the "Ingoldsby Legends"—are known to be perfectly authentic; as are the following, the account of which I have received from a highly respectable servant, residing in a family with whom I am well acquainted: she informs me that she was, not very long since, living with a Colonel and Mrs. W——, who, being at Carlisle, engaged a furnished house, which they obtained at an exceedingly cheap rate, because nobody liked to live in it. This family, however, met with no annoyance, and attached no importance to the rumor which had kept the house empty. There were, however, two rooms in it wholly unfurnished; and as the house was large, they were dispensed with till the recurrence of the race week, when, expecting company, these two rooms were temporarily fitted up for the use of the nurses and children. There were heavy Venetian blinds to the windows; and, in the middle of the night, the person who related the circumstance to me, was awakened by the distinct sound of these blinds being pulled up and down with violence, perhaps as many as twenty times. The fire had fallen low, and she could not see whether they were actually moved or not, but lay trembling in indescribable terror. Presently feet were heard in the room, and a stamping as if several men were moving about without stockings. While lying in this state of agony, she was comforted by hearing the voice of a nurse, who slept in another bed in the same chamber, exclaiming: "The Lord have mercy upon us!" This second woman then asked the first if she had courage to get out of bed and stir up the fire, so that they might be able to see; which by a great effort she did, the chimney being near her bed. There was, however, nothing to be discovered, everything being precisely as when they went to bed. On another occasion, when they were sitting in the evening at work, they distinctly heard some one counting money, and the chink of the pieces as they were laid down. The sound proceeded from the inner room of the two, but there was nobody there. This family left the house, and though a large and commodious one, she understood it remained unoccupied, as before.

A respectable citizen of Edinburgh, not long ago, went to America to visit his son, who had married and settled there. The morning after his arrival, he declared his determination to return immediately to Philadelphia, from which the house was at a considerable distance; and, on being interrogated as to the cause of this sudden departure, he said that in the previous night he had heard a man walking about his room, who had approached the bed, drawn back the curtains, and bent over him. Thinking it was somebody who had concealed himself there with ill intentions, he had struck out violently at the figure, when, to his horror, his arm passed unimpeded through it.

Other extraordinary things happened in that house, which had the reputation of being haunted, although the son had not believed it, and had therefore not mentioned the report to the father. One day the children said they had been running after "such a queer thing in the cellar; it was like a goat, and not like a goat; but it seemed to be like a shadow."

A few years ago, some friends of mine were taking a house

in this city, when the servants of the people who were leaving advised them not to have anything to do with it, for that there was a ghost in it that screamed dreadfully, and that they never could keep a stitch of clothes on them at night—the bed-coverings were always pulled off. My friends laughed heartily and took the house; but the cries and groans all over it were so frequent, that they at length got quite used to them. It is to be observed that the house was a *flat*, or *floor*, shut in; so that there could be no draughts of air nor access for tricks. Besides, it was a woman's voice, sometimes close to their ears, sometimes in a closet, sometimes behind their beds—in short, in all directions. Everybody heard it that went to the house.

The tenant that succeeded them, however, has never been troubled with it.

The story of the Brown Lady at the Marquis of T——'s, in Norfolk, is known to many. The Hon. H. W—— told me that a friend of his, while staying there, had often seen her, and had one day inquired of his host, "Who was the lady in brown that he had met frequently on the stairs?" Two gentlemen, whose names were mentioned to me, resolved to watch for her and intercept her. They at length saw her but she eluded them by turning down a staircase, and when they looked over she had disappeared. Many persons have seen her.

There is a Scotch family of distinction, who, I am told, are accompanied by an unseen attendant, whom they call "Spinning Jenny." She is heard spinning in their house in the country, and when they come into town she spins here; servants and all hear the sound of her wheel. I believe she accompanies them no further than to their own residences, not to those of other people. Jenny is supposed to be a former housemaid of the family, who was a great spinner, and they are so accustomed to her presence as to feel it no annoyance.

The following very singular circumstance was related to me by the daughter of the celebrated Mrs. S——: Mrs. S—— and her husband were travelling into Wales, and had occasion to stop on their way, some days, at Oswestry. There they established themselves in a lodging, to reach the door of which they had to go down a sort of close, or passage. The only inhabitants of the house were the mistress, a very handsome woman, and two maids. Mr. and Mrs. S——, however, very soon had occasion to complain of the neglected state of the rooms, which were apparently never cleaned or dusted; though, strange to say, to judge by their own ears, the servants were doing nothing else all night, their sleep being constantly disturbed by the noise of rubbing, sweeping, and the moving of furniture. When they complained to these servants of the noise in the night, and the dirt of the rooms, they answered that the noise was not made by them, and that it was impossible for them to do their work, exhausted as they were by sitting up all night with their mistress, who could not bear to be alone when she was in bed. Mr. and Mrs. S—— afterward discovered that she had her room lighted up every night; and one day, as they were returning from a walk, and she happened to be going down the close before them, they heard her saying, as she turned her head sharply from side to side, "Are you there again? What, the devil! Go away, I tell you!" &c., &c. On applying to the neighbors for an explanation of these mysteries, the good people only shook their heads, and gave mysterious answers. Mr. and Mrs. S—— afterward learned that she was believed to have murdered a girl who formerly lived in her service.

There is nothing in the conduct of this unhappy woman which may not be perfectly well accounted for, by the supposition of a guilty conscience; but the noises heard by Mr. and Mrs. S—— at night, are curiously in accordance with a variety of similar stories, wherein this strange visionary repetition of the trivial actions of daily life, or of some particular incident, has been observed. The affair of Lord St. Vincent's was of this nature; and there is somewhere extant, an account of the ghost of Peter the Great, of Russia, having appeared to Doctor Doppelio, complaining to him of the sufferings he endured from having to act over again his former cruelties; a circumstance which exhibits a remarkable coincidence with the Glasgow dream, mentioned in a preceding chapter. We must, of course, attach a symbolical meaning to these phenomena, and conclude that these reactings are somewhat of the nature of our dreams. Certainly, there would need no stronger motive to induce us to spend the period allotted to us on earth, in those pure and innocent pleasures and occupations, which never weary or sicken the soul, than the belief that such a future awaits us!

A family in one of the English counties, was a few years ago terribly troubled by an unseen inmate who chiefly seemed to inhabit a large cellar, into which there was no entrance except the door which was kept locked. Here there would be a loud knocking—sometimes a voice crying—heavy feet walking, &c., &c. At first, the old trustworthy butler would summon his accolytes, and descend, armed with sword and blunderbuss; but no one was to be seen. They could often hear the feet following them up stairs from this cellar; and once, when the family had determined to watch, they found themselves accompanied up stairs not only by the sound of the feet, but by a *visible* shadowy companion! They rushed up, flew to their chamber, and shut the door, when instantly they felt and saw the handle turned in their hand by a hand outside. Windows and doors were opened in spite of locks and keys; but notwithstanding the most persevering investigations, the only clew to the mystery was the appearance of that spectral figure.

The knockings and sounds of people at work, asserted to be heard in mines, is a fact maintained by many very sensible men, overseers, and superintendents, &c., as well as by the workmen themselves; and there is a strong persuasion, I know, among the miners of Cornwall, and those of Mendip, that these visionary workmen are sometimes heard among them; on which occasions the horses evince their apprehensions by trembling and sweating; but as I have no means of verifying these reports, I do not dwell upon them further.

When the mother of George Canning, then Mrs. Hunn, was an actress in the provinces, she went, among other places, to Plymouth, having previously requested her friend, Mr. Bernard, of the theatre, to procure her a lodging. On her arrival Mr. B. told her that if she was not afraid of a ghost, she might have a comfortable residence at a very low rate, "For there is," said he, "a house belonging to our carpenter, that is reported to be haunted, and nobody will live in it. If you like to have it, you may, and for nothing, I believe, for he is so anxious to get a tenant; only you must not let it be known that you do not pay rent for it."

Mrs. Hunn, alluding to the theatrical apparitions, said it would not be the first time she had had to do with a ghost, and that she was very willing to encounter this one; so she had her luggage taken to the house in question, and the bed prepared. At her usual hour, she sent her maid and her children to bed, and, curious to see if there was any foundation for the rumor she had heard, she seated herself, with a couple of candles and a book, to watch the event. Beneath the room she occupied was the carpenter's workshop, which had two doors. The one which opened into the street was barred and bolted within; the other, a smaller one, opening into the passage, was only on the latch; and the house was, of course, closed for the night. She had read something more than half an hour, when she perceived a noise issuing from this lower apartment, which sounded very much like the sawing of wood. Presently other such noises as usually proceed from a carpenter's workshop were added, till by-and-by, there was a regular concert of knocking and hammering, and sawing and planing, &c.; the whole sounding like half a dozen busy men in full employment. Being a woman of considerable courage, Mrs. Hunn resolved, if possible, to penetrate the mystery; so taking off her shoes, that her approach might not be heard, with her candle in her hand, she very softly opened her door and descended the stairs, the noise continuing as loud as ever, and evidently proceeding from the workshop, till she opened the door, when instantly all was silent —all was still—not a mouse was stirring; and the tools and the wood, and everything else, lay as they had been left by the workmen when they went away. Having examined every part of the place, and satisfied herself that there was nobody there, and that nobody could get into it, Mrs. Hunn ascended to her room again, beginning almost to doubt her own senses, and question with herself whether she had really heard the noise or not, when it recommenced and continued, without intermission, for about half an hour. She however went to bed, and the next day told nobody what had occurred, having determined to watch another night before mentioning the affair to any one. As, however, this strange scene was acted over again, without her being able to discover the cause of it, she now mentioned the circumstance to the owner of the house and to her friend Bernard; and the former, who would not believe it, agreed to watch with her, which he did. The noise began as before, and he was so horror-struck that, instead of entering the workshop as she wished him to do, he rushed into the street. Mrs. Hunn continued to inhabit the house the whole summer; and, when referring afterward to the adventure, she observed that use was second nature, and that she was sure if any night these ghostly carpenters had not pursued their visionary labors, she should have been quite frightened, lest they should pay her a visit upstairs.

From many recorded cases, I find the vulgar belief, that buried money is frequently the cause of these disturbances, is strongly borne out by facts. This certainly does seem to us very strange, and can only be explained by the hypothesis suggested, that the soul awakes in the other world in exactly the same state in which it quitted this.

In the abovementioned instances, of what are called *haunted houses*, there is generally nothing seen; but those are equally abundant where the ghostly visiter is visible.

Two young ladies were passing the night in a house in the north, when the youngest, then a child, awoke and saw an old man, in a Kilmarnock nightcap, walking about their bedroom. She said, when telling the story in after-life, that she was not the least frightened—she was only surprised! but she found that her sister, who was several years older than herself, was in a state of great terror. He continued some time moving about, and at last went to a chest of drawers, where there lay a parcel of buttons, belonging to a travelling tailor who had been at work in the house. Whether the old man threw them down or not, she could not say; but, just then, they all fell rattling off the drawers to the floor, whereupon he disappeared. The next morning, when they mentioned the circumstance, she observed that the family looked at each other in a significant manner; but it was not till she was older she learned that the house was said to be haunted by this old man. "It never occurred to me," she said, "that it was a ghost. Who could have thought of a ghost in a Kilmarnock nightcap!"

At the Leipsic fair, lodgings are often very scarce, and on one occasion a stranger, who had arrived late in the evening, had some difficulty in finding a bed. At length he found a vacant chamber in the house of a citizen. It was one they made no use of, but they said he was welcome to it; and, weary and sleepy, he gladly accepted the offer. Fatigued as he was, however, he was disturbed by some unaccountable noises, of which he complained to his hosts in the morning. They pacified him by some excuses; but the next night, not long after he had gone to bed, he came down stairs in great haste, with his portmanteau on his shoulder, declaring he would not stay there another hour for the world; for that a lady, in a strange old-fashioned dress, had come into the room with a dagger in her hand, and made threatening gestures at him. He accordingly went away, and the room was shut up again; but some time afterward, a servant-girl in the family of this citizen, being taken ill, they were obliged to put her into that room, in order to separate her from the rest of the family. Here she recovered her health rapidly; and as she had never complained of any annoyance, she was asked, when she was quite well, whether anything particular had happened while she inhabited that chamber. "Oh, yes," she answered; "every night there came a strange lady into the room, who sat herself on the bed and stroked me with her hand, and I believe it is to her I owe my speedy recovery; but I could never get her to speak to me—she only sighs and weeps."

Not very long since, a gentleman set out, one fine midsummer's evening, when it is light all night in Scotland, to walk from Montrose to Brechin. As he approached a place called Dunn, he observed a lady walking on before, which, from the lateness of the hour, somewhat surprised him. Sometime afterward, he was found by the early laborers lying on the ground, near the churchyard, in a state of insensibility. All he could tell them was, that he had followed this lady till she had turned her head and looked round at him, when, seized with horror, he had fainted. "Oh," said they, "you have seen the lady of Dunn." What is the legend attached to this lady of Dunn, I do not know.

Monsieur De S. had been violently in love with Hippolyte Clairon, the celebrated French actress, but she rejected his suit, in so peremptory a manner, that even when he was at the point of death, she refused his earnest entreaties, that she would visit him. Indignant at her cruelty, he declared that he would haunt her, and he certainly kept his word. I believe she never saw his ghost, but he appears to have been always near her; at least, on several occasions when other people doubted the fact, he signalized his presence at her bidding, by various sounds, and this, wherever she happened to be at the moment. Sometimes it was a cry, at others, a shot, and at others, a clapping of hands or music. She seems to have been slow to believe in the extra-natural character of these noises; and even when she was ultimately convinced, to have been divided between horror on the one hand, and diversion, at the oddness of the circumstance, on the other. The sounds were heard by everybody in her vicinity; and I am informed by Mr. Charles Kirkpatrick Sharpe, that the margrave of Anspach, who was subsequently her lover, and Mr. Keppel Craven, were perfectly well acquainted with the circumstances of this haunting, and entertained no doubt of the facts above alluded to.

The ghost known by the designation of "the White Lady," which is frequently seen in different castles or palaces belonging to the royal family of Prussia, has been mentioned in another publication, I think. She was long supposed to be a Countess Agnes, of Orlamunde; but a picture of a princess called Bertha, or Perchta von Rosenberg, discovered some time since, was thought so exceedingly to resemble the apparition, that it is now a disputed point which of the two ladies it is, or whether it is or is not the same apparition that is seen at different places. Neither of these ladies appears to have been very happy in their lives: but the opinion of its being the Princess Bertha, who lived in the fifteenth century, was somewhat countenanced by the circumstance, that at a period when, in consequence of the war, an annual benefit which she had bequeathed to the poor was neglected, the apparition seemed to be unusually disturbed, and was seen more frequently. She is often observed before a death; and one of the Fredericks said, shortly before his decease, that he should "not live long, for he had met the White Lady." She wears a widow's band and veil, but it is sufficiently transparent to show her features, which do not express happiness, but placidity. She has only been twice heard to speak. In December, 1628, she appeared in the palace at Berlin, and was heard to say, "*Veni, judica vivos et mortuos! Judicium mihi adhuc superest.*"—"Come, judge the quick and the dead! I wait for judgment." On the other occasion, which is more recent, one of the princesses at the castle of Neuhaus, in Bohemia, was standing before a mirror, trying on a new head-dress, when, on asking her waiting-maid what the hour was, the white lady suddenly stepped from behind a screen and said: "Zehn uhr ist es ihr liebden!"—"It is ten o'clock, your love!" which is the mode in which the sovereign princes address each other, instead of "your highness." The princess was much alarmed, soon fell sick, and died in a few weeks. She has frequently evinced displeasure at the exhibition of impiety or vice; and there are many records of her different appearances to be found in the works of Balbinus and of Erasmus Francisci; and in a publication called "The Iris," published in Frankfort in 1819, the editor, George Doring, who is said to have been a man of great integrity, gives the following account of one of her later appearances, which he declares he received just as he gives it, from the lips of his own mother, on whose word and judgment he could perfectly rely; and shortly before his death, an inquiry being addressed to him with regard to the correctness of the narration, he vouched for its authenticity.

It seems that the elder sister of his mother was companion

to one of the ladies of the court, and that the younger ones were in the habit of visiting her frequently. Two of these (Doring's mother and another), aged fourteen and fifteen, were once spending a week with her, when she being out and they alone with their needlework, chattering about the court diversions, they suddenly heard the sound of a stringed instrument, like a harp, which seemed to proceed from behind a large stove that occupied one corner of the room. Half in fear and half in fun, one of the girls took a yard measure that lay beside them, and struck the spot, whereupon the music ceased, but the stick was wrested from her hand. She became alarmed; but the other, named Christina, laughed and said she must have fancied it, adding that the music doubtless proceeded from the street, though they could not descry any musicians. To get over her fright, of which she was half ashamed, the former now ran out of the room to visit a neighbor for a few minutes; but when she returned, she found Christina lying on the floor in a swoon, who, on being revived with the aid of the attendants who had heard a scream, related, that no sooner had her sister left her than the sound was repeated, close to the stove, and a white figure had appeared and advanced toward her, whereupon she had screamed and fainted.

The lady who owned the apartments flattered herself that this apparition betokened that a treasure was hidden under the stove, and, imposing silence on the girls, she sent for a carpenter and had the planks lifted. The floor was found to be double, and below was a vault, from which issued a very unwholesome vapor, but no treasure was found, nor anything but a quantity of quick-lime. The circumstance being now made known to the king, he expressed no surprise; he said that the apparition was doubtless that of a countess of Orlamunde, who had been buried alive in that vault. She was the mistress of a margrave of Brandenburg, by whom she had two sons. When the prince became a widower, she expected he would marry her; but he urged as an objection that he feared, in that case, her sons might hereafter dispute the succession with the lawful heirs. In order to remove this obstacle out of her way, she poisoned the children; and the margrave, disgusted and alarmed, had her walled up in that vault for her pains. He added that she was usually seen every seven years, and was preceded by the sound of a harp, on which instrument she had been a proficient; and also that she more frequently appeared to children than to adults,—as if the love she had denied her own offspring in life was now her torment, and that she sought a reconciliation with childhood in general. I know from the best authority that the fact of these appearances is not doubted by those who have the fullest opportunities of inquiry and investigation; and I remember seeing in the English papers, a few years since, a paragraph copied from the foreign journals, to the effect that the White Lady had been seen again, I think at Berlin.

The following very curious relation I have received from the gentleman to whom the circumstance occurred, who is a professional man residing in London:—

"I was brought up by a grandfather and four aunts, all ghost-seers and believers in supernatural appearances. The former had been a sailor, and was one of the crew that sailed round the world with Lord Anson. I remember, when I was about eight years old, that I was awakened by the screams of one of these ladies, with whom I was sleeping, which summoned all the family about her to inquire the cause of the disturbance. She said that she had 'seen Nancy by the side of the bed, and that she was slipping into it.' We had scarcely got down stairs in the morning, before intelligence arrived that that lady had died, precisely at the moment my aunt said she saw her. Nancy was her brother's wife. Another of my aunts, who was married and had a large family, foretold my grandfather's death, at a time that we had no reason to apprehend it. He, also, had appeared at her bedside; he was then alive and well, but he died a fortnight afterward. But it would be tedious were I to enumerate half the instances I could recall of a similar description; and I will therefore proceed to the relation of what happened to myself.

"I was, some few years since, invited to pass a day and

night at the house of a friend in Hertfordshire, with whom I was intimately acquainted. His name was B——, and he had formerly been in business as a saddler, in Oxford street, where he realized a handsome fortune, and had now retired to enjoy his *otium cum dignitate*, in the rural and beautiful village of Sarratt.

"It was a gloomy Sunday, in the month of November, when I mounted my horse for the journey, and there was so much appearance of rain, that I should certainly have selected some other mode of conveyance, had I not been desirous of leaving the animal in Mr. E——'s straw-yard for the winter. Before I got as far as St. John's wood, the threatening clouds broke, and by the time I reached Watford I was completely soaked. However, I proceeded, and arrived at Sarratt before my friend and his wife had returned from church. The moment they did so, they furnished me with dry clothes, and I was informed that we were to dine at the house of Mr. D——, a very agreeable neighbor. I felt some little hesitation about presenting myself in such a costume, for I was decked out in a full suit of Mr. B——'s, who was a stout man, of six feet in height, while I am rather of the diminutive order; but my objections were overruled; we went, and my appearance added not a little to the hilarity of the party. At ten o'clock we separated, and I returned with Mr. and Mrs. B—— to their house, where I was shortly afterward conducted to a very comfortable bed-room.

"Fatigued with my day's ride, I was soon in bed, and soon asleep, but I do not think I could have slept long before I was awakened by the violent barking of dogs. I found that the noise had disturbed others as well as myself, for I heard Mr. B——, who was lodged in the adjoining room, open his window and call to them to be quiet. They were obedient to his voice, and as soon as quietness ensued I dropped asleep again; but I was again awakened by an extraordinary pressure upon my feet; *that I was perfectly awake, I declare;* the light that stood in the chimney-corner shone strongly across the foot of the bed, and I saw the figure of a well-dressed man in the act of stooping, and supporting himself in so doing by the bedclothes. He had on a blue coat, with bright gilt buttons, but I saw no head; the curtains at the foot of the bed, which were partly looped back, just hung so as to conceal that part of his person. At first I thought it was my host, and as I had dropped my clothes, as is my habit, on the floor at the foot of the bed, I supposed he was come to look after them, which rather surprised me: but, just as I had raised myself upright in bed, and was about to inquire into the occasion of his visit, the figure passed on. I then recollected that I had locked the door; and, becoming somewhat puzzled, I jumped out of bed; but I could see nobody; and on examining the room I found no means of ingress but the door through which I had entered, and one other; both of which were locked on the inside. Amazed and puzzled I got into bed again, and sat some time ruminating on the extraordinary circumstance, when it occurred to me that I had not looked under the bed; so I got out again, fully expecting to find my visiter, whoever he was, there; but I was disappointed. So, after looking at my watch, and ascertaining that it was ten minutes past two, I stepped into bed again, hoping now to get some rest. But, alas! sleep was banished for that night; and after turning from side to side, and making vain endeavors at forgetfulness, I gave up the point, and lay till the clocks struck seven, perplexing my brain with the question of who my midnight visiter could be, and also how he had got in and how he had got out of my room. About eight o'clock I met my host and his wife at the breakfast-table, when, in answer to their hospitable inquiries of how I had passed the night, I mentioned, first, that I had been awaked by the barking of some dogs, and that I had heard Mr. B—— open his window and call to them. He answered that two strange dogs had got into the yard and had disturbed the others. I then mentioned my midnight visiter, expecting that they would either explain the circumstance, or else laugh at me and declare I must have dreamed it. But, to my surprise, my story was listened to with grave attention, and they related to me the tradition with which this spectre, for such I found they deemed it to be, was supposed to be connected. This was to the effect, that many years ago a gentleman so attired had been murdered there, under some frightful circumstances, and that his head had been cut off. On perceiving that I was very unwilling to accept this explanation of the mystery, for, in spite of my family peculiarity, I had always been an entire disbeliever in supernatural appearances, they begged me to prolong my visit for a day or two, when they would introduce me to the rector of the parish, who could furnish me with such evidence with regard to circumstances of a similar nature, as would leave no doubt on my mind as to the possibility of their occurrence. But I had made an engagement to dine at Watford, on my way back, and I confess, moreover, that after what I had heard I did not feel disposed to encounter the chance of another visit from the mysterious stranger; so I declined the proffered hospitality, and took my leave.

"Some time after this, I happened to be dining at C—— street, in company with some ladies resident in the same county, when, chancing to allude to my visit to Sarratt, I added, that I had met with a very extraordinary adventure there, which I had never been able to account for, when one of these ladies immediately said that she hoped I had not had a visit from the headless gentleman, in a blue coat and gilt buttons, who was said to have been seen by many people in that house.

"Such is the conclusion of this marvellous tale as regards myself; and I can only assure you that I have related facts as they occurred, and that I had never heard a word about this apparition in my life, till Mr. B—— related to me the tradition above alluded to. Still, as I am no believer, in supernatural appearances, I am constrained to suppose that the whole affair was the product of my imagination.

"I must add, that Mr. B—— mentioned some strange circumstances connected with another house in the county, inhabited by a Mr. M——, which were corroborated by the ladies above alluded to. Both parties agreed that, from the unaccountable noises, &c., &c., which were heard there, that gentleman had the greatest difficulty in persuading any servants to remain with him. "A—— W—— M——.

"*C—— street, 5th September*, 1846."

This is one of those curious instances of determined skepticism that fully justify the patriarch's prediction.

The following interesting letter, written by a member of a very distinguished English family, will furnish its own explanation:—

"As you express a wish to know what degree of credit is to be attached to a garbled tale which has been sent forth, after a lapse of between thirty and forty years, as an 'accredited ghost-story,' I will state the facts as they were recalled to my mind last year by a daughter of Sir William A. C——, who sent the book to me, requesting me to tell her if there was any foundation for the story, which she could scarcely believe, since she had never heard my mother allude to it. I read the narrative with surprise, it being evidently not furnished by any of the family, nor indeed by any one who was with us at the time! yet, though full of mistakes in names, &c., &c., some particulars come so near the truth as to puzzle me. The facts are as follows:—

"Sir James, my mother, with myself and my brother Charles, went abroad toward the end of the year 1786. After trying several different places, we determined to settle at Lille, where we found the masters particularly good, and where we had also letters of introduction to several of the best French families. There Sir James left us, and, after passing a few days in an uncomfortable lodging, we engaged a nice, large family house, which we liked very much, and which we obtained at a very low rent, even for that part of the world.

"About three weeks after we were established in our new residence, I walked one day with my mother to the bankers, for the purpose of delivering our letter of credit from Sir Robert Herries, and drawing some money, which, being paid in heavy five-franc pieces, we found we could not carry, and therefore requested the banker to send, saying, 'We live in the Place du Lion D'or.' Whereupon he looked surprised, and observed that he knew of no house there fit for us, 'except, indeed,' he added, 'the one that has been long uninhabited, on account of the *revenan* that walks about it.' He said this quite seriously, and in a natural tone of voice, in spite of which we laughed, and were quite entertained at the idea of a ghost; but at the same time we begged him not to mention the thing to our servants, lest they should take any fancies into their heads; and my mother and I resolved to say nothing about the matter to any one. 'I suppose it is the ghost,' said my mother, laughing, 'that wakes us so often by walking over our heads.' We had, in fact, been awakened several nights by a heavy foot, which we supposed to be that of one of the men-servants, of whom we had three English and four French; of women-servants we had five English, and all the rest were French. The English ones, men and women, every one of them, returned ultimately to England with us.

"A night or two afterward, being again awakened by the step, my mother asked Creswell, 'Who slept in the room above us?' 'No one, my lady,' she replied—'it is a large, empty garret.'

"About a week or ten days after this, Creswell came to my mother, one morning, and told her that all the French servants talked of going away, because there was a *revenant* in the house; adding that there seemed to be a strange story attached to the place, which was said, together with some other property, to have belonged to a young man, whose guardian, who was also his uncle, had treated him cruelly and confined him in an iron cage; and as he had subsequently disappeared, it was conjectured he had been murdered. This uncle, after inheriting the property, had suddenly quitted the house and sold it to the father of the man of whom we had hired it. Since that period, though it had been several times let, nobody had ever stayed in it above a week or two, and for a considerable time past it had had no tenant at all.

"'And do you really believe all this nonsense, Creswell?' said my mother.

"'Well, I don't know, my lady,' answered she; 'but there's the iron cage in the garret over your bed-room, where you may see it, if you please.'

"Of course we rose to go; and as just at that moment an old

officer, with his Croix de St. Louis, called on us, we invited him to accompany us and we ascended together. We found, as Creswell had said, a large empty garret with bare brick walls; and in the further corner of it stood an iron cage, such as wild beasts are kept in, only higher; it was about four feet square, and eight in height, and there was an iron ring in the wall at the back, to which was attached an old rusty chain with a collar fixed to the end of it. I confess it made my blood creep when I thought of the possibility of any human being having inhabited it! And our old friend expressed as much horror as ourselves, assuring us that it must certainly have been constructed for some such dreadful purpose. As, however, we were no believers in ghosts, we all agreed that the noises must proceed from somebody who had an interest in keeping the house empty; and since it was very disagreeable to imagine that there were secret means of entering it at night, we resolved, as soon as possible, to look out for another residence, and in the meantime to say nothing about the matter to anybody. About ten days after this determination, my mother, observing one morning that Creswell, when she came to dress her, looked exceedingly pale and ill, inquired if anything was the matter with her. 'Indeed, my lady,' she answered, 'we have been frightened to death, and neither I nor Mrs. Marsh can sleep again in the room we are now in.'

"'Well,' returned my mother, 'you shall both come and sleep in the little spare room next us; but what has alarmed you?'

"'Some one, my lady, went through our room in the night; we both saw the figure, but we covered our heads with the bed-clothes, and lay in a dreadful fright till morning.'

"On hearing this, I could not help laughing, upon which Creswell burst into tears; and seeing how nervous she was, we comforted her by saying we had heard of a good house, and that we should very soon abandon our present habitation.

"A few nights afterward, my mother requested me and Charles to go to her bed-room and fetch her frame, that she might prepare her work for the next day. It was after supper, and we were ascending the stairs by the light of a lamp which was always kept burning, when we saw going up before us a tall, thin figure, with hair flowing down his back, and wearing a loose powdering gown. We both at once concluded it was my sister Hannah, and called out: 'It won't do, Hannah—you can not frighten us!' Upon which the figure turned into a recess in the wall; but, as there was nobody there when we passed, we concluded that Hannah had contrived, somehow or other, to slip away and make her escape by the back stairs. On telling this to my mother, she said: 'It is very odd, for Hannah went to bed with a headache before you came in from your walk;' and sure enough, on going to her room, there we found her fast asleep; and Alice, who was at work there, assured us that she had been so for more than an hour. On mentioning this circumstance to Creswell, she turned quite pale and exclaimed that that was precisely the figure she and Marsh had seen in their bed-room.

"About this time, my brother Harry came to spend a few days with us, and we gave him a room up another pair of stairs, at the opposite end of the house. A morning or two after his arrival, when he came down to breakfast, he asked my mother angrily whether she thought he went to bed drunk and could not put out his own candle, that she sent those French rascals to watch him. My mother assured him that she never thought of doing such a thing; but he persisted in the accusation, adding: 'Last night I jumped up and opened the door, and, by the light of the moon through the skylight, I saw the fellow in his loose gown at the bottom of the stairs. If I had not been in my shirt, I would have gone after him and made him remember coming to watch me.'

"We were now preparing to quit the house, having secured another, belonging to a gentleman who was going to spend some time in Italy; but, a few days before our removal, it happened that Mr. and Mrs. Atkyns, some English friends of ours, called, to whom we mentioned these circumstances, observing how extremely unpleasant it was to live in a house that somebody found means of getting into, though how they contrived it we could not discover, nor what their motive could be except it was to frighten us; adding, that nobody could sleep in the room Marsh and Creswell had been obliged to give up. Upon this Mrs. Atkyns laughed heartily, and said she should like, of all things, to sleep there, if my mother would allow her, adding, that with her little terrier she should not be afraid of any ghost that ever appeared. As my mother had, of course, no objection to this fancy of hers, she requested Mrs. Atkyns to ride home with the groom, in order that the latter might bring her night-things before the gates of the town would be shut, as they were then residing a little way in the country. Mr. Atkyns smiled and said she was very bold; but he made no difficulties, and sent the things,—and his wife retired with her dog to her room when we retired to ours, apparently without the least apprehension.

"When she came down in the morning, we were immediately struck at seeing her look very ill; and on inquiring if she too had been frightened, she said she had been awakened in the night by something moving in her room, and that, by the light of the night-lamp, she saw most distinctly a figure, and that the dog, which was spirited and flew at everything, never stirred, although she had endeavored to make him. We saw clearly that she had been very much alarmed; and when Mr. Atkyns came, and endeavored to dissipate the feeling by persuading her that she might have dreamed it, she got quite angry. We could not help thinking that she had actually seen something; and my mother said, after she was gone, that though she could not bring herself to believe it was really a ghost, still she earnestly hoped that she might get out of the house without seeing this figure, which frightened people so much.

"We were now within three days of the one fixed for our removal. I had been taking a long ride, and, being tired, had fallen asleep the moment I lay down; but, in the middle of the night, I was suddenly awakened—I can not tell by what, for the steps over our heads we had become so used to that it no longer disturbed us. Well, I awoke. I had been lying with my face toward my mother, who was asleep beside me, and, as one usually does on awaking, I turned to the other side, where, the weather being warm, the curtain of the bed was undrawn, as it was, also, at the foot; and I saw standing by a chest of drawers, which were betwixt me and the window, a thin, tall figure, in a loose powdering gown, one arm resting on the drawers, and the face turned toward me. I saw it quite distinctly by the night-light, which burned clearly. It was a long, thin, pale, young face, with, oh, such a melancholy expression as can never be effaced from my memory! I was, certainly, very much frightened; but my great horror was, lest my mother should awake and see the figure. I turned my head gently toward her, and heard her breathing high in a sound sleep. Just then the clock on the stairs struck four. I dare say it was nearly an hour before I ventured to look again, and when I did take courage to turn my eyes toward the drawers, there was nothing; yet I had not heard the slightest sound, though I had been listening with the greatest intensity.

"As you may suppose, I never closed my eyes again; and glad I was when Creswell knocked at the door, as she did every morning, for we always locked it, and it was my business to get out of bed and let her in; but on this occasion, instead of doing so, I called out, 'Come in; the door is not fastened;' upon which she answered that it was, and I was obliged to get out of bed and admit her as usual.

"When I told my mother what had happened, she was very grateful to me for not waking her, and commended me much for my resolution; but as she was always my first object, that was not to be wondered at. She however resolved not to risk another night in the house; and we got out of it that very day, after instituting, with the aid of the servants, a thorough search, with a view to ascertain if there was any possible means of getting into the rooms except by the usual modes of ingress; but our search was vain—none could be discovered.

"I think, from the errors in the names, &c., that the publisher of the 'Accredited Ghost-Stories' must have obtained his account from the inhabitants of Lille."

Considering the number of people that were in the house,

the fearlessness of the family, and their disinclination to believe in what is called *the supernatural*, together with the great interest the owner of this large and handsome residence must have had in discovering the trick, if there had been one, I think it is difficult to find any other explanation of this strange story, than that the sad and disappointed spirit of this poor, injured, and probably murdered boy, had never been disengaged from its earthly relations, to which regret for its frustrated hopes and violated rights still held it attached.

There is a story told by Pliny the younger, of a house at Athens, in which nobody could live, from its being haunted. At length the philosopher Athenadorus took it; and the first night he was there, he seems to have comported himself very much as the courageous Mrs. Canning did, on a similar occasion, at Plymouth. He sent his servants to bed, and set himself seriously to work with his writing materials, determined that fancy should not be left free to play him false. For some time all was still, and his mind was wholly engaged in his labors, when he heard a sound like the rattling of chains—which was the sound that had frightened everybody out of the house; but Athenadorus closed his ears, kept his thoughts collected, and wrote on, without lifting up his eyes. The noise, however, increased; it approached the door; it entered the room; then he looked round, and beheld the figure of an old man, lean, haggard, and dirty, with dishevelled hair, and a long beard, who held up his finger and beckoned him. Athenadorus made a gesture with his own hand in return, signifying that he should wait, and went on with his writing. Then the figure advanced and shook his chains over the philosopher's head, who, on looking up, saw him beckoning as before; whereupon he arose and followed him. The apparition walked slowly, as if obstructed by his chains; and having conducted him to a certain spot in the court, which separated the two divisions of an ancient Greek house, he suddenly disappeared. Athenadorus gathered together some grass and leaves, in order to mark the place; and the next day he recommended the authorities to dig there, which they did, and found the skeleton of a human being encircled with chains. It being taken up, and the rights of sepulture duly performed, the house was no longer disturbed.

This was, probably, some poor prisoner also; and in his desire to direct notice to his body, we see the prejudices of his age and country surviving dissolution. Grose, the antiquary, who is, as I have before observed, very facetious on the subject of ghosts, remarks that "Dragging chains is not the custom of English ghosts, chains and black vestments being chiefly the accoutrements of foreign spectres, seen in arbitrary governments." Now, this is a very striking observation. Grose's studies had, doubtless, introduced him to many histories of this description; and the different characteristics of these apparitions, under different governments, is a circumstance in remarkable conformity with the views of those who have been led to take a much more serious view of the subject. They appear as they lived, and as they conceive of themselves; and when rapport or receptivity enable them to see, and to render themselves visible to those yet living in the flesh, it is by so appearing that they tell their story, and ask for sympathy and assistance. I say enable them *to see*, because there seem many reasons for concluding that they do not, under ordinary circumstances, see us, any more than we see them. Whether it be rapport with certain inhabitants, or whether the phenomenon be dependent on certain periods, or any other condition, we can not tell; but I have met with several accounts of houses in which an annoyance of this sort has recurred more than once, at different intervals, sometimes at a distance of seven or ten years, the intermediate time being quite free from it.

One of the most melancholy and impressive circumstances of this sort I have met with, occurred to Mrs. L——, a lady with whose family I am acquainted; Mrs. L—— herself having been kind enough to furnish me with the particulars: A few years since, she took a furnished house in Stevenson street, North Shields, and she had been in it but a very few hours before she was perplexed by hearing feet in the passage, though, whenever she opened the door, she could see nobody. She went to the kitchen, and asked the servant if she had not heard the same sound. She said she had not, but that there seemed to be strange noises in the house. When Mrs. L—— went to bed, she could not go to sleep for the noise of a child's rattle, which seemed to be inside her curtains. It rattled round her head, first on one side, then on the other; then there were sounds of feet, and of a child crying, and a woman sobbing; and, in short, so many strange noises that the servant became frightened and went away. The next girl Mrs. L—— engaged came from Leith, and was a stranger to the place; but she had only passed a night in the house, when she said to her mistress, "This is a troubled house you've got into, ma'am;" and she described, among the rest, that she had repeatedly heard her own name called by a voice near her, though she could see nobody.

One night Mrs. L—— heard a voice, like nothing human, close to her, cry, "Weep! weep! weep!" Then there was a sound like some one struggling for breath, and again "Weep! weep! weep!" Then the gasping, and a third time, "Weep! weep! weep!" She stood still, and looked steadfastly on the spot whence the voice proceeded, but could see nothing; and her little boy, who held her hand, kept saying, "What is that, mamma? What is that?" She describes the sound as most frightful. All the noises seemed to suggest the idea of childhood, and of a woman in trouble. One night, when it was crying round her bed, Mrs. L—— took courage and adjured it; upon which the noise ceased, for that time, but there was no answer. Mr. L—— was at sea when she took the house, and when he came home he laughed at the story at first, but soon became so convinced the account she gave was correct, that he wanted to have the boards taken up, because, from the noises seeming to hover much about one spot, he thought perhaps some explanation of the mystery might be found. But Mrs. L—— objected that if anything of a painful nature were discovered she should not be able to continue in the house, and as she must pay the year's rent, she wished, if possible, to make out the time.

She never saw anything but twice; once, the appearance of

a child seemed to fall from the ceiling, close to her, and then disappear; and another time she saw a child run into a closet in a room at the top of the house; and it was most remarkable that a small door in that room, which was used for going out on to the roof, always stood open. However often they shut it, it was opened again immediately by an unseen hand, even before they got out of the room; and this continued the whole time they were in the house; while, night and day, some one in creaking shoes was heard pacing backward and forward in the room over Mr. and Mrs. L——'s heads.

At length the year expired; and to their great relief they quitted the house; but five or six years afterward, a person who had bought it having taken up the floor of that upper room to repair it, there was found, close to the small door above alluded to, the skeleton of a child. It was then remembered that some years before a gentleman of somewhat dissolute habits had resided there, and that he was supposed to have been on very intimate terms with a young woman-servant who lived with him, but there had been no suspicion of anything more criminal.

About six years ago, Mr. C——, a gentleman engaged in business in London, heard of a good country-house in the neighborhood of the metropolis, which was to be had at a low rent. It was rather an old-fashioned place, and was surrounded by a garden and pleasure-ground; and having taken a lease of it for seven years, furnished as it was, his family removed thither, and he joined them once or twice a week, as his business permitted.

They had been some considerable time in the house without the occurrence of anything remarkable, when one evening, toward dusk, Mrs. C——, on going into what was called the oak bedroom, saw a female figure near one of the windows. It was apparently a young woman with dark hair hanging over her shoulders, a silk petticoat, and a short, white robe, and she appeared to be looking eagerly through the window, as if expecting somebody. Mrs. C—— clapped her hand upon her eyes, "as thinking she had seen something she ought not to have seen," and when she looked again the figure had disappeared.

Shortly after this, a young girl who filled the situation of under nursery-maid, came to her in great agitation, saying that she had had a terrible fright, from seeing a very ugly old woman looking in upon her as she passed the window in the lobby. The girl was trembling violently, and almost crying, so that Mrs. C—— entertained no doubts of the reality of her alarm. She, however, thought it advisable to laugh her out of her fear, and went with her to the window, which looked into a closed court, but there was no one there, neither had any of the other servants seen such a person. Soon after this, the family began to find themselves disturbed with strange, and frequently very loud, noises during the night. Among the rest, there was something like the beating of a crow-bar upon the pump in the above-mentioned court; but, search as they would, they could discover no cause for the sound. One day, when Mr. C—— had brought a friend from London to stay the night with him, Mrs. C—— thought proper to go up to the oak bedroom, where the stranger was to sleep, for the purpose of inspecting the arrangements for his comfort, when, to her great surprise, some one seemed to follow her up to the fireplace, though, on turning round, there was nobody to be seen. She said nothing about it, however, and returned below, where her husband and the stranger were sitting. Presently, one of the servants (not the one mentioned above) tapped at the door and requested to speak with her, and Mrs. C—— going out, she told her, in great agitation, that in going up stairs to the visiter's room, a footstep had followed her all the way to the fireplace, although she could see nobody. Mrs. C—— said something soothing, and that matter passed, she, herself, being a good deal puzzled, but still unwilling to admit the idea that there was anything extra-natural in these occurrences. Repeatedly, after this, these footsteps were heard in different parts of the house, when nobody was to be seen; and often, while she was lying in bed, she heard them distinctly approach her door, when, being a very courageous woman, she would start out with a loaded pistol in her hand, but there was never any one to be seen. At length it was impossible to conceal from herself and her servants that these occurrences were of an extraordinary nature, and the latter, as may be supposed, felt very uncomfortable. Among other unpleasant things, while sitting all together in the kitchen, they used to see the latch lifted and the door open, though no one came in that they could see; and when Mr. C—— himself watched for these events, although they took place, and he was quite on the alert, he altogether failed in detecting any visible agent.

One night, the same servant who had heard the footsteps following her to the bedroom fireplace, happening to be asleep in Mrs. C——'s chamber, she became much disturbed, and was heard to murmur, "Wake me! wake me!" as if in great mental anguish. Being aroused, she told her mistress a dream she had had, which seemed to throw some light upon these mysteries. She thought she was in the oak bedroom, and at one end of it she saw a young female in an old-fashioned dress, with long dark hair, while in another part of the room was a very ugly old woman, also in old-fashioned attire. The latter addressing the former said, "What have you done with the child, Emily? What have you done with the child?" To which the younger figure answered, "Oh, I did not kill it. He was preserved, and grew up, and joined the —— regiment, and went to India." Then addressing the sleeper, the young lady continued, "I have never spoken to mortal before; but I will tell you all. My name is Miss Black; and this old woman is Nurse Black. Black is not her name, but we call her so because she has been so long in the family." Here the old woman interrupted the speaker by coming up and laying her hand on the dreaming girl's shoulder, while she said something; but she could not remember what, for, feeling excruciating pain from the touch, she had been so far aroused as to be sensible she was asleep, and to beg to be wholly awakened.

As the old woman seemed to resemble the figure that one of the other servants had seen looking into the window, and the young one resembled that she had herself seen in the oak chamber, Mrs. C—— naturally concluded that there was something extraordinary about this dream, and she consequently took an early opportunity of inquiring in the neighborhood what was known as to the names or circumstances of the former inhabitants of this house; and, after much investigation, she learned that, about seventy or eighty years before, it had been in the possession of a Mrs. Ravenhall, who had a niece, named Miss Black, living with her. This niece Mrs. C—— supposed might be the younger of the two persons who was seen. Subsequently, she saw her again in the same room, wringing her hands, and looking with a mournful significance to one corner. They had the boards taken up on that spot, but nothing was found.

One of the most curious incidents, connected with this story, remains to be told. After occupying the house three years, they were preparing to quit it—not on account of its being haunted, but for other reasons—when on awaking one morning, a short time before their departure, Mrs. C—— saw, standing at the foot of her bed, a dark-complexioned man, in a working dress, a fustian jacket, and red comforter round his neck—who, however, suddenly disappeared. Mr. C—— was lying beside her at the time, but asleep. This was the last apparition seen. But the strange thing is, that a few days after this, it being necessary to order in a small quantity of coals to serve till their removal, Mr. C—— undertook to perform the commission on his way to London. Accordingly, the next day, she mentioned to him that the coals had arrived; which he said was very fortunate, since he had entirely forgotten to order them. Wondering whence they had come, Mrs. C—— hereupon inquired of the servants, who none of them knew anything about the matter; but on interrogating a person in the village, by whom they had frequently been provided with this article, he answered that they had been ordered by a dark man, in a fustian jacket and red comfort, who had called for the purpose.

After this last event, Mr. and Mrs. C—— quitted the house; but I have heard that its subsequent tenants encountered some similar annoyances, although I have no means of ascertaining the particulars.

But perhaps one of the most remarkable cases of haunting in modern times, is that of Willington, near Newcastle, in my account of which, however, I find myself anticipated by Mr. Howitt; and as he has had the advantage of visiting the place, which I have not, I shall take the liberty of borrowing his description of it, prefacing the account with the following letter from Mr. Proctor, the owner of the house, who it will be seen vouches for the general authenticity of the narrative. The letter was written in answer to one from me, requesting some more precise information than I had been able to obtain:—

"Josh. Proctor hopes C. Crowe will excuse her note having remained two weeks unanswered, during which time J. P. has been from home, or particularly engaged. Feeling averse to add to the publicity the circumstances occurring in his house, at Willington, have already obtained, J. P. would rather not furnish additional particulars; but if C. C. is not in possession of the number of 'Howitt's Journal,' which contains a variety of details on the subject, he will be glad to forward her one. He would, at the same time, assure C. Crowe of the strict accuracy of that portion of W. Howitt's narrative which is extracted from 'Richardson's Table Book.' W. Howitt's statements, derived from his recollection of verbal communications with branches of J. Proctor's family, are likewise essentially correct, though, as might be expected in some degree, erroneous circumstantially.

"J. P. takes leave to express his conviction that the unbelief of the educated classes in apparitions of the deceased and kindred phenomena is not grounded on a fair philosophic examination of the facts, which have induced the popular belief of all ages and countries; and that it will be found by succeeding ages to have been nothing better than unreasoning and unreasonable prejudice.

"*Willington, near Newcastle-on-Tyne,*
7th mo. 22, 1847."

"VISITS TO REMARKABLE PLACES.

"BY WILLIAM HOWITT.

"THE HAUNTED HOUSE AT WILLINGTON, NEAR NEWCASTLE-ON-TYNE.

"We have of late years settled it as an established fact that ghosts and haunted houses were the empty creation of ignorant times. We have comfortably persuaded ourselves that such fancies only hovered in the twilight of superstition, and that in these enlightened days they had vanished for ever. How often has it been triumphantly referred to, as a proof that all such things were the offspring of ignorance, that nothing of the kind is heard of now? What shall we say, then, to the following facts? Here we have ghosts and a haunted house still. We have them in the face of our vaunted noonday light—in the midst of a busy and a populous neighborhood—in the neighborhood of a large and most intelligent town—and in a family neither ignorant nor in any other respect superstitious. For years have these ghosts and hauntings disturbed the quiet of a highly respectable family, and continue to haunt and disturb, spite of the incredulity of the wise, the investigations of the curious, and the anxious vigilance of the suffering family itself.

"Between the railway running from Newcastle-on-Tyne to North Shields, and the river Tyne, there lie in a hollow some few cottages, a parsonage, a mill, and a miller's house: these constitute the hamlet of Willington. Just above these the railway is carried across the valley on lofty arches, and from it you look down on the mill and cottages, lying at a considerable depth below. The mill is a large steam flour-mill, like a factory, and the miller's house stands near it, but not adjoining it. None of the cottages which lie between these premises and the railway, either, are in contact with them. The house stands on a sort of little promontory, round which runs the channel of a water-course, which appears to fill and empty with the tides. On one side of the mill and house, slopes away upward a field to a considerable distance, where it is terminated by other enclosures; on the other stands a considerable extent of ballast-hill—*i. e.*, one of the numerous hills on the banks of the Tyne made by the deposite of ballast from the vessels trading thither. At a distance, the top of the mill seems about level with the country around it. The place lies about half-way between Newcastle and North Shields.

"This mill is, I believe, the property of, and is worked by, Messrs. Unthank and Procter. Mr. Joseph Procter resides on the spot in the house just by the mill, as already stated. He is a member of the society of friends—a gentleman in the very prime of life—and his wife, an intelligent lady, is of a family of friends in Carlisle. They have several young children. This very respectable and well-informed family, belonging to a sect which of all others is most accustomed to control, to regulate, and to put down even the imagination—the last people in the world, as it would appear, in fact, to be affected by any mere imaginary terrors or impressions—have for years been persecuted by the most extraordinary noises and apparitions.

"The house is not an old house, as will appear; it was built about the year 1800. It has no particularly spectral look about it. Seeing it in passing, or within, ignorant of its real character, one should by no means say that it was a place likely to have the reputation of being haunted. Yet looking down from the railway, and seeing it and the mill lying in a deep hole, one might imagine various strange noises likely to be heard in such a place in the night, from vessels on the river—from winds sweeping and howling down the gulley in which it stands—from engines in the neighborhood connected with coal-mines, one of which, I could not tell where, was making at the time I was there a wild sighing noise, as I stood on the hill above. There is not any passage, however, known of under the house, by which subterranean noises could be heard; nor are they merely noises that are heard,—distinct apparitions are declared to be seen.

"Spite of the unwillingness of Mr. Procter, that these mysterious circumstances should become quite public, and averse as he is to make known himself these strange visitations, they were of such a nature that they soon became rumored over the whole neighborhood. Numbers of people hurried to the place to inquire into the truth of them, and at length a remarkable occurrence brought them into print. What this occurrence was, the pamphlet which appeared, and which was afterward reprinted in 'The Local Historian's Table-Book,' published by Mr. M. A. Richardson, of Newcastle, and which I here copy, will explain. It will be seen that the writer of this article has the fullest faith in the reality of what he relates, as, indeed, vast numbers of the best informed inhabitants of the neighborhood have.

"AUTHENTIC ACCOUNT OF A VISIT TO THE HAUNTED HOUSE AT WILLINGTON.

"Were we to draw an inference from the number of cases of reported visitatations from the invisible world that have been made public of late, we might be led to imagine that the days of supernatural agency were about to recommence, and that ghosts and hobgoblins were about to resume their sway over the fears of mankind. Did we, however, indulge in such an apprehension, a glance at the current tone of the literature and philosophy of the day, when treating of these subjects, would show a measure of unbelief regarding them as scornful and uncompromising as the veriest atheist or materialist could desire Notwithstanding the prevalence of this feeling among the educated classes, there is a curiosity and interest manifested in every occurrence of this nature, that indicate a lurking faith at bottom, which an affected skepticism fails entirely to conceal. We feel, therefore, that we need not apologise to our readers for introducing the following particulars of a *visit* to a house in this immediate neighborhood, which had become notorious for some years previous, as being 'haunted;' and several of the reputed deeds, or misdeeds, of its supernatural visitant had been published far and wide by rumor's thousand tongues. We deem it as worthy to be chronicled as the doings of its contempory *genii* at Windsor, Dublin, Liverpool, Carlisle, and Sun derland, and which have all likewise hitherto failed, after public investigation, to receive a solution consistent with a rejection of spiritual agency.

"We have visited the house in question, which is well known

to many of our readers, as being near a large steam corn-mill, in full view of Willington viaduct, on the Newcastle and Shields railway; and it may not be irrelevant to mention that it is quite detached from the mill, or any other premises, and has no cellaring under it. The proprietor of the house, who lives in it, declines to make public the particulars of the disturbance to which he has been subjected, and it must be understood that the account of the visit we are about to lay before our readers is derived from a friend to whom Dr. Drury presented a copy of his correspondence on the subject, with power to make such use of it as he thought proper. We learned that the house had been reputed, at least one room in it, to have been haunted forty years ago, and had afterward been undisturbed for a long period, during some years of which quietude the present occupant lived in it unmolested. We are also informed that about the time that the premises were building, viz., in 1800 or 1801, there were reports of some deed of darkness having been committed by some one employed about them. We should extend this account beyond the limits we have set to ourselves, did we now enter upon a full account of the strange things which have been seen and heard about the place by several of the neighbors, as well as those which are reported to have been seen, heard, and felt, by the inmates, whose servants have been changed, on that account, many times. We proceed, therefore, to give the following letters which have been passed between individuals of undoubted veracity, leaving the reader to draw his own conclusions on the subject.

"(Copy, No. 1.)

"*17th June*, 1840.

"To Mr. Procter:

"Sir: Having heard from indisputable authority, viz., that of my excellent friend, Mr. Davison, of Low Willington, farmer, that you and your family are disturbed by most unaccountable noises at night, I beg leave to tell you that I have read attentively Wesley's account of such things, but with, I must confess, no great belief; but an account of this report coming from one of your sect, which I admire for candor and simplicity, my curiosity is excited to a high pitch, which I would fain satisfy. My desire is to remain alone in the house all night with no companion but my own watch-dog, in which, as far as courage and fidelity are concerned, I place much more reliance than upon any three young gentlemen I know of. And it is also my hope that, if I have a fair trial, I shall be able to unravel this mystery. Mr. Davison will give you every satisfaction if you take the trouble to inquire of him concerning me.

"I am, sir, yours most respectfully,

"EDWARD DRURY.

"At C. C. Embleton's, Surgeon,
"*No.* 10 *Church street, Sunderland.*

"(COPY, No. 2.)

"Joseph Procter's respects to Edward Drury, whose note he received a few days ago, expressing a wish to pass a night in his house at Willington. As the family is going from home on the 23d instant, and one of Unthank and Procter's men will sleep in the house, if Edward Drury feel inclined to come on or after the 24th, to spend a night in it, he is at liberty so to do, with or without his faithful dog, which, by-the-by, can be of no possible use, except as company. At the same time, Joseph Procter things it best to inform him that particular disturbances are far from frequent at present, being only occasional, and quite uncertain, and therefore the satisfaction of Edward Drury's curiosity must be considered as problematical. The best chance will be afforded by sitting up alone in the third story, till it be fairly daylight, say two or three, A. M.

"*Willington, 6th mo. 21st,* 1840.

"Joseph Procter will leave word with T. Maun, foreman, to admit Edward Drury.

"Mr. Procter left home with his family on the 23d of June, and got an old servant, who was then out of place in consequence of ill-health, to take charge of the house during their absence. Mr. Procter returned alone, on account of business, on the 3d of July, on the evening of which day Mr. Drury and his companion also unexpectedly arrived. After the house had been locked up, every corner of it was minutely examined. The room out of which the apparition issued is too shallow to contain any person. Mr. Drury and his friend had lights by them, and were satisfied that there was no one in the house besides Mr. Procter, the servant, and themselves.

"(Copy, No. 3.)

"Monday Morning, *July 6th*, 1840.

"To Mr. Procter:

"Dear Sir: I am sorry I was not at home to receive you yesterday, when you kindly called to inquire for me. I am happy to state, that I am really surprised that I have been so little affected as I am, after that horrid and most awful affair. The only bad effect that I feel is a heavy dullness in one of my ears, the right one. I call it heavy dullness because I not only do not hear distinctly, but feel in it a constant noise. This I never was affected with before; but I doubt not it will go off. I am persuaded that no one went to your house at any time more *disbelieving in respect to seeing anything peculiar;* and now no one can be more satisfied than myself. I will, in the course of a few days, send you a full detail of all I saw and heard. Mr. Spence and two other gentlemen came down to my house in the afternoon to hear my detail; but, sir, could I account for these noises from natural causes, yet so firmly am I persuaded of the horrid apparition, that I would affirm that what I saw with my eyes was a punishment to me for my scoffing and unbelief; that I am assured that, as far as the horror is concerned, they are happy that believe and have not seen. Let me trouble you, sir, to give me the address of your sister, from Cumberland, who was alarmed, and also of your brother. I would feel a satisfaction in having a line from them; and, above all things, it will be a great cause of joy to me, if you never allow your young family to be in that horrid house again. Hoping you will write a few lines at your leisure,

"I remain, dear sir, yours very truly,

"Edward Drury.

"(Copy, No. 4.)

"Willington, *7th mo.* 9, 1840.

"Respected Friend, E. Drury: Having been at Sunderland, I did not receive thine of the 6th till yesterday morning. I am glad to hear thou art getting well over the effects of thy unlooked-for visitation. I hold in respect thy bold and manly assertion of the truth, in the face of that ridicule and ignorant conceit with which that which is called the supernatural, in the present day, is usually assailed.

"I shall be glad to receive thy detail, in which it will be needful to be very particular in showing that thou couldst not be asleep or attacked by nightmare, or mistake a reflection of the candle, as some sagaciously suppose.

"I remain, respectfully, thy friend,

"Josh. Procter.

"P. S.—I have about thirty witnesses to various things which can not be satisfactorily accounted for on any other principle than that of spiritual agency.

"(Copy, No. 5.)

"Sunderland, *July* 13, 1840.

"Dear Sir: I hereby, according to promise in my last letter, forward you a true account of what I heard and saw at your house, in which I was led to pass the night from various rumors circulated by most respectable parties—particularly from an account by my esteemed friend Mr. Davison, whose name I mentioned to you in a former letter. Having received your sanction to visit your mysterious dwelling, I went on the 3d of July, accompanied by a friend of mine, T. Hudson. This was not according to promise, nor in accordance with my first intent, as I wrote to you I would come alone; but I felt gratified at your kindness in not alluding to the liberty I had taken, as it ultimately proved for the best. I must here mention that, not expecting you at home, I had in my pocket a brace of pistols, determining in my mind to let one of them drop before the miller, as if by accident, for fear he should presume to play tricks upon me; but, after my interview with you, I felt there was no occasion for weapons, and did not load them, after you had allowed us to inspect as minutely as we pleased every portion of the house. I sat down on the third story landing, fully expecting to account for any noises that I might hear, in a philosophical manner. This was about eleven o'clock, P. M. About ten minutes to twelve, we both heard a noise, as if a number of people were pattering with their bare feet upon the floor; and yet so singular was the noise, that I could not minutely determine whence it proceeded. A few minutes afterward we heard a noise, as if some one was knocking with his knuckles among our feet; this was followed by a hollow cough from the very room from which the apparition proceeded. The only noise after this, was as if a person was rustling against the wall in coming up stairs. At a quarter to one, I told my friend that, feeling a little cold, I would like to go to bed, as we might hear the noise equally well there; he replied that he would not go to bed till daylight. I took up a note which I had accidentally dropped, and began to read it, after which I took out my watch to ascertain the time, and found that it wanted ten minutes to one. In taking my eyes from the watch, they became riveted upon a closet-door, which I distinctly saw open, and saw also the figure of a female attired in grayish garments, with the head inclining downward, and one hand pressed upon the chest as if in pain, and the other, viz., the right hand, extended toward the floor, with the index finger pointing downward. It advanced with an apparently cautious step across the floor toward me; immediately as it approached my friend, who was slumbering, its right hand was extended toward him: I then rushed at it, giving, as Mr. Procter states, a most awful yell; but, instead of grasping it, I fell upon my friend, and I recollected nothing distinctly for nearly three hours afterward. I have since learned that I was carried down stairs in an agony of fear and terror.

"I hereby certify that the above account is strictly true and correct in every respect.

"EDWARD DRURY.

"*North Shields.*

"The following more recent case of an apparition seen in the window of the same house from the outside, by four credible witnesses, who had the opportutiy of scrutinizing it for more than ten minutes, is given on most unquestionable authority. One of these witnesses is a young lady, a near connection of the family, who, for obvious reasons, did not sleep in the house; another, a respectable man, who has been many years employed in, and is foreman of, the manufactory; his daughter, aged about seventeen; and his wife, who first saw the object and called out the others to view it. The appearance presented was that of a bareheaded man, in a flowing robe like a surplice, who glided backward and forward about three feet from the floor, or level with the bottom of the second story window, seeming to enter the wall on each side, and thus present a side view in passing. It then stood still in the window, and a part of the body came through both the blind, which was close down, and the window, as its luminous body intercepted the view of the framework of the window. It was semi-transparent, and as bright as a star, diffusing a radiance all around. As it grew more dim, it assumed a blue tinge, and gradually faded away from the head downward. The foreman passed twice close to the house under the window, and also went to inform the family, but found the house locked up. There was no moonlight, nor a ray of light visible anywhere about, and no person near. Had any magic lantern been used, it could not possibly have escaped detection; and it is obvious nothing of that kind could have been employed on the inside, as in that case the light could only have been thrown upon the blind, and not so as to intercept the view both of the blind and of the window from without. The owner of the house slept in that room, and must have entered it shortly after this figure had disappeared.

"It may well be supposed what a sensation the report of the visit of Mr. Drury and its result must have created. It flew far and wide, and when it appeared in print, still wider; and, what was not a little singular, Mr. Procter received, in consequence, a great number of letters from individuals of different ranks and circumstances, including many of much property, informing him that their residences were, and had been for years, subject to annoyances of precisely a similar character.

"So, the ghosts and the hauntings are not gone, after all! We have turned our backs on them, and, in the pride of our philosophy, have refused to believe in them; but they have persisted in remaining, notwithstanding!

"These singular circumstances being at various times related by parties acquainted with the family at Willington, I was curious, on a tour northward some time ago, to pay this haunted house a visit, and to solicit a night's lodging there. Unfortunately the family was absent, on a visit to Mrs. Procter's relatives in Carlisle, so that my principal purpose was defeated; but I found the foreman and his wife, mentioned in the foregoing narrative, living just by. They spoke of the facts above detailed with the simple earnestness of people who had no doubts whatever on the subject. The noises and apparitions in and about this house seemed just like any other facts connected with it—as matters too palpable and positive to be questioned, any more than that the house actually stood, and the mill ground. They mentioned to me the circumstance of the young lady, as above stated, who took up her lodging in their house, because she would no longer encounter the annoyances of the haunted house—and what trouble it had occasioned the family in procuring and retaining servants.

"The wife accompanied me into the house, which I found in charge of a recently-married servant and her husband, during the absence of the family. This young woman—who had, previous to her marriage, lived some time in the house—had never seen anything, and therefore had no fear. I was shown over the house, and especially into the room on the third story, the main haunt of the unwelcome visiters, and where Dr. Drury had received such an alarm. This room, as stated, was and had been for some time abandoned as a bed-room, from its bad character, and was occupied as a lumber-room.

"At Carlisle, I again missed Mr. Procter: he had returned to Willington, so that I lost the opportunity of hearing from him or Mrs. Procter any account of these singular matters. I saw, however, various members of his wife's family, most intelligent people, of the highest character for sound and practical sense, and they were unanimous in their confirmation of the particulars I had heard, and which are here related.

"One of Mrs. Procter's brothers—a gentleman in middle life, and of a peculiarly sensible, sedate, and candid disposition, a person apparently most unlikely to be imposed on by fictitious alarms or tricks—assured me that he had himself, on a visit there, been disturbed by the strangest noises; that he had resolved, before going, that if any such noises occurred, he would speak, and demand of the invisible actor who he was, and why he came thither: but the occasion came, and he found himself unable to fulfil his intention. As he lay in bed one night, he heard a heavy step ascend the stairs toward his room, and some one striking, as it were, with a thick stick on the banisters, as he went along. It came to his door, and he essayed to call, but his voice died in his throat. He then sprang from his bed, and, opening the door, found no one there—but now heard the same heavy steps deliberately descending, though invisible, the steps before his face, and accompanying the descent with the same loud blows on the banisters.

"My informant now proceeded to the room door of Mr. Procter, who he found had also heard the sounds, and who now also arose, and with a light they made a speedy descent below, and a thorough search there, but without discovering anything that could account for the occurrence.

"The two young ladies, who, on a visit there, had also been annoyed by this invisible agent, gave me this account of it: The first night, as they were sleeping in the same bed, they felt the bed lifted up beneath them. Of course, they were much alarmed. They feared lest some one had concealed himself there for the purpose of robbery. They gave an alarm, search was made, but nothing was found. On another night, their bed was violently shaken, and the curtains suddenly hoisted up* all

* It is remarkable that this hoisting of the bed-curtains is similar to an incident recorded in the account of the visit of Lord Tyrone's ghost to Lady Beresford.

round to the very tester, as if pulled by cords, and as rapidly let down again, several times! Search again produced no evidence of the cause. The next, they had the curtains totally removed from the bed, resolving to sleep without them, as they felt as though evil eyes were lurking behind them. The consequences of this, however, were still more striking and terrific. The following night, as they happened to awake, and the chamber was light enough (for it was summer) to see everything in it, they both saw a female figure, of a misty substance, and bluish-gray hue, come out of the wall at the bed's head, and through the head-board, in a horizontal position, and lean over them. They saw it most distinctly—they saw it as a female figure come out of, and again pass into, the wall. Their terror became intense, and one of the sisters from that night refused to sleep any more in the house, but took refuge in the house of the foreman during her stay; the other shifting her quarters to another part of the house. It was the young lady who slept at the foreman's who saw, as above related, the singular apparition of the luminous figure in the window, along with the foreman and his wife.

"It would be too long to relate all the forms in which this nocturnal disturbance is said by the family to present itself. When a figure appears, it is sometimes that of a man, as already described, which is often very luminous, and passes through the walls as though they were nothing. This male figure is well known to the neighbors by the name of "Old Jeffrey!" At other times, it is the figure of a lady, also in gray costume, and as described by Mr. Drury. She is sometimes seen sitting wrapped in a sort of mantle, with her head depressed, and her hands crossed on her lap. The most terrible fact is, that she is without eyes.

"To hear such sober and superior people gravely relate to you such things, gives you a very odd feeling. They say that the noise made is often like that of a pavior with his rammer thumping on the floor. At other times it is coming down stairs, making a similar loud sound. At others it coughs, sighs, and groans, like a person in distress; and, again, there is the sound of a number of little feet pattering on the floor of the upper chamber, where the apparition has more particularly exhibited itself, and which, for that reason, is solely used as a lumber-room. Here these little footsteps may be often heard as if careering a child's carriage about, which in bad weather is kept up there. Sometimes, again, it makes the most horrible laughs. Nor does it always confine itself to the night. On one occasion, a young lady, as she assured me herself, opened the door in answer to a knock, the housemaid being absent, and a lady in fawn-colored silk entered, and proceeded up stairs. As the young lady, of course, supposed it a neighbor come to make a morning call on Mrs. Procter, she followed her up to the drawing-room, where, however, to her astonishment, she did not find her, nor was anything more seen of her.

"Such are a few of the 'questionable shapes' in which this troublesome guest comes. As may be expected, terror of it is felt by the neighboring cottagers, though it seems to confine its malicious disturbance almost solely to the occupants of this one house. There is a well, however, near to which no one ventures after it is dark, because it has been seen near it.

"It is useless to attempt to give any opinion respecting the real causes of these strange sounds and sights. How far they may be real or imaginary, how far they may be explicable by natural causes or not—the only thing which we have here to record is, the very singular fact of a most respectable and intelligent family having for many years been continually annoyed by them, as well as their visiters. They express themselves as most anxious to obtain any clew to the true cause, as may be seen by Mr. Procter's ready acquiescence in the experiment of Mr. Drury. So great a trouble is it to them, that they have contemplated the necessity of quitting the house altogether, though it would create great inconvenience as regarded business. And it only remains to be added that we have not heard very recently whether these visitations are still continued, though we have a letter of Mr. Procter's to a friend of ours, dated September, 1844, in which he says: 'Disturbances have for a length of time been only very unfrequent, which is a comfort, as the elder children are getting old enough (about nine or ten years) to be more injuriously affected by anything of the sort.'

"Over these facts let the philosophers ponder, and if any of them be powerful enough to exorcise 'Old Jeffrey,' or the bluish-gray and misty lady, we are sure that Mr. Joseph Procter will hold himself deeply indebted to them. We have lately heard that Mr. Procter has discovered an old book, which makes it appear that the very same 'hauntings' took place in an old house, on the very same spot, at least two hundred years ago."

To the above information, furnished by Mr. Howitt, I have to subjoin that the family of Mr. Procter are now quitting the house, which he intends to divide into small tenements for the work-people. A friend of mine who lately visited Willington, and who went over the house with Mr. Procter, assures me that the annoyances still continue, though less frequent than formerly. Mr. Procter informed her that the female figure generally appeared in a shroud, and that it had been seen in that guise by one of the family only a few days before. A wish being expressed by a gentleman visiting Mr. Procter that some natural explanation of these perplexing circumstances might be discovered, the latter declared his entire conviction, founded on an experience of fifteen years, that no such elucidation was possible.

CHAPTER XIV.

SPECTRAL LIGHTS, AND APPARITIONS ATTACHED TO CERTAIN FAMILIES.

In commencing another chapter, I take the opportunity of repeating what I have said before, viz., that in treating of these phenomena, I find it most convenient to assume what I myself believe—that they are to be explained by the existence and appearance of what are called GHOSTS; but in so doing, I am not presuming to settle the question: if any one will examine into the facts and furnish a better explanation of them, I shall be ready to receive it.

In the meantime, assuming this hypothesis, there is one phenomenon frequently attending their appearance, which has given rise to a great deal of thoughtless ridicule, but which, in the present state of science, merits very particular attention. Grose, whom Dr. Hibbert quotes with particular satisfaction, says: "I can not learn that ghosts carry tapers in their hands, as they are sometimes depicted; though the room in which they appear, even when without fire or candle, is frequently said to be as light as day."

Most persons will have heard of this peculiarity attending the appearance of ghosts. In the case of Professor Dorrien's apparition, mentioned in a former chapter, Professor Oeder saw it, when there was no light in the room, by a flame which proceeded from itself. When he had the room lighted, he saw it no longer, the light of the lamp rendering invisible the more delicate phosphorescent light of the spectre: just as the bright glare of the sun veils the feebler lustre of the stars, and obscures to our senses many chemical lights which are very perceptible in darkness. Hence the notion, so available to those who satisfy themselves with scoffing without inquiring, that broad daylight banishes apparitions, and that the belief in them is merely the offspring of physical as well as moral darkness.

I meet with innumerable cases in which this phosphorescent light is one of the accompaniments, the flame sometimes proceeding visibly from the figure; while in others, the room appeared pervaded with light, without its seeming to issue from any particular object.

I remember a case of the servants in a country-house, in Aberdeenshire, hearing the door-bell ring after their mistress was gone to bed; on coming up to open it, they saw through a window that looked into a hall that it was quite light, and that their master, Mr. F——, who was at the time absent from home, was there in his travelling dress. They ran to tell their mistress what they had seen; but when they returned, all was dark, and there was nothing unusual to be discovered. That night Mr. F—— died at sea, on his voyage to London.

A gentleman, some time ago, awoke in the middle of a dark winter's night, and perceived that his room was as light as if it were day. He awoke his wife and mentioned the circumstance, saying he could not help apprehending that some misfortune had occurred to his fishing-boats, which had put to sea. The boats were lost that night.

Only last year, there was a very curious circumstance happened in the south of England, in which these lights were seen. I give the account literally as I extracted it from the newspaper, and also the answer of the editor to my further inquiries. I know nothing more of this story; but it is singularly in keeping with others proceeding from different quarters.

"A Ghost at Bristol.—We have this week a ghost-story to relate. Yes, a ghost-story; a real ghost-story, and a ghost-story without, as yet, any clew to its elucidation. After the dissolution of the Calendars, their ancient residence, adjoining and almost forming a part of All-Saint's church, Bristol, was converted into a vicarage-house, and it is still called by that name, though the incumbents have for many years ceased to reside there. The present occupants are Mr. and Mrs. Jones, the sexton and sextoness of the church, and one or two lodgers;

and it is to the former and their servant-maid that the strange visiter has made his appearance, causing such terror by his nightly calls, that all three have determined on quitting the premises, if indeed they have not already carried their resolution into effect. Mr. and Mrs. Jones's description of the disturbance as given to the landlord, on whom they called in great consternation, is as distinct as any ghost-story could be. The nocturnal visiter is heard walking about the house when the inhabitants are in bed; and Mr. Jones, who is a man of by no means nervous constitution, declares he has several times seen a light flickering on one of the walls. Mrs. Jones is equally certain that she has heard a man with creaking shoes walking in the bed-room above her own, when no man was on the premises (or at least ought to be), and "was nearly killed with the fright." To the servant-maid, however, was vouchsafed the unenvied honor of seeing this restless night-visiter; she declares she has repeatedly had her bed-room door unbolted at night between the hours of twelve and two o'clock—the period when such beings usually make their promenades—by something in human semblance; she can not particularize his dress, but describes it as something antique, and of a fashion "lang syne gane." and to some extent corresponding to that of the ancient Calendars, the former inhabitants of the house. She further says he is a "whiskered gentleman" (we give her own words)—which whiskered gentleman has gone the length of shaking her bed, and she believes would have shaken herself also, but that she invariably puts her head under the clothes when she sees him approach. Mrs. Jones declares she believes in the appearance of the whiskered gentleman, and she had made up her mind, the night before she called on her landlord, to leap out of the window (and it is not a trifle that will make people leap out of the windows) as soon as he entered the room. The effect of the 'flickering light' on Mr. Jones was quite terrific, causing excessive trembling, and the complete doubling up of his whole body into a round ball, like."—*Bristol Times.*

"BRISTOL TIMES OFFICE, *June* 3, 1846.

"MADAM: In reply to your inquiries respecting the ghost-story, I have to assure you that the whole affair remains wrapped in the same mystery as when chronicled in the pages of the *Bristol Times.*

"I am, madam, yours obediently,

"THE EDITOR."

I subsequently wrote to Mrs. Jones, who I found was not a very dexterous scribe; but she confirmed the above account—adding, however, that the Rev. Mr. ——, the clergyman of the parish, said I had better write to him about it, and that he does not believe in such things. Of course he does not, and it would have been useless to have asked his opinion.

There never was, perhaps, a more fearless human being than Madame Gottfried, the empoisonneuse of Bremen; at least, she felt no remorse—she feared nothing but discovery; and yet, when after years of successful crime she was at length arrested, she related that soon after the death of her first husband, Miltenburg, whom she had poisoned, as she was standing, in the dusk of the evening, in her drawing-room, she suddenly saw a bright light hovering at no great distance above the floor, which advanced toward her bed-room door and then disappeared. This phenomenon occurred on three successive evenings. On another occasion, she saw a shadowy appearance hovering near her—"Ach! denke ich, das ist Miltenburg, seine erscheinung!"—(Alas! thought I, that is the ghost of Miltenburg!) Yet did not this withhold her murderous hand.

The lady who met with the curious adventure in Petersburgh, mentioned in a former chapter, had no light in her room; yet she saw the watch distinctly by the old woman's light, though of what nature it was, she does not know. Of the lights seen over graves, familiarly called "corpse-candles," I have spoken elsewhere—as also of the luminous form perceived by Rilling in the garden at Colmar, as mentioned by Baron von Reichenbach. Most people have heard the story of the Radiant Boy seen by Lord Castlereagh—an apparition which the owner of the castle admitted to have been visible to many others. Dr. Kerner mentions a similar fact, wherein an advocate and his wife were awakened by a noise and a light, and saw a beautiful child enveloped by the sort of glory that is seen surrounding the heads of saints. It disappeared, and they never had a repetition of the phenomenon, which they afterward heard was believed to recur every seven years in that house, and to be connected with the cruel murder of a child by its mother.

To these instances I will add an account of the ghost seen in C—— castle, copied from the handwriting of C—— M—— H—— in a book of manuscript extracts, dated C—— castle, December 22, 1824, and furnished to me by a friend of the family:—

"In order to introduce my readers to the haunted room, I will mention that it forms part of the old house, with windows looking into the court, which in early times was deemed a necessary security against an enemy. It adjoins a tower built by the Romans for defence; for C—— was properly more a border tower than a castle of any consideration. There is a winding staircase in this tower, and the walls are from eight to ten feet thick.

"When the times became more peaceable, our ancestors enlarged the arrow-slit windows, and added to that part of the building which looks toward the river Eden; the view of which, with its beautiful banks, we now enjoy. But many additions and alterations have been made since that.

"To return to the room in question, I must observe that it is by no means remote or solitary, being surrounded on all sides by chambers that are constantly inhabited. It is accessible by a passage cut through a wall eight feet in thickness, and its dimensions are twenty-one by eighteen. One side of the wainscoting is covered with tapestry; the remainder is decorated with old family-pictures, and some ancient pieces of embroidery, probably the handiwork of nuns. Over a press, which has doors of Venetian glass, is an ancient oaken figure, with a battle-axe in his hand, which was one of those formerly placed on the walls of the city of Carlisle, to represent guards. There used to be, also, an old-fashioned bed and some dark furniture in this room; but, so many were the complaints of those who slept there, that I was induced to replace some of these articles of furniture by more modern ones, in the hope of removing a certain air of gloom, which I thought might have given rise to the unaccountable reports of apparitions and extraordinary noises which were constantly reaching us. But I regret to say I did not succeed in banishing the nocturnal visiter, which still continues to disturb our friends.

"I shall pass over numerous instances, and select one as being especially remarkable, from the circumstance of the apparition having been seen by a clergyman well known and highly respected in this county, who, not six weeks ago, repeated the circumstances to a company of twenty persons, among whom were some who had previously been entire disbelievers in such appearances.

"The best way of giving you these particulars, will be by subjoining an extract from my journal, entered at the time the event occurred.

"Sept. 8, 1803.—Among other guests invited to C—— castle, came the Rev. Henry A——, of Redburgh, and rector of Greystoke, with Mrs. A——, his wife, who was a Miss S——, of Ulverstone. According to previous arrangements, they were to have remained with us for some days; but their visit was cut short in a very unexpected manner. On the morning after their arrival, we were all assembled at breakfast, when a chaise and four dashed up to the door in such haste that it knocked down part of the fence of my flower-garden. Our curiosity was, of course, awakened to know who could be arriving at so early an hour; when, happening to turn my eyes toward Mr. A——, I observed that he appeared extremely agitated. 'It is our carriage!' said he; 'I am very sorry, but we must absolutely leave you this morning.'

"We naturally felt and expressed considerable surprise, as well as regret at this unexpected departure; representing that we had invited Colonel and Mrs. S——, some friends whom

Mr. A—— particularly desired to meet, to dine with us on that day. Our expostulations, however, were vain; the breakfast was no sooner over than they departed, leaving us in consternation to conjecture what could possibly have occasioned so sudden an alteration in their arrangements. I really felt quite uneasy lest anything should have given them offence; and we reviewed all the occurrences of the preceding evening in order to discover, if offence there was, whence it had arisen. But our pains were vain; and after talking a great deal about it for some days, other circumstances banished it from our minds.

"It was not till we some time afterward visited the part of the country in which Mr. A—— resides, that we learned the real cause of his sudden departure from C——. The relation of the fact, as it here follows, is in his own words:—

"Soon after we went to bed, we fell asleep: it might have been between one and two in the morning when I awoke. I observed that the fire was totally extinguished; but although that was the case, and we had no light, I saw a glimmer in the centre of the room, which suddenly increased to a bright flame. I looked out, apprehending that something had caught fire, when, to my amazement, I beheld a beautiful boy, clothed in white, with bright locks, resembling gold, standing by my bedside, in which position he remained some minutes, fixing his eyes upon me with a mild and benevolent expression. He then glided gently away toward the side of the chimney, where it is obvious there is no possible egress, and entirely disappeared. I found myself again in total darkness, and all remained quiet until the usual hour of rising. I declare this to be a true account of what I saw at C—— castle, upon my word as a clergyman."

I am acquainted with some of the family, and with several of the friends of Mr. A——, who is still alive, though now an old man, and I can most positively assert that his own conviction, with regard to the nature of this appearance, has remained ever unshaken. The circumstance made a lasting impression upon his mind, and he never willingly speaks of it; but when he does, it is always with the greatest seriousness, and he never shrinks from avowing his belief, that what he saw admits of no other interpretation than the one he then put upon it.

Now, let us see whether in this department of the phenomenon of ghost-seeing, namely, the lights that frequently accompany the apparitions, there is anything so worthy of ridicule as Grose and other such commentators seem to think.

Of God, the uncreated, we know nothing; but the created spirit, man, we can not conceive of independent of some organism or organ, however different that organ may be to those which form our means of apprehension and communication at present. This organ, we may suppose to be that pervading ether which is now the germ of what St. Paul calls the *spiritual body*, the *astral spirit* of the mystics, the *nerve-spirit* of the clear-seers; the fundamental body, of which the external fleshly body is but the copy and husk—an organ comprehending all those distinct ones which we now possess in the one universal, or, as some of the German physiologists call it, the *central* sense, of which we occasionally obtain some glimpses in somnambulism, and in other peculiar states of nervous derangement; especially where the ordinary senses of sight, hearing, feeling, &c., are in abeyance; an effect which Dr. Ennemoser considers to be produced by a change of polarity, the external periphery of the nerves taking on a negative state; and which Dr. Passavent describes as the retreating of the ether from the external to the internal, so that the nerves no longer receive impressions, or convey information to the brain; a condition which may be produced by various causes, as excess of excitement, great elevation of the spirit, as we see in the ecstatics and martyrs, over-irritation producing consequent exhaustion; and also artificially, by certain manipulations, narcotics, and other influences. All somnambules of the highest order—and when I make use of this expression, I repeat that I do not allude to the subjects of mesmeric experiments, but to those extraordinary cases of disease, the particulars of which have been recorded by various continental physicians of eminence—all persons in that condition describe themselves as hearing and seeing, not by their ordinary organs, but by some means the idea of which they can not convey further than that they are pervaded by light, and that this is not the *ordinary* physical light is evident, inasmuch as they generally see best in the dark, a remarkable instance of which I myself witnessed.

I never had the slightest idea of this internal light, till, in the way of experiment, I inhaled the sulphuric ether; but I am now very well able to conceive it: for, after first feeling an agreeable warmth pervading my limbs, my next sensation was to find myself, I can not say in this heavenly light, for the light was in *me*—I was pervaded by it: it was not perceived by my eyes, which were closed, but perceived internally, I can not tell how. Of what nature this heavenly light was—and I can not forbear calling it *heavenly*, for it was like nothing on earth—I know not, nor how far it may be related to those luminous emanations occasionally seen around ecstatics, saints, martyrs, and dying persons; or to the flames seen by somnambules issuing from various objects, or to those observed by Von Reichenbach's patients proceeding from the ends of the fingers, &c. But at all events, since the process which maintains life is of the nature of combustion, we have no reason to be amazed at the presence of luminous emanations; and as we are the subjects of various electrical phenomena, nobody is surprised when, on combing their hair or pulling off their silk-stockings, they hear a crackling noise, or even see sparks.

Light, in short, is a phenomenon which seems connected with all forms of life; and I need not here refer to that emitted by glow-worms, fire-flies, and those marine animals which illuminate the sea. The eyes also of many animals shine with a light which is not merely a reflected one—as has been ascertained by Rengger, a German naturalist, who found himself able to distinguish objects in the most profound darkness, by the flaming eyes of a South American monkey.

"The seeing of a clear-seer," says Dr. Passavent, "may be called a *solar* seeing, for he lights and inter-penetrates his object with his *own* organic light, viz., his nervous ether, which becomes the organ of the spirit;" and under certain circumstances this organic light becomes visible, as in those above alluded to. Persons recovering from deep swoons and trances, frequently describe themselves as having been in this region of light—this light of the spirit, if I may so call it—this palace of light, in which it dwells, which will hereafter be its proper light; for the physical or solar light, which serves us while in the flesh, will be no longer needed, when out of it, nor probably be perceived by the spirit, which will then, I repeat, be a light to itself: and as this organic light—this germ of our future spiritual body—occasionally becomes partially visible now, there can not, I think, be any great difficulty in conceiving that it may, under given circumstances, be so hereafter.

The use of the word *light*, in the Scriptures, must not be received in a purely symbolical sense. We shall dwell in light, or we shall dwell in darkness, in proportion as we have shaken off the bonds that chain us to the earth; according, in short, to our moral state, we shall be pure and bright, or impure and dark.

Monsieur Arago mentions, in his treatise on lightning and the electrical fluid, that all men are not equally susceptible of it, and that there are different degrees of receptivity, verging from total insensibility to the extreme opposite; and he also remarks that animals are more susceptible to it than men. He says the fluid will pass through a chain of persons, of whom perhaps one (though forming only the second link) will be wholly insensible of the shock. Such persons would be rarely struck by lightning, while another would be in as great danger from a flash as if he were made of metal. Thus it is not only the situation of a man, during a storm, but also his physical constitution, that regulates the amount of his peril. The horse and the dog are particularly susceptible.

Now, this varying susceptibility is analogous to, if not the very same, that causes the varying susceptibility to such phenomena as I am treating of; and, accordingly, we know that in all times, horses and dogs have been reputed to have the faculty of seeing spirits: and when persons who have the second-sight see a vision, these animals, if in contact with them, perceive it also, and frequently evince symptoms of great terror.

We also here find the explanation of another mystery, namely, what the Germans call ***ansteckung***, and the English (skeptics when alluding to these phenomena) ***contagion***—meaning simply ***contagious fear***; but, as when several persons form a chain, the shock from an electrical machine will pass through the whole of them—so, if one person is in such a state as to become sensible of an apparition or some similar phenomenon, he may be able to communicate that power to another; and thus has arisen the conviction among the highlanders, that a seer, by touching a person near him, enables him frequently to participate in his vision.

A little girl, in humble life, called Mary Delves, of a highly nervous temperament, has been frequently punished for saying that the cat was on fire, and that she saw flames issuing from various persons and objects.

With regard to the perplexing subject of corpse-lights, there would be little difficulty attending it if they always remained stationary over the graves; but it seems very well established that that is not the case. There are numerous stories, proceeding from very respectable quarters, proving the contrary; and I have heard two from a dignitary of the church, born in Wales, which I will relate:—

A female relation of his had occasion to go to Aberystwith, which was about twenty miles from her home, on horseback; and she started at a very early hour for that purpose, with her father's servant. When they had nearly reached the half-way, fearing the man might be wanted at home, she bade him return, as she was approaching the spot where the servant of the lady she was going to visit was to meet her, in order to escort her the other half.

The man had not long left her, when she saw a light coming toward her, the nature of which she suspected. It moved, according to her description, steadily on, about three feet from the ground. Somewhat awestruck, she turned her horse out of the bridle-road, along which it was coming, intending to wait till it had passed; but, to her dismay, just as it came opposite to her, it stopped, and there remained perfectly fixed for nearly half an hour, at the end of which period it moved on as before.

The servant presently came up, and she proceeded to the house of her friend, where she related what she had seen. A few days afterward, the very servant who came to meet her was taken ill and died: his body was carried along that road; and, at the very spot where the light had paused, an accident occurred, which caused a delay of half an hour.

The other story was as follows: A servant in the family of Lady Davis, my informant's aunt, had occasion to start early for market. Being in the kitchen, about three o'clock in the morning, taking his breakfast alone, when everybody else was in bed, he was surprised at hearing a sound of heavy feet on the stairs above; and, opening the door to see who it could be, he was struck with alarm at perceiving a great light, much brighter than could have been shed by a candle, at the same time that he heard a violent thump, as if some very heavy body had hit the clock, which stood on the landing. Aware of the nature of the light, the man did not await its further descent, but rushed out of the house—whence he presently saw it issue from the front door, and proceed on its way to the churchyard.

As his mistress, Lady Davis, was at that period in her bed, ill, he made no doubt that her death impended; and when he returned from the market at night, his first question was, whether she was yet alive: and though he was informed she was better, he declared his conviction that she would die, alleging as his reason what he had seen in the morning—a narration which led everybody else to the same conclusion.

The lady, however, recovered; but, within a fortnight, another member of the family died: and as his coffin was brought down the stairs, the bearers ran it violently against the clock—upon which the man instantly exclaimed, "That is the very noise I heard!"

I could relate numerous stories wherein the appearance of a ghost was accompanied by a light; but as there is nothing that distinguishes them from those above mentioned, I will not dilate further on this branch of the subject, on which, perhaps, I have said enough to suggest to the minds of my readers that, although we know little *how* such things are, we do know enough of analogous phenomena to enable us to believe, at least, their possibility.

I confess I find much less difficulty in conceiving the existence of such facts as those above described, than those of another class, of which we meet with occasional instances.

For example, a gentleman of fortune and station, in Ireland, was one day walking along the road, when he met a very old man, apparently a peasant, though well dressed, and looking as if he had on his Sunday habiliments. His great age attracted the gentleman's attention the more, that he could not help wondering at the alertness of his movements, and the ease with which he was ascending the hill. He consequently accosted him, inquiring his name and residence; and was answered that his name was Kirkpatrick, and that he lived at a cottage, which he pointed out. Whereupon the gentleman expressed his surprise that he should be unknown to him, since he fancied he had been acquainted with every man on his estate. "It is odd you have never seen me before," returned the old man, "for I walk here every day."

"How old are you?" asked the gentleman.

"I am one hundred and five," answered the other; "and have been here all my life."

After a few more words, they parted; and the gentleman, proceeding toward some laborers in a neighboring field, inquired if they knew an old man of the name of Kirkpatrick. They did not; but on addressing the question to some older tenants, they said, "Oh, yes;" they had known him, and had been at his funeral; he had lived at the cottage on the hill, but had been dead twenty years.

"How old was he when he died?" inquired the gentleman, much amazed. "He was eighty-five," said they: so that the old man gave the age that he would have reached had he survived to the period of this rencontre.

This curious incident is furnished by the gentleman himself and all he can say is, that it certainly occurred, and that he is quite unable to explain it. He was in perfect health at the time, and had never heard of this man in his life, who had been dead several years before the estate came into his possession.

The following is another curious story. The original will be found in the register of the church named, from which it has been copied for my use:—

EXTRACT FROM THE REGISTER IN BRISLEY CHURCH, NORFOLK.

"DECEMBER 12, 1706.—I, Robert Withers, M. A., vicar of Gately, do insert here a story which I had from undoubted hands; for I have all the moral certainty of the truth of it possible:—

"Mr. Grose went to see Mr. Shaw on the 2d of August last. As they sat talking in the evening, says Mr. Shaw: 'On the 21st of the last month, as I was smoking a pipe, and reading in my study, between eleven and twelve at night, in comes Mr. Naylor (formerly fellow of St. John's college, but had been dead full four years). When I saw him, I was not much affrighted, and I asked him to sit down, which accordingly he did for about two hours, and we talked together. I asked him how it fared with him. He said, "Very well."—"Were any of our old acquaintances with him?"—"No!" (at which I was much alarmed), "but Mr. Orchard will be with me soon, and yourself not long after." As he was going away, I asked him if he would not stay a little longer, but he refused. I asked him if he would call again. "No;" he had but three days' leave of absence, and he had other business.'

"N. B.—Mr. Orchard died soon after. Mr. Shaw is now dead: he was formerly fellow of St. John's college—an ingenious, good man. I knew him there; but at his death he had a college-living in Oxfordshire, and here he saw the apparition."

An extraordinary circumstance occurred some years ago, in which a very pious and very eminent Scotch minister, Ebenezer Brown of Inverkeithing, was concerned. A person of ill character in the neighborhood having died, the family very shortly afterward came to him to complain of some exceedingly unpleasant circumstances connected with the room in which the dissolution had taken place, which rendered it unin habitable, and requesting his assistance. All that is known by his family of what followed, is that he went and entered the room alone; came out again, in a state of considerable excitement and in a great perspiration; took off his coat and re-entered the room; a great noise and I believe voices were then heard by the family, who remained the whole time at the door; when he came out finally, it was evident that something very extraordinary had taken place; what it was, he said, he could never disclose; but that perhaps after his death some paper might be found upon the subject. None, however, as far as I can learn, has been discovered.

A circumstance of a very singular nature is asserted to have occurred, not very many years back, in regard to a professor in the college of A——, who had seduced a girl and married another woman. The girl became troublesome to him; and being found murdered, after having been last seen in his company, he was suspected of being some way concerned in the crime. But the strange thing is, that, from that period, he retired every evening at a particular hour to a certain room, where he stayed a great part of the night, and where it was declared that *her* voice was distinctly heard in conversation with him: a strange, wild story, which I give as I have it, without pretending to any explanation of the belief that seems to have prevailed, that he was obliged to keep this fearful tryst.

Visitations of this description — which seem to indicate that the deceased person is still, in some way incomprehensible to us, an inhabitant of the earth — are more perplexing than any of the stories I meet with. In the time of Frederick II. of Prussia, the cook of a catholic priest residing at a village named Quarrey, died, and he took another in her place; but the poor woman had no peace or rest from the interference of her predecessor, insomuch that she resigned her situation, and the minister might almost have done without any servant at all. The fires were lighted, and the rooms swept and arranged, and all the needful services performed, by unseen hands. Numbers of people went to witness the phenomena, till at length the story reached the ears of the king, who sent a captain and a lieutenant of his guard to investigate the affair. As they approached the house, they found themselves preceded by a march, though they could see no musicians; and when they entered the parlor and witnessed what was going on, the captain exclaimed: "If that doesn't beat the devil!" upon which he received a smart slap on the face, from the invisible hand that was arranging the furniture.

In consequence of this affair, the house was pulled down, by the king's orders, and another residence built for the minister at some distance from the spot.

Now, to impose on Frederick II. would have been no slight matter, as regarded the probable consequences; and the officers of his guard would certainly not have been disposed to make the experiment; and it is not likely that the king would have ordered the house to be pulled down without being thoroughly satisfied of the truth of the story.

One of the most remarkable stories of this class I know—excepting indeed the famous one of the Grecian bride—is that which is said to have happened at Crossen, in Silesia, in the year 1659, in the reign of the Princess Elizabeth Charlotte. In the spring of that year, an apothecary's man, called Christopher Monig—a native of Serbest, in Anhalt—died, and was buried with the usual ceremonies of the Lutheran church. But, to the amazement of everybody, a few days afterward, he, at least what seemed to be himself, appeared in the shop, where he would sit himself down, and sometimes walk, and take from the shelves boxes, pots, and glasses, and set them again in other places; sometimes try and examine the goodness of the medicines, weigh them with the scales, pound the drugs with a mighty noise—nay, serve the people that came with bills to the shop, take their money and lay it up in the counter: in a word, do all things that a journeyman in such cases used to do. He looked very ghostly upon his former companions, who were afraid to say anything to him, and his master being sick at that time, he was very troublesome to him. At last he took a cloak that hung in the shop, put it on and walked abroad, but minding nobody in the streets; he entered into some of the citizen's houses, especially such as he had formerly known, yet spoke to no one but to a maid-servant, whom he met with hard by the church-yard, whom he desired to go home and dig in a lower chamber of her master's house, where she would find an inestimable treasure. But the girl, amazed at the sight of him, swooned away; whereupon he lifted her up, but left a mark upon her, in so doing, that was long visible. She fell sick in consequence of the fright, and having told what Monig had said to her, they dug up the place indicated, but found nothing but a decayed pot with a hemarites or bloodstone in it. The affair making a great noise, the reigning princess caused the man's body to be taken up, which being done, it was found in a state of putrefaction, and was reinterred. The apothecary was then recommended to remove everything belonging to Monig—his linen, clothes, books, &c.—after which the apparition left the house and was seen no more.

The fact of the man's reappearance in this manner was considered to be so perfectly established at the time, that there was actually a public disputation on the subject in the academy of Leipsic. With regard to the importance the apparition attached to the bloodstone, we do not know but that there may be truth in the persuasion that this gem is possessed of some occult properties of much more value than its beauty.

The story of the Grecian bride is still more wonderful, and yet it comes to us so surprisingly well authenticated, inasmuch as the details were forwarded by the prefect of the city in which the thing occurred, to the proconsul of his province, and by the latter were laid before the emperor Hadrian—and as it was not the custom to mystify Roman emperors—we are constrained to believe that what the prefect and proconsul communicated to him, they had good reason for believing themselves.

It appears that a gentleman, called Demostrates, and Charito, his wife, had a daughter called Philinnion, who died; and that about six months afterward, a youth named Machates, who had come to visit them, was surprised on retiring to the apartments destined to strangers, by receiving the visits of a young maiden who eats and drinks and exchanges gifts with him. Some accident having taken the nurse that way, she, amazed by the sight, summons her master and mistress to behold their daughter, who is there sitting with the guest.

Of course, they do not believe her; but at length, wearied by her importunities, the mother follows her to the guest's chamber; but the young people are now asleep, and the door closed; but looking through the keyhole, she perceives what she believes to be her daughter. Still unable to credit her senses, she resolves to wait till morning before disturbing them; but when she comes again the young lady had departed; while Machates, on being interrogated, confesses that Philinnion had been with him, but that she had admitted to him that it was unknown to her parents. Upon this, the amazement and agitation of the mother were naturally very great; especially when Machates showed her a ring which the girl had given him, and a bodice which she had left behind her; and his amazement was no less, when he heard the story they had to tell. He, however, promised that if she returned the next night, he would let them see her; for he found it impossible to believe that his bride was their dead daughter. He suspected, on the contrary, that some thieves had stripped her body of the clothes and ornaments in which she had been buried, and that the girl who came to his room had bought them. When, therefore, she arrived, his servant having had orders to summon the father and mother, they came; and perceiving that it was really their daughter, they fell to embracing her, with tears. But she reproached them for the intrusion, declaring that she had been permitted to spend three days with this stranger, in the house of her birth; but that now she must go to the appointed place; and immediately fell down dead, and the dead body lay there visible to all.

The news of this strange event soon spread abroad, the house was surrounded by crowds of people, and the prefect was obliged to take measures to avoid a tumult. On the following morning, at an early hour, the inhabitants assembled in the theatre, and thence they proceeded to the vault, in order to ascertain if the body of Philinnion was where it had been deposited six months before. It was not; but on the bier there lay the ring and cap which Machates had presented to her the first night she visited him; showing that she had returned there in the interim. They then proceeded to the house of Democrates, where they saw the body, which it was decreed must now be buried without the bounds of the city. Numerous religious ceremonies and sacrifices followed, and the unfortunate Machates, seized with horror, put an end to his own life.

The following very singular circumstance occurred in this country toward the latter end of the last century, and excited, at the time, considerable attention; the more so, as it was asserted by everybody acquainted with the people and the locality, that the removal of the body was impossible by any recognised means; besides, that no one would have had the hardihood to attempt such a feat:—

"Mr. William Craighead, author of a popular system of arithmetic, was parish-schoolmaster of Monifieth, situate upon the estuary of the Tay, about six miles east from Dundee. It would appear that Mr. Craighead was then a young man, fond of a frolic, without being very scrupulous about the means, or calculating the consequences. There being a lykewake in the neighborhood, according to the custom of the times, attended by a number of his acquaintance, Craighead procured a confederate, with whom he concerted a plan to draw the watchers from the house, or at least from the room where the corpse lay. Having succeeded in this, he dexterously removed the dead body to an outer house, while his companion occupied the place of the corpse in the bed where it had lain. It was agreed upon between the confederates, that when the company were reassembled Craighead was to join them, and, at a concerted signal the impostor was to rise, shrouded like the dead man, while the two were to enjoy the terror and alarm of their companions. Mr. Craighead came in, and, after being some time seated, the signal was made, but met no attention; he was rather surprised; it was repeated, and still neglected. Mr. Craighead, in his turn, now became alarmed; for he conceived it impossible that his companion could have fallen asleep in that situation; his uneasiness became insupportable; he went to the bed, and found his friend lifeless! Mr. Craighead's feelings, as may well be imagined, now entirely overpowered him, and the dreadful fact was disclosed. Their agitation was extreme, and it was far from being alleviated when every attempt to restore animation to the thoughtless young man proved abortive. As soon as their confusion would permit, an inquiry was made after the original corpse, and Mr. Craighead and another went to fetch it in, but it was not to be found. The alarm and consternation of the company were now redoubled; for some time a few suspected that some hardy fellow among them had been attempting a Rowland for an Oliver, but when every knowledge of it was most solemnly denied by all present, their situation can be more easily imagined than described; that of Mr. Craighead was little short of distraction. Daylight came without relieving their agitation; no trace of the corpse could be discovered, and Mr. Craighead was accused as the *primum mobile* of all that had happened: he was incapable of sleeping, and wandered several days and nights in search of the body, which was at last discovered in the parish of Tealing, deposited in a field, about six miles distant from the place whence it was removed.

"It is related that this extraordinary affair had a strong and lasting effect upon Mr. Craighead's mind and conduct; that he immediately became serious and thoughtful, and ever after conducted himself with great prudence and sobriety."

Among what are called *superstitions*, there are a great many curious ones attached to certain families; and from some members of these families I have been assured that experience has rendered it impossible for them to forbear attaching importance to these persuasions.

A very remarkable circumstance occurred lately in this part of the world, the facts of which I had an opportunity of being well acquainted with.

One evening, somewhere about Christmas, of the year 1844, a letter was sent for my perusal, which had been just received from a member of a distinguished family, in Perthshire. The friend who sent it me, an eminent literary man, said, "Read the enclosed; and we shall now have an opportunity of observing if any event follows the prognostics." The information contained in the letter was to the following effect: —

Miss D——, a relative of the present Lady C——, who had been staying some time with the earl and countess, at their seat near Dundee, was invited to spend a few days at C—— castle, with the earl and countess of A——. She went: and while she was dressing for dinner, the first evening of her arrival, she heard a strain of music under her window, which finally resolved itself into a well-defined sound of a drum. When her maid came up stairs, she made some inquiries about the drummer that was playing near the house; but the maid knew nothing on the subject. For the moment, the circumstance passed from Miss D——'s mind; but recurring to her again during the dinner, she said, addressing Lord A——, "My lord, who is your drummer?" — upon which his lordship turned pale, Lady A—— looked distressed, and several of the company (who all heard the question) embarrassed; while the lady, perceiving that she had made some unpleasant allusion, although she knew not to what their feelings referred, forbore further inquiry till she reached the drawing-room, when, having mentioned the circumstance again to a member of the family, she was answered, "What! have you never heard of the drummer-boy?" — "No," replied Miss D——; "who in the world is he?" — "Why," replied the other, "he is a person who goes about the house playing his drum whenever there is a death impending in the family. The last time he was heard was shortly before the death of the last countess (the earl's former wife), and that is why Lord A—— became so pale when you mentioned it. 'The drummer' is a very unpleasant subject in this family, I assure you!"

Miss D—— was naturally much concerned, and, indeed, not a little frightened at this explanation, and her alarm being augmented by hearing the sounds on the following day, she took her departure from C—— castle and returned to Lord C——'s, stopping on her way to call on some friends, where she related this strange circumstance to the family, through whom the information reached me.

This affair was very generally known in the north, and we awaited the event with interest. The melancholy death of the countess about five or six months afterward, at Brighton, sadly verified the prognostic. I have heard that a paper was found in her desk after her death, declaring her conviction that the drum was for her; and it has been suggested that probably the thing preyed upon her mind and caused the catastrophe: but in the first place, from the mode of her death, that does not appear to be the case; in the second, even if it were, the fact of the verification of the prognostic remains unaffected; besides which, those who insist upon taking refuge in this hypothesis must admit that, before people living in the world like Lord and Lady A——, could attach so much importance to the prognostic as to entail such fatal effects, they must have had very good reason for believing in it.

The legend connected with "the drummer" is, that either himself, or some officer whose emissary he was, had become an object of jealousy to a former Lord A——, and that he was put to death by being thrust into his own drum and flung from the window of the tower in which Miss D——'s room was situated. It is said that he threatened to haunt them if they took his life; and he seems to have been as good as his word, having been heard several times in the memory of persons yet living.

There is a curious legend attached to the family of G——, of R——, to the effect that, when a lady is confined in that house, a little old woman enters the room when the nurse is absent, and strokes down the bedclothes; after which the patient, according to the technical phrase, "never does any good," and dies. Whether the old lady has paid her visits or not I do not know, but it is remarkable that the results attending several late confinements there have been fatal.

There was a legend, in a certain family, that a single swan was seen on a particular lake before a death. A member of this family told me that on one occasion, the father, being a widower, was about to enter into a second marriage. On the wedding-day, his son appeared so exceedingly distressed, that the bridegroom was offended, and, expostulating with him, was told by the young man that his low spirits were caused by his having seen the swan. He (the son) died that night quite unexpectedly.

Besides Lord Littleton's dove, there are a great many very curious stories recorded in which birds have been seen in a room when a death was impending; but the most extraordinary prognostic I know is that of "the black dog," which seems to be attached to some families:—

A young lady of the name of P——, not long since was sitting at work, well and cheerful, when she saw, to her great surprise, a large black dog close to her. As both door and window were closed, she could not understand how he had got in; but when she started up to put him out, she could no longer see him.

Quite puzzled, and thinking it must be some strange illusion, she sat down again and went on with her work, when, presently, he was there again. Much alarmed, she now ran out and told her mother, who said she must have fancied it, or be ill. She declered neither was the case; and, to oblige her, the mother agreed to wait outside the door, and if she saw it again, she was to call her. Miss P—— re-entered the room, and presently there was the dog again; but when she called her mother, he disappeared. Immediately afterward, the mother was taken ill and died. Before she expired, she said to her daughter, "Remember the black dog!"

I confess I should have been much disposed to think this a spectral illusion, were it not for the number of corroborative instances; and I have only this morning read in the review of a work called "The Unseen World," just published, that there is a family in Cornwall who are also warned of an approaching death by the apparition of a black dog: and a very curious example is quoted, in which a lady newly married into the family, and knowing nothing of the tradition, came down from the nursery to request her husband would go up and drive away a black dog that was lying on the child's bed. He went up, and found the child dead!

I wonder if this phenomenon is the origin of the French phrase "*bête noir*," to express an annoyance, or an augury of evil?

Most persons will remember the story of Lady Fanshawe, as related by herself—namely, that while paying a visit to Lady Honor O'Brien, she was awakened the first night she slept there by a voice, and, on drawing back the curtain, she saw a female figure standing in the recess of the window, attired in white, with red hair and a pale and ghastly aspect. "She looked out of the window," says Lady Fanshawe, "and cried in a loud voice, such as I never before heard, 'A horse!—a horse!—a horse!' and then with a sigh, which rather resembled the wind than the voice of a human being, she disappeared. Her body appeared to me rather like a thick cloud than a real solid substance. I was so frightened," she continues, "that my hair stood on end, and my night-cap fell off. I pushed and shook my husband, who had slept all the time, and who was very much surprised to find me in such a fright, and still more so when I told him the cause of it, and showed him the open window. Neither of us slept any more that night, bnt he talked to me about it, and told me how much more frequent such apparitions were in that country than in England."

This was, however, what is called a *banshee:* for in the morning Lady Honor came to them, to say that one of the family had died in the night, expressing a hope that they had not been disturbed: "for," said she, "whenever any of the O'Briens is on his death-bed, it is usual for a woman to appear at one of the windows every night till he expires; but when I put you into this room, I did not think of it." This apparition was connected with some sad tale of seduction and murder.

I could relate many more instances of this kind, but I wish as much as possible to avoid repeating cases already in print; so I will conclude this chapter with the following account of "Pearlin Jean," whose persevering annoyances, at Allanbank, were so thoroughly believed and established, as to have formed at various times a considerable impediment to letting the place. I am indebted to Mr. Charles Kirkpatrick Sharpe for the account of Jean, and the anecdote that follows.

A housekeeper, called Bettie Norrie, that lived many years at Allanbank, declared she and various other people had frequently seen Jean, adding that they were so used to her, as to be no longer alarmed at her noises.

"In my youth," says Mr. Sharpe, "Pearlin Jean was the most remarkable ghost in Scotland, and my terror when a child. Our old nurse, Jenny Blackadder, had been a servant at Allanbank, and often heard her rustling in silks up and down stairs, and along the passage. She never saw her—but her husband did.

"She was a French woman, whom the first baronet of Allanbank (then Mr. Stuart) met with at Paris, during his tour to finish his education as a gentleman. Some people said she was a nun, in which case she must have been a sister of charity, as she appears not to have been confined to a cloister. After some time, young Stuart became either faithless to the lady, or was suddenly recalled to Scotland by his parents, and had got into his carriage, at the door of the hotel, when his Dido unexpectedly made her appearance, and stepping on the fore-wheel of the coach to address her lover, he ordered the postillion to drive on; the consequence of which was, that the lady fell, and one of the wheels going over her forehead, killed her!

"In a dusky autumnal evening, when Mr. Stuart drove under the arched gateway of Allanbank, he perceived Pearlin Jean sitting on the top, her head and shoulders covered with blood.

"After this, for many years, the house was haunted: doors shut and opened with great noise at midnight; and the rustling of silks, and pattering of high-heeled shoes, were heard in bedrooms and passages. Nurse Jenny said there were seven ministers called together at one time, to *lay* the spirit; 'but they did no mickle good, my dear.'

"The picture of the ghost was hung between those of her lover and his lady, and kept her comparatively quiet; but when taken away, she became worse-natured than ever. This portrait was in the present Sir J—— G——'s possession. I am unwilling to record its fate.

"The ghost was designated 'Pearlin,' from always wearing a great quantity of that sort of lace.*

"Nurse Jenny told me that when Thomas Blackadder was her lover (I remember Thomas very well), they made an assignation to meet one moonlight night in the orchard at Allanbank. True Thomas, of course, was the first comer; and, seeing a female figure, in a light-colored dress, at some distance, he ran forward with open arms to embrace his Jenny. Lo, and behold! as he neared the spot where the figure stood, it vanished; and presently he saw it again, at the very end of the orchard, a considerable way off. Thomas went home in a fright; but Jenny, who came last, and saw nothing, forgave him, and they were married.

"Many years after this, about the year 1790, two ladies paid a visit at Allanbank—I think the house was then let—and passed a night there. They had never heard a word about the ghost; but they were disturbed the whole night with something walking backward and forward in their bedchamber. This I had from the best authority.

"Sir Robert Stuart was created a baronet in the year 1687.

"Lady Stapleton, grandmother of the late Lord le Despencer, told me that the night Lady Susan Fane (Lord Westmoreland's daughter) died in London, she appeared to her father, then at Merriworth, in Kent. He was in bed, but had not fallen asleep. There was a light in the room; she came in, and sat down on a chair at the foot of the bed. He said to her, 'Good God, Susan! how came you here? What has brought you from town?' She made no answer; but rose directly, and went to the door, and looked back toward him very earnestly: then she retired, shutting the door behind her. The next morning he had notice of her death. This, Lord Westmoreland himself told to Lady Stapleton, who was by birth a Fane, and his near relation."

* "A species of lace made of thread."—JAMIESON.

CHAPTER XV.

APPARITIONS SEEKING THE PRAYERS OF THE LIVING.

WITH regard to the appearance of ghosts, the frequency of haunted houses, presentiments, prognostics, and dreams, if we come to inquire closely, it appears to me that all parts of the world are much on an equality—only, that where people are most engaged in business or pleasure, these things are, in the first place, less thought of and less believed in, consequently less observed; and when they *are* observed, they are readily explained away: and in the second place—where the external life, the life of the brain, wholly prevails—either they do not happen, or they are not perceived—the rapport not existing, or the receptive faculty being obscured.

But, although the above phenomena seem to be equally well known in all countries, there is one peculiar class of apparitions of which I meet with no records but in Germany. I allude to ghosts, who, like those described in the "Seeress of Prevorst," seek the prayers of the living. In spite of the positive assertions of Kerner, Eschenmayer, and others, that after neglecting no means to investigate the affair, they had been forced into the conviction that the spectres that frequented Frederica Hauffe were not subjective illusions, but real outstanding forms, still, as she was in the somnambulic state, many persons remain persuaded that the whole thing was delusion. It is true, that as those parties were not there, and as all those who did go to the spot came to a different conclusion, this opinion being only the result of preconceived notions or prejudices, and not of calm investigation, is of no value whatever; nevertheless, it is not to be denied that these narrations are very extraordinary; but, perplexing as they are, they by no means stand alone. I find many similar ones noticed in various works, where there has been no somnambule in question. In all cases, these unfortunate spirits appear to have been waiting for some one with whom they could establish a rapport, so as to be able to communicate with them; and this waiting has sometimes endured a century or more. Sometimes they are seen by only one person, at other times by several, with varying degrees of distinctness, appearing to one as a light, to another as a shadowy figure, and to a third as a defined human form. Other testimonies of their presence—as sounds, footsteps, lights, visible removing of solid articles without a visible agent, odors, &c.—are generally perceived by many; in short, the sounds seem audible to all who come to the spot, with the exception of the voice, which in most instances is only heard by the person with whom the rapport is chiefly established. Some cases are related, where a mark like burning is left on the articles seen to be lifted. This is an old persuasion, and has given rise to many a joke. But, upon the hypothesis I have offered, the thing is simple enough: the mark will probably be of the same nature as that left by the electrical fluid;—and it is this particular, and the lights that often accompany spirits, that have caused the notion of material flames, sulphur, brimstone, &c., to be connected with the idea of a future state. According to our views, there can be no difficulty in conceiving that a happy and blessed spirit would emit a mild radiance; while anger or malignity would necessarily alter the character of the effulgence.

As whoever wishes to see a number of these cases may have recourse to my translation of the "Seeress of Prevorst," I will here only relate one, of a very remarkable nature, that occurred in the prison of Weinsberg, in the year 1835.

Dr. Kerner, who has published a little volume containing a report of the circumstances, describes the place where the thing happened to be such a one as negatives at once all possibility of trick or imposture. It was in a sort of block-house or fortress—a prison within a prison—with no windows but what looked into a narrow passage, closed with several doors. It was on the second floor; the windows were high up, heavily barred with iron, and immovable without considerable mechanical force. The external prison is surrounded by a high wall, and the gates are kept closed day and night. The prisoners in different apartments are of course never allowed to communicate with each other, and the deputy-governor of the prison and his family, consisting of a wife, niece, and one maid-servant, are described as people of unimpeachable respectability and veracity. As depositions regarding this affair were laid before the magistrates, it is on them I found my narration.

On the 12th September, 1835, the deputy-governor or keeper of the jail, named Mayer, sent in a report to the magistrates that a woman called Elizabeth Eslinger was every night visited by a ghost, which generally came about eleven o'clock, and which left her no rest, as it said she was destined to release it, and it always invited her to follow it; and as she would not, it pressed heavily on her neck and side till it gave her pain. The persons confined with her pretended also to have seen this apparition.

Signed "MAYER."

A woman named Rosina Schahl, condemned to eight days' confinement for abusive language, deposed, that about eleven o'clock, Eslinger began to breathe hard as if she was suffocating; she said a ghost was with her, seeking his salvation. "I did not trouble myself about it, but told her to wake me when it came again. Last night I saw a shadowy form, between four and five feet high, standing near the bed; I did not see it move. Eslinger breathed very hard, and complained of a pressure on the side. For several days she has neither ate nor drank anything.

Signed "SCHAHL."

"COURT RESOLVES,

"That Eslinger is to be visited by the prison physician, and a report made as to her mental and bodily health.

"Signed by the magistrates,

"ECKHARDT,
"THEURER,
"KNORR.

"REPORT.

"Having examined the prisoner, Elizabeth Eslinger, confined here since the beginning of September, I found her of sound mind, but possessed with one fixed idea, namely, that she is and has been for a considerable time troubled by an apparition, which leaves her no rest, coming chiefly by night, and requiring her prayers to release it. It visited her before she came to the prison, and was the cause of the offence that brought her here. Having now, in compliance with the orders of the supreme court, observed this woman for eleven weeks, I am led to the conclusion that there is no deception in this case, and also that the persecution is not a mere monomaniacal idea of her own, and the testimony not only of her fellow-prisoners, but that of the deputy-governor's family, and even of persons in distant houses, confirms me in this persuasion.

"Eslinger is a widow, aged thirty-eight years, and declares that she never had any sickness whatever, neither is she aware of any at present; but she has always been a ghost-seer, though never till lately had any communication with them; that now, for eleven weeks that she has been in the prison, she is nightly disturbed by an apparition, that had previously visited her in her own house, and which had been once seen also by a girl of fourteen—a statement which this girl confirms. When at home, the apparition did not appear in a defined human form, but as a pillar of cloud, out of which proceeded a hollow voice, signifying to her that she was to release it, by her prayers, from the cellar of a woman in Wimmenthal, named Singhaasin, whither it was banished, or whence it could not free itself. She (Eslinger) says that she did not then venture to speak to it, not knowing whether to address it as *Sie*, *Ihr*, or *Du* (that is, whether she should address it in the second or third person—which custom among the Germans has rendered a very important point of etiquette. It is to be remembered that this woman was a peasant, without education, who had been brought into trouble by treasure-seeking, a pursuit in which she hoped to be assisted by this spirit. This digging for buried treasure is a strong passion in Germany.

"The ghost now comes in a perfect human shape, and is dressed in a loose robe, with a girdle, and has on its head a four-cornered cap. It has a projecting chin and forehead, fiery, deep-set eyes, a long beard, and high cheek-bones, which look as if they were covered with parchment. A light radiates about and above his head, and in the midst of this light she sees the outlines of the spectre.

"Both she and her fellow-prisoners declare, that this apparition comes several times in a night, but always between the evening and morning bell. He often comes through the closed door or window, but they can then see neither door nor window, nor iron bars; they often hear the closing of the door, and can see into the passage when he comes in or out that way, so that if a piece of wood lies there they see it. They hear a shuffling in the passage as he comes and goes. He most frequently enters by the window, and they then hear a peculiar sound there. He comes in quite erect. Although their cell is entirely closed, they feel a cool wind* when he is near them. All sorts of noises are heard, particularly a crackling. When he is angry, or in great trouble, they perceive a strange mouldering, earthy smell. He often pulls away the coverlet, and sits on the edge of the bed. At first the touch of his hand was icy cold, since he became brighter it is warmer; she first saw the brightness of his finger-ends; it afterward spread further. If she stretches out her hand she can not feel him, but when he touches her she feels it. He sometimes takes her hands and lays them together, to make her pray. His sighs and groans are like a person in despair; they are heard by others as well as Eslinger. While he is making these sounds, she is often praying aloud, or talking to her companions, so they are sure it is not she who makes them. She does not see his mouth move when he speaks. The voice is hollow and gasping. He comes to her for prayers, and he seems to her like one in a mortal sickness, who seeks comfort in the prayers of others. He says he was a catholic priest in Wimmenthal, and lived in the year 1414."

* It is to be observed that this is the sensation asserted to be felt by Reichenbach's patients on the approach of the magnet.

(Wimmenthal is still catholic; the woman Eslinger herself is a Lutheran, and belongs to Backnang.)

"He says, that among other crimes, a fraud committed conjointly with his father, on his brothers, presses sorely on him; he can not get quit of it; it obstructs him. He always entreated her to go with him to Wimmenthal, whither he was banished, or consigned, and pray there for him.

"She says she can not tell whether what he says is true; and does not deny that she thought to find treasures by his aid. She has often told him that the prayers of a sinner, like herself, can not help him, and that he should seek the Redeemer; but he will not forbear his entreaties. When she says these things, he is sad, and presses nearer to her, and lays his head so close that she is obliged to pray into his mouth. *He seems hungry for prayers.* She has often felt his tears on her cheek and neck; they felt icy cold; but the spot soon after burns, and they have a bluish red mark. (These marks are visible on her skin.)

"One night this apparition brought with him a large dog, which leaped on the beds, and was seen by her fellow-prisoners also, who were much terrified, and screamed. The ghost, however, spoke, and said, 'Fear not; this is my father.' He had since brought the dog with him again, which alarmed them dreadfully, and made them quite ill.

"Both Mayer and the prisoners asserted, that Eslinger was scarcely seen to sleep, either by night or day, for ten weeks. She ate very little, prayed continually, and appeared very much wasted and exhausted. She said she saw the spectre alike, whether her eyes were opened or closed, which showed that it was a magnetic perception, and not *seeing* by her bodily organs. It is remarkable that a cat belonging to the jail, being shut up in this room, was so frightened when the apparition came, that it tried to make its escape by flying against the walls; and finding this impossible, it crept under the coverlet of the bed, in extreme terror. The experiment was made again, with the same result; and after this second time the animal refused all nourishment, wasted away, and died.

"In order to satisfy myself," says Dr. Kerner, "of the truth of these depositions, I went to the prison on the night of the 15th of October, and shut myself up without light in Eslinger's cell. About half-past eleven I heard a sound as of some hard body being flung down, but not on the side where the woman was, but the opposite; she immediately began to breathe hard, and told me the spectre was there. I laid my hand on her head, and adjured it as an evil spirit to depart. I had scarcely spoken the words when there was a strange rattling, crackling noise, all round the walls, which finally seemed to go out through the window; and the woman said that the spectre had departed.

"On the following night it told her that it was grieved at being addressed as an evil spirit, which it was not, but one that deserved pity; and that what it wanted was prayers and redemption.

"On the 18th of October, I went to the cell again, between ten and eleven, taking with me my wife, and the wife of the keeper, Madame Mayer. When the woman's breathing showed me the spectre was there, I laid my hand on her, and adjured it, in gentle terms, not to trouble her further. The same sort of sound as before commenced, but it was softer, and this time continued all along the passage, where there was certainly nobody. We all heard it.

"On the night of the 20th I went again, with Justice Heyd. We both heard sounds when the spectre came, and the woman could not conceive why we did not see it. We could not; but we distinctly felt a cool wind blowing upon us when, according to her account, it was near, although there was no aperture by which air could enter."

On each of these occasions Dr. Kerner seems to have remained about a couple of hours.

Madame Mayer now resolved to pass a night in the cell, for the purpose of observation; and she took her niece, a girl aged nineteen, with her: her report is as follows:—

"It was a rainy night, and, in the prison, pitch dark. My niece slept sometimes; I remained awake all night, and mostly sitting up in bed.

"About midnight I saw a light come in at the window; it

was a yellowish light, and moved slowly; and though we were closely shut in, I felt a cool wind blowing on me. I said to the woman, 'The ghost is here, is he not?' She said 'Yes,' and continued to pray, as she had been doing before. The cool wind and the light now approached me; my coverlet was quite light, and I could see my hands and arms; and at the same time I perceived an indescribable odor of putrefaction; my face felt as if ants were running over it. (Most of the prisoners described themselves as feeling the same sensation when the spectre was there.) Then the light moved about, and went up and down the room; and on the door of the cell I saw a number of little glimmering stars, such as I had never before seen. Presently, I and my niece heard a voice which I can compare to nothing I ever heard before. It was not like a human voice. The words and sighs sounded as if they were drawn up out of a deep hollow, and appeared to ascend from the floor to the roof in a column; while this voice spoke, the woman was praying aloud: so I was sure it did not proceed from her. No one could produce such a sound. They were strange, superhuman sighs and entreaties for prayers and redemption.

"It is very extraordinary that, whenever the ghost spoke, I always *felt it beforehand.* [Proving that the spirit had been able to establish a rapport with this person. She was in a magnetic relation to him.] We heard a crackling in the room also. I was perfectly awake, and in possession of my senses; and we are ready to make oath to having seen and heard these things."

On the 9th of December, Madame Mayer spent the night again in the cell, with her niece and her maid-servant; and her report is as follows:—

"It was moonlight, and I sat up in bed all night, watching Eslinger. Suddenly I saw a white shadowy form, like a small animal, cross the room. I asked her what it was; and she answered, 'Don't you see it's a lamb? It often comes with the apparition.' We then saw a stool, that was near us, lifted and set down again on its legs. She was in bed, and praying the whole time. Presently, there was such a noise at the window that I thought all the panes were broken. She told us it was the ghost, and that he was sitting on the stool. We then heard a walking and shuffling up and down, although I could not see him; but presently I felt a cool wind blowing on me, and out of this wind the same hollow voice I had heard before, said, 'In the name of Jesus, look on me!'

"Before this, the moon was gone, and it was quite dark; but when the voice spoke to me, I saw a light around us, though still no form. Then there was a sound of walking toward the opposite window, and I heard the voice say, 'Do you see me now?' And then, for the first time, I saw a shadowy form, stretching up as if to make itself visible to us, but could distinguish no features.

"During the rest of the night, I saw it repeatedly, sometimes sitting on the stool, and at others moving about; and I am perfectly certain that there was no moonlight now, nor any other light from without. How I saw it, I can not tell; it is a thing not to be described.

"Eslinger prayed the whole time, and the more earnestly she did so, the closer the spectre went to her. It sometimes sat upon her bed.

"About five o'clock, when he came near to me, and I felt the cool air, I said, 'Go to my husband, in his chamber, and leave a sign that you have been there!' He answered distinctly, 'Yes.' Then we heard the door, which was fast locked, open and shut; and we saw the shadow float out (for he floated rather than walked), and we heard the shuffling along the passage.

"In a quarter of an hour we saw him return, entering by the window; and I asked him if he had been with my husband, and what he had done. He answered by a sound like a short, low, hollow laugh. Then he hovered about without any noise, and we heard him speaking to Eslinger, while she still prayed aloud. Still, as before, I always knew when he was going to speak. After six o'clock, we saw him no more. In the morning, my husband mentioned, with great surprise, that his chamber door, which he was sure he had fast bolted and locked, even taking out the key when he went to bed, he had found wide open."

On the 24th, Madame Mayer passed the night there again; but on this occasion she only saw a white shadow coming and going, and standing by the woman, who prayed unceasingly. She also heard the shuffling.

Between prisoners and the persons in authority who went to observe, the number of those who testify to this phenomenon is considerable; and, although the amount of what was perceived varied according to the receptivity of the subject in each case, the evidence of all is perfectly coincident as to the character of the phenomena. Some saw only the light; others distinguished the form in the midst of it; all heard the sound, and perceived the mouldering earthy smell.

That the receptivity of the women was greater than that of the men, after what I have elsewhere said, should excite no surprise; the preponderance of the sympathetic system in them being sufficient to account for the difference.

Frederica Follen, from Lowenstein, who was eight weeks in the same cell with Eslinger, was witness to all the phenomena, though she only once arrived at seeing the spectre in its perfect human form, as the latter saw it; but it frequently spoke to her, bidding her amend her life, and remember that it was one who had tasted of death that give her this counsel. This circumstance had a great effect upon her.

When any of them swore, the apparition always evinced much displeasure, grasped them by the throat, and forced them to pray. Frequently, when he came or went, they said it sounded like a flight of pigeons.

Catherine Sinn, from Mayenfels, was confined in an adjoining room for a fortnight. After her release, she was interrogated by the minister of her parish, and deposed that she had known nothing of Eslinger, or the spectre; "but every night, being quite alone, I heard a rustling and a noise at the window, which looked only into the passage. I felt and heard, though I could not see anybody, that some one was moving about the room; these sounds were accompanied by a cool wind, though the place was closely shut up. I heard also a crackling, and a shuffling, and a sound as if gravel were thrown; but could find none in the morning. Once it seemed to me that a hand was laid softly on my forehead. I did not like staying alone, on account of these things, and begged to be put into a room with others; so I was placed with Eslingen and Follen. The same things continued here, and they told me about the ghost; but not being alone, I was not so frightened. I often heard him speak; it was hollow and slow, not like a human voice; but I could seldom catch the words. When he left the prison, which was generally about five in the morning, he used to say, 'Pray!' and when he did so, he would add, 'God reward you!' I never saw him distinctly till the last morning I was there; then I saw a white shadow standing by Eslinger's bed.

Signed "CATHERINE SINN.

"MINISTER BINDER, Mayenfels."

It would be tedious, were I to copy the depositions of all the prisoners, the experience of most of them being similar to the above. I will therefore content myself with giving an abstract of the most remarkable particulars.

Besides the crackling, rustling as of paper, walking, shuffling, concussions of the windows and of their beds, &c., &c., they heard sometimes a fearful cry, and not unfrequently the bed-coverings were pulled from them; it appearing to be the object of the spirit to manifest himself thus to those to whom he could not make himself visible; and as I find this pulling off the bed-clothes, and heaving up the bed as if some one were under it, repeated in a variety of cases, foreign and English, I conclude the motive to be the same. Several of the women heard him speak.

All these depositions are contained in Dr. Kerner's report to the magistrates; and he concludes by saying, that there can be no doubt of the fact of the woman Elizabeth Eslinger suffering these annoyances, by whatever name people may choose to call them.

Among the most remarkable phenomena, is the real or apparent opening of the door, so that they could see what was in the passage. Eslinger said that the spirit was often surrounded by a light, and his eyes looked fiery; and there sometimes came with him two lambs, which occasionally appeared as stars. He often took hold of Eslinger, and made her sit up, put her hands together, that she might pray; and once he appeared to take a pen and paper from under his gown, and wrote, laying it on her coverled.

It is extremely curious that, on two occasions, Eslinger saw Dr. Kerner and Justice Heyd enter with the ghost, when they were not there in the body, and both times Heyd was enveloped in a black cloud. The ghost, on being asked, told Eslinger that the cloud indicated that trouble was impending. A few days afterward his child died very unexpectedly, and Dr. Kerner now remembered, that the first time Eslinger said she had seen Heyd in this way, his father had died directly afterward. Kerner attended both patients, and was thus associated in the symbol. Follen also saw these two images, and spoke, believing the one to be Dr. Kerner himself.

On other occasions she saw strangers come in with the ghost, whom afterward, when they *really* came in the body, she recognised. This seems to have been a sort of second sight.

Dr. K. says, I think justly enough, that if Eslinger had been feigning, she never would have ventured on what seemed so improbable.

Some of the women, after the spectre had visibly leaned over them, or had spoken into their ears, were so affected by the odor he diffused that they vomited, and could not eat till they had taken an emetic; and those parts of their persons that he touched became painful and swollen, an effect I find produced in numerous other instances.

The following particulars are worth observing, in the evidence of a girl sixteen years of age, called Margaret Laibesberg, who was confined for ten days for plucking some grapes in a vineyard. She says she knew nothing about the spectre, but that she was greatly alarmed the first night at hearing the door burst open and something come shuffling in. Eslinger bade her not fear, and said that it would not injure her. The girl, however, being greatly terrified every night, and hiding her head under the bed-clothes, on the fourth Eslinger got out of her own bed, and, coming to her, said: "Do, in the name of God, look at him! He will do you no harm, I assure you."—"Then," says the girl, "I looked out from under the clothes, and I saw two white forms, like two lambs—so beautiful that I could have looked at them for ever. Between them stood a white, shadowy form, as tall as a man, but I was not able to look longer, for my eyes failed me." The terrors of this girl were so great, that Eslinger had repeatedly occasion to get out of bed and fetch her to lie with herself. When she could be induced to look, she always saw the figure, and he bade her also pray for him. Whenever he touched her, which he did on the forehead and eyes, she felt pain, but says nothing of any subsequent swelling. Both this girl and another, called Neidhardt, who was brought in on the last day of Margaret L——'s imprisonment, testified that on the previous night they had heard Eslinger ask the ghost why he looked so angry; and that they had heard him answer that it was "because she had on the preceding night neglected to pray for him as much as usual," which neglect arose from two gentlemen having passed the night in the cell.

When on the tenth day the girl Margaret L—— was released, she said that there was something so awful to her in this apparition, that she had firmly resolved and vowed to be pious and lead henceforth a virtuous life.

Some of them seem to have felt little alarm; Maria Bar, aged forty-one, said: "I was not afraid, for I have a good conscience." The offences for which these women were confined appear to have been very slight ones, such as quarrelling, &c.

In a room that opened into the same passage, men were shut up for disputing with the police, neglect of regulations, and similar misdemeanors. These persons not only heard the noises as above described, such as the walking, shuffling, opening and shutting the door, &c., &c., but some of them saw the ghost. Christian Bauer deposed that he had never heard anything about the ghost, but that, being disturbed by a knocking and rustling toward three o'clock on the second morning of his incarceration, he looked up and saw a white figure bending over him, and heard a strange hollow voice say: "You must needs have patience!" He said he thought it must be his grandfather, at which Stricker, his companion, laughed. Stricker deposed that he heard a hollow voice say: "You must needs have patience;" and that Bauer told him that there was a white apparition near him, and that he supposed it was his grandfather. Bauer said that he was frightened the first night, but got used to it and did not mind.

It is worthy of observation, that when they heard the door of the women's room open, they also heard the voice of Eslinger praying, which seems as if the door not only appeared to open, but actually did so. We have already seen that this spirit could open doors. In the "Seeress of Prevorst," the doors were constantly *audibly* and *visibly* opened, as by an unseen hand, when she saw a spectre enter; and I know to an absolute certainty that the same phenomenon takes place in a house not far from where I am writing; and this, sometimes, when there are two people sleeping in the room—a lady and gentleman. The door having been fast locked when they went to bed, the room thoroughly examined, and every precaution taken—for they are unwilling to believe in the spiritual character of the disturbances that annoy them—they are aroused by a consciousness that it is opening, and they do find it open, on rising to investigate the fact.

One of the most remarkable proofs, either of the force of volition or of the electrical powers of the apparition that haunted Eslinger, or else of his power to imitate sounds, was the real, or apparent, violent shaking of the heavy, iron-barred window, which it is asserted the united efforts of six men could not shake at all when they made the experiment.

The supreme court having satisfied itself that there was no imposture in this case, it was proposed that some men of science should be invited to investigate the strange phenomenon, and endeavor if possible to explain it. Accordingly, not only Dr. Kerner himself and his son, but many others, passed nights in the prison for this purpose. Among these, besides some ministers of the Lutheran church, there was an engraver called Duttenhofer; Wagner, an artist; Kapff, professor of mathematics at Heilbronn; Frass, a barrister; Doctors Seyffer and Sicherer, physicians; Heyd, a magistrate; Baron von Hugel, &c., &c.: but their perquisitions elicited no more than has been already narrated—all heard the noises, most of them saw the lights, and some saw the figure. Duttenhofer and Kapff saw it without a defined outline; it was itself bright, but did not illuminate the room. Some of the sounds appeared to them like the discharging of a Leyden jar. There was also a throwing of gravel, and a heavy dropping of water, but neither to be found. Professor Kapff says that he was quite cool and self-possessed, till there was such a violent concussion of the heavy, barred window, that he thought it must have come in; then both he and Duttenhofer felt horror-struck.

As they could not see the light emitted by the spectre when the room was otherwise lighted, they were in the dark; but they took every care to ascertain that Eslinger was in her bed while these things were going on. She prayed aloud the whole time, unless when speaking to them. By the morning, she used to be dreadfully exhausted, from this continual exertion.

It is also mentioned that the straw on which she lay was frequently changed and examined, and every means taken to ascertain that there was nothing whatever in her possession that could enable her to perform any sort of jugglery. Her fellow-prisoners were also invited to tell all they knew or could discover; and a remission of their sentences promised to those who would make known the imposition, if there was one.

Dr. Sicherer, who was accompanied by Mr. Frass, says that, having heard of these phenomena, which he thought the more unaccountable from the circumstances of the woman's age and condition, &c.—she being a healthy, hard-working person, aged thirty-eight, who had never known sickness—he was very desirous of inquiring personally into the affair.

While they were in the court of the prison, waiting for admittance, they heard extraordinary noises, which could not be accounted for, and during the night there was a repetition of those above described—especially the apparent throwing of gravel, or peas, which seemed to fall so near him that he involuntarily covered his face. Then followed the feeling of a cool wind; and then the oppressive odor, for which, he says, he can find no comparison, and which almost took away his breath. He was perfectly satisfied that it was no smell originating in the locality or the state of the prison. Simultaneously with the perception of this odor, he saw a thick, gray cloud, of no defined shape, near Eslinger's bed. When this cloud disappeared, the odor was no longer perceptible. It was a fine moonlight night, and there was light enough in the room to distinguish the beds, &c.

The same phenomena recurred several times during the night: Eslinger was heard, each time the ghost was there, praying and reciting hymns. They also heard her say, "Don't press my hands so hard together!"—"Don't touch me!" &c. The voice of the spirit they did not hear. Toward three or four o'clock, they heard heavy blows, footsteps, opening and shutting of the door, and a concussion of the whole house, that made them think it was going to fall on their heads. About six o'clock, they saw the phantom again; and altogether these phenomena recurred at least ten times in the course of the night.

Dr. Sicherer concludes by saying that he had undertaken the investigation with a mind entirely unprepossessed; and that in the report he made, at the desire of the supreme court, he had recorded his observations as conscientiously as if he had been upon a jury. He adds that he had examined everything; and that neither in the person of the woman, nor in any other of the inmates of the prison, could he find the smallest grounds for suspicion, nor any clew to the mystery, which, in a scientific point of view, appeared to him utterly inexplicable. Dr. Sicherer's report is dated Heilbronn, January 8, 1836.

Mr. Fraas, who accompanied him, confirms the above statement in every particular, with the addition that he several times saw a light, of a varying circumference, moving about the room;

and that it was while he saw this, that the woman told him the ghost was there. He also felt an oppression of the breath and a pressure on his forehead each time before the apparition came, especially once, when, although he had carefully abstained from mentioning his sensations, she told him it was standing close at his head. He stretched out his hand, but perceived nothing, except a cool wind and an overpowering smell.

Dr. Seyffer being there one night, with Dr. Kerner, in order to exclude the possibility of light entering through the window, they stopped it up. They, however, saw the phosphorescent light of the spectre, as before. It moved quietly about, and remained a quarter of an hour. The room was otherwise perfectly dark; the sounds accompanying it were like the dropping of water and the discharge of a Leyden jar. They fully ascertained that these phenomena did not proceed from the woman.

I have already given the depositions of Madame Mayer, the wife of the deputy-governor or keeper of the prison, who is spoken of as a highly respectable person. Mayer himself, however, though quite unable to account for all these extraordinary proceedings, found great difficulty in believing that there was anything supernatural in the affair; and he told Eslinger that, if she wished him to be convinced, she must send the ghost to do it!

He says: "The night after I had said this, I went to bed and to sleep, little expecting such a visiter; but, toward midnight, I was awakened by something touching my left elbow. This was followed by a pain; aud in the morning, when I looked at the place, I saw several blue spots. I told Eslinger that this was not enough, and that she must tell the ghost to touch my other elbow. This was done on the following night, and, at the same time, I perceived a smell like putrefaction. The blue spots followed." (It will be remembered that Eslinger had blue spots also.)

Mayer continues to say that the spectre made known its presence in his chamber by various sounds, such as were heard in the other part of the house. He never saw the figure distinctly, but his wife did: she always prayed when it was there. He, however, felt the cool wind that they all described.

The ghost told Eslinger that he should continue his visits to the prison after she had quitted it, and he did so. The second night after her release, they felt his approach, especially from the cool wind, and Madame Mayer desired him to testify his presence to her husband. Immediately there were sounds like a wind-instrument, and these were repeated at her desire.

The prisoners also heard and felt the apparition after Eslinger's departure; and Mayer says he is perfectly assured that in this jail, where the inmates were frequently changed, everybody was locked up, and every place thoroughly examined, it was utterly impossible for any trick to be played: besides which, all parties agreed that the sounds were often of a description that could not have been produced by any known means.

But it was not to the prison alone that this apparition confined his visits. To whomsoever Eslinger sent him, he went—testifying his presence by the same signs as above described. He visited the chambers of several of the magistrates, of a teacher named Neuffer, of the referendary burgher, of a citizen named Rummel, and many others. Of these, some only perceived his presence by the noises, the cool air, the smell, or the touch; others saw the light also, and others perceived the figure with more or less distinctness.

A Mr. Dorr, of Heilbronn, seems to have scoffed very much at these rumors, and Dr. Kerner bade Eslinger ask the ghost to convince him, which she did.

Mr. Dorr says: "When I heard these things talked of, I always laughed at them, and was thought very sensible for so doing. Now I shall be laughed at in my turn, no doubt." He then relates that, on the morning of the 30th of December, 1835, he awoke, as usual, about five o'clock, and was thinking of some business he had in hand, when he became conscious that there was something near him, and he felt as if it blew cold upon him. He started up, thinking some animal had got into his room, but could find nothing. Next he heard a noise, like sparks from an electrical machine, and then a report close to his right ear. Had there been anything visible, it was light enough to see it. This report was frequently heard in the prison.

Wherever the apparition once made a visit, he generally continued to go for several successive nights. He also visited Professor Kapff at Heilbronn, and Baron von Hugel at Eschenau, without being desired to do so by Eslinger; and Neuffer, whom he also went to, she knew nothing of.

When he visited Dr. Kerner's chamber, his wife, who had prided herself on her incredulity, and boasted of being born on St. Thomas's day, was entirely converted, for she not only heard him, but saw him distinctly. He visited them for several nights, accompanied by the noises and the light.

One night, while lying awake observing these phenomena, they fancied they heard their horse come out of his stable, which was under their room. In the morning, he was found standing outside, with his halter on; it was not broken, and it was evident that the horse had not got loose by any violence. Moreover, the door of the stable was closed behind him, as it had been at night when he was shut up.

Dr. Kerner's sister, who came from a distance to visit them, had heard very little about this affair, yet she was awakened by a sound that seemed like some one trying to speak into her ear; and, looking up, she saw two stars, like those described by Margaret Laibesberg. She observed that they emitted no rays. She also felt the cool air, and perceived the corpse-like odor. This odor accompanied the ghost even when it appeared at Heilbronn.

It is remarkable that some of these persons, both men and women, felt themselves unable to move or call out while the spectre was there, and that they were relieved the moment he went away. They appeared to be magnetized; but this feeling was by no means universal. Many were perfectly composed and self-possessed the whole time, and made their observations to each other. All agreed that the speaking of the apparition seemed like that of a person making efforts to speak. Now, as we are to presume that he did not speak by means of organs, as we do, but that he imitated the sounds of words as he imitated other sounds, by some means with which we are unacquainted — for since the noises were heard by everybody within hearing, we must suppose that they actually existed — we, who know the extreme difficulty of imitating human speech, may conceive how this imitation should be very defective.

Dutthenhofer and others remarked that there was no echo from the sounds, as well as that the phosphorescence shed no light around; and though the spectre could touch *them*, or produce the sensation that he did, they could not feel *him*: but, as in all similar cases, could thrust their hands through what appeared to be his body. The sensation of his falling tears, and the marks they left, seem most unaccountable; and yet, in the records of a ghost that haunted the countess of Eberstein, in 1685, we find the same thing asserted. This account was made public by the authority of the consistorial court, and with the consent of the family.

At length, on the 11th of February, the ghost took his departure from Eslinger; at least, after that day he was no more seen or heard by her or anybody else. He had always entreated her to go to Wimmenthal, where he had formerly lived, to pray for him; and, after she was released from the jail, by the advice of her friends, she did it. Some of them accompanied her, and they saw the apparition near her while she was kneeling in the open air, though not all with equal distinctness. A very respectable woman, called Wörner — a stranger to Eslinger, whom she says she never saw or spoke to till that day — offered to make oath that she had accompanied her to Wimmenthal, and that, with the other friends, she had stood about thirty paces off, quite silent and still, while the woman knelt and prayed; and that she had seen the apparition of a man, accompanied by two smaller spectres, hovering near her. "When the prayer was ended, he went close to her, and there was a light like a falling star; then I saw something like a white cloud, that seemed to float away: and after that, we saw no more."

Eslinger had been very unwilling to undertake this expedition: she took leave of her children before she started, and evidently expected mischief would befall her; and now, on approaching her, they found her lying cold and insensible. When they had revived her, she told them that, on bidding her farewell, before he ascended—which he did, accompanied by two bright infantine forms—the ghost had asked her to give him her hand; and that, after wrapping it in her handkerchief, she had complied. "A small flame had arisen from the handkerchief when he touched it; and we found the marks of his fingers like burns, but without any smell." This, however, was not the cause of her fainting; but she had been terrified by a troop of frightful animals that she saw rush past her, when the spirit floated away.

From this time, nobody, either in the prison or out of it, was troubled with this apparition.

This is certainly a very extraordinary story; and what is more extraordinary, such cases do not seem to be very uncommon in Germany. I meet with many recorded: and an eminent German scholar of my acquaintance tells me that he has also heard of several, and was surprised that we have no similar instances here. If these things occurred merely among the Roman catholics, we might be inclined to suppose that they had some connection with their notion of purgatory: but, on the contrary, it appears to be among the Lutheran population they chiefly occur—insomuch that it has even been suggested that the omission of prayers for the dead, in the Lutheran church, is the cause of the phenomenon. But, on the other hand, as in the present case, and in several others, the person that revisits the earth was of the catholic persuasion when alive, we are bound to suppose that he had the benefit of his own church's prayers.

I am here assuming that all the above strange phenomena were really produced by the agency of an apparition. If they were not, what were they? The three physicians, who were among the visiters, must have been perfectly aware of the contagious nature of some forms of nervous disorder, and from the previous incredulity of two of them, they must have been quite prepared to regard these phenomena from that point of view; yet they seem unable to bring them under the category of sensuous illusions.

The apparently electrical nature of the lights, and of several of the sounds, is very remarkable, as are also the swellings produced on some of the persons by the touch of the ghost, which remind us of Professer Hofer's case, mentioned in a former chapter. The apparition of the dog and the lambs also, strange as they are, are by no means isolated cases. These appearances seem to be symbolical: the father had been evil, and had led his son to do evil, and he appeared in the degraded form of a dog; and the innocence of the children, who had been, probably, in some way wronged, was symbolized by their appearing as lambs. "If I had lived as a beast," said an apparition to the Seeress of Provorst, "I should appear as a beast." These symbolical transfigurations can not appear very extravagant to those who accept the belief of many theologians, that the serpent of the garden of Eden was an evil spirit incarnated in that degraded form.

How far the removal of the horse out of the stable was connected with the rest of the phenomena, it is impossible to say; but a similar circumstance has very lately occurred with regard to a dog that was locked up in the house in this neighborhood, which I have several times alluded to, where footsteps and rustlings are heard, doors are opened, and a feeling that some one is blowing or breathing upon them is felt by the inhabitants.

The holes burnt in the handkerchief are also quite in accordance with many other relations of the kind, especially that of the maid of Orlach, and also that of the Hammerschan family, mentioned in "Stilling's Pneumatology," when a ghost who had been, as he said, waiting one hundred and twenty years for some one to release him by their prayers, was seen to take a handkerchief, on which he left the marks of his five fingers, appearing like burnt spots. A bible that he touched was marked in the same manner; and these two mementoes of the apparition were carefully retained in the family. This particularity, also, reminds us of Lord Tyrone's leaving the marks of his hand on Lady Beresford's wrist, on which she ever afterward wore a black riband. In several instances I find it reported that when an apparition is requested to render himself visible to, or to enter into communication with, other persons besides those to whom he addresses himself, he answers that it is impossible; and in other cases, that he could do it, but that the consequences to those persons would be pernicious. This, together with the circumstance of their waiting so long for the right person, tends strongly to support the hypothesis that an intense magnetic rapport is necessary to any facility of intercourse. It also appears that the power of establishing this rapport with one or more persons, varies exceedingly among these denizens of a spiritual world, some being only able to render themselves audible, others to render themselves visible to one person, while a few seem to possess considerably greater powers or privileges.

Another particular to be observed is, that in many instances, if not in all, these spirits are what the Germans call *gebannt*, that is, *banned*, or *proscribed*, or, as it were, *tethered* to a certain spot, which they can occasionally leave, as Anton did the cellar at Wimmenthal, to which he was *gebannt*, but from which they can not free themselves. To this spot they seem to be attached, as by an invisible chain, whether by the memory of a crime committed there, or by a buried treasure, or even by its being the receptacle of their own bodies. In short, it seems perfectly clear, admitting them to be apparitions of the dead, that, whatever the bond may be that keeps them down, they can not quit the earth; they are, as St. Martin says, *remainers*, not *returners*, and this seems to be the explanation of haunted houses.

In the year 1827, Christian Eisengrun, a respectable citizen of Neckarsteinach, was visited by a ghost of the above kind, and the particulars were judically recorded. He was at Eherbach, in Baden, working as a potter, which was his trade, in the manufactory of Mr. Gehrig, when he was one night awakened by a noise in his chamber, and, on looking up, he saw a faint light, which presently assumed a human form, attired in a loose gown; he could see no head. He had his own head under the clothes; but it presently spoke, and told him that he was destined to release it, and for that purpose he must go to the catholic churchyard of Neckarsteinach, and there, for twenty-one successive days, repeat the following verse from the New Testament, before the stone sepulchre there:—

"For what man knoweth the things of a man, save the spirit of man which is in him? So, the things of God knoweth no man, but the spirit of God."—1 Cor. ii. 11.

The ghost having repeated his visits and his request, the man consulted his master what he should do, and he advised him not to trifle with the apparition, but to do what he required, adding that he had known many similar instances. Upon this, Eisengrun went to Neckarsteinach, and addressed himself to the catholic priest there, named Seitz, who gave him the same counsel, together with his blessing and also a hymn of Luther's, which he bade him learn and repeat, as well as the verse, when he visited the sepulchre.

As there was only one stone sepulchre in the churchyard, Eisengrun had no difficulty in finding it; and while he performed the service imposed on him by the ghost, the latter stood on the grave with his hands folded as if in prayer; but when he repeated the hymn, he moved rapidly backward and forward, but still not overstepping the limits of the stone. The man, though very frightened, persevered in the thing for the time imposed, twenty-one days; and during this period he saw the perfect form of the apparition, which had no covering on its head except very white hair. It always kept its hands folded, and had large eyes, in which he never perceived any motion; this filled him with horror. Many persons went to witness the ceremony.

The surviving nephews and nieces of the apparition brought an action against Eisengrun, and they contrived to have him seized and carried to the magistrate's house, one day, at the time he should have gone to the churchyard. But the ghost came and beckoned, and made signs to him to follow him, till the man was so much affected and terrified that he burst into tears. The two magistrates could not see the spectre, but feeling themselves affected with a cold shudder, they consented to his going.

He was then publicly examined in court, together with the offended family and a number of witnesses; and the result was, that he was permitted to continue the service for the twenty-one days, after which he never saw or heard more of the ghost, who had been formerly a rich timber-merchant. The terror and anxiety attendant on these daily visits to the churchyard, affected Eisengrun so much, that it was some time before he recovered his usual health. He had all his life been a ghost-seer, but had never had communication with any before this event.

The catholic priest, in this instance, appears to have been more liberal than the deceased timber-merchant, for the latter did not seem to like the Lutheran hymn which the former prescribed. His dissatisfaction, however, may have arisen from their making any addition to the formula he had himself indicated.

CHAPTER XVI.

THE POLTERGEIST OF THE GERMANS, AND POSSESSION.

WITH regard to the so-called *hauntings*, referred to in the preceding chapter, there seems reason to believe that the invisible guest was formerly a dweller upon earth, in the flesh, who is prevented by some circumstance which we are not qualified to explain, from pursuing the destiny of the human race, by entering freely into the next state prepared for him. He is like an unfortunate caterpillar that can not entirely free itself from the integuments of its reptile life which chain it to the earth, while its fluttering wings vainly seek to bear it into the region to which it now belongs. But there is another kind of *haunting*, which is still more mysterious and strange, though by no means unfrequent, and which, from the odd, sportive, mischievous nature of the disturbances created, one can scarcely reconcile to our notions of what we understand by the term *ghost;* for in those cases where the unseen visitant appears to be the spirit of a person deceased, we see evidences of grief, remorse, and dissatisfaction, together with, in many instances, a disposition to repeat the acts of life—or at least to simulate a repetition of them: but there is nothing sportive or mischievous, nor, except where an injunction is disobeyed or a request refused, are there generally any evidences of anger or malignity. But in the other cases alluded to, the annoyances appear rather like the tricks of a mischievous imp. I refer to what the Germans call the *poltergeist*, or racketing spectre, for the phenomenon is known in all countries, and has been known in all ages.

Since hearing of the phenomenon of the electric girl, which attracted so much attention and occasioned so much controversy in Paris lately, and other similar cases which have since reached me, I feel doubtful whether some of these strange circumstances may not have been connected with electricity in one form or another. The famous story of what is familiarly called the Stockwell ghost, for example, might possibly be brought under this category. I have heard some people assert that the mystery of this affair was subsequently explained away, and the whole found to be a trick: but that is a mistake. Some years ago, I was acquainted with persons whose parents were living on the spot at that time, who knew all the details, and to them it remained as great a mystery as ever; not the smallest light had ever been thrown upon it. People are so glad to get rid of troublesome mysteries of this description, that they are always ready to say, "The trick has been found out!" and those who pride themselves on not believing idle stories, are to the last degree credulous when "the idle story" flatters their skepticism.

The circumstances of the so-called Stockwell ghost, which I extract from a report published at the time, are as follows:—

The pamphlet was entitled: "An authentic, candid, and Circumstantial Narrative of the astonishing Transactions at Stockwell, in the County of Surrey, on Monday and Tuesday, the 6th and 7th days of January, 1772; containing a Series of the most surprising and unaccountable Events that ever happened, which continued, from first to last, upward of twenty hours, and at different places: published with the consent and approbation of the family and other parties concerned, to authenticate which the original copy is signed by them.

"Before we enter upon a description of the most extraordinary transactions that perhaps ever happened, we shall begin with an account of the parties who were principally concerned, and, in justice to them, give their characters, by which means the impartial world may see what credit is due to the following narrative:—

"The events, indeed, are of so strange and singular a nature, that we can not be at all surprised the public should be doubtful of the truth of them, more especially as there have been too many impositions of this sort; but, let us consider, here are no sinister ends to be answered, no contributions to be wished for, nor would be accepted, as the parties are in reputable situations and good circumstances, particularly Mrs. Golding, who is a lady of an independent fortune: Richard Fowler and his wife might be looked upon as an exception to this assertion; but, as their loss was trivial, they must be left out of the question, except so far as they appear corroborating evidences. Mr. Pain's maid lost nothing.

"How or by what means these transactions were brought about, has never transpired: we have only to rest our confidence on the veracity of the parties, whose descriptions have been most strictly attended to, without the least deviation: nothing here offered is either exaggerated or diminished—the whole stated in the clearest manner, just as they occurred: as such only we lay them before the candid and impartial public.

"Mrs. Golding, an elderly lady at Stockwell, in Surrey, at whose house the transactions began, was born in the same parish (Lambeth), has lived in it ever since, and has always been well known and respected as a gentlewoman of unblemished honor and character. Mrs. Pain, a niece of Mrs. Golding, has been married several years to Mr. Pain, a farmer, at Brixton causeway, a little above Mr. Angel's—has several children, and is well known and respected in the parish. Mary Martin, Mr. Pain's servant, an elderly woman, has lived two years with them and four years with Mrs. Golding, where she came from. Richard Fowler lives almost opposite to Mr. Pain, at the Brick pound—an honest, industrious, and sober man. And Sarah Fowler, wife to the above, is an industrious and sober woman.

"These are the subscribing evidences that we must rest the truth of the facts upon; yet there are numbers of other persons who were eye-witnesses of many of the transactions during the time they happened, all of whom must acknowledge the truth of them.

"Another person who bore a principal part in these scenes was Ann Robinson, Mrs. Golding's maid, a young woman about twenty years old, who had lived with her but one week and three days. So much for the *historiæ personæ*, and now for the narrative.

"On Monday, January the 6th, 1772, about ten o'clock in the forenoon, as Mrs. Golding was in her parlor, she heard the china and glasses in the back kitchen tumble down and break; her maid came to her and told her the stone plates were falling from the shelf; Mrs. Golding went into the kitchen and saw them broke. Presently after, a row of plates from the next shelf fell down likewise, while she was there, and nobody near them; this astonished her much, and while she was thinking about it, other things in different places began to tumble about, some of them breaking, attended with violent noises all over the house; a clock tumbled down and the case broke; a lantern that hung on the staircase was thrown down and the glass broken to pieces; an earthen pan of salted beef broke to pieces and the beef fell about: all this increased her surprise and brought several persons about her, among whom was Mr. Rowlidge, a carpenter, who gave it as his opinion that the foundation was giving way and that the house was tumbling down, occasioned by the too great weight of an additional room erected above: so ready are we to discover natural causes for everything! But no such thing happened, as the reader will find; for whatever was the cause, that cause ceased almost as soon as Mrs. Golding and her maid left any place, and followed them wherever they went. Mrs. Golding ran into Mr. Gresham's house, a gentleman living next door to her, where she fainted.

"In the interim, Mr. Rowlidge and other persons were removing Mrs. Golding's effects from her house, for fear of the consequences he had prognosticated. At this time all was quiet; Mrs. Golding's maid, remaining in the house, was gone up stairs, and when called upon several times to come down, for fear of the dangerous situation she was thought to be in, she answered very coolly, and after some time came down as deliberately, without any seeming fearful apprehensions.

"Mrs. Pain was sent for from Brixton Causeway, and desired to come directly, as her aunt was supposed to be dead: this was the message to her. When Mrs. Pain came, Mrs. Goldiug was come to herself, but very faint.

"Among the persons who were present was Mr. Gardner, a surgeon, of Clapham, whom Mrs. Pain desired to bleed her aunt, which he did. Mrs. Pain asked him if the blood should be thrown away: he desired it might not, as he would examine it when cold. These minute particulars would not be taken notice of, but as a chain to what follows. For the next circumstance is of a more astonishing nature than anything that had preceded it: the blood that was just congealed, sprang out of the basin upon the floor, and presently after the basin broke to pieces! This china basin was the only thing broke belonging to Mr. Gresham; a bottle of rum that stood by it broke at the same time.

"Among the things that were removed to Mr. Gresham's, was a tray full of china, a japan bread-basket, some mahogany waiters, with some bottles of liquors, jars of pickles, &c., and a pier-glass, which was taken down by Mr. Saville (a neighbor of Mrs. Golding's); he gave it to one Robert Hames, who laid it on the grass-plat at Mrs. Gresham's: but, before he could put it out of his hands, some parts of the frame on each side flew off! It rained at that time; Mrs. Golding desired it might be brought into the parlor, where it was put under a sideboard, and a dressing-glass along with it. It had not been there long, before the glasses and china which stood on the sideboard began to tumble about and fall down, and broke both the glasses to pieces. Mr. Saville and others being asked to drink a glass of wine or rum, both the bottles broke in pieces before they were uncorked!

"Mrs. Golding's surprise and fear increasing, she did not know what to do, or where to go. Wherever she and her maid were, these strange, destructive circumstances followed her, and how to help or free herself from them was not in her power or any other person's present. Her mind was one confused chaos, lost to herself and everything about her—drove from her own home, and afraid there would be no other to receive her. At last she left Mr. Gresham's and went to Mr. Mayling's, a gentleman at the next door; here she stayed about three quarters of an hour, during which time nothing happened. Her maid stayed at Mr. Gresham's to put up what few things remained unbroken of her mistress's, in a back apartment, when a jar of pickles that stood upon a table turned upside down; then a jar of raspberry jam broke to pieces; next two mahogany waiters and a quadrille-box likewise broke in pieces.

"Mrs. Pain, not choosing her aunt should stay too long at Mr. Mayling's, for fear of being troublesome, persuaded her to go to her house at Rush Common, near Brixton Causeway, where she would endeavor to make her as happy as she could, hoping by this time all was over, as nothing had happened at that gentleman's house while she was there. This was about two o'clock in the afternoon.

"Mr. and Miss Gresham were at Mr. Pain's house when Mrs. Pain, Mrs. Golding, and her maid, went there. It being about dinner-time, they all dined together; in the interim, Mrs. Golding's servant was sent to her house to see how things remained. When she returned, she told them nothing had happened since they left it. Some time after, Mr. Gresham and miss went home, everything remaining quiet at Mr. Pain's; but about eight o'clock in the evening a fresh scene began. The first thing that happened was, a whole row of pewter dishes, except one, fell from off a shelf to the middle of the floor, rolled about a little while, then settled; and, what is almost beyond belief, as soon as they were quiet, turned upside down! They were then put on the dresser, and went through the same a second time. Next fell a whole row of pewter plates from off the second shelf over the dresser to the ground, and, being taken up and put on the dresser one in another, they were thrown down again.

"The next thing was, two eggs that were upon one of the pewter shelves, one of them flew off, crossed the kitchen, struck a cat on the head, and then broke in pieces.

"Next, Mary Martin, Mrs. Pain's servant, went to stir the kitchen fire; she got to the right-hand side of it, being a large chimney, as is usual in farmhouses. A pestle and mortar that stood nearer the left-hand end of the chimney-shelf, jumped about six feet on the floor! Then went candlesticks and other brasses, scarcely anything remaining in its place. After this, the glasses and china were put down on the floor for fear of undergoing the same fate: they presently began to dance and tumble about, and then broke to pieces. A teapot that was among them flew to Mrs. Golding's maid's foot, and struck it.

"A glass tumbler that was put on the floor jumped about two feet and then broke. Another that stood by it jumped about at the same time, but did not break till some hours after, when it jumped again, and then broke. A china bowl that stood in the parlor jumped from the floor to behind a table that stood there. This was most astonishing, as the distance from where it stood was between seven and eight feet, but was not broke. It was put back by Richard Fowler to its place, where it remained some time, and then flew to pieces.

"The next thing that followed was a mustard-pot, that jumped out of a closet and was broke. A single cup that stood upon the table (almost the only thing remaining) jumped up, flew across the kitchen, ringing like a bell, and then was dashed to pieces against the dresser. A candlestick that stood on the chimney-shelf flew across the kitchen to the parlor-door, at about fifteen feet distance. A teakettle under the dresser was thrown out about two feet; another kettle, that stood at one end of the range, was thrown against the iron that is fixed to prevent children from falling into the fire. A tumbler with rum-and-water in it, that stood upon a waiter upon a table in the parlor, jumped about ten feet, and was broke. The table then fell down, and along with it a silver tankard belonging to Mrs. Golding—the waiter in which stood the tumbler, and a candlestick. A case-bottle then flew to pieces.

"The next circumstance was, a ham that hung in one side of the kitchen-chimney raised itself from the hook and fell down to the ground. Some time after, another ham, that hung on the other side of the chimney, likewise underwent the same fate. Then a flitch of bacon, which hung up in the same chimney, fell down.

"All the family were eye-witnesses to these circumstances, as well as other persons, some of whom were so alarmed and shocked, that they could not bear to stay, and were happy in getting away, though the unhappy family were left in the midst of their distresses. Most of the genteel families around were continually sending to inquire after them, and whether all was over or not. Is it not surprising that some among them had not the inclination and resolution to try to unravel this most intricate affair, at a time when it would have been in their power to have done so? There certainly was sufficient time for so doing, as the whole, from first to last, continued upward of twenty hours.

"At all the times of action, Mrs. Golding's servant was walking backward and forward, in either the kitchen or parlor, or wherever some of the family happened to be. Nor could they get her to sit down five minutes together, except at one time for about half an hour toward the morning, when the family were at prayers in the parlor; then all was quiet: but in the midst of the greatest confusion, she was as much composed as at any other time, and with uncommon coolness of temper advised her mistress not to be alarmed or uneasy, as she said these things could not be helped. Thus she argued, as if they were common occurrences, which must happen in every family!

"This advice surprised and startled her mistress almost as much as the circumstances that occasioned it. For how can we suppose that a girl of about twenty years old (an age when female timidity is too often assisted by superstition) could remain in the midst of such calamitous circumstances (except they proceed from causes best known to herself), and not be struck with the same terror as every other person was who was present? These reflections led Mr. Pain (and, at the end of the transactions, likewise Mrs. Golding) to think that she was not altogether so unconcerned as she appeared to be; but, hitherto, the whole remains mysterious and unrivalled.

"About ten o'clock at night, they sent over the way to Richard Fowler, to desire he would come and stay with them. He came and continued till one in the morning, and was so terrified that he could remain no longer.

"As Mrs. Golding could not be persuaded to go to bed, Mrs. Pain at that time (one o'clock) made an excuse to go up stairs to her youngest child, under pretence of getting it to sleep, but she really acknowledges it was through fear, as she declares she could not sit up to see such strange things going on, as everything, one after another, was broke, till there was not above two or three cups and saucers remaining out of a considerable quantity of china, &c., which was destroyed to the amount of some pounds.

"About five o'clock on Tuesday morning, Mrs. Golding went up to her niece, and desired her to get up, as the noises and destruction were so great, she could continue in the house no longer. At this time all the tables, chairs, drawers, &c., were tumbling about. When Mrs. Pain came down, it was amazing beyond all description. Their only security then was to quit the house, for fear of the same catastrophe as had been expected the morning before at Mrs. Golding's. In consequence of this resolution, Mrs. Golding and her maid went over the way to Richard Fowler's. When Mrs. Golding's maid had seen her safe to Richard Fowler's, she came back to Mrs. Pain, to help her to dress the children in the barn, where she had carried them for fear of the house falling. At this time all was quiet. They then went to Fowler's, and then began the same scene as had happened at the other places. It must be remarked, all was quiet here as well as elsewhere, till the maid returned.

"When they got to Mr. Fowler's, he began to light a fire in his back room. When done, he put the candle and candlestick upon a table in the fore-room. This apartment Mrs. Golding and her maid had passed through. Another candlestick, with a tin lamp in it, that stood by it, were both dashed together, and fell to the ground. A lantern, with which Mrs. Golding was lighted across the road, sprang from a hook to the ground, and a quantity of oil spilled on the floor. The last thing was, the basket of coals tumbled over, the coals rolling about the room

The maid then desired Richard Fowler not to let her mistress remain there, as she said wherever she was the same things would follow. In consequence of this advice, and fearing greater losses to himself, he desired she would quit his house; but first begged her to consider within herself, for her own and the public's sake, whether or not she had been guilty of some atrocious crime, for which Providence was determined to pursue her on this side of the grave: for he could not help thinking she was the object that was to be made an example to posterity, by the all-seeing eye of Providence, for crimes which but too often none but that Providence can penetrate, and by such means as these bring to light.

"Thus was the poor gentlewoman's measure of affliction complete, not only to have undergone all which has been related, but to have added to it the character of a bad and wicked woman, when till this time she was esteemed as a most deserving person. In candor to Fowler, he could not be blamed. What could he do? what would any man have done that was so circumstanced? Mrs. Golding soon satisfied him: she told him she would not stay in his house or any other person's, as her conscience was quite clear, and she could as well wait the will of Providence in her own house as in any other place whatever; upon which she and her maid went home. Mr. Pain went with them. After they had got to Mrs. Golding's the last time, the same transactions once more began upon the remains that were left.

"A nine-gallon cask of beer, that was in the cellar, the door being open, and no person near it, turned upside down. A pail of water, that stood on the floor, boiled like a pot! A box of candles fell from a shelf in the kitchen to the floor; they rolled out, but none were broke: and a round mahogany table overset in the parlor.

"Mr. Pain then desired Mrs. Golding to send her maid for his wife to come to them. When she was gone, all was quiet Upon her return she was immediately discharged, and no disturbances have happened since. This was between six and seven o'clock on Tuesday morning.

"At Mrs. Golding's were broke the quantity of three pailfuls of glass, china, &c. At Mrs. Pain's they filled two pails.

"Thus ends the narrrative—a true, circumstantial, and faithful account of which we have laid before the public; and have endeavored as much as possible, throughout the whole, to state only facts, without presuming to obtrude any opinion on them. If we have in part hinted anything that may appear unfavorable to the girl, it is not from a determination to charge her with the cause, right or wrong, but only from a strict adherence to truth, most sincerely wishing this extraordinary affair may be unravelled.

"The above narrative is absolutely and strictly true, in witness whereof we have set our hands this eleventh day of January, 1772:—

"Mary Golding,
"John Pain,
"Mary Pain,
"Richard Fowler,
"Sarah Fowler,
"Mary Martin.

"The original copy of this narrative, signed as above, with the parties' own hands, was put into the hands of Mr. Marks, bookseller, in St. Martin's Lane, to satisfy persons who choose to inspect the same."

Such phenomena as this of the Stockwell ghost are by no means uncommon, and I am acquainted with many more instances than I can allude to here. One occurred very lately in the neighborhood of London, as I learned from the following newspaper paragraph. I subsequently heard that the little girl had been sent away; but whether the phenomena then ceased, or whether she carried the disturbance with her, I have not been able to ascertain, nor does it appear certain that she had anything to do with it:—

A Mischievous and Mysterious Ghost.—(From a correspondent.)—The whole of the neighborhood of Black Lion-lane, Bayswater, is ringing with the extraordinary occurrences that have recently happened in the house of a Mr. Williams, in the

Moscow-road, and which bear a strong resemblance to the celebrated Stockwell ghost affair in 1772. The house is inhabited by Mr. and Mrs. Williams, a grown-up son and daughter, and a little girl between ten and eleven years of age. On the first day, the family, who are remarkable for their piety, were startled all at once by a mysterious movement among the things in the sitting-rooms and kitchen, and other parts of the house. At one time, without any visible agency, one of the jugs came off the hook over the dresser, and was broken; then followed another, and next day another. A china teapot, with the tea just made in it, and placed on the mantel-piece, whisked off on to the floor, and was smashed. A pewter one, which had been substituted immediately after, did the same, and, when put on the table, was seen to hop about as if bewitched, and was actually held down while the tea was made for Mr. Williams's breakfast, before leaving for his place of business. When for a time all had been quiet, off came from its place on the wall, a picture in a heavy gilt frame, and fell to the floor without being broken. All was now amazement and terror, for the old people are very superstitious, and ascribing it to a supernatural agency, the other pictures were removed, and stowed away on the floor. But the spirit of locomotion was not to be arrested. Jugs and plates continued at intervals to quit their posts, and skip off their hooks and shelves into the middle of the room, as though they were inspired by the magic flute, and at supper, when the little girl's mug was filled with beer, the mug slided off the table on to the floor. Three times it was replaced, and three times it moved off again. It would be tedious to relate the fantastic tricks which have been played by household articles of every kind. An Egyytian vase jumped off the table suddenly, when no soul was near, and was smashed to pieces. The tea-kettle popped off the fire into the grate as Mr. Williams had filled the teapot, which fell off the chimney-piece. Candlesticks, after a dance on the table, flew off, and ornaments from the shelves, and bonnets and cap-boxes flung about in the oddest manner. A looking-glass hopped off a dressing-table, followed by combs and brushes and several bottles, and a great pincushion has been remarkably conspicuous for its incessant jigs from one part to another. The little girl, who is a Spaniard, and under the care of Mr. and Mrs. Williams, is supposed by their friends to be the cause of it all, however extraordinary it may seem in one of her age, but up to the present time it continues a mystery, and the *modus operandi* is invisible."—*Morning Post.*

To imagine that these extraordinary effects were produced by the voluntary agency of the child, furnishes one of those remarkable instances of the credulity of the skeptical, to which I have referred. But when we read a true statement of the effects involuntarily exhibited by Angelique Cottin, we begin to see that it is just possible the other strange phenomena may be provided by a similar agency.

The French Academy of Sciences had determined, as they had formerly done by Mesmerism, that the thing should not be true. Monsieur Arago was nonsuited; but although it is extremely possible that either the phenomenon had run its course and arrived at a natural termination, or that the removal of the girl to Paris had extinguished it, there appears no doubt that it had previously existed.

Angelique Cottin was a native of La Perriere, aged fourteen, when, on the 15th of January, 1846, at eight o'clock in the evening, while weaving silk-gloves at an oaken frame, in company with other girls, the frame began to jerk, and they could not by any efforts keep it steady. It seemed as if it were alive, and becoming alarmed, they called in the neighbors, who would not believe them; but desired them to sit down and go on with their work. Being timid, they went one by one, and the frame remained still till Angelique approached, when it recommenced its movements, while she was also attracted by the frame: thinking she was bewitched or possessed, her parents took her to the presbytery that the spirit might be exorcised. The curate, however, being a sensible man, refused to do it, but set himself, on the contrary, to observe the phenomenon, and being perfectly satisfied of the fact, he bade them take her to a physician.

Meanwhile, the intensity of the influence, whatever it was,

augmented; not only articles made of oak, but all sorts of things were acted upon by it and reacted upon her, while persons who were near her, even without contact, frequently felt electric shocks. The effects, which were diminished when she was on a carpet or a waxed cloth, were most remarkable when she was on the bare earth. They sometimes entirely ceased for two or three days, and then recommenced. Metals were not affected. Anything touched by her apron or dress would fly off, although a person held it; and Monsieur Hebert, while seated on a heavy tub or trough, was raised up with it. In short, the only place she could repose on, was a stone covered with cork; they also kept her still by isolating her. When she was fatigued the effects diminished. A needle suspended horizontally, oscillated rapidly with the motion of her arm, without contact, or remained fixed, while deviating from the magnetic direction. Great numbers of enlightened medical and scientific men witnessed these phenomena, and investigated them with every precaution to prevent imposition. She was often hurt by the violent involuntary movements she was thrown into, and was evidently afflicted by chorea.

Unfortunately, her parents, poor and ignorant, insisted much against the advice of the doctors, on exhibiting her for money; and under these circumstances, she was brought to Paris; and nothing is more probable than that after the phenomena had really ceased, the girl may have been induced to simulate what had originally been genuine. The thing avowedly ceased altogether on the 10th of April, and there has been no return of it.

In 1831, a young girl, also aged fourteen, who lived as under nursery-maid in a French family, exhibited the same phenomena, and when the case of Angelique Cottin was made public, her master published hers. He says that things of such an extraordinary nature occurred as he dare not repeat, since none but an eye-witness could believe them. The thing lasted for three years, and there was ample time for observation.

In the year 1686, a man at Brussels, called Breekmans, was similarly affected. A commission was appointed by the magistrates to investigate his condition; and, being pronounced a sorcerer, he would have been burnt, had he not luckily made his escape.

Many somnambulic persons are capable of giving an electric shock; and I have met with one person, not somnambulic, who informs me that he has frequently been able to do it by an effort of the will.

Dr. Ennemoser relates the case of a Mademoiselle Emmerich, sister to the professor of theology at Strasburg, who also possessed this power. This young lady, who appears to have been a person of very rare merit and endowments, was afflicted with a long and singular malady, originating in a fright, in the course of which she exhibited many very curious phenomena, having fallen into a state of natural somnambulism, accompanied by a high degree of lucidity. Her body became so surcharged with electricity, that it was necessary to her relief to discharge it; and she sometimes imparted a complete battery of shocks to her brother and her physician, or whoever was near her, and that frequently when they did not touch her. Professor Emmerich mentions also that she sent him a smart shock, one day, when he was several rooms off. He started up and rushed into her chamber, where she was in bed; and as soon as she saw him she said, laughing: "Ah, you felt it, did you?" Mademoiselle Emmerich's illness terminated in death.

Cotugno, a surgeon, relates that, having touched with his scalpel the intercostal nerve of a mouse that had bitten his leg, he received an electric shock; and where the torpedo abounds, the fishermen, in pouring water over the fish they have caught for the purpose of washing them, know if one is among them by the shock they sustain.

A very extraordinary circumstance, which we may possibly attribute to some such influence as the above, occurred at Rambouillet in November, 1846. The particulars are furnished by a gentleman residing on the spot at the time, and were published by the Baron Dupotel—who, however, attempts no explanation of the mystery:—

One morning some travelling merchants, or pedlars, came to the door of a farmhouse, belonging to a man named Bottel, and asked for some bread, which the maid-servant gave them, and they went away. Subsequently one of the party returned to ask for more, and was refused. The man, I believe, expressed some resentment and uttered vague threats, but she would not give him anything and he departed. That night at supper the plates began to dance and roll off the table, without any visible cause, and several other unaccountable phenomena occurred; and the girl going to the door and chancing to place herself just where the pedlar had stood, she was seized with convulsions and an extraordinary rotatory motion. The carter who was standing by laughed at her, and out of bravado placed himself on the same spot, when he felt almost suffocated, and was so unable to command his movements that he was overturned into a large pool in front of the house.

Upon this they rushed to the curé of the parish for assistance; but he had scarcely said a prayer or two before he was attacked in the same manner, though in his own house; and his furniture beginning to oscillate and crack as if it were bewitched, the poor people were frightened out of their wits.

By-and-by the phenomena intermitted, and they hoped all was over; but presently it began again, and this occurred more than once before it subsided wholly.

On the 8th December, 1836, at Stuttgard, Carl Fischer, a baker's boy, aged seventeen, of steady habits and good character, was fixed with a basket on his shoulders, in some unaccountable way, in front of his master's house. He foresaw the thing was to happen when he went out with his bread very early in the morning; earnestly wished that the day was over, and told his companion that if he could only cross the threshold, on his return, he should escape it. It was about six when he did return; and his master, hearing a fearful noise which he could not describe—"as if proceeding from a multitude of beings"—looked out of the window, where he saw Carl violently struggling and fighting with his apron, though his feet were immoveably fixed to one spot. A hissing sound proceeded from his mouth and nose, and a voice, which was neither his nor that of any person present, was heard to cry, "Stand fast,

Carl!" The master says that he could not have believed such a thing; and he was so alarmed that he did not venture into the street, where numerous persons were assembled. The boy said he must remain there till eleven o'clock; and the police kept guard over him till that time, as the physician said he must not be interfered with, and the people sought to push him from the spot. When the time had expired, he was carried to the hospital, where he seemed exceedingly exhausted and fell into a profound sleep.

I meet with numerous extraordinary records of a preternatural ringing of all the bells in a house; sometimes occurring periodically for a considerable time, and continuing after precautions have been taken which precluded the possibility of trick or deception, the wires being cut, and vigilant eyes watching them; and yet they rung on, by day or night, just the same.

It is certainly very difficult to conceive, but at the same time it is not impossible, that such strange phenomena as that of the Stockwell ghost, and many similar ones, may be the manifestations of some extraordinary electrical influence; but there are other cases of poltergeist which it is impossible to attribute to the same cause, since they are accompanied by evident manifestations of will and intelligence. Such was the instance related in Southey's Life of Wesley, which occurred in the year 1716, beginning with a groaning, and subsequently proceeding to all manner of noises, lifting of latches, clattering of windows, knockings of a most mysterious kind, &c., &c. The family were not generally frightened, but the young children, when asleep, showed symptoms of great terror. This annoyance lasted, I think, two or three months, and then ceased. As in most of these cases, the dog was extremely frightened, and hid himself when the visitations commenced.

In the year 1838, a circumstance of the same kind occurred in Paris, in the Rue St. Honoré; and not very long ago there was one in Caithness, in which most unaccountable circumstances transpired. Among the rest, stones were flung, which never hit people, but fell at their feet, in rooms perfectly closed on all sides. A gentleman who witnessed these extraordinary phenomena, related the whole story to an advocate of my acquaintance, who assured me that, however impossible he found it to credit such things, he should certainly place entire reliance on that gentleman's word in any other case.

Then there is the famous story of the drummer of Tedworth;* and the persecution of Professor Schuppart, at Giessen, in Upper Hesse, which continued, with occasional intermission, for six years. This affair began with a violent knocking at the door one night; next day stones were sent whizzing through closed rooms in all directions, so that, although no one was struck, the windows were all broken; and no sooner were new panes put in, than they were broken again. He was persecuted with slaps on the face, by day and by night, so that he could get no rest; and when two persons were appointed by the authorities to sit by his bed to watch him, they got the slaps also. When he was reading at his desk, his lamp would suddenly rise up and remove to the other end of the room — not as if thrown, but evidently carried. His books were torn to pieces and flung at his feet; and when he was lecturing, this mischievous sprite would tear out the leaf he was reading; and it is very remarkable, that the only thing that seemed available as a protection, was a drawn sword brandished over his head by himself or others, which was one of the singularities attending the case of the drummer of Tedworth. Schuppart narrated all these circumstances in his public lectures, and nobody ever disputed the facts.

A remarkable case of this sort occurred in the year 1670, at Keppock, near Glasgow. There, also, stones were thrown which hit nobody, but the annoyance only continued eight days; and there are several more to be found recorded in works of that period. The disturbance that happened in the house of Gilbert Cambell, at Glenluce, excited considerable notice. Here, as elsewhere, stones were thrown; but, as in most simi-

* There was also a remarkable case of this sort at Mr. Chaves, in Devonshire, in the year 1810, where affidavits were made before the magistrates attesting the facts, and large rewards offered for discovery, but in vain. The phenomena continued several months, and the spiritual agent was frequently seen in the form of some strange animal.

lar instances I meet with, no human being was damaged—the license of these spirits, or goblins, or whatever they be, seeming to extend no further than worrying and tormenting their victims. In this case, however, the spirit spoke to them, though he was never seen. The annoyance commenced in November, of the year 1654, I think, and continued till April, when there was some intermission till July, when it recommenced. The loss of the family from the things destroyed was ruining; for their household goods and chattels were rendered useless, their food was polluted and spoiled, and their very clothes cut to pieces while on their backs, by invisible hands; and it was in vain that all the ministers about the country assembled to exorcise this troublesome spirit, for whoever was there the thing continued exactly the same.

At length poor Cambell applied to the synod of presbyters for advice; and a meeting was convened in October, 1655, and a solemn day of humiliation was imposed through the whole bounds of the presbytery, for the sake of the afflicted family. Whether it was owing to this or not, there ensued an alleviation from that time till April, and from April till August they were entirely free, and hoped all was over; but then it began again worse than ever, and they were dreadfully tormented through the autumn; after which the disturbance ceased, and although the family lived in the house many years afterward, nothing of the sort ever happened again.

There was another famous case, which occurred at a place called Ring-Croft, in Kirkcudbright, in the year 1695. The afflicted family bore the name of Mackie. In this instance, the stones did sometimes hit them, and they were beaten as if by staves; they, as well as strangers who came to the house, were lifted off the ground by their clothes; their bed coverings were taken off their beds; things were visibly carried about the house by invisible hands; several people were hurt, even to the effusion of blood, by stones and blows; there were fire-balls seen about the house, which were several times ignited; people, both of the family and others, felt themselves grasped as if by a hand; then there was groaning, crying, whistling, and a voice that frequently spoke to them. Crowds of people went to the house; but the thing continued just the same whether there were many or few, and sometimes the whole building shook as if it were coming down.

A day of humiliation was appointed in this case also, but without the least effect. The disturbance commenced in February, and ended on the 1st of May. Numberless people witnessed the phenomenon, and the account of it is attested by fourteen ministers and gentlemen.

The same sort of thing occurred in the year 1659, in a place inhabited by an evangelical bishop, called Schlotterbeck. It began in the same manner, by throwing of stones and other things, many of which came through the roof, insomuch that they believed at first that some animal was concealed there. However, nothing could be found, and the invisible guest soon proceeded to other annoyances similar to those above mentioned; and though they could not see him, his footsteps were for ever heard about the house. At length, wearied out, the bishop applied to the government for aid; and they sent him a company of soldiers to guard the house by day and night, out of which he and his family retired. But the goblin cared no more for the soldiers than it had done for the city watch; the thing continued without intermission, whoever was there, till it ceased of its own accord. There was a house at Aix-la-Chapelle that was for several years quite uninhabitable from a similar cause.

I could mention many other cases, and, as I have said before, they occur in all countries; but these will suffice as specimens of the class. It is in vain for people who were not on the spot to laugh, and assert that these were the mischievous tricks of servants or others, when those who were there, and who had such a deep interest in unravelling the mystery, and such abundance of time and opportunity for doing it, could find no solution whatever. In many of the above cases, the cattle were unloosed, the horses were turned out of their stables, and uniformly all the animals in the way exhibited great terror, sweating and trembling, while the visitation continued.

Since we can not but believe that man forms but one class in an immense range of existences, do not these strange occurrences suggest the idea that occasionally some individual out of this gamut of beings comes into rapport with us, or crosses our path like a comet, and that, while certain conditions last, it can hover about us, and play these *puckish*, mischievous tricks, till the charm is broken, and then it re-enters its own sphere, and we are cognizant of it no more!

But one of the most extraordinary examples of this kind of annoyance is that which occurred, in the year 1806, in the castle of Prince Hohenlohe, in Silesia. The account is given at length by Councillor Hahn, of Ingelfingen, who witnessed the circumstances; and in consequence of the various remarks that have been since made on the subject, in different publications, he has repeatedly reasserted the facts in letters, which have been printed and laid before the public. I can not, therefore, see what right we have to disbelieve a man of honor and character, as he is said to be, merely because the circumstances he narrates are unaccountable, more especially as the story, strange as it is, by no means stands alone in the annals of demonology. The following details were written down at the time the events occurred, and they were communicated by Councillor Hahn to Dr. Kerner in the year 1828:—

"After the campaign of the Prussians against the French, in the year 1806, the reigning prince of Hohenlohe gave orders to Councillor Hahn, who was in his service, to proceed to Slawensick, and there to wait his return. His serene highness advanced from Leignitz toward his principality, and Hahn also commenced his journey toward Upper Silesia on the 19th November. At the same period, Charles Kern, of Kuntzlau, who had fallen into the hands of the French, being released on parole, and arriving at Leignitz in an infirm condition, he was allowed to spend some time with Hahn, while awaiting his exchange.

"Hahn and Kern had been friends in their youth, and their destinies having brought them both at this time into the Prussian states, they were lodged together in the same apartment of the castle, which was one on the first floor, forming an angle at the back of the building, one side looking toward the north and the other to the east. On the right of the door of this room was a glass door, which led into a chamber divided from those which followed by a wainscot partition. The door in this wainscot, which communicated to those adjoining rooms, was entirely closed up, because in them all sorts of household utensils were kept. Neither in this chamber, nor in the sitting-room which preceded it, was there any opening whatever which could furnish the means of communication from without; nor was there anybody in the castle besides the two friends, except the prince's two coachmen and Hahn's servant. The whole party were fearless people; and as for Hahn and Kern, they believed in nothing less than ghosts or witches, nor had any previous experience induced them to turn their thoughts in that direction. Hahn, during his collegiate life, had been much given to philosophy—had listened to Fichte, and earnestly studied the writings of Kant. The result of his reflections was a pure materialism; and he looked upon created man, not as an aim, but merely as a means to a yet undeveloped end. These opinions he has since changed, like many others who think very differently in their fortieth year to what they did in their twentieth. The particulars here given are necessary in order to obtain credence for the following extraordinary narrative; and to establish the fact that the phenomena were not merely accepted by ignorant superstition, but coolly and courageously investigated by enlightened minds. During the first days of their residence in the castle, the two friends, living together in solitude, amused their long evenings with the works of Schiller, of whom they were both great admirers; and Hahn usually read aloud. Three days had thus passed quietly away, when, as they were sitting at the table, which stood in the middle of the room, about nine o'clock in the evening, their reading was interrupted by a small shower of lime which fell around them. They looked at the ceiling, concluding it must have come thence, but could perceive no abraded parts; and while they were yet seeking to ascertain whence the lime had proceeded, there suddenly fell several larger pieces, which were quite cold, and appeared as if they had belonged to the external wall. At length, concluding the lime must have fallen from some part of the wall, giving up further inquiry, they went to bed, and slept quietly till morning, when, on awaking, they were somewhat surprised at the quantity which strewed the floor, more especially as they could still discover no part of the walls or ceiling from which it could have fallen. But they thought no more of the matter till evening, when, instead of the lime falling as before, it was thrown, and several pieces struck Hahn. At the same time they heard heavy blows, sometimes below, and sometimes over their heads, like the sound of distant guns; still, attributing these sounds to natural causes, they went to bed as usual, but the uproar prevented their sleeping, and each accused the other of occasioning it by kicking with his feet against the foot-board of his bed, till, finding that the noise continued when they both got out and stood together in the middle of the room, they were satisfied that this was not the case. On the following evening, a third noise was added, which resembled the faint and distant beating of a drum. Upon this, they requested the governess of the castle to send them the key of the apartments above and below, which was brought them by her son; and while he and Kern went to make their investigations, Hahn remained in their own room. Above, they found an empty room; below, a kitchen. They knocked, but the noise they made was very different to that which Hahn continued all the while to hear around him. When they returned, Hahn said, jestingly, 'The place is haunted!' On this night, when they went to bed, with a light burning, they heard what seemed like a person walking about the room with slippers on, and a stick, with which he struck the floor as he moved step by step. Hahn continued to jest, and Kern to laugh, at the oddness of these circumstances, for some time, when they both, as usual, fell asleep, neither in the slightest degree disturbed by these events, nor inclined to attribute them to any supernatural cause. But on the following evening the affair became more inexplicable: various articles in the room were thrown about;

knives, forks, brushes, caps, slippers, padlocks, funnel, snuffers, soap—everything, in short, that was moveable; while lights darted from the corners, and everything was in confusion; at the same time, the lime fell and the blows continued. Upon this, the two friends called up the servants, Knittel, the castle watch, and whoever else was at hand, to be witnesses of these mysterious operations. In the morning all was quiet, and generally continued so till after midnight. One evening, Kern going into the chamber to fetch something, and hearing an uproar that almost drove him backward to the door, Hahn caught up the light, and both rushed into the room, where they found a large piece of wood lying close to the wainscot. But supposing this to be the cause of the noise, who had set it in motion? For Kern was sure the door was shut, even while the noise was making; neither had there been any wood in the room. Frequently, before their eyes, the knives and snuffers rose from the table, and fell, after some minutes, to the ground; and Hahn's large shears were once lifted in this manner between him and one of the prince's cooks, and falling to the ground, stuck into the floor. As some nights, however, passed quite quietly, Hahn was determined not to leave the rooms; but when, for three weeks, the disturbance was so constant that they could get no rest, they resolved on removing their beds into the large room above, in hopes of once more enjoying a little quiet sleep. Their hopes were vain—the thumping continued as before; and not only so, but articles flew about the room which they were quite sure they had left below. 'They may fling as they will,' cried Hahn, 'sleep I must;' while Kern began to undress, pondering on these matters as he walked up and down the room. Suddenly Hahn saw him stand, as if transfixed, before the looking-glass on which he had accidentally cast his eyes. He had so stood for some time, when he was seized with a violent trembling, and turned from the mirror with his face as white as death. Hahn, fancying the cold of an uninhabited room had seized him, hastened to throw a cloak over him, when Kern, who was naturally very courageous, recovered himself, and related, though with trembling lips, that as he had accidentally looked in the glass, he had seen a white female figure looking out of it; she was in front of his own image, which he distinctly saw behind her. At first he could not believe his eyes; he thought it must be fancy, and for that reason he had stood so long; but when he saw that the eyes of the figure moved, and looked into his, a shudder had seized him, and he had turned away. Hahn, upon this, advanced with firm steps to the front of the mirror, and called upon the apparition to show itself to him; but he saw nothing, although he remained a quarter of an hour before the glass, and frequently repeated his exhortation. Kern then related that the features of the apparition were very old, but not gloomy or morose; the expression was that of indifference; but the face was very pale, and the head was wrapped in a cloth which left only the features visible.

"By this time it was four o'clock in the morning; sleep was banished from their eyes, and they resolved to return to the lower room and have their beds brought back again: but the people who were sent to fetch them returned, declaring they could not open the door, although it did not appear to be fastened. They were sent back again; but a second and a third time they returned with the same answer. Then Hahn went himself, and opened it with the greatest ease. The four servants, however, solemnly declared that all their united strength could make no impression on it.

"In this way a month had elapsed: the strange events at the castle had got spread abroad: and among others who desired to convince themselves of the facts were two Bavarian officers of dragoons, namely, Captain Cornet and Lieutenant Magerle, of the regiment of Minuci. Magerle offering to remain in the room alone, the others left him; but scarcely had they passed into the next apartment, when they heard Magerle storming like a man in a passion, and cutting away at the tables and chairs with his sabre, whereupon the captain thought it advisable to return, in order to rescue the furniture from his rage. They found the door shut, but he opened it on their summons, and related, in great excitement, that as soon as they had quitted the room, some cursed thing had begun to fling lime and other matters at him, and, having examined every part of the room without being able to discover the agent of the mischief, he had fallen into a rage and cut madly about him.

"The party now passed the rest of the evening together in the room, and the two Bavarians closely watched Hahn and Kern in order to satisfy themselves that the mystery was no trick of theirs. All at once, as they were quietly sitting at the table, the snuffers rose into the air and fell again to the ground behind Magerle, and a leaden ball flew at Hahn and hit him upon the breast, and presently afterward they heard a noise at the glass-door, as if somebody had struck his fist through it, together with a sound of falling glass. On investigation they found the door entire, but a broken drinking-glass on the floor. By this time the Bavarians were convinced, and they retired from the room to seek repose in one more peaceful.

"Among other things, the following, which occurred to Hahn, is remarkable. One evening about eight o'clock, being about to shave himself, the implements for the purpose, which were lying on a pyramidal stand in a corner of the room, flew at him, one after the other—the soap-box, the razor, the brush, and the soap—and fell at his feet, although he was standing several paces from the pyramid. He and Kern, who was sitting at the table, laughed, for they were now so accustomed to these events that they only made them subjects of diversion. In the meantime, Hahn poured some water, which had been standing on the stove, in a basin, observing, as he dipped his finger into it, that it was of a nice heat for shaving. He seated himself before the table and strapped his razor, but when he attempted to prepare the lather, the water was clean vanished out of the basin. Another time, Hahn was awakened by goblins throwing at him a squeezed-up piece of sheet-lead in which tobacco had been wrapped, and when he stooped to pick it up, the self-same piece was flung at him again. When this was repeated a third time, Hahn flung a heavy stick at his invisible assailant.

"Dorfel, the book-keeper, was frequently a witness to these strange events. He once laid his cap on the table by the stove; when, being about to depart, he sought for it, it had vanished. Four or five times he examined the table in vain; presently afterward he saw it lying exactly where he had placed it when he came in. On the same table, Knittel having once placed his cap and drawn himself a seat, suddenly, although there was nobody near the table, he saw the cap flying through the room to his feet, where it fell.

"Hahn now determined to find out the secret himself, and for this purpose seated himself, with two lights before him, in a position where he could see the whole of the room and all the doors and windows it contained;—but the same things occurred, even when Kern was out, the servants in the stables, and nobody in the room but himself; and the snuffers were as usual flung about, although the closest observation could not detect by whom.

"The forest-master, Radzensky, spent a night in the room, but, although the two friends slept, he could get no rest. He was bombarded without intermission, and in the morning his bed was found full of all manner of household articles.

"One morning, in spite of all the drumming and flinging, Hahn was determined to sleep; but a heavy blow on the wall close to his bed soon awoke him from his slumbers. A second time he went to sleep, and was awaked by a sensation as if some person had dipped his finger in water and was sprinkling his face with it. He pretended to sleep again, while he watched Kern and Knittel, who were sitting at the table; the sensation of sprinkling returned, but he could find no water on his face.

"About this time, Hahn had occasion to make a journey as far as Breslau; and when he returned he heard the strangest story of all. In order not to be alone in this mysterious chamber, Kern had engaged Hahn's servant, a man of about forty years of age, and of entire singleness of character, to stay with him. One night as Kern lay in his bed, and this man was standing near the glass-door in conversation with him, to his utter amazement he beheld a jug of beer, which stood on a table in the room at some distance from him, slowly lifted to a height of about three feet, and the contents poured into a glass that was standing there also, until the latter was half full. The jug was then gently replaced, and the glass lifted and emptied as by some one drinking; while John, the servant, exclaimed in terrified surprise, 'Lord Jesus! it swallows!' The glass was quietly replaced, and not a drop of beer was to be found on the floor. Hahn was about to require an oath of John in confirmation of this fact; but forbore, seeing how ready the man was to take one, and satisfied of the truth of the relation.

"One night Knetsch, an inspector of the works, passed the night with the two friends, and in spite of the unintermitting flinging they all three went to bed. There were lights in the room, and presently all three saw two napkins, in the middle of the room, rise slowly up to the ceiling, and, having there spread themselves out, flutter down again. The china bowl of a pipe belonging to Kern flew about and was broken. Knives and forks were flung, and at last one of the latter fell on Hahn's head, though fortunately with the handle downward: and having now endured this annoyance for two months, it was unanimously resolved to abandon this mysterious chamber, for this night at all events. John and Kern took up one of the beds and carried it into the opposite room, but they were no sooner gone than a pitcher for holding chalybeate-water flew to the feet of the two who remained behind, although no door was open, and a brass candlestick was flung to the ground. In the opposite room the night passed quietly, although some sounds still issued from the forsaken chamber. After this there was a cessation to these strange proceedings, and nothing more remarkable occurred, with the exception of the following circumstance. Some weeks after the above-mentioned removal, as Hahn was returning home and crossing the bridge that leads to the castle-gate, he heard the foot of a dog behind him. He looked round, and called repeatedly on the name of a grayhound that was much attached to him, thinking it might be her; but, although he still heard the foot, even when he ascended the stairs, as he could see nothing, he concluded it was an illusion. Scarcely, however, had he set his foot within the room, than Kern advanced and took the door out of his hand, at the same time calling the dog by name,—immediately adding, however, that he thought he had seen the dog, but that he had no sooner called her than she disappeared. Hahn then inquired if he had really seen the dog. 'Certainly I did,' replied Kern, 'she was close behind you—half within the door—and that was the reason I took it out of your hand, lest, not observing her, you should have shut it suddenly and crushed her. It was a white dog, and I took it for Flora.' Search was immediately made for the dog, but she was found locked up in the stable and had not been out of it the whole day. It is certainly remarkable—even supposing Hahn to have been deceived with respect to the footsteps—that Kern should have seen a white dog behind him, before he had heard a word on the subject from his friend, especially as there was no such animal in the neighborhood; besides, it was not yet dark, and Kern was very sharp-sighted.

"Hahn remained in the castle for half a year after this, without experiencing anything extraordinary; and even persons who had possession of the mysterious chambers were not subjected to any annoyance.

"The riddle, however, in spite of all the perquisitions and investigations that were set on foot remained unsolved—no explanation of these strange events could be found; and even supposing any motive could exist, there was nobody in the neighborhood clever enough to have carried on such a system of persecution, which lasted so long, that the inhabitants of the chamber became almost indifferent to it.

"In conclusion, it is only necessary to add that Councillor Hahn wrote down this account for his own satisfaction, with the strictest regard to truth. His words are:—

"'I have described these events exactly as I heard and saw them: from beginning to end I observed them with the most entire self-possession. I had no fear, nor the slightest tendency to it; yet the whole thing remains to me perfectly inexplicable. Written the 19th of November, 1808.

"'AUGUSTUS HAHN, *Councillor*.'

"Doubtless many natural explanations of these phenomena will be suggested by those who consider themselves above the weakness of crediting stories of this description. Some say that Kern was a dexterous juggler, who contrived to throw dust in the eyes of his friend Hahn; while others affirm that both Hahn and Kern were intoxicated every evening! I did not fail to communicate these objections to Hahn, and here insert his answer:—

"'After the events alluded to, I resided with Kern for a quarter of a year in another part of the castle of Slawensick (which has since been struck by lightning, and burnt), without finding a solution of the mystery, or experiencing a repetition of the annoyance, which discontinued from the moment we quitted those particular apartments. Those persons must suppose me very weak, who can imagine it possible that, with only one companion, I could have been the subject of his sport for two months without detecting him. As for Kern himself, he was, from the first, very anxious to leave the rooms; but as I was unwilling to resign the hope of discovering some natural cause for these phenomena, I persisted in remaining; and the thing that at last induced me to yield to his wishes was the vexation at the loss of his china-pipe, which had been flung against the wall and broken. Besides, jugglery requires a juggler, and I was frequently quite alone when these events occurred. It is equally absurd to accuse us of intoxication. The wine there was too dear for us to drink at all, and we confined ourselves wholly to weak beer. All the circumstances that happened are not set down in the narration; but my recollection of the whole is as vivid as if it had occurred yesterday. We had also many witnesses, some of whom have been mentioned. Councillor Klenk also visited me at a later period, with every desire to investigate the mystery; and when, one morning, he had mounted on a table, for the purpose of doing so, and was knocking at the ceiling with a stick, a powder-horn fell upon him, which he had just before left on the table in another room. At that time Kern had been for some time absent. I neglected no possible means that could have led to a discovery of the secret; and at least as many people have blamed me for my unwillingness to believe in a supernatural cause as the reverse. Fear is not my failing, as all who are acquainted with me know; and, to avoid the possibility of error, I frequently asked others what they saw when I was myself present; and their answers always coincided with what I saw myself. From 1809 to 1811 I lived in Jacobswald, very near the castle where the prince himself was residing. I am aware that some singular circumstances occurred while he was there; but as I did not witness them myself, I can not speak of them more particularly.

"'I am still as unable as ever to account for those events, and I am content to submit to the hasty remarks of the world, knowing that I have only related the truth, and what many persons now alive witnessed as well as myself.

"'COUNCILLOR HAHN.

"'INGELFINGEN, *August* 24, 1828.'"*

The only key to this mystery ever discovered was, that after the destruction of the castle by lightning, when the ruins were removed, there was found the skeleton of a man without a coffin. His skull had been split, and a sword lay by his side!

Now, I am very well aware how absurd and impossible these events will appear to many people, and that they will have recourse to any explanation rather than admit them for facts. Yet, so late as the year 1835, a suit was brought before the sheriff of Edinburgh, in which Captain Molesworth was defendant, and the landlord of the house he inhabited (which was at Trinity, about a couple of miles from Edinburgh) was plaintiff, founded upon circumstances not so varied, certainly, but quite as inexplicable. The suit lasted two years, and I have been favored with the particulars of the case by Mr. M—— L——, the advocate employed by the plaintiff, who spent many hours in examining the numerous witnesses, several of whom were officers of the army, and gentlemen of undoubted honor and capacity for observation.

Captain Molesworth took the house of a Mr. Webster, who

* Translated from the original German.—C. C.

resided in the adjoining one, in May or June, 1835; and when he had been in it about two months, he began to complain of sundry extraordinary noises, which, finding it impossible to account for, he took it into his head (strangely enough) were made by Mr. Webster. The latter naturally represented that it was not probable he should desire to damage the reputation of his own house, and drive his tenant out of it, and retorted the accusation. Still, as these noises and knockings continued, Captain Molesworth not only lifted the boards in the room most infected, but actually made holes in the wall which divided his residence from Mr. Webster's, for the purpose of detecting the delinquent—of course without success. Do what they would, the thing went on just the same: footsteps of invisible feet, knockings, and scratchings, and rustlings, first on one side, and then on the other, were heard daily and nightly. Sometimes this unseen agent seemed to be knocking to a certain tune, and if a question were addressed to it which could be answered numerically—as, "How many people are there in this room?" for example—it would answer by so many knocks. The beds, too, were occasionally heaved up, as if somebody were underneath, and where the knockings were, the wall trembled visibly, but, search as they would, no one could be found.

Captain Molesworth had had two daughters, one of whom, named Matilda, had lately died; the other, a girl between twelve and thirteen, called Jane, was sickly, and generally kept her bed; and, as it was observed that, wherever she was, these noises most frequently prevailed, Mr. Webster, who did not like the *mala fama* that was attaching itself to his house, declared that she made them, while the people in the neighborhood believed that it was the ghost of Matilda, warning her sister that she was soon to follow.

Sheriff's officers, masons, justices of peace, and the officers of the regiment quartered at Leith, who were friends of Captain Molesworth, all came to his aid, in hopes of detecting or frightening away his tormentor, but in vain. Sometimes it was said to be a trick of somebody outside the house, and then they formed a cordon round it; and next, as the poor sick girl was suspected, they tied her up in a bag—but it was all to no purpose.

At length, ill and wearied out by the annoyances and the anxieties attending the affair, Captain Molesworth quitted the house, and Mr. Webster brought an action against him for the damages committed by lifting the boards, breaking the walls, and firing at the wainscoat, as well as for the injury done to his house by saying it was haunted, which prevented other tenants taking it.

The poor young lady died, hastened out of the world, it is said, by the severe measures used while she was under suspicion; and the persons that have since inhabited the house have experienced no repetition of the annoyance.

The manner in which these strange persecutions attach themselves to certain persons and places, seems somewhat analogous to another class of cases, which bear a great similarity to what was formerly called POSSESSION: and I must here observe that many German physicians maintain that, to this day, instances of genuine possession occur, and there are several works published in their language on the subject; and for this malady they consider magnetism the only remedy, all others being worse than useless. Indeed, they look upon *possession* itself as a demono-magnetic state, in which the patient is in rapport with mischievous or evil spirits; as, in the *agatho* (or good) magnetic state, which is the opposite pole, he is in rapport with good ones: and they particularly warn their readers against confounding this infliction with cases of epilepsy or mania. They assert that, although instances are comparatively rare, both sexes and all ages are equally subject to this misfortune; and that it is quite an error to suppose, either, that it has ceased since the resurrection of Christ, or that the expression used in the Scriptures, "possessed by a devil," meant merely insanity or convulsions.

This disease, which is not contagious, was well known to the Greeks; and in later times Hoffmann has recorded several well-established instances. Among the distinguishing symptoms, they reckon the patient's speaking in a voice that is not his own; frightful convulsions and motions of the body, which arise suddenly, without any previous indisposition; blasphemous and obscene talk; a knowledge of what is secret, and of the future; a vomiting of extraordinary things, such as hair, stones, pins, needles, &c., &c. I need scarcely observe that this opinion is not universal in Germany; still, it obtains among many who have had considerable opportunities for observation.

Dr. Bardili had a case in the year 1830, which he considered decidedly to be one of possession. The patient was a peasant-woman, aged thirty-four, who never had any sickness whatever, and the whole of whose bodily functions continued perfectly regular while she exhibited the following strange phenomena: I must observe that she was happily married, and had three children—was not a fanatic, and bore an excellent character for regularity and industry—when, without any warning or perceptible cause, she was seized with the most extraordinary convulsions, while a strange voice proceeded from her, which assumed to be that of an unblessed spirit, who had formerly inhabited a human form. While these fits were on her, she entirely lost her own individuality, and became this person: on returning to herself, her understanding and character were as entire as before. The blasphemy and cursing, and barking and screeching, were dreadful. She was wounded and injured severely by the violent falls and blows she gave herself; and when she had an intermission, she could do nothing but weep over what they told her had passed, and the state in which she saw herself. She was, moreover, reduced to a skeleton; for when she wanted to eat, the spoon was turned round in her hand, and she often fasted for days together.

This affliction lasted for three years; all remedies failed, and the only alleviation she obtained was by the continued and earnest prayers of those about her, and her own: for although this demon did not like prayers, and violently opposed her kneeling down, even forcing her to outrageous fits of laughter, still they had a power over him. It is remarkable that pregnancy, confinement, and the nursing her child, made not the least difference in this woman's condition: all went on regularly, but the demon kept his post. At length, being magnetized, the patient fell into a partially somnambulic state, in which another voice was heard to proceed from her, being that of her protecting spirit, which encouraged her to patience and hope, and promised that the evil guest would be obliged to vacate his quarters. She often now fell into a magnetic state without the aid of a magnetizer. At the end of three years she was entirely relieved and as well as ever.

In the case of Rosina Wildin, aged ten years, which occurred at Pleidelsheim, in 1834, the demon used to announce himself by crying out, "Here I am again!" Whereupon the weak, exhausted child, who had been lying like one dead, would rage and storm in a voice like a man's, perform the most extraordinary movements and feats of violence and strength, till he would cry out, "Now I must be off again!" This spirit spoke generally in the plural number, for he said she had another besides himself, a dumb devil, who plagued her most. "He it is that twirls her round and round, distorts her features, turns her eyes, locks her teeth, &c. What he bids me, I must do!" This child was at length cured by magnetism.

Barbara Rieger, of Steinbach, aged ten, in 1834, was possessed by two spirits, who spoke in two distinctly different male voices and dialects; one said he had formerly been a mason, the other gave himself out for a deceased provisor; the latter of whom was much the worst of the two. When they spoke, the child closed her eyes, and when she opened them again, she knew nothing of what they had said. The mason confessed to have been a great sinner, but the provisor was proud and hardened, and would confess nothing. They often commanded food, and made her eat it, which, when she recovered her individuality, she felt nothing of, but was very hungry. The mason was very fond of brandy and drank a great deal; and if not brought when he ordered it, his raging and storming was dreadful. In her own individuality the child had the greatest aversion to this liquor. They treated her for worms, and other disorders, without the least effect; till at length, by magnetism, the mason was cast out. The provisor was more tenacious, but finally they got rid of him too, and the girl remained quite well.

In 1835, a respectable citizen, whose full name is not given, was brought to Dr. Kerner. He was aged thirty-seven, and till the last seven years had been unexceptionable in conduct and character. An unaccountable change had, however, come over him in his thirtieth year, which made his family very unhappy; and at length, one day, a strange voice suddenly spoke out of him, saying that he was the late magistrate S——, and that he had been in him six years. When this spirit was driven out, by magnetism, the man fell to the earth, and was almost torn to pieces by the violence of the struggle; he then lay for a space as if dead, and arose quite well and free.

In another case, a young woman at Gruppenbach, was quite in her senses, and heard the voice of her demon (who was also a deceased person) speak out of her, without having any power to suppress it.

In short, instances of this description seem by no means rare; and if such a phenomenon as possession ever did exist, I do not see what right we have to assert that it exists no longer, since, in fact, we know nothing about it; only, that being determined to admit nothing so contrary to the ideas of the present day, we set out by deciding that the thing is impossible

Since these cases occur in other countries, no doubt they must do so in this; and, indeed, I have met with one instance much more remarkable in its details than any of those abovementioned, which occurred at Bishopwearmouth, near Sunderland, in the year 1840; and as the particulars of this case have been published and attested by two physicians and two surgeons, not to mention the evidence of numerous other persons, I think we are bound to accept the facts, whatever interpretation we may choose to put upon them.

The patient, named Mary Jobson, was between twelve and thirteen years of age; her parents, respectable people in humble life, and herself an attendant on a Sunday-school. She became ill in November, 1839, and was soon afterward seized with terrific fits, which continued, at intervals, for eleven weeks.

It was during this period that the family first observed a strange knocking, which they could not account for. It was sometimes in one place, and sometimes in another; and even about the bed, when the girl lay in a quiet sleep, with her hands folded outside the clothes. They next heard a strange voice, which told them circumstances they did not know, but which they afterward found to be correct. Then there was a noise like the clashing of arms, and such a rumbling that the tenant below thought the house was coming down; footsteps where nobody was to be seen, water falling on the floor, no one knew whence, locked doors opened, and above all, sounds of ineffably sweet music. The doctors and the father were suspicious, and every precaution was taken, but no solution of the mystery could be found. This spirit, however, was a good one, and it preached to them, and gave them a great deal of good advice. Many persons went to witness this strange phenomenon, and some were desired to go by the voice, when in their own homes. Thus Elizabeth Gauntlett, while attending to some domestic affairs at home, was startled by hearing a voice say, "Be thou faithful, and thou shalt see the works of thy God, and shalt hear with thine ears!" She cried out, "My God! what can this be!" and presently she saw a large white cloud near her. On the same evening the voice said to her, "Mary Jobson, one of your scholars is sick; go and see her, and it will be good for you." This person did not know where the child lived, but having inquired the address, she went: and at the door she heard the same voice bid her go up. On entering the room she heard another voice, soft and beautiful, which bade her be faithful, and said, "I am the Virgin Mary." This voice promised her a sign at home; and accordingly, that night, while reading the Bible, she heard it say, "Jemima, be not afraid; it is I: if you keep my commandments it shall be well with you." When she repeated her visit the same things occurred, and she heard the most exquisite music.

The same sort of phenomena were witnessed by everybody who went—the immoral were rebuked, the good encouraged. Some were bidden instantly to depart, and were forced to go.

The voices of several deceased persons of the family were also heard, and made revelations.

Once the voice said, "Look up, and you shall see the sun and moon on the ceiling!" and immediately there appeared a beautiful representation of these planets in lively colors, viz., green, yellow, and orange. Moreover, these figures were permanent; but the father, who was a long time skeptical, insisted on whitewashing them over; however, they still remained visible.

Among other things, the voice said, that though the child appeared to suffer, she did not; that she did not know where her body was; and that her own spirit had left it, and another had entered; and that her body was made a speaking trumpet. The voice told the family and visiters many things of their distant friends, which proved true.

The girl twice saw a divine form standing by her bedside who spoke to her, and Joseph Ragg, one of the persons who had been invited by the voice to go, saw a beautiful and heavenly figure come to his bedside about eleven o'clock at night, on the 17th of January. It was in male attire, surrounded by a radiance; it came a second time on the same night. On each occasion it opened his curtains and looked at him benignantly, remaining about a quarter of an hour. When it went away, the curtains fell back into their former position. One day, while in the sick child's room, Margaret Watson saw a lamb, which passed through the door and entered a place where the father, John Jobson, was; but he did not see it.

One of the most remarkable features in this case is the beautiful music which was heard by all parties, as well as the family, including the unbelieving father; and indeed it seems to have been, in a great degree, this that converted him at last. This music was heard repeatedly during a space of sixteen weeks: sometimes it was like an organ, but more beautiful; at others there was singing of holy songs, in parts, and the words distinctly heard. The sudden appearance of water in the room too was most unaccountable; for they felt it, and it was really water. When the voice desired that water should be sprinkled, it immediately appeared as if sprinkled. At another time, a sign being promised to the skeptical father, water would suddenly appear on the floor; this happened "not once, but twenty times."

During the whole course of this affair, the voices told them that there was a miracle to be wrought on this child; and accordingly on the 22d of June, when she was as ill as ever and they were only praying for her death, at five o'clock the voice ordered that her clothes should be laid out, and that everybody should leave the room except the infant, which was two years and a half old. They obeyed; and having been outside the door a quarter of an hour, the voice cried, "Come in!" and when they entered, they saw the girl completely dressed and quite well, sitting in a chair with the infant on her knee, and she had not had an hour's illness from that time till the report was published, which was on the 30th of January, 1841.

Now, it is very easy to laugh at all this, and assert that these things never happened, because they are absurd and impossible; but while honest, well-meaning, and intelligent people, who were on the spot, assert that they did, I confess I find myself constrained to believe them, however much I find in the case which is discrepant with my notions. It was not an affair of a day or an hour—there was ample time for observation—for the phenomena continued from the 9th of February to the 22d of June; and the determined unbelief of the father regarding the possibility of spiritual appearances, insomuch that he ultimately expressed great regret for the harshness he had used, is a tolerable security against imposition. Moreover, they pertinaciously refused to receive any money or assistance whatever, and were more likely to suffer in public opinion than otherwise by the avowal of these circumstances.

Dr. Clanny, who publishes the report with the attestations of the witnesses, is a physician of many years' experience, and is also, I believe, the inventor of the improved Davy lamp; and he declares his entire conviction of the facts, assuring his readers that "many persons holding high rank in the established church, ministers of other denominations, as well as many lay-members of society, highly respected for learning and piety, are equally satisfied." When he first saw the child lying on her back, apparently insensible, her eyes suffused with florid blood, he felt assured that she had a disease of the brain; and he was not in the least disposed to believe in the mysterious part of the affair, till subsequent investigation compelled him to do so: and that his belief is of a very decided character we may feel assured, when he is content to submit to all the obloquy he must incur by avowing it.

He adds that, since the girl has been quite well, both her family and that of Joseph Ragg have frequently heard the same heavenly music as they did during her illness; and Mr. Torbock, a surgeon, who expresses himself satisfied of the truth of the above particulars, also mentions another case, in which he, as well as a dying person he was attending, heard divine music just before the dissolution.

Of this last phenomenon—namely, sounds as of heavenly music being heard when a death was occurring—I have met with numerous instances.

From the investigation of the above case, Dr. Clanny has arrived at the conviction that the spiritual world do occasionally identify themselves with our affairs; and Dr. Drury asserts that, besides this instance, he has met with another circumstance which has left him firmly convinced that we live in a world of spirits, and that he has been in the presence of an unearthly being, who had "passed that bourne from which," it is said, "no traveller returns."*

But the most extraordinary case I have yet met with is the following; because it is one which can not, by any possibility, be attributed to disease or illusion. It is furnished to me from the most undoubted authority, and I give it as I received it, with the omission of the names. I have indeed, in this instance, thought it right to change the initial, and substitute G. for the right one—the particulars being of a nature which demand the greatest delicacy, as regards the parties concerned:—

* Alluding, I conclude, to the affair at Willington.

"Mrs. S. C. Hall, in early life, was intimately acquainted with a family, one of whom, Richard G——, a young officer in the army, was subject to a harassing visitation of a kind that is usually regarded as supernatural. Mrs. H. once proposed to pay a visit to her particular friend, Catherine G——, but was told that it would not be convenient exactly at that time, as Richard was on the point of coming home. She thought the inconvenience consisted in the want of a bed-room, and spoke of sleeping with Miss G——, but found that the objection really lay in the fact of Richard being 'haunted,' which rendered it impossible for anybody else to be comfortable in the same house with him. A few weeks after Richard's return, Mrs. Hall heard of Mrs. G——'s being extremely ill; and found, on going to call, that it was owing to nothing but the distress the old lady suffered in consequence of the strange circumstance connected with her son. It appeared that Richard, wherever he was — at home, in camp, in lodgings, abroad, or in his own country — was liable to be visited in his bed-room at night by certain extraordinary noises. Any light he kept in the room was sure to be put out. Something went beating about the walls and his bed, making a great noise, and often shifting close to his face, but never becoming visible. If a cage-bird was in his room, it was certain to be found dead in the morning. If he kept a dog in the apartment, it would make away from him as soon as released, and never come near him again. His brother, even his mother, had slept in the room, but the visitation took place as usual. According to Miss G——'s report, she and other members of the family would listen at the bed-room door, after Richard had gone to sleep, and would hear the noises commence; and they would then hear him sit up and express his vexation by a few military execrations. The young man, at length, was obliged by this pest to quit the army and go upon half-pay. Under its influence he became a sort of Cain; for, wherever he lived, the annoyance was so great that he was quickly obliged to remove. Mrs. Hall heard of his having ultimately gone to settle in Ireland, where, however, according to a brother whom she met about four years ago, the visitation which afflicted him in his early years was in no degree abated."

This can not be called a case of possession, but seems to be one of a rapport, which attaches this invisible tormentor to his victim.

CHAPTER XVII.

MISCELLANEOUS PHENOMENA.

In a former chapter, I alluded to the forms seen floating over graves, by Billing, Pfeffel's amanuensis. By some persons, this luminous form is seen only as a light, just as occurs in many of the apparition cases I have related. How far Baron Reichenbach is correct in his conclusion, that these figures are merely the result of the chemical process going on below, it is impossible for any one at present to say. The fact that these lights do not always hover over the graves, but sometimes move from them, militates against this opinion, as I have before observed; and the insubstantial nature of the form which reconstructed itself after Pfeffel had passed his stick through it proves nothing, since the same thing is asserted of all apparitions I meet with, let them be seen where they may, except in such very extraordinary cases as that of the Bride of Corinth, supposing that story to be true.

At the same time, although these cases are not made out to be chemical phenomena, neither are we entitled to class them under the head of what is commonly understood by the word *ghost;* whereby we comprehend a shadowy shape, informed by an intelligent spirit. But there are some cases, a few of which I will mention, that it seems extremely difficult to include under one category or the other.

The late Lieutenant-General Robertson, of Lawers, who served during the whole of the American war, brought home with him, at its termination, a negro, who went by the name of Black Tom, and who continued in his service. The room appropriated to the use of this man, in the general's town residence (I speak of Edinburgh), was on the ground floor; and he was heard frequently to complain that he could not rest in it, for that every night the figure of a headless lady, with a child in her arms, rose out of the hearth and frightened him dreadfully. Of course nobody believed this story, and it was supposed to be the dream of intoxication, as Tom was not remarkable for sobriety; but, strange to say, when the old mansion was pulled down to build Gillespie's hospital, which stands on its site, there was found, under the hearth-stone in that apartment, a box containing the body of a female, from which the head had been severed; and beside her lay the remains of an infant, wrapped in a pillow-case trimmed with lace. She appeared, poor lady, to have been cut off in the "blossom of her sins;" for she was dressed, and her scissors were yet hanging by a riband to her side, and her thimble was also in the box, having, apparently, fallen from the shrivelled finger.

Now, whether we are to consider this a ghost, or a phenomenon of the same nature as that seen by Billing, it is difficult to decide. Somewhat similar is the following case, which I have borrowed from a little work entitled "Supernaturalism in New England." Not only does this little extract prove that the same phenomena, be they interpreted as they may, exist in all parts of the world, but I think it will be granted me that, although we have not here the confirmation that time furnished in the former instance, yet it is difficult to suppose that this unexcitable person should have been the subject of so extraordinary a spectral illusion.

"Whoever has seen Great pond, in the east parish of Haverhill, has seen one of the very loveliest of the thousand little lakes or ponds of New England. With its soft slopes of greenest verdure—its white and sparkling sand-rim—its southern hem of pine and maple, mirrored, with spray and leaf, in the glassy water—its graceful hill-sentinels round about, white with the orchard-bloom of spring, or tasselled with the corn of autumn—its long sweep of blue waters, broken here and there by picturesque headlands—it would seem a spot, of all others, where spirits of evil must shrink, rebuked and abashed, from the presence of the beautiful. Yet here, too, has the shadow of the supernatural fallen. A lady of my acquaintance, a staid, unimaginative church-member, states that, a few years ago, she was standing in the angle formed by two roads, one of which traverses the pond-shore, the other leading over the hill which rises abruptly from the water. It was a warm summer evening, just at sunset. She was startled by the appearance of a horse and cart, of the kind used a century ago in New England, driving rapidly down the steep hill-side, and crossing the wall a few yards before her, without noise or displacing of a stone. The driver sat sternly erect, with a fierce countenance, grasping the reins tightly, and looking neither to the right nor the left. Behind the cart, and apparently lashed to it, was a woman of gigantic size, her countenance convulsed with a blended expression of rage and agony, writhing and struggling, like Laocoon in the folds of the serpent. Her head, neck, feet, and arms, were naked; wild locks of gray hair streamed back from temples corrugated and darkened. The horrible cavalcade swept by across the street, and disappeared at the margin of the pond."

Many persons will have heard of the "Wild Troop of Rodenstein," but few are aware of the curious amount of evidence there is in favor of the strange belief which prevails among the inhabitants of that region. The story goes, that the former possessors of the castles of Rodenstein and Schnellert were robbers and pirates, who committed, in conjunction, all manner of enormities; and that, to this day, the troop, with their horses and carriages, and dogs, are heard, every now and then, wildly rushing along the road between the two castles. This sounds like a fairy tale; yet so much was it believed, that, up to the middle of the last century, regular reports were made to the authorities in the neighborhood of the periods when the troop had passed. Since that, the landgericht, or court leet, has been removed to Furth, and they trouble themselves no longer about the Rodenstein troop; but a traveller, named Wirth, who a few years ago undertook to examine into the affair, declares the people assert that the passage of the visionary cavalcade still continues; and they assured him that certain houses, that he saw lying in ruins, were in that state because, as they lay directly in the way of the troop, they were uninhabitable. There is seldom anything seen; but the noise of carriage-wheels, horses' feet, smacking of whips, blowing of horns, and the voice of these fierce hunters of men urging them on, are the sounds by which they recognise that the troop is passing from one castle to the other; and at a spot which was formerly a blacksmith's, but is now a carpenter's, the invisible lord of Rodenstein still stops to have his horse shod. Mr. Wirth copied several of the depositions out of the court records, and they are brought down to June, 1764. This is certainly a strange story; but it is not much more so than that of the black man, which I know to be true.

During the seven years' war in Germany, a drover lost his life in a drunken squabble on the high road. For some time there was a sort of rude tombstone, with a cross on it, to mark the spot where his body was interred; but this has long fallen, and a milestone now fills its place. Nevertheless, it continues commonly asserted by the country people, and also by various travellers, that they have been deluded in that spot by seeing, as they imagine, herds of beasts, which, on investigation, prove to be merely visionary. Of course, many people look upon this as a superstition; but a very singular confirmation of the story occurred in the year 1826, when two gentlemen and two ladies were passing the spot in a post-carriage. One of these was a clergyman, and none of them had ever heard of the phenomenon said to be attached to the place. They had been discussing the prospects of the minister, who was on his way to a vicarage, to which he had just been appointed, when they saw a large flock of sheep, which stretched quite across the road, and was accompanied by a shepherd and a long-haired black dog. As to meet cattle on that road was nothing uncommon, and indeed they had met several droves in the course of the day, no remark was made at the moment, till, suddenly, each looked at the other and said, "What is become of the sheep?" Quite perplexed at their sudden disappearance, they called to the postillion to stop, and all got out in order to mount a little elevation and look around; but still unable to discover them, they now bethought themselves of asking the postillion where they were, when, to their infinite surprise, they learned that he had not seen them. Upon this, they bade him quicken his pace, that they might overtake a carriage that had passed them shortly before, and inquire if that party had seen the sheep; but they had not.

Four years later, a postmaster, named J——, was on the same road, driving a carriage, in which were a clergyman and his wife, when he saw a large flock of sheep near the same spot. Seeing they were very fine wethers, and supposing them to have been bought at a sheep-fair that was then taking place a few miles off, J—— drew up his reins and stopped his horse, turning at the same time to the clergyman to say, that he wanted to inquire the price of the sheep, as he intended going next day to the fair himself. While the minister was asking him what sheep he meant, J—— got down and found himself in the midst of the animals, the size and beauty of which astonished him. They passed him at an unusual rate, while he made his way through them to find the shepherd, when, on getting to the end of the flock, they suddenly disappeared. He then first learned that his fellow-travellers had not seen them at all.

Now, if such cases as these are not pure illusions, which I confess I find it difficult to believe, we must suppose that the animals and all the extraneous circumstances are produced by the magical will of the spirit, either acting on the constructive imagination of the seers, or else actually constructing the ethereal forms out of the elements at its command, just as we have supposed an apparition able to present himself with whatever dress or appliances he conceives; or else we must conclude these forms to have some relation to the mystery called PALINGNESIA, which I have previously alluded to, although the motion and change of place render it difficult to bring them under this category. As for the animals, although the drover was slain, they were not; and therefore, even granting them to have souls, we can not look upon them as the apparitions of the flock. Neither can we consider the numerous instances of armies seen in the air to be apparitions; and yet these phenomena are so well established that they have been accounted for by supposing them to be atmospherical reflections of armies elsewhere, in actual motion. But how are we to account for the visionary troops which are not seen in the air, but on the very ground on which the seers themselves stand, which was the case especially with those seen in Havarah park, near Ripley, in the year 1812? These soldiers wore a white uniform, and in the centre was a personage in a scarlet one.

After performing several evolutions, the body began to march in perfect order to the summit of a hill, passing the spectators at the distance of about one hundred yards. They amounted to several hundreds, and marched in a column, four deep, across about thirty acres; and no sooner were they passed, than another body, far more numerous, but dressed in dark clothes, arose and marched after them, without any apparent hostility. Both parties having reached the top of the hill, and there formed what the spectators called an L, they disappeared down the other side, and were seen no more; but at that moment a volume of smoke arose like the discharge of a park of artillery, which was so thick that the men could not, for two or three minutes, discover their own cattle. They then hurried home to relate what they had seen, and the impression made on them is described as so great, that they could never allude to the subject without emotion.

One of them was a farmer of the name of Jackson, aged forty-five; the other was a lad of fifteen, called Turner: and they were at the time herding cattle in the park. The scene seems to have lasted nearly a quarter of an hour, during which time they were quite in possession of themselves, and able to make remarks to each other on what they saw. They were both men of excellent character and unimpeachable veracity, insomuch that nobody who knew them doubted that they actually saw what they described, or, at all events, believed that they did. It is to be observed, also, that the ground is not swampy, nor subject to any exhalations.

About the year 1750, a visionary army of the same description was seen in the neighborhood of Inverness, by a respectable farmer, of Glenary, and his son. The number of troops was very great, and they had not the slightest doubt that they were otherwise than substantial forms of flesh and blood. They counted at least sixteen pairs of columns, and had abundance of time to observe every particular. The front ranks marched seven abreast, and were accompanied by a good many women and children, who were carrying tin cans and other implements of cookery. The men were clothed in red, and their arms shone brightly in the sun. In the midst of them was an animal — a deer or a horse, they could not distinguish which — that they were driving furiously forward with their bayonets. The younger of the two men observed to the other that every now and then the rear ranks were obliged to run to overtake the van; and the elder one, who had been a soldier, remarked that that was always the case, and recommended him, if he ever served, to try and march in the front. There was only one mounted officer: he rode a gray dragoon horse, and wore a gold-laced hat and blue hussar cloak, with wide, open sleeves, lined with red. The two spectators observed him so particularly, that they said afterward they should recognise him anywhere. They were, however, afraid of being ill-treated, or forced to go along with the troops, whom they concluded had come from Ireland, and landed at Kyntyre; and while they were climbing over a dike to get out of their way, the whole thing vanished.

Some years since, a phenomenon of the same sort was observed at Paderborn, in Westphalia, and seen by at least thirty persons, as well as by horses and dogs, as was discovered by the demeanor of these animals. In October, 1836, on the very same spot, there was a review of twenty thousand men; and the people then concluded that the former vision was a second-sight.

A similar circumstance occurred in Stockton forest, some years ago; and there are many recorded elsewhere — one especially, in the year 1686, near Lanark, where, for several afternoons, in the months of June and July, there were seen, by numerous spectators, companies of men in arms, marching in order by the banks of the Clyde, and other companies meeting them, &c., &c.; added to which there were showers of bonnets, hats, guns, swords, &c., which the seers described with the greatest exactness. All who were present could not see these things, and Walker relates that one gentleman, particularly, was turning the thing into ridicule, calling the seers "damned witches and warlocks, with the second-sight!" — boasting that "the devil a thing he could see!" — when he suddenly exclaimed, with fear and trembling, that he now saw it all; and entreated those who did not see, to say nothing — a change that may be easily accounted for, be the phenomenon of what nature it may, by supposing him to have touched one of the seers, when the faculty would be communicated like a shock of electricity.

With regard to the palinganesia, it would be necessary to establish that these objects had previously existed, and that, as Oetinger says, the earthly husk having fallen off, "the volatile essence had ascended perfect in form, but void of substance."

The notion supported by Baron Reichenbach, that the lights seen in churchyards and over graves are the result of a process going on below, is by no means new, for Gaffarillus suggested the same opinion in 1650; only he speaks of the appearances over graves and in churchyards as shadows, *ombres*, as they appeared to Billing; and he mentions, casually, as a thing frequently observed, that the same visionary forms are remarked on ground where battles have been fought, which he thinks arise out of a process between the earth and the sun. When a limb has been cut off, some somnambules still discern the form of the member as if actually attached.

But this magical process is said to be not only the work of the elements, but also possible to man; and that as the forms of plants can be preserved after the substance is destroyed, so can that of man be either preserved or reproduced from the elements of his body. In the reign of Louis XIV., three alchemists, having distilled some earth taken from the cemetery of the Innocents, in Paris, were forced to desist, by seeing the forms of men appearing in their vials, instead of the philosopher's stone, which they were seeking; and a physician, who, after dissecting a body, and pulverizing the cranium (which was then an article admitted into the materia medica), had left the powder on the table of his laboratory, in charge of his assistant, the latter, who slept in an adjoining room, was awakened in the night by hearing a noise, which, after some search, he ultimately traced to the powder—in the midst of which he beheld, gradually constructing itself, a human form! First appeared the head, with two open eyes, then the arms and hands, and, by degrees, the rest of the person, which subsequently assumed the clothes it had worn when alive! The man was, of course, frightened out of his wits—the rather, as the apparition planted itself before the door, and would not let him go away till it had made its own exit, which it speedily did. Similar results have been said to arise from experiments performed on blood. I confess I should be disposed to consider these apparitions, if ever they appeared, cases of genuine ghosts, brought into rapport by the operation, rather than forms residing in the bones or blood. At all events, these things are very hard to believe; but seeing we were not there, I do not think we have any right to say they did not happen; or at least that some phenomena did not occur, that were open to this interpretation.

It is highly probable that the seeing of those visionary armies and similar prodigies is a sort of second-sight; but having admitted this, we are very little nearer an explanation. Granting that, as in the above experiments, the essence of things may retain the forms of the substance, this does not explain the seeing that which has not yet taken place, or which is taking place at so great a distance, that neither Oetinger's essence nor the superficial films of Lucretius can remove the difficulty.

It is the fashion to say that second-sight was a mere superstition of the highlanders, and that no such thing is ever heard of now; but those who talk in this way know very little of the matter. No doubt, if they set out to look for seers, they may not find them; such phenomena, though known in all countries and in all ages, are *comparatively* rare, as well as uncertain and capricious, and not to be exercised at will: but I know of too many instances of the existence of this faculty in families, as well as of isolated cases occurring to individuals above all suspicion, to entertain the smallest doubt of its reality. But the difficulty of furnishing evidence is considerable: because, when the seers are of the humbler classes, they are called impostors and not believed; and when they are of the higher, they do not make the subject a matter of conversation, nor choose to expose themselves to the ridicule of the foolish; and consequently the thing is not known beyond their own immediate friends. When the young duke of Orleans was killed, a lady, residing here, saw the accident, and described it to her husband at the time it was occurring in France. She had frequently seen the duke, when on the continent.

Captain N—— went to stay two days at the house of Lady T——. After dinner, however, he announced that he was under the necessity of going away that night, nor could he be induced to remain. On being much pressed for an explanation, he confided to some of the party that, during the dinner, he had seen a female figure with her throat cut, standing behind Lady T——'s chair. Of course, it was thought an illusion, but Lady T—— was not told of it, lest she should be alarmed. That night the household was called up for the purpose of summoning a surgeon—Lady T—— had cut her own throat!

Mr. C——, who, though a Scotchman, was an entire skeptic with regard to the second-sight, was told by a seer whom he had been jeering on the subject, that, within a month, he (Mr. C——) would be a pall-bearer at a funeral; that he would go by a certain road, but that, before they had crossed the brook, a man in a drab coat would come down the hill and take the pall from him. The funeral occurred, Mr. C—— was a bearer, and they went by the road described; but he firmly resolved that he would disappoint the seer by keeping the pall while they crossed the brook; but shortly before they reached it, the postman overtook them, with letters, which in that part of the country arrived but twice a week, and Mr. C——, who was engaged in some speculations of importance, turned to received them—at which moment the pall was taken from him, and on looking round, he saw it was by a man in a drab coat!

A medical friend of mine, who practised some time at Deptford, was once sent for to a girl who had been taken suddenly ill. He found her with inflammation of the brain, and the only account the mother could give of it was, that shortly before, she had run into the room, crying, "Oh, mother, I have seen Uncle John drowned in his boat under the fifth arch of Rochester bridge!" The girl died a few hours afterward; and, on the following night, the uncle's boat ran foul of the bridge, and he was drowned, exactly as she had foretold.

Mrs. A——, an English lady, and the wife of a clergyman, relates that, previous to her marriage, she with her father and mother being at the seaside, had arranged to make a few days' excursion to some races that were about to take place; and that the night before they started, the father having been left alone, while the ladies were engaged in their preparations, they found him, on descending to the drawing-room, in a state of considerable agitation—which, he said, had arisen from his having seen a dreadful face at one corner of the room. He described it as a bruised, battered, crushed, discolored face, with the two eyes protruding frightfully from their sockets; but the features were too disfigured to ascertain if it were the face of any one he knew. On the following day, on their way to the races, an accident occurred; and he was brought home with his own face exactly in the condition he had described. He had never exhibited any other instance of this extraordinary faculty, and the impression made by the circumstance lasted the remainder of his life, which was unhappily shortened by the injuries he had received.

The late Mrs. V——, a lady of fortune and family, who resides near Loch Lomond, possessed this faculty in an extraordinary degree, and displayed it on many remarkable occasions. When her brother was shipwrecked in the channel, she was heard to exclaim, "Thank God, he is saved!" and described the scene with all its circumstances.

Colonel David Steward, a determined believer in what he calls the supernatural, in his book on the highlanders, relates the following fact as one so remarkable, that "credulous minds" may be excused for believing it to have been prophetic. He says that, late in an autumnal evening of the year 1773, the son of a neighbor came to his father's house, and soon after his arrival inquired for a little boy of the family, then about three years old. He was shown up to the nursery, and found the nurse putting a pair of new shoes on the child, which she complained did not fit. "Never mind," said the young man, "they will fit him before he wants them" — a prediction which not only offended the nurse, but seemed at the moment absurd, since the child was apparently in perfect health. When he joined the party in the drawing-room, he being much jeered upon this new gift of second-sight, explained that the impression he had received originated in his having just seen a funeral passing the wooden bridge which crossed a stream at a short distance from the house. He first observed a crowd of people, and on coming nearer he saw a person carrying a small coffin, followed by about twenty gentlemen, all of his acquaintance, his own father and a Mr. Stewart being among the number. He did not attempt to join the procession, which he saw turn off into the churchyard: but knowing his own father could not be actually there, and that Mr. and Mrs. Stewart were then at Blair, he felt a conviction that the phenomenon portended the death of the child: a persuasion which was verified by its suddenly expiring on the following night;—and Colonel Stewart adds that the circumstances and attendants at the funeral were precisely such as the young man had described. He mentions, also, that this gentleman was not a seer; that he was a man of education and general knowledge; and that this was the first and only vision of the sort he ever had.

I know of a young lady who has three times seen funerals in this way.

The old persuasion that fasting was a means of developing

the spirit of prophecy, is undoubtedly well founded, and the annals of medicine furnish numerous facts which establish it. A man condemned to death at Viterbo, having abstained from food in the hope of escaping execution, became so clairvoyant, that he could tell what was doing in any part of the prison; the expression used in the report is that he "saw through the walls:" this, however, could not be with his natural organs of sight.

It is worthy of observation, that idiots often possess some gleams of this faculty of second-sight or presentiment; and it is probably on this account that they are in some countries held sacred. Presentiment, which I think may very probably be merely the vague and imperfect recollection of what we *knew* in our sleep, is often observed in drunken people.

In the great plague at Basle, which occurred toward the end of the sixteenth century, almost everybody who died called out in their last moments the name of the person that was to follow them next.

Not long ago, a servant girl on the estate of D——, of S——, saw with amazement five figures ascending a perpendicular cliff, quite inaccessible to human feet; one was a boy wearing a cap with red binding. She watched them with great curiosity till they reached the top, where they all stretched themselves on the earth, with countenances expressive of great dejection. While she was looking at them they disappeared, and she immediately related her vision. Shortly afterward, a foreign ship, in distress, was seen to put off a boat with four men and a boy: the boat was dashed to pieces in the surf, and the five bodies, exactly answering the description she had given, were thrown on shore at the foot of the cliff, which they had perhaps climbed in the spirit!

How well what we call clairvoyance was known, though how little understood, at the period of the witch persecution, is proved by what Dr. Henry More says in his "Antidote against Atheism":—

"We will now pass to those supernatural effects which are observed in them that are bewitched or possessed; and such as foretelling things to come, telling what such and such persons speak or do, as exactly as if they were by them, when the party possessed is at one end of the town, and sitting in a house within doors, and those parties that act and confer together are without, at the other end of the town; to be able to see some and not others; to play at cards with one certain person, and not to discern anybody else at the table beside him; to act and talk, and go up and down, and tell what will become of things, and what happens in those fits of possession; and then, as soon as the possessed or bewitched party is out of them, to remember nothing at all, but to inquire concerning the welfare of those whose faces they seemed to look upon just before, when they were in their fits;"—a state which he believes to arise from the devil's having taken possession of the body of the magnetic person, which is precisely the theory supported by many fanatical persons in our own day. Dr. More was not a fanatic: but these phenomena, though very well understood by the ancient philosophers, as well as by Paracelsus, Van Helmont, Cornelius Agrippa, Jacob Behmen, a Scotch physician (called Maxwell) who published on the subject in the seventeenth century, and manyothers, were still, when observed, looked upon as the effects of diabolical influence by mankind in general.

When Monsieur Six Deniers, the artist, was drowned in the Seine in 1846, after his body had been vainly sought, a somnambule was applied to, in whose hands they placed a portfolio belonging to him; and being asked where the owner was, she evinced great terror, held up her dress as if walking in the water, and said that he was between two boats, under the Pont des Arts, with nothing on but a flannel waistcoat: and there he was found.

A friend of mine knows a lady who, early one morning—being in a natural state of clairvoyance without magnetism—saw the porter of the house where her son lodged ascend to his room with a carving-knife, go to his bed where he lay asleep, lean over him, then open a chest, take out a fifty-pound note, and retire. On the following day, she went to her son and asked him if he had any money in the house; he said, "Yes, I have fifty pounds:" whereupon she bade him seek it, but it was gone. They stopped payment of the note; but did not prosecute, thinking the evidence insufficient. Subsequently, the porter being taken up for other crimes, the note was found crumpled up at the bottom of an old purse belonging to him.

Dr. Ennemoser says that there is no doubt of the ancient Sibyls having been *clairvoyant* women, and that it is impossible so much value could have been attached to their books, had not their revelations been verified.

A maid-servant residing in a family in Northumberland, one day last winter was heard to utter a violent scream immediately after she had left the kitchen. On following her to inquire what had happened, she said that she had just seen her father in his night-clothes, with a most horrible countenance, and she was sure something dreadful had happened to him. Two days afterward there arrived a letter, saying he had been seized with *delirium tremens*, and was at the point of death; which accordingly ensued.

There are innumerable cases of this sort recorded in various collections, not to mention the much more numerous ones that meet with no recorder; and I could myself mention many more, but these will suffice—one, however, I will not omit, for, though historical, it is not generally known. A year before the rebellion broke out, in consequence of which Lord Kilmarnock lost his head, the family were one day startled by a scream, and on rushing out to inquire what had occurred, they found the servants all assembled, in amazement, with the exception of one maid, who they said had gone up to the garrets to hang some linen on the lines to dry. On ascending thither, they found the girl on the floor, in a state of insensibility; and they had no sooner revived her than, on seeing Lord Kilmarnock bending over her, she screamed and fainted again. When ultimately recovered, she told them that while hanging up her linen, and singing, the door had burst open and his lordship's bloody head had rolled in. I think it came twice. This event was so well known at the time, that on the first rumors of the rebellion,

Lord Saltoun said, "Kilmarnock will lose his head." It was answered, "that Kilmarnock had not joined the rebels." "He will, and will be beheaded," returned Lord Saltoun.

Now, in these cases we are almost compelled to believe that the phenomenon is purely subjective, and there is no veritable outstanding object seen; yet, when we have taken refuge in this hypothesis, the difficulty remains as great as ever; and is to me much more incomprehensible than ghost-seeing, because in the latter we suppose an external agency acting in some way or other on the seer.

I have already mentioned that Oberlin, the good pastor of Ban de la Roche, himself a ghost-seer, asserted that everything earthly had its counterpart, or antitype, in the other world, not only organized, but unorganized matter. If so, do we sometimes see these antitypes?

Dr. Ennemoser, in treating of second-sight—which, by the way, is quite as well known in Germany, and especially in Denmark, as in the highlands of Scotland—says, that as in natural somnambulism there is a partial internal vigilance, so does the seer fall, while awake, into a dream-state. He suddenly becomes motionless and stiff: his eyes are open, and his senses are, while the vision lasts, unperceptive of all external objects; the vision may be communicated by the touch, and sometimes persons at a distance from each other, but connected by blood or sympathy, have the vision simultaneously. He remarks, also, that, as we have seen in the above case of Mr. C——, any attempt to frustrate the fulfilment of the vision never succeeds, inasmuch as the attempt appears to be taken into the account.

The seeing in glass and in crystals is equally inexplicable; as is the magical seeing of the Egyptians. Every now and then we hear it said that this last is discovered to be an imposition, because some traveller has either actually fallen into the hands of an impostor—and there are impostors in all trades—or because the phenomenon was imperfectly exhibited; a circumstance which, as in the exhibitions of clairvoyants and somnambulists, where all the conditions are not under command, or even recognised, must necessarily happen. But not to mention the accounts published by Mr. Lane and Lord Prudhoe, whoever has read that of Monsieur Léon Laborde must be satisfied that the thing is an indisputable fact. It is, in fact, only another form of the seeing in crystals, which has been known in all ages, and of which many modern instances have occurred among somnambulic patients.

We see by the forty-fourth chapter of Genesis that it was by his cup that Joseph prophesied: "Is not this it in which my lord drinketh, and whereby indeed he divineth?" But, as Dr. Passavent observes, and as we shall presently see, in the anecdote of the boy and the gipsy, the virtue does not lie in the glass nor in the water, but in the seer himself, who may possess a more or less developed faculty. The external objects and ceremonies being only the means of concentrating the attention and intensifying the power.

Monsieur Léon Laborde witnessed the exhibition, at Cairo, before Lord P——'s visit; the exhibitor, named Achmed, appeared to him a respectable man, who spoke simply of his science, and had nothing of the charlatan about him. The first child employed was a boy eleven years old, the son of a European; and Achmed having traced some figures on the palm of his hand, and poured ink over them, bade him look for the reflection of his own face. The child said he saw it; the magician then burnt some powders in a brazier, and bade him tell him when he saw a soldier sweeping a place; and while the fumes from the brazier diffused themselves, he pronounced a sort of litany. Presently the child threw back his head, and screaming with terror, sobbed out, while bathed in tears, that he had seen a dreadful face. Fearing the boy might be injured, Monsieur Laborde now called up a little Arab servant, who had never seen or heard of the magician. He was gay and laughing, and not at all frightened; and the ceremony being repeated, he said he saw the soldier sweeping in the front of a tent. He was then desired to bid the soldier bring Shakspere, Colonel Cradock, and several other persons; and he described every person and thing so exactly as to be entirely satisfactory. During the operations the boy looked as if intoxicated, with his eyes fixed and the perspiration dripping from his brow. Achmed disenchanted him by placing his thumbs on his eyes. He gradually recovered, and gayly related all he had seen, which he perfectly remembered.

Now this is merely another form of what the Laplanders, the African magicians, and the Schaamans of Siberia, do by taking narcotics and turning round till they fall down in a state of insensibility, in which condition they are clear-seers, and besides vaticinating, describe scenes, places, and persons, they have never seen. In Barbary they anoint their hands with a black ointment, and then holding them up in the sun, they see whatever they desire, like the Egyptians.

Lady S—— possesses somewhat of a singular faculty, naturally. By walking rapidly round a room several times, till a certain degree of vertigo is produced, she will name to you any person you have privately thought of or agreed upon with others. Her phrase is: "I *see*" so and so.

Monsieur Laborde purchased the secret of Achmed, who said he had learned it from two celebrated scheicks of his own country, which was Algiers. Monsieur L. found it connected with both physics and magnetism, and practised it himself afterward with perfect success; and he affirms, positively, that under the influence of a particular organization and certain ceremonies, among which he can not distinguish which are indispensable and which are not, that a child, without fraud or collusion, can see, as through a window or peep-hole, people moving, who appear and disappear at their command, and with whom they hold communication—and they remember everything after the operation. He says: "I narrate, but explain nothing; I produced those effects, but can not comprehend them; I only affirm in the most positive manner that what I relate is true. I performed the experiment in various places, with various subjects, before numerous witnesses, in my own room or other rooms, in the open air, and even in a boat on the Nile. The exactitude and detailed descriptions of persons, places, and scenes, could by no possibility be feigned."

Moreover, Baron Dupotet has very lately succeeded in obtaining these phenomena in Paris, from persons not somnambulic selected from his audience,—the chief difference being that they did not recollect what they had seen when the crisis was over.

Cagliostro, though a charlatan, was possessed of this secret, and it was his great success in it that chiefly sustained his reputation; the spectators, convinced he could make children see distant places and persons in glass, were persuaded he could do other things, which appeared to them no more mysterious. Dr. Dee was perfectly honest with regard to his mirror, in which he could *see* by concentrating his mind on it; but, as he could not remember what he saw, he employed Kelly to *see* for him, while he himself wrote down the revelations: and Kelly was a rogue, and deceived and ruined him.

A friend of Pfeffel's knew a boy, apprenticed to an apothecary at Schoppenweyer, who, having been observed to amuse himself by looking into vials filled with water, was asked what he saw; when it was discovered that he possessed this faculty of *seeing* in glass, which was afterward very frequently exhibited for the satisfaction of the curious. Pfeffel also mentions another boy who had this faculty, and who went about the country with a small mirror, answering questions, recovering stolen goods, &c. He said that he one day fell in with some gipsies, one of whom was sitting apart and staring into this glass. The boy, from curiosity, looked over his shoulder and exclaimed that he saw "a fine man who was moving about;" whereupon the gipsy, having interrogated him, gave him the glass; "for," said he, "I have been staring in it long enough, and can see nothing but my own face."

It is almost unnecessary to observe that the sacred books of the Jews and of the Indians testify to their acquaintance with this mode of divination, as well as many others.

Many persons will have heard or read an account of Mr. Canning and Mr. Huskisson having seen, while in Paris, the visionary representation of their own deaths in water, as exhibited to them by a Russian or Polish lady there: as I do not, however, know what authority there is for this story, I will not insist on it here. But St. Simon relates a very curious circumstance of this nature, which occurred at Paris, and was related to him by the duke of Orleans, afterward regent. The latter said that he had sent on the preceding evening for a man, then in Paris, who pretended to exhibit whatever was desired in a glass of water. He came, and a child of seven years old, belonging to the house, being called up, they bade her tell what she saw doing in certain places. She did; and as they sent to these places and found her report correct, they bade her next describe under what circumstances the king would die, without, however, asking when the death would take place.

The child knew none of the court, and had never been at Versailles; yet she described everything exactly—the room, bed, furniture, and the king himself, Madame de Maintenon, Fagon, the physician, the princes and princesses—everybody, in short, including a child, wearing an order, in the arms of a lady whom she recognised as having seen; this was Madame de Ventadour.

It was remarkable that she omitted the dukes de Bourgogne and Berry, and Monseigneur, and also the duchess de Bourgogne. Orleans insisted they must be there, describing them; but she always said "*No.*" These persons were then all well, but they died before the king. She also saw the children of the prince and princess of Conti, but not themselves—which was correct, as they also died shortly after this occurrence.

Orleans then wished to see his own destiny; and the man said, if he would not be frightened he could show it to him, as if painted on the wall; and after fifteen minutes of conjuration, the duke appeared, of the natural size, dressed as usual, but with a *couronne fermée* or closed crown on his head, which they could not comprehend, as it was not that of any country they knew of. It covered his head, had only four circles, and nothing at the top. They had never seen such a one. When he became regent, they understood that that was the interpretation of the prediction.

In connection with this subject, the aversion to glass frequently manifested by dogs is well worthy of observation.

When facts of this kind are found to be recorded or believed in, in all parts of the world, from the beginning of it up to the present time, it is surely vain for the so-called *savants* to deny them; and, as Cicero justly says in describing the different kinds of magic, "What we have to do with is the facts, since of the cause we know little. Neither," he adds, "are we to repudiate these phenomena, because we sometimes find them imperfect, or even false, any more than we are to distrust that the human eye sees, although some do this very imperfectly, or not at all."

We are part spirit and part matter: by the former we are allied to the spiritual world and to the absolute spirit; and as nobody doubts that the latter can work magically, that is, by the mere act of will—for by the mere act of will all things were created, and by its constant exertion all things are sustained—why should we be astonished that we, who partake of the Divine nature and were created after God's own image, should also, within certain limits, partake of this magical power? That this power has been frequently abused, is the fault of those who, being capable, refuse to investigate, and deny the existence of these and similar phenomena; and, by thus casting them out of the region of legitimate science, leave them to become the prey of the ignorant and designing.

Dr. Ennemoser, in his very learned work on magic, shows us that all the phenomena of magnetism and somnambulism, and all the various kinds of divination, have been known and practised in every country under the sun; and have been intimately connected with, and indeed may be traced up to the fountain-head of every religion.

What are the limits of these powers possessed by us while in the flesh—how far they may be developed—and whether, at the extreme verge of what we can effect, we begin to be aided by God or by spirits of other spheres of existence bordering on ours—we know not; but, with respect to the morality of these practices, it suffices that what is good in act or intention, must come of good; and what is evil in act or intention, must come of evil: which is true now, as it was in the time of Moses and the prophets, when miracles and magic were used for purposes holy and unholy, and were to be judged accordingly. God works by natural laws, of which we yet know very little, and, in some departments of his kingdom, nothing; and whatever appears to us supernatural, only appears so from our ignorance; and whatever faculties or powers he has endowed us with, it must have been designed we should exercise and cultivate for the benefit and advancement of our race: nor can I for one moment suppose that, though like everything else, liable to abuse, the legitimate exercise of these powers, if we knew their range, would be useless, much less pernicious or sinful.

Of the magical power of WILL, as I have said before, we know nothing; and it does not belong to a purely rationalistic age to acknowledge what it can not understand. In all countries men have arisen, here and there, who *have* known it, and some traces of it have survived both in language and in popular superstitions. "If ye have faith as a grain of mustard-seed, ye shall say unto this mountain, 'Remove hence,' and it shall remove; and nothing shall be impossible to you. Howbeit, this kind goeth not out but by prayer and fasting." And, *veuillez et croyez*—will and believe—was the solution Puysegur gave of his magical cures; and no doubt the explanation of those affected by royal hands is to be found in the fact that they believed in *themselves;* and having *faith*, they could exercise *will.* But, with the belief in the divine right of kings, the faith and the power would naturally expire together.

With respect to what Christ says, in the above-quoted passage, of *fasting*, numerous instances are extant, proving that clear-seeing and other magical or spiritual powers are sometimes developed by it.

Wilhelm Krause, a doctor of philosophy and a lecturer at Jena, who died during the prevalence of the cholera, cultivated these powers and preached them. I have not been able to obtain his works, they being suppressed as far as is practicable by the Prussian government. Krause could leave his body, and, to all appearance, die whenever he pleased. One of his disciples, yet living, Count von Eberstein, possesses the same faculty.

Many writers of the sixteenth century were well acquainted with the power of will, and to this was attributed the good or evil influence of blessings and curses. They believed it to be of great effect in curing diseases, and that by it alone life might be extinguished. That, *subjectively*, life may be extinguished, we have seen by the cases of Colonel Townshend, the dervish that was buried, Hermotinus, and others: for doubtless the power that could perform so much, could, under an adequate motive, have performed more: and since all things in nature, spiritual and material, are connected, and that there is an unceasing interaction between them, we being members of one great whole, only individualized by our organisms, it is possible to conceive that the power which can be exerted on our own organism might be extended to others: and since we can not conceive man to be an isolated being—the only intelligence besides God—none above us and none below—but must, on the contrary, believe that there are numerous grades of intelligences, it seems to follow, of course, that we must stand in some kind of relation to them, more or less intimate; nor is it at all surprising that with some individuals this relation should be more intimate than with others. Finally, we are not entitled to deny the existence of this magical or spiritual power, as exerted by either incorporated or unincorporated spirits, because we do not comprehend how it can be exerted; since, in spite of all the words that have been expended on the subject, we are equally ignorant of the mode in which our own will acts upon our own muscles. We know the fact, but not the mode of it.

CHAPTER XVIII.

CONCLUSION.

Of the power of the mind over matter, we have a remarkable example in the numerous well-authenticated instances of the *stigmata*. As in most cases this phenomenon has been connected with a state of religious exaltation, and has been appropriated by the Roman church as a miracle, the fact has been in this country pretty generally discredited, but without reason. Ennemoser, Passavent, Schubert, and other eminent German physiologists, assure us that not only is the fact perfectly established, as regards many of the so-called saints, but also that there have been indubitable modern instances, as in the case of the ecstaticas of the Tyrol, Catherine Emmerich (commonly called the Nun of Dulmen), Maria Morl, and Domenica Lazzari, who have all exhibited the stigmata.

Catherine Emmerich, the most remarkable of the three, began very early to have visions, and to display unusual endowments. She was very pious; could distinguish the qualities of plants, reveal secrets or distant circumstances, and knew people's thoughts; but was, however, extremely sickly, and exhibited a variety of extraordinary and distressing symptoms, which terminated in her death. The wounds of the crown of thorns round her head, and those of the nails in her hands and feet, were as perfect as if painted by an artist, and they bled regularly on Fridays. There was also a double cross on her breast. When the blood was wiped away, the marks looked like the puncture of flies. She seldom took any nourishment but water; and, having been but a poor cow-keeper, she discoursed, when in the ecstatic state, as if inspired.

I am well aware that on reading this, many persons who never saw her, will say it was all imposture. It is very easy to say this; but it is as absurd as presumptuous to pronounce on what they have had no opportunity of observing. I never saw these women either; but I find myself much more disposed to accept the evidence of those who did, than of those who only "do not believe, because they do not believe."

Neither Catherine Emmerich nor the others made their sufferings a source of profit, nor had they any desire to be exhibited—but quite the contrary. She could see in the dark as well as the light, and frequently worked all night at making clothes for the poor, without lamp or candle.

There have been instances of magnetic patients being stigmatized in this manner. Madame B. von N—— dreamed one night that a person offered her a red and a white rose, and that she chose the latter. On awaking she felt a burning pain in her arm, and by degrees there arose there the figure of a rose perfect in form and color. It was rather raised above the skin. The mark increased in intensity till the eighth day, after which it faded away, and by the fourteenth was no longer perceptible.

A letter from Moscow, addressed to Dr. Kerner, in consequence of reading the account of the "Nun of Dulmen," relates a still more extraordinary case. At the time of the French invasion, a Cossack having pursued a Frenchman into a *cul de sac*—an alley without an outlet—there ensued a terrible conflict between them, in which the latter was severely wounded. A person who had taken refuge in this close and could not get away, was so dreadfully frightened, that when he reached home, there broke out on his body the very same wounds that the Cossack had inflicted on his enemy!

The signatures of the fœtus are analogous facts; and if the mind of the mother can thus act on another organism, why not the minds of the saints, or of Catherine Emmerich, on their own? From the influence of the mother on the child, we have but one step to that asserted to be possible between two organisms not visibly connected; for the difficulty therein lies, that we do not see the link that connects them, though doubtless it exists. Dr. Blacklock, who lost his eyesight at an early period, said that, when awake, he distinguished persons by hearing and feeling them; but when asleep, he had a distinct impression of another sense. He then seemed to himself united to them by a kind of distant contact, which was effected by threads passing from their bodies to his, which seems to be but a metaphorical expression of the fact; for, whether the connection be maintained by an all-pervading ether, or be purely dynamic, that the intertraction exists between both organic and inorganic bodies, is made evident wherever there is sufficient excitability to render the effects sensible.

Till very lately, the powers of the divining-rod were considered a mere fable; yet, that this power exists, though not in the rod, but in the person that holds it, is now perfectly well established. Count Tristan, who has written a book on the subject, says that about one in forty have it, and that a complete course of experiments has proved the phenomenon to be electric. The rod seems to serve, in some degree, the same purpose as the magical mirror and conjurations, and it is also serviceable in presenting a result visible to the eye of the spectator. But numerous cases are met with, in which metals or water are perceived beneath the surface of the earth, without the intervention of the rod. A man, called Bléton, from Dauphiny, possessed this divining power in a remarkable degree, as did a Swiss girl, called Katherine Beutler. She was strong and healthy, and of a phlegmatic temperament, yet so susceptible of these influences that, without the rod, she pointed out and traced the course of water, veins of metal, coal-beds, salt-mines, &c. The sensations produced were sometimes on the soles of her feet, sometimes on her tongue, or in her stomach. She never lost the power wholly, but it varied considerably in intensity at different times, as it did with Bleton. She was also rendered sensible of the bodily pains of others, by laying her hand on the affected part, or near it; and she performed several magnetic cures.

A person now alive, named Dussange, in the Maçonnés, possesses this power. He is a simple, honest man, who can give no account of his own faculty. The Abbés Chatelard and Paramelle can also discover subterraneous springs; but they say it is effected by means of their geological science. Monsieur D——, of Cluny, however, found the faculty of Dussange much more to be relied on. The Greeks and Romans made hydroscopy an art; and there are works alluded to as having existed on this subject, especially one by Marcellus. The caduceus of Mercury, the wand of Circe, and the wands of the Egyptian sorcerers, show that the wand or rod was always looked upon as a symbol of divination. One of the most remarkable instances of the use of the divining-rod, is that of Jacques Aymar.

On the 5th of July, 1692, a man and his wife were murdered in a cellar at Lyons, and their house was robbed. Having no clew whatever to the criminal, this peasant, who had the reputation of being able to discover murderers, thieves, and stolen articles, by means of the divining-rod, was sent for from Dauphiny. Aymar undertook to follow the footsteps of the assassins, but he said he must first be taken into the cellar where the murder was committed. The procurator royal conducted him thither; and they gave him a rod out of the first wood that came to hand. He walked about the cellar, but the rod did not move till he came to the spot where the man had been killed. Then Aymar became agitated, and his pulse beat as if he were in a high fever; and all these symptoms were augmented when he approached the spot on which they had found the body of the woman. From this, he, of his own accord, went into a sort of shop where the robbery had been committed; thence he proceeded into the street, tracing the assassin, step by step, first to the court of the archbishop's palace, then out of the city, and along the right side of the river. He was escorted all the way by three persons appointed for the purpose, who all testified that sometimes he detected the traces of three accomplices, sometimes only of two. He led the way to the house of a gardener, where he insisted that they had touched a table and one of three bottles that were yet standing upon it. It was at first denied; but two children, of nine or ten years old, said that three men had been there, and had been served with wine in that bottle. Aymar then traced them to the river where they had embarked in a boat; and, what is very extraordinary, he tracked them as surely on the water as on the land. He followed them wherever they had gone ashore, went straight to the places they had lodged at, pointed out their beds, and the very utensils of every description that they had used. On arriving at Sablon, where some troops were encamped, the rod and his own sensations satisfied him that the assassins were there; but fearing the soldiers would ill treat him, he refused to pursue the enterprise further, and returned to Lyons. He was, however, promised protection, and sent back by water, with letters of recommendation. On reaching Sablon, he said they were no longer there; but he tracked them into Languedoc, entering every house they had stopped at, till he at length reached the gate of the prison, in the town of Beaucaire, where he said one of them would be found. They brought all the prisoners before him, amounting to fifteen; and the only one his rod turned on was a little *Bossu*, or deformed man, who had just been brought in for a petty theft. He then ascertained that the two others had taken the road to Nimes, and offered to follow them; but as the man denied all knowledge of the murder, and declared he had never been at Lyons, it was thought best that they should return there; and as they went the way they had come, and stopped at the same houses, where he was recognised, he at length confessed that he had travelled with two men who had engaged him to assist in the crime. What is very remarkable, it was found necessary that Jacques Aymar should walk in front of the criminal, for when he followed him he became violently sick. From Lyons to Beaucaire is forty-five miles.

As the confession of the *Bossu* confirmed all Aymar had asserted, the affair now created an immense sensation; and a great variety of experiments were instituted, every one of which proved perfectly satisfactory. Moreover, two gentlemen, one of them the controller of the customs, were discovered to possess this faculty, though in a minor degree. They now took Aymar back to Beaucaire, that he might trace the other two criminals; and he went straight again to the prison-gate, where he said that now another would be found. On inquiry, however, it was discovered that a man had been there to inquire for the *Bossu*, but was gone again. He then followed them to Toulon, and finally to the frontier of Spain, which set a limit to further researches. He was often so faint and overcome with the effluvia, or whatever it was that guided him, that the perspiration streamed from his brow, and they were obliged to sprinkle him with water to prevent his fainting.

He detected many robberies in the same way. His rod moved whenever he passed over metals or water, or stolen goods; but he found that he could distinguish the track of a murderer from all the rest, by the horror and pain he felt. He made this discovery accidentally, as he was searching for water. They dug up the ground, and found the body of a woman that had been strangled.

I have myself met with three or four persons in whose hands the rod turned visibly; and there are numerous very remarkable cases recorded in different works. In the Hartz, there is a race of people who support themselves entirely by this sort of divination; and as they are paid very highly, and do nothing else, they are generally extremely worthless and dissipated.

The extraordinary susceptibility to atmospheric changes in certain organisms, and the faculty by which a dog tracks the foot of his master, are analogous facts to those of the divining-rod. Mr. Boyle mentions a lady who always perceived if a person that visited her came from a place where snow had lately fallen. I have seen one who, if a quantity of gloves are given her, can tell to a certainty to whom each belongs; and a particular friend of my own, on entering a room, can distinguish perfectly who has been sitting in it, provided these be persons he is familiarly acquainted with. Numerous extraordinary stories are extant respecting this kind of faculty in dogs.

Doubtless not only our bodies, but all matter, sheds its atmosphere around it; the sterility of the ground where metals are found is notorious; and it is asserted that, to some persons, the vapors that emanate from below are visible, and that, as the height of the mountains round a lake furnishes a measure of its depth, so does the height to which these vapors ascend show

how far below the surface the mineral treasures or the waters lie. The effect of metals on somnambulic persons is well known to all who have paid any attention to these subjects; and surely may be admitted, when it is remembered that Humboldt has discovered the same sensibility in zoophytes, where no traces of nerves could be detected; and, many years ago, Frascatorius asserted that symptoms resembling apoplexy were sometimes induced by the proximity of a large quantity of metal. A gentleman is mentioned who could not enter the mint at Paris without fainting. In short, so many well-attested cases of idiosyncratic sensibilities exist, that we have no right to reject others because they appear incomprehensible.

Now, we may not only easily conceive, but we know it to be a fact, that fear, grief, and other detrimental passions, vitiate the secretions,* and augment transpiration; and it is quite natural to suppose that, where a crime has been committed which necessarily aroused a number of turbulent emotions, exhalations perceptible to a very acute sense may for some time hover over the spot; while the anxiety, the terror, the haste, in short, the general commotion of system, that must accompany a murderer in his flight, is quite sufficient to account for his path being recognisable by such an abnormal faculty, "for the wicked flee when no man pursueth." We also know that a person perspiring with open pores is more susceptible than another to contagion; and we have only to suppose the pores of Jacques Aymar so constituted as easily to imbibe the emanations shed by the fugitive, and we see why he should be affected by the disagreeable sensations he describes.

The disturbing effect of odors on some persons, which are quite innoxious to others, must have been observed by everybody. Some people do actually almost "die of a rose in aromatic pain." Boyle says that, in his time, many physicians avoided giving drugs to children, having found that external applications, to be imbibed by the skin, or by respiration, were suffi-

* In the "Medical Annals," a case is recorded of a young lady whose axillary excretions were rendered so offensive, by the fright and horror she had experienced in seeing some of her relations assassinated in India, that she was unable to go into society.

cient; and the homeopaths occasionally use the same means now. Sir Charles Bell told me that Mr. F——, a gentleman well known in public life, had only to hold an old book to his nose to produce all the effects of a cathartic. Elizabeth Okey was oppressed with most painful sensations when near a person whose frame was sinking. Whenever this effect was of a certain intensity, Dr. Elliotson observed that the patient invariably died.

Herein lies the secret of amulets and talismans, which grew to be a vain superstition, but in which, as in all popular beliefs, there was a germ of truth. Somnambulic persons frequently prescribe them; and absurd as it may seem to many, there are instances in which their efficacy has been perfectly established, be the interpretation of the mystery what it may. In a great plague which occurred in Moravia, a physician, who was constantly among the sufferers, attributed the complete immunity of himself and his family to their wearing amulets composed of the powder of toads, "which," says Boyle, "caused an emanation adverse to the contagion." A Dutch physician mentions, that in the plague at Nimeguen, the pest seldom attacked any house till they had used soap in washing their linen. Wherever this was done it appeared immediately.

In short, we are the subjects, and so is everything around us, of all manner of subtle and inexplicable influences: and if our ancestors attached too much importance to these ill-understood arcana of the night-side of nature, we have attached too little. The sympathetic effects of multitudes upon each other, of the young sleeping with the old, of magnetism on plants and animals, are now acknowledged facts: may not many other asserted phenomena that we yet laugh at be facts also, though probably too capricious in their nature—by which I mean, depending on laws beyond our apprehension—to be very available? For I take it, that as there is no such thing as chance, but all would be certainty if we knew the whole of the conditions, so no phenomena are really capricious and uncertain: they only appear so to our ignorance and shortsightedness.

The strong belief that formerly prevailed in the efficacy of sympathetic cures, can scarcely have existed, I think, without some foundation: nor are they a whit more extraordinary than the sympathetic falling of pictures and stopping of clocks and watches, of which such numerous well-attested cases are extant that several learned German physiologists of the present day pronounce the thing indisputable. I have myself heard of some very perplexing instances.

Gaffarillus alludes to a certain sort of magnet, not resembling iron, but of a black-and-white color, with which if a needle or knife were rubbed, the body might be punctured or cut without pain. How can we know that this is not true? Jugglers who slashed and cauterized their bodies for the amusement of the public were supposed to avail themselves of such secrets.

How is it possible for us, either, to imagine that the numerous recorded cases of the *Blood Ordeal,* which consisted in the suspected assassin touching the body of his victim, can have been either pure fictions or coincidences? Not very long ago, an experiment of a frightful nature is said to have been tried in France on a somnambulic person, by placing on the epigastric region a vial filled with the arterial blood of a criminal just guillotined. The effect asserted to have been produced was the establishment of a rapport between the somnambule and the deceased which endangered the life of the former.

Franz von Baader suggests the hypothesis of a *vis sanguinis ultra mortem,* and supposes that a rapport or *communio vitæ* may be established between the murderer and his victim; and he conceives the idea of this mutual relation to be the true interpretation of the sacrificial rites common to all countries, as also of the *Blutschuld,* or the requiring blood for blood.

With regard to the blood ordeal, the following are the two latest instances of it recorded to have taken place in this country; they are extracted from "Hargrave's State Trials:"—

"Evidence having been given with respect to the death of Jane Norkott, an ancient and grave person, minister of the parish in Hertfordshire where the murder took place, being sworn, deposed. that the body being taken up out of the grave, and the four defendants being present, were required, each of them, to touch the dead body. Okeman's wife fell upon her knees, and prayed God to show token of her innocency. The appellant did touch the body, whereupon the brow of the deceased, which was before of a livid and carrion color, began to have a dew, or gentle sweat on it, which increased by degrees till the sweat ran down in drops on the face, the brow turned to a lively and fresh color, and the deceased opened one of her eyes and shut it again, and this opening the eye was done three several times; she likewise thrust out the ring, or marriage finger, three times, and pulled it in again, and blood dropped from the finger on the grass.

"Sir Nicholas Hyde, the chief justice, seeming to doubt this evidence, he asked the witness who saw these things besides him, to which he, the witness, answered, 'My lord, I can not swear what others saw, but I do believe the whole company saw it; and if it had been thought a doubt, proof would have been made, and many would have attested with me. My lord,' added the witness, observing the surprise his evidence awakened, 'I am minister of the parish, and have long known all the parties, but never had displeasure against any of them, nor they with me, but as I was minister. The thing was wonderful to me, but I have not interest in the matter, except as called on to testify to the truth. My lord, my brother, who is minister of the next parish, is here present, and, I am sure, saw all that I have affirmed.'"

Hereupon, the brother, being sworn, he confirmed the above evidence in every particular, and the first witness added, that having dipped his finger into what appeared to be blood, he felt satisfied that it was really so. It is to be observed, that this extraordinary circumstance must have occurred, if it occurred at all, when the body had been upward of a month dead; for it was taken up in consequence of various rumors implicating the prisoners, after the coroner's jury had given in a verdict of *felo de se*. On their first trial, they were acquitted, but an appeal being brought, they were found guilty and executed. It was on this latter occasion that the above strange evidence was given, which, being taken down at the time by Sir John Maynard, then sergeant-at-law, stands recorded, as I have observed, in Hargrave's edition of "State Trials."

The above circumstances occurred in the year 1628, and in 1688 the blood ordeal was again had recourse to in the trial of Sir Philip Stansfield for parricide, on which occasion the body had also been buried, but for a short time. Certain suspicions arising, it was disinterred and examined by the surgeons, and, from a variety of indications, no doubt remained that the old man had been murdered, nor that his son was guilty of his death. When the body had been washed and arrayed in clean linen, the nearest relations and friends were desired to lift it and replace it in the coffin; and when Sir Philip placed his hand under it, he suddenly drew it back, stained with blood, exclaiming, "Oh, God!" and letting the body fall, he cried, "Lord, have mercy upon me!" and went and bowed himself over a seat in the church, in which the corpse had been inspected. Repeated testimonies are given to this circumstance in the course of the trial; and it is very remarkable that Sir John Dalrymple, a man of strong intellect, and wholly free from superstition, admits it as an established fact in his charge to the jury.

In short, we are all, though in different degrees, the subjects of a variety of subtle influences, which, more or less, neutralize each other, and many of which, therefore, we never observe; and frequently when we do observe the effects, we have neither time nor capacity for tracing the cause; and when in more susceptible organisms such effects are manifested, we content ourselves with referring the phenomena to disease or imposture. The exemption, or the power, whichever it may be, by which certain persons or races are enabled to handle venomous animals with impunity, is a subject that deserves much more attention than it has met with; but nobody thinks of investigating secrets that seem rather curious than profitable; besides which, to believe these things implies a reflection on one's sagacity. Yet, every now and then, I hear of facts so extraordinary, which come to me from undoubted authority, that I can see no reason in the world for rejecting others that are not much more so. For example, only the other day, Mr. B. C——, a gentleman well known in Scotland, who has lived a great deal abroad, informed me, that having frequently heard of the singular phenomenon to be observed by placing a scorpion and a mouse together under a glass, he at length tried the experiment; and the result perfectly established what he had been previously unable to believe. Both animals were evidently frightened, but the scorpion made the first attack, and stung the mouse, which defended itself bravely, and killed the scorpion. The victory, however, was not without its penalties, for the mouse swelled to an unnatural size, and seemed in danger of dying from the poison of its defeated antagonist, when it relieved itself and was cured by eating the scorpion, which was thus proved to be an antidote to its own venom; furnishing a most interesting and remarkable instance of isopathy.

There is a religious sect in Africa, not far from Algiers, who eat the most venomous serpents alive, and certainly, it is said, without extracting their fangs. They declare they enjoy the privilege from their founder. The creatures writhe and struggle between their teeth; but possibly, if they do bite them, the bite is innocuous.

Then, not to mention the common expedients of extracting the poisonous fangs, or forcing the animal by repeated bitings to exhaust their venom, the fact seems too well established to be longer doubted, that there are persons in whom the faculty of charming, or, in other words, disarming serpents, is inherent, as the psylli and marsi of old, and the people mentioned by Bruce, Hassequist, and Lempriere, who were themselves eye-witnesses of the facts they relate. With respect to the marsi, it must be remembered, that Heliogabalus made their priests fling venomous serpents into the circus when it was full of people, and that many perished by the bites of these animals, which the marsi had handled with impunity. The modern charmers told Bruce that their immunity was born with them; and it was established beyond a doubt, during the French expedition into Egypt, that these people go from house to house to destroy serpents, as men do rats in this country. They declare that some mysterious instinct guides them to the animals, which they immediately seize with fury and tear to pieces with their hands and teeth. The negroes of the Antilles can smell a serpent which they do not see, and of whose presence a European is quite insensible; and Madame Calderon de la Barca mentions, in her letters from Mexico, some singular cases of exemption from the pernicious effects of venomous bites; and further relates, that in some parts of America, where rattle-snakes are extremely abundant, they have a custom of innoculating children with the poison, and that this is a preservative from future injury. This may or may not be true; but it is so much the fashion in these days to set down to the account of fable everything deviating from our daily experience, that travellers may repeat these stories for ages before any competent person will take the trouble of verifying the report. However, taking the evidence altogether, it appears clear that there does exist in some persons a faculty of producing in these animals a sort of numbness, or *engourdissement*, which renders them for the time incapable of mischief; though of the nature of the power we are utterly ignorant, unless it be magnetic. The senses of animals, although generally resembling ours, are yet extremely different in various instances; and we know that many of them have one faculty or another exalted to an intensity of which we have no precise conception. Galen asserted, on the authority of the marsi and psylli themselves, that they obtained their immunity by feeding on the flesh of venomous animals: but Pliny, Elian, Silius Italicus, and others, account for the privilege by attributing it to the use of some substance of a powerful nature, with which they rubbed their bodies; and most modern travellers incline to the same explanation. But if this were the elucidation of the mystery, I suspect it would be easily detected.

It is observable that in all countries where a secret of this sort exists, there is always found some custom which may be looked upon as either the cause or the consequence of the discovery. In Hindostan, for example, in order to test the truth of an accusation, the cobra capello is flung into a deep pot of earth with a ring; and if the supposed criminal succeeds in extracting the ring without being bitten by the serpent, he is accounted innocent. So the sacred asps in Egypt inflicted death upon the wicked, but spared the good. Dr. Allnut mentions that he saw a negro in Africa touch the protruded tongue of a snake with the black matter from the end of his pipe, which he said was tobacco-oil. The effects were as rapid as a shock of electricity. The animal never stirred again, but stiffened, and was as rigid and hard as if it had been dried in the sun.

It is related of Machamut, a Moorish king, that he fed on poisons till his bite became fatal and his saliva venomous. Cœlius Rhodiginus mentions the same thing of a woman who was thus mortal to all her lovers; and Avicenna mentions a man whose bite was fatal in the same way.

The boy that was found in the forest of Arden, in 1563, and who had been nourished by a she-wolf, made a great deal of money for a short time, after he was introduced to civilized life, by exempting the flocks and herds of the shepherds from the peril they nightly ran of being devoured by wolves. This he did by stroking them with his hands, or wetting them with his saliva, after which they for some time enjoyed an immunity. His faculty was discovered from the circumstance of the beasts he kept never being attacked. It left him, however, when he was about fourteen, and the wolves ceased to distinguish him from other human beings.

However, my readers will, I think, ere now have supped full with *wonders*, if not with *horrors*—and it is time I should bring this book to a conclusion. If I have done no more, I trust I shall at least have afforded some amusement; but I shall be better pleased to learn that I have induced any one, if it be *but* one, to look upon life and death, and the mysteries that attach to both, with a more curious and inquiring eye than they have hitherto done. I can not but think that it would be a great step if mankind could familiarize themselves with the idea that they are spirits incorporated for a time in the flesh; but that the dissolution of the connection between soul and body, though it changes the external conditions of the former, leaves its moral state unaltered. What a man has made himself, he will be; his state is the result of his past life, and his heaven or hell is in himself. At death we enter upon a new course of life, and what that life shall be depends upon ourselves. If we have provided oil for our lamps, and fitted ourselves for a noble destiny and the fellowship of the great and good spirits that have passed away, such will be our portion; and if we have misused our talent, and sunk our souls in the sensual pleasures or base passions of this world, we shall carry our desires and passions with us, to make our torment in the other—or perhaps be tethered to the earth by some inextinguishable remorse or disappointed scheme, like those unhappy spirits I have been writing about—and that perhaps for hundreds of years; for, although they be evidently freed from many of the laws of space and matter, while unable to leave the earth, they are still the children of time and have not entered into eternity. It is surely absurd to expect that because our bodies have decayed and fallen away, or been destroyed by an accident, that a miracle is to be wrought in our favor, and that the miser's love of gold, or the profligate's love of vice, is to be immediately extinguished, and be superseded by inclinations and tastes better suited to his new condition! New circumstances do not so rapidly engender a new mind here, that we should hope they will do so there: more especially as, in the first place, we do not know what facilities of improvement may remain in us; and in the second, since the law that like seeks like must be undeviating, the blind will seek the blind, and not those who could help them to light.

I think, too, that if people would learn to remember that they are spirits, and acquire the habit of conceiving of themselves as individuals, apart from the body, that they would not only be better able to realize this view of a future life, but they would also find it much less difficult to imagine, that, since they belong to the spiritual world on the one hand, quite as much as they belong to the material world on the other, that these extraordinary faculties, which they occasionally see manifested by certain individuals, or in certain states, may possibly be but faint rays of those properties which are inherent in spirit, though temporarily obscured by its connection with the flesh—and designed to be so, for the purposes of this earthly existence. The most ancient nations of the world knew this, although we have lost sight of it, as we learn by the sacred books of the Hebrews.

According to the *Cabbalah*, "Mankind are endowed by nature, not only with the faculty of penetrating into the regions of the supersensuous and invisible, but also of working magically above and below, or in the worlds of light and darkness. As the Eternal fills the world, sees, and is not seen, so does the soul *(N'schamach)* fill the body, and sees without being seen. The soul perceives that which the bodily eye can not. Sometimes a man is seized suddenly with a fear, for which he can not account, which is because the soul descries an impending misfortune. The soul possesses also the power of working with the elementary matter of the earth, so as to annihilate one form and produce another. Even by the force of imagination, human beings can injure other things; yea, even to the slaying of a man!" (The new platonist, Paracelsus, says the same thing.) The "Cabbalah" teaches that there have in all times existed men endowed with powers, in a greater or less degree, to work good or evil; for, to be a virtuoso in either, requires a peculiar spiritual vigor: thence, such men as heroes and priests in the kingdom of Tumah (the kingdom of the clean and unclean). "If a man therefore sets his desires on what is godly, in proportion as his efforts are not selfish, but purely a seeking of holiness, he will be endowed, by the free grace of God, with supernatural faculties; and it is the highest aim of existence, that man should regain his connection with his inward, original source, and exalt the material and earthly into the spiritual." The highest degree of this condition of light and spirit is commonly called "the holy ecstasy," which is apparently the degree attained by the ecstatics of the Tyrol.

I am very far from meaning to imply that it is our duty, or in any way desirable, that we should seek to bring ourselves into this state of holy ecstasy, which seems to involvo some derangement of the normal relations between the soul and body;

but it is at least equally unwise in us to laugh at, or deny it or its proximate conditions, where they really exist. It appears perfectly clear that, as by giving ourselves up wholly to our external and sensuous life, we dim and obscure the spirit of God that is in us—so, by annihilating, as far as in us lies, the necessities of the body, we may so far subdue the flesh as to loosen the bonds of the spirit, and enable it to manifest some of its inherent endowments. Ascetics and saints have frequently done this voluntarily; and disease, or a peculiar constitution. sometimes does this for us involuntarily: and it is far from desirable that we should seek to produce such a state by either means, but it *is* extremely desirable that we should avail ourselves of the instruction to be gained by the simple knowledge that such phenomena have existed and been observed in all ages; and that thereby our connection with the spiritual world may become a demonstrated fact to all who choose to open their eyes to it.

With regard to the cases of apparitions I have adduced, they are not, as I said before, one hundredth part of those I could have brought forward, had I resorted to a few of the numerous printed collections that exist in all languages.

Whether the view I acknowledge myself to take of the facts be or not the correct one—whether we are to look to the region of the psychical or the hyperphysical for the explanation—the facts themselves are certainly well worthy of observation; the more so, as it will be seen that, although ghosts are often said to be out of fashion, such occurrences are, in reality, as rife as ever: while, if these shadowy forms be actually visiters from the dead, I think we can not too soon lend an attentive ear to the tale their reappearance tells us.

That we do not all see them, or that those who promise to come do not all keep tryst, amounts to nothing. We do not know why they can come, nor why they can not; and as for not seeing them, I repeat, we must not forget how many other things there are that we do not see: and since, in science, we know that there are delicate manifestations which can only be rendered perceptible to our organs by the application of the most delicate electrometers, is it not reasonable to suppose that there may exist certain susceptible or diseased organisms, which, judiciously handled, may serve as electrometers to the healthy ones?

As my book is designed as an inquiry, with a note of interrogation I characteristically bid adieu to my readers.

C. C.

THE END.

THE POETICAL WORKS

OF

PERCY BYSSHE SHELLEY.

EDITED BY G. G. FOSTER.

THE FIRST COMPLETE AMERICAN EDITION.

In one volume, 16mo.

"Shelley has a private nook in my affections. He is so unlike all other poets that I can not mate him. He is like his own 'skylark' among birds. He does not keep ever up in the thin air with Byron, like the eagle, nor sing with Keats low and sweetly like the thrush, nor, like the dove sitting always upon her nest, brood with Wordsworth over the affections. He begins to sing when the morning wakes him, and as he grows wild with his own song, he mounts upward,

'And singing ever soars, and soaring ever singeth;'

and it is wonderful how he loses himself, like the delirious bird in the sky, and with a verse which may be well compared for its fine delicacy with her little wings, penetrates its far depths fearlessly and full of joy. There is something very new in this mingled trait of fineness and sublimity. Milton and Byron seem made for the sky. Their broad wings always strike the air with the same solemn majesty. But Shelley, near the ground, is a very 'bird in a bower,' running through his merry compass as if he never dreamed of the upward and invisible heavens. Withal, Shelley's genius is too fiery to be moody. He was a melancholy man, but it was because he was crossed in the daily walk of life, and such anxieties did not touch his imagination. It was above—far, far above them. His poetry was not, like that of other poets, linked with his common interests; and if it 'unbound the serpent of care from his heart,' as doubtless it did, it was by making him forget that it was there. He conceived and wrote in a wizard circle. The illiberal world was the last thing remembered, and its annoying prejudices gall him as they might in the exercise of his social duties, never followed over the fiery limit of his fancy. Never have we seen such pure abstraction from earthliness as in the temper of his poetry. It is the clear, intellectual lymph, unalloyed and unpolluted."—*N. P. Willis.*

NAPOLEON'S MAXIMS OF WAR,

Translated by Col. D'Aguilar.

WITH NOTES.

In one vol., 32mo. Price 50 cents.

"THE science of war, in its legitimate sense, is entitled to encouragement, and study, and we recommend that every man of military mind, should possess himself of a copy of 'Napoleon's Maxims.' The work is also one of interest to the general reader, containing, as it does, numerous brief historical facts connected with the most celebrated battles, and men of military renown of almost every age."—*Recruit.*

"IT is a work of no little interest to those who wish to understand the principles upon which the greatest captain of the age carried on his operations, and who also desire to understand the errors committed by the inferior intellects brought into the field against him."—*Penn. Inquirer.*

"THIS work appears in its first American edition, with a recommendation from Gen. Scott, speaking of its utility to military men. That, indeed, is apparent enough; but it has occurred to us that the perusal of the little work, with its full illustrative notes, must be of great advantage also to the general reader, who desires to understand the tactics of the great Emperor. It will be a good companion to Thiers' History, now publishing."—*U. S. Sat. Post.*

Ingram Content Group UK Ltd.
Milton Keynes UK
UKHW051814260323
419150UK00005BA/175

9 781016 303828